MR. BOSTON

Official Bartender's Guide

75th Anniversary Edition

Edited by
Jonathan Pogash
with
Rick Rodgers

Photography by Ben Fink

WILEY

John Wiley & Sons, Inc.

Anyone who is pregnant or in a vulnerable health group should avoid recipes
that use raw egg whites or lightly cooked eggs.

CONTENTS

Introduction · iv

Acknowledgments · xi

BAR BASICS · 1

COCKTAIL CLASSICS · 27

BRANDY · 49

GIN · 71

RUM · 121

TEQUILA · 151

VODKA · 169

WHISKIES · 193

CORDIALS AND LIQUEURS · 231

SHOOTERS · 243

FROZEN DRINKS · 253

HOT DRINKS · 269

EGGNOGS AND PUNCHES · 281

WINE AND BEER IN MIXED DRINKS· 297

NONALCOHOLIC DRINKS · 307

Resources · 315

Glossary · 322

Index · 329

INTRODUCTION

Welcome!

We are pleased as punch to present the 68th edition of the *Mr. Boston Official Bartender's Guide*. For over three-quarters of a century, the "little red book" has been the go-to manual for making perfect drinks. It has been endorsed, consulted, and considered a basic tool by both professional and avocational bartenders. In fact, over 11 million copies have been printed since the very first printing of what was then called the *Old Mr. Boston Deluxe Official Bartender's Guide*. That rare, hard-to-find first edition, which debuted soon after the repeal of Prohibition, was compiled and edited by Leo Cotton, a purchasing agent for the Mr. Boston® liquor brand. Mr. Cotton was as meticulous about his work as he was passionate about cocktails. His foreword in the original book remains timeless:

> With repeal came the inevitable avalanche of cocktail books, most of them published without regard to accuracy or completeness. A survey proved the need for a cocktail book that would be authentic and accurate. The task of compiling this *Official Bartenders Guide* was thereupon undertaken and now after almost one year of tedious work it is presented to the thousands of bartenders throughout the country and to that portion of the

American public who desire a truly official source of information for home mixing.

The *Official Bartenders Guide* was compiled and edited in collaboration with four old time Boston Bartenders whose background and experience make them authorities on the correct ingredients to be used and the proper manner of serving cocktails. This experience plus the fact that every cocktail has been actually tested makes this truly an *Official Bartenders Guide*.

Leo Cotton's enthusiasm was such that his editing side job became a near-full-time vocation; he updated the *Official Bartenders Guide* through its 49th edition until he retired in 1970.

Though Leo Cotton died in 1990, his spirit lives on in this latest edition. The current cocktail renaissance, which began in the early 1990s, has brought with it a return to classicism in the art of cocktail making. The popularity of cocktails has increased dramatically over the last decade. What began as the "cocktail revolution" is now a whole new "cocktail culture." Every major city has cocktail lounges where the drinks are crafted with care from the very best ingredients. Newspapers such as the *New York Times* and the *Washington Post* have regular and well-read columns on the appreciation of fine spirits. Websites on every aspect of imbibing abound.

All of which amounts to the enjoyment of a heck of a lot of spirits. According to the Distilled Spirits Council of the United States, distilled spirits grew in 2010 after a slight slump the year before, with sales up 2 percent to $19.1 billion and volume also rising 2 percent to 190.7 million cases. The council also reported that despite a weakening economy, growth is expected to continue this year as consumers migrate away from beer to cocktails.

What on earth is in all those cocktails that we are drinking? Just about everything. Spirits distributors have responded to our enthusiasm with flavors old and new, bringing out explosively exciting products like elderflower liqueur and organic spirits and, at the same time, bolstering lost categories like rye, pisco, cachaça, crème de violette, and Old Tom Gin.

Categorically, vodka is still the most popular spirit for the masses, representing about 31 percent of the market, but other spirits like rum and whiskies have increased their sales. Rum, too, has taken off in a new direction that's positively old in origin—thanks to a renaissance in using sugarcane instead of molasses. If you see the words "rhum agricole" on a bottle or menu, it refers to how pure-cane rum is known on the French island of Martinique, while Brazilians call their pure-cane spirit "cachaça." Batavia arrack, a Javanese ancestor of rum, made from sugarcane and fermented red rice, is showing up on more bar menus, especially when the establishment's accent is on Asian cooking. In fact, it was named one of the "New Staples" by the *New York Times*.

On the whiskey front, rye has returned from its post-Prohibition banishment with such a vengeance that producers can't make enough of it. And new small-batch whiskies seem to debut every year now, with distilleries offering an array of boutique finishes. Single-malt Scotch and bourbon are still going strong.

How we're mixing these spirits into cocktails today is also remarkable. Mixology has returned to its culinary roots, embracing the zeitgeist and techniques of today's chefs, including taking farm to glass—as opposed to table. Once bartenders start working with someone who understands flavor combinations, like a chef, the drinks become more flavor-driven than spirit-driven. And that means mixers are more important than ever. With the introduction of high-quality, all-natural tonics and artisan sparkling juices, many bartenders have abandoned their soda guns—and all of the high-fructose corn syrup con-coctions they spout—for "cleaner" mixers sweetened with cane sugar or agave nectar. This can change how drinks are made *and* how they taste.

All of which means that in this edition you won't find pre-fabricated mixers that didn't exist when this book was first published. In other words, you won't find references to "sour mix," "daiquiri mix," or "Collins mix." The use of superfine sugar has been almost entirely eliminated in favor of simple syrup (an easy-to-make combination of sugar and water), as the latter is more thoroughly mixed into a cocktail with less effort. When used with fresh citrus juices, it will make a highly supe-rior substitute to the quick-fix mixes that invaded this book through its many incarnations. And, in acknowledgment of the attention to detail that many bartenders practice behind the bar, we've included from-scratch versions of many delicious flavored syrups, from lemongrass syrup to homemade gren-adine, the better to bring your bartending skills up a notch. We've also been sure to include drinks in the current edition featuring spirits infused with tea, vanilla, and other flavors.

What you will find in this 68th edition are nearly 150 completely new recipes reflecting the most popular spirits, liqueurs, and juices of the moment. Scores of the best bar-tenders, bar chefs, and mixologists from around the world contributed recipes, tips, and advice for nothing more than thanks in print. We'd like to think their contributions were an homage to the book that first inspired many of them to start mixing drinks at the beginning of their careers.

In addition to the new recipes, the myriad details of the overall subtle changes that went into rebuilding this book might be lost on the novice or first-time reader of this guide. But our hope is that professional or veteran *Mr. Boston* readers will be pleasantly surprised by this lat-est incarnation. We'd like to think that Leo Cotton would be pleased to see how much of this book reflects the spirit of his original edition (which, by the way, didn't contain a single vodka cocktail).

By the time Cotton wrote the first edition of this book, the great-granddaddy of American cocktails, "Professor" Jerry Thomas, was long gone—and with him many of the techniques that set his service apart from lesser-mortal barmen back in the late nineteenth century. Indeed, ask any serious bartender or mixologist today who inspires their showmanship and creativity, and the answer will probably be "Jerry Thomas." Or perhaps it will be Thomas's twentieth-century incarnation, Dale DeGroff, who may not have single-handedly revived the cocktail classicism movement of the 1990s but certainly was and continues to be one of the most passionate, dynamic bartenders alive today.

Because DeGroff has spent more than twenty years traveling around the country educating a generation of modern mixologists—when not mixing drinks behind the bar— it seems appropriate to cite his "Five Commandments for Bartenders," which are universal to all cocktail professionals and those passionate about being a good host:

I: SET THE TONE

The rapport between a bartender and guest is set by the bartender. If a guest is short or less than cordial, you, the bartender—according to the social contract you uphold—cannot respond in kind. This is a one-sided contract weighted in favor of the guest, but in practice it is an opportunity for the bartender to do what he or she was hired to do best: turn difficult guests into friends, make great drinks, and even, on occasion, teach people how to have a good time.

II: BE OBSERVANT

Good bartenders need to sharpen their powers of observation and develop their ability to listen. In the first encounter with a guest, the bartender will determine not only the drink but the mood of the guest, if conversation is welcome or not, and generally why the guest has come. This is your opportunity to make the visit to your bar a success.

III: KNOW YOUR RECIPES

You're the chef of the bar and have the same responsibility to guests that the chef de cuisine has to diners. Are you putting the dash of Angostura bitters in your Manhattan? Do you use fresh lime juice in your Mojito? It took me a couple of years to get over the arrogance I developed in the first six months of bartending, then it took me several years after that to research the correct recipes for the 150 or so classic and popular drinks that are 90 percent of a bartender's regular repertoire.

IV: PERFECT YOUR CRAFT

The skill a bartender possesses in the handling of tools and the small theatrical elements he or she demonstrates, such as the flaming of citrus peels, can return huge dividends in both esteem and gratuity—not to mention return business. This is not a circus act but rather exuding a sense of confidence that impresses your guests. A bartender is most definitely on stage, so expect to be scrutinized down to your fingernails.

V: EXUDE GRAVITAS

A bartender's skill and cleverness in being many things to many people is one of the most compelling and challenging aspects of the job. The bartender is a source of information on the day's news and sporting events, as well as a glossary of where to dine, drink, see, and be seen. You have the ability to keep peace between customers in a light-handed way. Rudeness to a bar guest is never acceptable; there are myriad ways of reacting coolly to a difficult guest. And even the most difficult of guests can be handled with a professional demeanor, though sometimes help is required.

Before you continue reading, please take a moment to think about both the responsible use and serving of alcoholic drinks. The consumption of alcohol dates back many centuries and in many cultures throughout the world is part of social rituals associated with significant occasions and celebrations. The majority of adults who choose to drink do not abuse alcohol and are aware that responsible drinking is key to their own enjoyment, health, and safety, as well as that of others, particularly when driving. Be a responsible drinker, and if you're under the legal drinking age, our nonalcoholic drinks chapter is the only one for you.

So, congratulations! You're well on your way to enhancing your expertise as a professional bartender or a properly prepared host. Let's raise a proverbial glass in honor of Mr. Boston, as he was introduced in his 1935 debut:

Sirs—May we now present to you Old Mr. Boston in permanent form. We know you are going to like him. He is a jolly fellow, one of those rare individuals, everlastingly young, a distinct personality and famous throughout the land for his sterling qualities and genuine good fellowship. His friends number in the millions those who are great and those who are near great even as you and I. He is jovial and ever ready to accept the difficult role of "Life of the Party," a sympathetic friend who may be relied upon in any emergency. Follow his advice and there will be many pleasant times in store for you.

Gentlemen, Old Mr. Boston.

Cheers!
JONATHAN POGASH
RICK RODGERS
May, 2011

ACKNOWLEDGMENTS

The editors would like to thank the following superstars who joined forces to produce the seventy-fifth anniversary edition of the *Mr. Boston Official Bartender's Guide*:

There are so many people at John Wiley & Sons to thank: First and foremost, our editor, Pamela Chirls, for her motivation, wisdom, and enthusiasm. Jillian Gaffney, for keeping the pieces of the puzzle that is a manuscript under control. And to Memo Productions for their elegant design that tips a glass to the past.

Photographer Ben Fink and food stylist Jamie Kimm brought the cocktails to life in the thirst-inducing photos with talent and flair.

Jack Kavanagh, Peter Collins, and our friends at *The Sazerac Company*, for keeping the traditions of the Mr. Boston Official Bartender's Guild alive and very much in the modern age.

Hal Wolin, bartender and member of *The Cocktail Guru* team, for assisting with testing and evaluating recipes.

Anthony Giglio and Jim Meehan, for their past editing of this book and their tips on this current edition.

The United States Bartenders Guild (USBG), for creating a community of like-minded professional bartenders. And to the many USBG members (whose names are given with their drinks) who generously contributed cocktail recipes to this book.

Jonathan would like to thank:

My mentor, gaz regan, for teaching me about classic cocktails and proper bar technique . . . and for ensuring I always buy him a drink whenever I see him.

My father, Jeff Pogash, not only a mentor, but an inspiration, for nudging me into the wild and wacky liquor business without even batting an eyelash . . . and for placing a drop of Champagne on my lips when I was born. Foreshadowing? I think so.

Rick Rodgers, my conspirator on this edition, for keeping me on track and for allowing my words to dazzle on the page . . . and for his endless humor whilst under an innumerable amount of deadlines.

And to my beautiful wife, Megan FitzGerald (and our newest addition), Benjamin Zen Fitz Gerald Pogash, for her love, dedication, and endless support throughout. I love you!

Rick would like to thank:

Pam Chirls (again) for the invitation to work with her on the book that brought me full-circle to my former career as a food service professional/bartender. Jillian Gaffney (again), for taking the time to show me new tricks with my Mac.

My partner, Patrick Fisher, who mixed many a Rob Roy on the rocks with orange bitters for me during the writing of this book. Come to think of it, he's mixed me a few before and after, too.

My late father, Dick Rodgers, whose spirit guided me to find his 1963 edition of Mr. Boston hidden away in his bar. The memories of our cocktail-time chats always bring a smile.

To my dear friend Carl Raymond, for pointing me to Astor Center in New York City and their excellent mixology program, and where I discovered the talented Jonathan Pogash.

Thanks, Jonathan, for proving to me that it is never too late to relearn long-forgotten skills, and for making me the best bartender in Maplewood, New Jersey. I am far from the only guy in town with crème de violette and pimento liqueur—which says volumes about the state of mixology today.

BAR BASICS

EQUIPMENT

The right tools make mixing drinks easier, but some tasks simply can't be done without the right gizmo.

Boston Shaker Two-piece set comprised of a 16-ounce mixing glass and a slightly larger metal container that acts as a cover for the mixing glass when shaking cocktails. The mixing glass can be used alone for stirring drinks that aren't shaken. This is the shaker of choice for professional bartenders.

Barspoon Long-handled shallow spoon with a twisted handle, used for a number of bartending techniques beyond stirring. The handle's curves help rotate the spoon during mixing, and the spoon bowl guides poured liqueurs into position for layered drinks.

Hawthorne Strainer Perforated metal strainer for the metal half of a Boston shaker, held in place by a wire coil.

Julep Strainer Perforated spoon-shaped strainer used in conjunction with a mixing glass.

Cocktail Shaker Two-part container with a tight-fitting lid. While styles vary widely, the most common shaker (also called a cobbler) has a top with a built-in lidded spout that serves as a strainer. The metal *Parisian-style shaker*, preferred by many home bartenders, has a sleek Art Deco look, lacks the top spout, and must be used in conjunction with a Hawthorne strainer.

Electric Blender Absolutely necessary to make frozen drinks, puree fruit, and even crush ice for certain recipes. Choose a top-quality blender with a heavy base, as lightweight blenders tend to "walk" when blending thick mixtures.

Cutting Board Either wood or plastic, it is used to cut fruit upon for garnishes.

Paring Knife Small, sharp knife to prepare fruit for garnishes.

Channel Tool Use this gadget to create relatively thin ribbons of citrus zest for twists.

Muddler Looks like a pestle, the flat end of which is used to crush and combine ingredients in a serving glass or mixing glass. Can be made of wood, metal, or even hard rubber.

Microplane Grater Useful for zesting fruit or grating nutmeg.

Bottle Opener Essential for opening bottles that aren't twist-off.

"Church Key" This metal tool is pointed at one end to punch holes in the tops of cans (these days most likely to be fruit juices), while the blunt end is used to open bottles.

Corkscrew There are a myriad of styles from which to choose. Professionals use the "waiter's corkscrew," which looks like a penknife, the "Screwpull," or the "rabbit corkscrew." The "winged corkscrew," found in most homes, is considered easiest to use but often destroys the cork.

Citrus Reamer This tool for juicing fruit comes in two styles. The strainer bowl style has the pointed cone on top, or there is the wooden handle style with the cone attached, which must be used with a wire strainer to remove the seeds. However, if you plan to use a lot of fresh fruit juice (and nothing is better for your drinks than freshly squeezed lemons or limes), get an inexpensive electric juicer or a metal standing lever-type juicer to whip through mountains of citrus.

Jigger Essential for precise measuring, it typically has two cone-shaped metal cups conjoined at the narrow ends. The best ones are marked to represent a quantity of fluid ounces (quarter, half, whole, etc.), fractionalized by lines etched in the metal. While jiggers come in a variety of sizes, the most useful jigger has 1½ ounces (1 jigger) and 1 ounce (1 pony). For smaller measurements in an unmarked jigger, just half-fill the larger cup for ¾ ounce, and the smaller cup in the same way for ½ ounce. Glass jiggers, which usually hold 2 ounces, are clearly marked, but could break in a busy professional bar. For consistency's sake, get out of the habit (if you have it) of free-pouring drinks, and take out the jigger every time you make a cocktail.

Measuring Spoons and Cups A set of measuring spoons (in 1 tablespoon, 1 teaspoon, ½ teaspoon, and ¼ teaspoon sizes) will be needed for smaller amounts of ingredients that are not measured by the fluid ounce. When measuring large amounts of liquids for punches or hot drinks, transparent liquid measuring cups in 1-cup and 2-cup capacities will come in handy.

Ice Bucket with Scoop and Tongs A bar without ice is like a car without gas. Use the scoop—never the glass—to gather ice in a mixing glass or shaker and tongs to add single cubes to a prepared drink.

Lewis Bag A heavy canvas bag with a mallet used to crush ice. Put ice cubes in the bag, close it, and pound away. It is low-tech, but it works.

Wire Sieve Used in conjunction with a Hawthorne strainer to ensure that the solids are removed from shaken cocktails. The strainer should be fit over the glass without an immoderate amount of overhang.

Miscellaneous Accoutrements Sipsticks or stirrers, straws, cocktail napkins, coasters, and cocktail picks.

GLASSWARE

Clean, polished glasses show off good drinks to great advantage. The best glasses should be thin-lipped, transparent, and sound off in high registers when "pinged." In practice, these five glasses could be used to make most of the mixed drinks and cocktails found in this book:

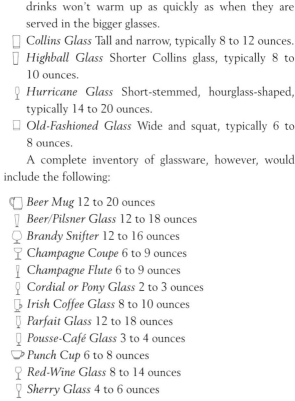

> ⅄ *Cocktail Glass* Also known as a martini glass, this glass used to hold 3 to about 4 ounces, but now it holds at least 6 ounces and often much more. The drinks in this book are formulated for the classic-sized cocktail glasses, which are worth the effort to find, as chilled drinks won't warm up as quickly as when they are served in the bigger glasses.

> ☐ *Collins Glass* Tall and narrow, typically 8 to 12 ounces.

> ☐ *Highball Glass* Shorter Collins glass, typically 8 to 10 ounces.

> ♀ *Hurricane Glass* Short-stemmed, hourglass-shaped, typically 14 to 20 ounces.

> ☐ *Old-Fashioned Glass* Wide and squat, typically 6 to 8 ounces.

A complete inventory of glassware, however, would include the following:

- 🍺 *Beer Mug* 12 to 20 ounces
- 🍺 *Beer/Pilsner Glass* 12 to 18 ounces
- 🍷 *Brandy Snifter* 12 to 16 ounces
- ⅄ *Champagne Coupe* 6 to 9 ounces
- 🍾 *Champagne Flute* 6 to 9 ounces
- ♀ *Cordial or Pony Glass* 2 to 3 ounces
- 🍮 *Irish Coffee Glass* 8 to 10 ounces
- 🥃 *Parfait Glass* 12 to 18 ounces
- 🥂 *Pousse-Café Glass* 3 to 4 ounces
- 🍵 *Punch Cup* 6 to 8 ounces
- 🍷 *Red-Wine Glass* 8 to 14 ounces
- ⅄ *Sherry Glass* 4 to 6 ounces

⎕ *Shot Glass* 1 to 3 ounces
♀ *White-Wine Glass* 8 to 14 ounces

THE WELL-STOCKED BAR

Nobody ever said stocking a home bar is easy or inexpensive, which is probably why so few people bother to do it. In the last few years, the best bartenders have upgraded their basic ingredients, and many barkeepers are known not just by the excellence of their spirits, but also by the variety and quality of their mixers and flavorings. You may be surprised to find how easy it is to make some of these ingredients at home.

Here are some of the things you'll need for a well-stocked bar.

Bitters Distilled or infused from herbs, roots, and other flavorful botanicals, these liquids have highly concentrated flavors. They contain alcohol but are used in such small quantities, drop by drop, that they aren't intoxicating. The "big three" bitters, which every bartender worth his or her salt stocks, are:

Angostura bitters: Known generically as aromatic bitters, they were first developed in Venezuela in 1824 as a cure for seasickness, illustrating how bitters were originally considered medicine.

Peychaud's bitters: The classic bitters of New Orleans, their spicy flavor is essential for Sazeracs.

Orange bitters: For some unfathomable reason, orange bitters, distilled from Seville sour orange peels and other flavorings, fell out of fashion. They have returned with a vengeance, mainly thanks to the efforts of mixologist gaz regan, who created Regan's Orange Bitters No. 6, which are now readily available to add a fragrant citrus note to many cocktails.

Beyond this trio, bitters expand into a panoply of flavors, some of them fruity (grapefruit, lemon, peach, and rhubarb) and others decidedly savory (such as mole, tobacco, and more). Whiskey-barrel and tiki bitters are specialty flavors that some bartenders wouldn't be without to make their signature drinks.

Fruit Juices Quite simply, the easiest way to improve your cocktails is to always use freshly squeezed lemon and lime juice, essential ingredients in countless cocktails. (OK, there are some people for whom a Gimlet wouldn't be itself without Rose's bottled sweetened lime juice, but that is the lone exception, and it is highly recommended to make your Gimlet with fresh juice and simple syrup.) A Salty Dog is never better than when made with fresh grapefruit juice. Supply your bar with an efficient juicer and use room-temperature fruit, as chilled citrus retains its juice. If you only have cold fruit, warm it in a bowl of hot water for about fifteen minutes before juicing. You can expect to get about 3 tablespoons of juice from a large lemon and 2 tablespoons from a large lime. Fresh orange and grapefruit juices are preferred but if unavailable, refrigerated are fine.

Some packaged juices, including pineapple, pomegranate, tropical juices such as passion fruit and guava (easily found at Latino markets), and cranberry, are perfectly acceptable. And frankly, even with an expeller juicer, they would difficult for the busy bartender to prepare. Keep canned tomato juice on hand for Bloody Marys. For a large amount of servings, buy big cans, but individual cans are perfect for keeping leftovers to a minimum.

Savory Ingredients Many cocktails (one might say the majority) have a fruity or sweet/sour element. Yet the beloved Bloody Mary is a fine example of a savory cocktail, zinged with Worcestershire, hot red pepper sauce, and often horseradish. Coarse (kosher) salt, often used in conjunction with spices or other flavorings, can rim a glass with crunchy/salty coating, as anyone who has drunk a Margarita can attest. Some recipes go so far as to recommend a particular kind of salt for its color and texture. See page 19 for tips on how to correctly rim a glass.

Sweetening Ingredients Here's another quick and easy tip for ratcheting up your cocktails: Sweeten your cocktails with homemade simple syrup. The sugar is already dissolved, and you will never serve a cocktail with undissolved sugar crystals again.

Simple syrup is nothing more complicated than boiling together equal parts of granulated sugar and water. Make the recipe on page 25 and store the syrup in the refrigerator. Simple syrup can also be purchased, but it is ridiculously easy to make yourself. Also, you can vary the sugar or add flavorings to make a wide range of other syrups, such as Demerara, chile, lemongrass, and honey.

You may already have some other sweeteners in your pantry. Agave nectar has sweetness similar to simple syrup, and some bartenders use it in their cocktails as a substitute. Maple syrup shows up in some drinks, but for the strongest maple flavor, use Grade B, not the more delicate Grade A.

When not homemade, flavored syrups can be purchased in an almost dizzying array of fruit, nut, and other flavors. Use top-quality beverage syrups, such as the ones intended for coffee. Imported brands, often made with natural ingredients and without corn syrup, can be the best. Orgeat (pronounced OR-zat), found in a number of "tiki" drinks, is a nutty syrup that also has some floral notes; almond syrup is an acceptable substitute. Grenadine, with its magenta color and sweet flavor, is another grocery store item that is simple to make in your kitchen, and the difference is eye-opening (page 26). Falernum, hailing from the Caribbean, has an exotic taste and aroma redolent of tropical spices. It comes in alcoholic and nonalcoholic versions, but most bartenders prefer the former for its truer flavor.

It is worth stocking superfine (also called bartenders') sugar for when you might be out of simple syrup or for rimming glasses. One-half ounce of simple syrup contains about

1½ teaspoons superfine sugar. Just be sure to add the superfine sugar to the glass, mixing glass, or shaker before any other ingredients, and stir or shake the drink well to be sure that the sugar dissolves. Sugar cubes are used in a few drinks, such as Irish Coffee and some flamed cocktails, so keep a box handy.

Piña Colada fans will want to stock cream of coconut, a canned sweetened product (not to be confused with coconut milk or creamed coconut, used in Indian and Southeast Asian cooking).

Dairy and Egg Ingredients Half-and-half is often used in cocktails to give them a luscious creaminess. Milk is used less often. Unsalted butter should be stocked during cold weather, as it is called for in Hot Buttered Rum. Use Grade A unsalted butter. If you have access to an artisan butter from a local dairy, use it.

Heavy cream should be stocked for rich cream drinks and to whip as a topping. Hand-whipped cream is always preferable to the kind squirted from a canister, especially the commercial presweetened version, although the latter may be the only kind stored at very busy bars. Keep in mind that the preferred topping for Irish Coffee and other hot drinks is a floated cap of lightly whipped cream, and not a tall, stiff peak.

To lightly whip cream, pour 1 cup heavy cream into a chilled bowl. If you want sweetened cream, add 2 tablespoons confectioners' sugar. Using an electric mixer on high speed or a thin-wire whisk, whip just until the cream is thickened but still pourable. Cover and refrigerate until ready to use, up to 1 day. If the cream separates, whip it until it thickens again. This makes enough cream for three or four drinks.

Eggs—whole, or singly yolk or white—give a cocktail a luscious texture and foamy top. There is concern about the use of raw eggs and possible contamination from salmonella and other potentially harmful bacteria. Always use fresh, uncracked large Grade A eggs (preferably organic, cage-free, or free-range), stored in the refrigerator. You can also use prepasteurized shell eggs, refrigerated egg substitute, or reconstituted dried egg whites. One egg equals 1/4 cup.

Sodas This is another common cocktail component where quality makes all the difference. Using a top-notch mixer, freshly opened from a single-serving bottle, instead of shot out of a soda gun, is an eye-opening experience. After all, in many cases, such as highballs, there are only two ingredients involved, so ensuring that each is as good as it can be will obviously improve the final result.

Soda Water: The bubbles in soda water are carbon dioxide, which can occur naturally (from mineral springs) or be introduced mechanically. Seltzer has the least amount of additives; club soda has minerals added for flavor. In general, buy soda water with plenty of fizz and a neutral taste that will cause minimum interference with the other cocktail's other ingredients.

Tonic (Quinine) Water: In the nineteenth century, quinine, a distillation of cinchona tree bark, was added to carbonated water as a preventative against malaria. The mixture wasn't delicious, and it was soon discovered that adding a shot of gin helped its palatability. Tonic water is now considered an essential mixer, if not medicine.

Flavored Soda: For cocktails that will separate yours from the rest of the pack, use artisan or small-batch versions of cola, lemon-lime, and other flavored sodas.

Garnishes A good number of cocktails are finished with some kind of fruit or savory garnish. (We'll not discuss nonedible doodads like paper umbrellas, but really, they might be appropriate for some retro drinks. Stock them according to your aesthetics.)

Versatile citrus fruits (lemons, limes, oranges, and sometimes grapefruits) add acidity, color, and aroma to drinks. Be sure to cut the fruit into sizeable pieces that will do the job—skimpy garnishes will not do. Fruit garnishes should be freshly made at the beginning of each shift or party and never allowed to get slimy. Keep cut garnishes refrigerated as much as possible. The most common citrus garnishes are:

Wheels: These fruit rounds are usually perched on the rim of the glass for visual appeal, and the drinker can squirt the juice from the fruit into the drink for extra flavor, if desired. Start by trimming about ½ inch off each end of the fruit.

To prepare fruit wheels, make a single cut along the length of the trimmed fruit, reaching into the center of the flesh. Cut the fruit crosswise into rounds about ⅛ inch thick. The incision in each wheel serves to help perch it on the glass.

To prepare fruit half-wheels, cut the trimmed fruit in half lengthwise. Turn the cut side of the fruit up, and make a single deep incision lengthwise into the center of the fruit. Turn the fruit cut side down, and cut crosswise into ⅛-inch-thick slices.

Wedges: Fruit chunks provide more juice than thin wheels. Trim about ½ inch off each end of the fruit. Cut each fruit in half lengthwise and place the fruit cut side up. Cut lengthwise into three wedges for a lime or four wedges for a lemon. When serving, cut an incision into the flesh side of the wedge if you want to perch it on the glass. This won't always be necessary, because a wedge is often squeezed and added directly to the drink.

Twists: A twist is nothing more than a piece of citrus zest actually twisted over the drink just before serving, for subtle fruit flavor. The most important thing to remember about preparing citrus twists is to only use the aromatic zest (the colored part of the fruit skin) and not the bitter white pith directly underneath. The traditional way to create citrus twists is to pare off the skin with a sharp paring knife and cut it into 2-inch lengths. (Any pith clinging to the skin can be scraped off with the knife.) That works, but a sturdy swivel-style vegetable peeler is much easier. For uniformly thin zest ribbons, use a channel zester.

There are a couple of ways to twist the twist. In the old-school method, hold the zest, peel (not pith) side down, in both hands just an inch or two above the drink. Twist your hands in opposite directions to wring the zest and express the citrus oils over the beverage surface. For a more contemporary one-handed technique, curve the twist between your thumb and forefinger, peel side down, and squeeze and pinch the twist to release the oils. In either case, to heighten the citrus flavor, rub the spent zest around the rim of the glass and drop it into the cocktail.

Flaming the citrus during the twisting process concentrates the oil's flavor and adds a little pyrotechnical drama. Gently bend the twist into a curve, holding it between your thumb and forefinger a few inches above the surface of the drink. Light a match with your free hand, and place it about $1/4$ inch under the zest. Squeeze the zest to bend it into a sharper curve, spraying the citrus oils into the flame and igniting them into tiny sparks. Add the twist to the drink.

Crusta and Horse's Neck cocktails use lemon or orange twists cut in a long, continuous spiral from a single fruit. This takes a very steady hand with a paring knife, but it can be accomplished with practice. If there was ever a time to use a vegetable peeler to remove the zest from a fruit, it is now. For both drinks, the zest spirals are inserted before adding ice. For a Crusta, curl the zest into a spiral and insert it on its side into the glass. For a Horse's Neck, hook one end of the zest over the rim of the glass (creating the "horse's neck"), letting the rest of the zest hang into the glass.

Other Fruit Garnishes According to the recipe, you may also need fresh berries, pineapple wedges, peaches, apples, bananas, or other fruits as edible garnishes. Some cocktails call for seasonal fresh fruit. In that case, choose a colorful assortment of the best produce available.

Cherries, Maraschino and Italian Preserved: There used to be only one kind of maraschino cherry, made in America, artificially flavored and unnaturally colored neon red. These were only inspired by and named for the famous European Marasca sour cherry and the equally famed Italian maraschino liqueur made from them, but in truth, they bore little resemblance to the real thing.

Today's craft bartenders use real marasca or amara cherries preserved in cherry syrup. You will find them at specialty markets and online. Luxardo is an excellent Italian brand. Unless a recipe specifically calls for imported marasca cherries, you can use either imported or domestic, but once you taste the Italian cherries, there will be no turning back. As an alternative, use cherries soaked in kirsch or brandy. They are almost as good, but the additional spirits will add a little alcoholic flavor to the cocktail.

Fresh Herbs and Savory Garnishes Mint sprigs are a familiar cocktail garnish, but you will also find other herbs in today's

TAKING STOCK

Here's what you'll need for a well-stocked bar.

Bitters

  Angostura bitters
  Peychaud's bitters
  Orange bitters

Fruit Juices

> Limes and lemons for freshly squeezed juices
> Oranges and grapefruits for freshly squeezed juices (refrigerated)
> Cranberry and pineapple juices (packaged)

Savory Ingredients

> Tomato juice and/or tomato-vegetable juice (canned)
> Prepared horseradish
> Hot red pepper sauces
> Worcestershire sauce

Sweetening Ingredients

> Simple syrup (page 25, or use store-bought)
> Superfine (bartenders') sugar
> Granulated sugar
> Sugar cubes
> Maple syrup, preferably Grade B, and agave nectar
> Cream of coconut (Coco Lopez)
> Various flavored syrups, homemade or store-bought
> Grenadine (page 26, or use store-bought)

Dairy/Egg Ingredients

> Half-and-half
> Heavy cream
> Milk
> Butter
> Large Grade A eggs

Sodas (preferably in individual-serving bottles)

> Soda water
> Tonic (quinine) water
> Various sodas, such as cola and lemon-lime

Garnishes

> Lemon wedges
> Lime wedges
> Assorted citrus wheels

Orange and lemon twists

Pineapple wedges and/or chunks

Maraschino cherries, preferably Italian preserved
  Marasca cherries

Pitted green olives

Celery sticks

Cocktail onions

Fresh herbs, such as mint, basil, and rosemary

cocktails. When muddling herbs, be sure to only use the leaves and not the strong-tasting stems.

Don't forget crisp celery stalks with the leaves attached for Bloody Marys, and cocktail onions for Gibsons.

TECHNIQUES

Chilling Glassware

Always chill before you fill—even your cocktail shaker—and mix the drink. There are two ways to make a cocktail glass cold:

1. Put the glasses in the refrigerator or freezer a couple of hours before using them.
2. Fill the glasses with ice and water and stir. Let stand while making the drink, then discard the ice water before filling the glasses.

Mixing Drinks

Any cocktail lover fondly clings to the image of a bartender vigorously shaking a drink, the ice making a syncopated rattle that is as melodic as any symphony. However, shaking is appropriate for many, but not all, drinks. Forget the old warning about "bruising the liquor," for spirits cannot be affected by shaking. However, shaking will effervesce the cocktail ingredients, and there are many times when you want the drink to remain clear. Mixing drinks can also be accomplished by stirring, as well as by two less common techniques, swizzling and rolling.

No matter which mixing procedure you use, remember that the ice does more than chill the drink. As the ice melts, it slightly dilutes and mellows the alcohol to actually make the drink more palatable. This is easy to test with deeply chilled vodka from the freezer—a habit that many people have affected to make a well-chilled martini. Pour one martini directly from the chilled bottle, and stir up another with ice in a mixing glass and strain it into a second glass. Taste them side by side. Thanks to the milder flavor, most people will prefer the ice-stirred drink. Even drinks that are served on the rocks are often shaken first and then strained into a glass over fresh ice to control the amount of melting (as the fresh ice won't melt as quickly as the shaken ice).

Shaking Drinks As a rule of thumb, shake any drink made with juices, syrup or sugar, egg, or cream to be sure that the ingredients are thoroughly combined. Pour the ingredients into the glass mixing part of the Boston shaker, with spirits first, then juices, and then the sweeteners and other flavorings, such as bitters. If you are trying to learn a drink recipe by heart, you can alter the sequence to go from largest amount of ingredients to the smallest, as that seems a reasonable and reliable way to remember a long list. Pouring the ingredients into the mixer glass before adding the ice premixes them before the more thorough shaking.

Now add ice to the mixer to fill it about two-thirds full, as you want to leave room for the ingredients to be able to move freely during shaking. Egg-based drinks, such as Flips, are an important exception. In their case, the ingredients are first combined and shaken without ice to make an emulsion and then the ice is added for a second shaking to chill the drink. And never shake a drink with soda, as the action will burst the bubbles, but add the soda to top off the drink after it is poured.

Place the metal half of the Boston shaker over the glass while it's sitting on the bar. Holding the glass firmly, clap the upturned end of the metal half twice with the heel of your free hand to form a seal. (To test the seal, lift the shaker by the metal top slightly off the bar to see if it holds; if not, repeat the procedure and try lifting again.)

Turn the conjoined shakers over so that the glass is on top and the metal half rests on the bar. Grasp the shakers with the metal half sitting securely in the palm of one hand and the other hand wrapped securely over the top of the glass half, then shake hard with the glass half of the set on top. (In case the seal breaks, the liquid stays in the bigger metal half.) Shake vigorously, for a count of eight, rendering the drink effervescent and with just the right amount of melting. With egg-based drinks, you may need to shake for about a minute, until you can see that the ingredients are mixed well and evenly colored.

After shaking, clasp one hand around the equator of the conjoined shakers and then, using the heel of your other hand, hit the metal shaker bluntly at the point where it meets the mixing glass to break the seal. If it doesn't work the first time, try again at another spot.

You can use a cobbler or Parisian shaker to shake drinks, but most professionals prefer the Boston shaker because it is sturdy, easy to clean, and the glass reveals how the drink is mixed at a glance.

Stirring Drinks When the drink is comprised of spirits alone, stir the ingredients so they remain clear and unclouded by shaking. After you've assembled your liquids and ice in the mixer glass, insert the barspoon, letting the handle of the spoon rest on the edge of the glass. Move the spoon around the edge of the glass in a circle for at least thirty seconds to completely chill the cocktail, while also allowing sufficient time for a small amount of the ice to melt.

Swizzling Any drinker knows the swizzle stick—the long decorative plastic rod jutting out of a tall (also called long) cocktail that serves as a stirrer. A proper swizzle stick is actually made from wood, getting its name from the long, straight branches of the Caribbean swizzlestick tree, or all spice bush. The swizzle stick lends its name to an entire category of iced thirst-quenchers that are stirred in a special way to frost the outside of the serving glass.

A barspoon, which is long enough to reach the bottom of the deepest glass, can be used as a swizzle stick. Pour the ingredients into the serving glass (usually a Collins or hurricane glass) and add the ice. Insert the barspoon. Place both palms around the twisted part of the handle. Move your hands back and forth and up and down to quickly rotate and lift the spoon until the glass is nicely frosted. When serving the drink, hold it by its rim with a cocktail napkin, so as not to mar the frosting.

Rolling Drinks This technique prevents drinks that call for thick juices or fruit purees from foaming. (It is also somewhat of a timesaver and gives the bartender an occasional break from shaking.) Pour the ingredients over ice in the mixing glass of a Boston shaker. Pour the drink back and forth between the glass and metal shaker half two or three times until combined. Strain the drink into the prepared serving glass.

Other Techniques

Coating a Glass Cocktails are created from a well-considered mix of ingredients, and sometimes a whisper of a particular spirit is all that is required. Coating the glass with a small amount of liquor accomplishes this step. Pour just a splash of the liquor into the serving glass, swirl to coat the inside, and pour out the excess liquor. (It is usually too much trouble to try to get these few drops back in their original bottle, so just discard them.) The exact amount of liquor will change with each recipe, depending on the desired flavor impact, but it will be small. Don't worry if it doesn't coat every inch of the glass interior. The idea is to provide background flavor in each sip.

Flaming Liquors The secret of setting brandy (or other high-alcohol spirits) aflame is first to warm it and its glass. Fill the glass with very hot tap (preferably boiling) water and let stand while heating the liquor. Next, heat the required spirits in a small saucepan over low heat. When the liquor is very warm, remove the saucepan from the heat. Discard the hot water from the glass. Pour the liquor into the warmed glass. Ignite the liquor with a match (preferably a long match) using extra care, as the invisible fumes above the liquor may ignite before the liquid itself. Let the flame burn out on its own, but don't let the flame burn too long or it will affect the flavor of the liquor. If it burns longer than 45 seconds or so, place a heatproof saucer over the top of the glass to cut off the oxygen and smother the flame.

Take precautions when flaming drinks. The flames shoot high suddenly. Look up and be sure there's nothing "en route" that can ignite. That includes your hair and sleeves. Have an open box of baking soda handy to pour over flames in case of accidents. Use pot holders to protect your hands from the hot glass and saucepan.

Floating Liqueurs Creating a rainbow effect in a glass with different colored cordials requires a special, but easy to master, pouring technique. Place a long barspoon, with rounded side of the spoon bowl facing up, in the glass at the level where you want the first liqueur. Let the tip of the spoon bowl touch the side of the glass. This breaks the velocity of liqueur as it pours and helps it spread evenly. Slowly pour the liqueur over the spoon bowl into the glass. For the next layer, place the tip of the spoon just at the surface of the poured liqueur and pour in the next cordial so it layers on top of the first. Repeat until all of the layers have been poured. You can also use this technique to float lightly whipped cream on top of a drink.

Muddling Fruits and Herbs This is a simple technique for mashing fruit and herbs, such as the lime and mint in a Mojito, in the bottom of the serving (or mixing) glass. Crushing releases more flavorful oils into the drink than shaking. Plastic or wooden muddlers are easily found at kitchenware shops. Use the wider, flat end of the muddler to do the mashing. Muddled drinks are often strained before serving, but in the case of the Caipirinha, the muddled ingredients sometimes remain in the serving glass.

Rimming a Glass Creating an edible crust around the edge of the serving glass is called rimming and is a direct connection to the antique Crusta cocktail, which used sugar for the encrusting. The technique was revived, with coarse salt instead of sugar, for the Margarita. In fact, until recently, the Margarita was the only cocktail that was regularly served in a rimmed glass, and even then as an option. Bartenders now regularly use rimming to add another layer of flavor to their specialty cocktails. The sugar or salt can be mixed with other ingredients, such as spices or herbs, for even more sensory pleasure.

Rimming separates the pros from the amateurs. The crust must only cling to the outside of the glass. If it is inside the glass, the inner crust will fall into the drink and overseason it. Use coarse (kosher, never iodized or fine) salt and superfine (granulated is fine) sugar for average use. Some drinks may have special requirements for particular ingredients, like sanding (coarse-crystal) sugar. Pour the salt or sugar into a small saucer to a depth of at least $1/8$ inch. Using a wedge of fresh citrus (chosen to complement the flavor of the drink) or a small amount of the required liquor on a paper towel, carefully moisten only the outside rim of the serving glass. Then, holding the glass sideways, dab the rim into the salt or sugar while turning the glass until the entire rim is covered. Finally, hold the glass over a sink and tap the glass gently against your free hand to knock off any excess rimming ingredients. The result is a delicately encrusted rim that looks almost frosted.

SERVING DRINKS

If you're the least bit theatrical, this is the time for it. Just remember: Always use the Hawthorne strainer (spring-form) with the metal part of the set for shaken drinks, and the julep strainer (holes) with the glass half for stirred cocktails.

Straining from the Metal Shaker Place the Hawthorne strainer in the mixer, acting as a cover. Then put your forefinger and middle finger over the strainer while grabbing the shaker with your thumb, ring, and pinky fingers. Hold the shaker tightly and strain slowly at first to avoid splashing out of the glass. When straining into a cocktail glass, pour the liquid in a circular motion around the inside of the glass to help avoid spillage. As the pour slows toward the last ounce, draw your hand up high over the middle of the cocktail glass, emptying the last of the liquid with a snap of the shaker.

Straining from the Glass Shaker Place the julep strainer over the top of the glass with the concave side facing up. Grab the glass toward the top with your thumb and last three fingers, and then curl your forefinger over the handle of the strainer, holding it firmly in place. Strain following the directions above.

Double-Straining Muddled or shaken cocktails sometimes contain tiny flecks of solid ingredients that must be removed before serving. Double-straining through a sieve does a better job than a single metal cocktail strainer. Hold a wire sieve over the prepared glass. With your other hand, pour the drink from the strainer-covered shaker through the sieve into the glass.

Opening Champagne or Sparkling Wine

When the bottle is well chilled, wrap it in a clean towel and undo the wire around the cork, holding the cork down with one hand while loosening the wire with the other—never letting go of the cork. Pointing the bottle away from people and priceless objects, grasp the bottle by the indentation on the bottom. Leveraging the pressure between both hands, slowly turn the bottle until the cork comes free with a gentle pop. The idea is to release as little carbon dioxide from the bottle as possible, as the more pop, the more gas is released into the air, reducing the amount of bubbles. Pour slowly into the center of the glass.

Opening Wine

Cut the seal neatly around the neck with a sharp knife just below the top. Peel off, exposing the cork. Wipe off the cork and bottle lip. Insert the corkscrew and turn until the corkscrew is completely inside the cork. With a steady pull, remove the cork. If the cork crumbles or breaks, pour the wine through a tea strainer into another container for serving. The host or hostess should taste the wine to check its quality before offering it to guests.

How Many Drinks to Plan

Whether you're hosting an intimate dinner party or throwing a bash for a crowd, the buying guide charts in this section can make it easy for you to determine how much liquor and wine you'll need. A rule of thumb is one drink per hour per person, with a little extra added as insurance. Remember, liquor has a long shelf life, even opened, so it is better to buy more and store leftovers than to run out.

With wine, open the bottles as needed, as unopened bottles can also be stored for another use, but opened bottles must be consumed in the next few days after the party. Always encourage the practice of designated driving at your festivities.

	For Four People	For Eight People	For Twelve People
LUNCH	4 cocktails/ wine before lunch	8 cocktails/ wine before lunch	12 cocktails/ wine before lunch
	4 glasses of wine with lunch	8 glasses of wine with lunch	12 glasses of wine with lunch
	4 liqueurs after lunch (optional)	8 liqueurs after lunch (optional)	8 liqueurs after lunch (optional)
COCKTAILS	6 cocktails/ wine per hour	12 cocktails/ wine per hour	18 cocktails/ wine per hour
DINNER	6 cocktails/ wine before dinner	12 cocktails/ wine before dinner	18 cocktails/ wine before dinner
	8 glasses of wine with dinner	16 glasses of wine with dinner	24 glasses of wine with dinner
	4 cocktails/ liqueurs after dessert	8 cocktails/ liqueurs after dessert	12 cocktails/ liqueurs after dessert
EVENING	6 cocktails/ wine per hour	12 cocktails/ wine per hour	18 cocktails/ wine per hour

How Many Bottles of Wine for Dinner

Table Wines, Champagnes, Sparkling Wines
average 2 servings, 5 ounces each, per person

People	4	6	8	10	12	20
750ml	2	2+	3+	4	5	8
1.5 liter	1	1+	2	2	2+	4

Generally, bottle quantities recommended provide some small overages
of wine from 10-ounces-per-guest formula; "+" indicates somewhat less
than the formula and you may desire to have an additional bottle on hand.

How Many Drinks Per Bottle

Cocktails, Mixed Drinks
1.5-ounce liquor servings

Bottles	1	2	4	6	8	10	12
750ml	16	33	67	101	135	169	203
Liter	22	45	90	135	180	225	270
1.5 liter	39	78	157	236	315	394	473

Table Wines, Champagnes, Sparkling Wines
5-ounce wine servings

Bottles	1	2	4	6	8	10	12
750ml	5	10	20	30	40	50	60
Liter	6	13	27	40	54	67	81
1.5 liter	10	20	40	60	81	101	121
3 liter	20	40	80	121	161	202	242
4 liter	27	54	108	162	216	270	324

MEASURES

Standard Bar Measurements (U.S. fluid ounces)

1 pony	= 1 ounce
1 ounce	= 3 centiliters
1 jigger shot	= 1½ ounces
1 mixing glass	= 16 ounces
1 splash	= ½ teaspoon

Other Measures

1 dash	= 6 drops
12 dashes	= ½ teaspoon
1 teaspoon	= ⅙ ounce
2 teaspoons	= ⅓ ounce
1 tablespoon	= ½ ounce
2 tablespoons	= 1 ounce
¼ cup	= 2 ounces
½ cup	= 4 ounces
1 cup or ½ pint	= 8 ounces
2 cups or 1 pint	= 16 ounces
4 cups, 2 pints, or 1 quart	= 32 ounces

Bottle Size Measures

Split	= 187 ml	= 6.4 ounces
Half-bottle	= 375 ml	= 12.7 ounces
Fifth	= 750 ml	= 25.4 ounces
Liter	= 1000 ml	= 33.8 ounces
Magnum	= 1.5 liters	= 2 wine bottles
Jeroboam	= 3 liters	= 4 wine bottles
Rehoboam	= 6 wine bottles	
Methuselah	= 8 wine bottles	
Salmanazar	= 12 wine bottles	
Balthazar	= 16 wine bottles	
Nebuchadnezzar	= 20 wine bottles	
Sovereign	= 34 wine bottles	

BASIC RECIPES

SIMPLE SYRUP

Makes about 1 c.

The bartender's sweetest ally. You can add other ingredients to the basic recipe to create an almost endless list of flavored syrups. (For an amazingly quick version that doesn't require cooking, use the Quick Simple Syrup variation.) Large bars can multiply this recipe to make as much as needs dictate, but don't make any less, as it keeps for weeks. While we encourage you to make simple syrup, superfine sugar will work at the proportion of 1½ teaspoons sugar to ½ ounce of syrup.

1 c. granulated sugar

Bring sugar and 1 c. water to a boil in small saucepan over high heat, stirring to dissolve sugar. Boil without stirring for 1 minute. Let cool. Pour into a very clean covered container and store in refrigerator for up to 2 months.

Chile Syrup: *Add 1 tbsp. crushed hot red pepper flakes to the hot syrup in the saucepan and let cool. Strain and store in refrigerator for up to 3 weeks.*

Cinnamon Syrup:

Substitute Demerara sugar for the granulated sugar. As soon as the syrup comes to a boil, add 4 (3-inch long) cinnamon sticks. Reduce heat to very low and simmer for 5 minutes. Let cool. Strain and store in refrigerator for up to 3 weeks.

Demerara Syrup:

This syrup gives a richer, molasses-like sweetness and an earthy color to cocktails. Substitute 1 c. Demerara sugar for the granulated sugar. Store in refrigerator for up to 2 months.

Ginger Syrup: *A deliciously spicy syrup that works in many cocktails beyond the predictable tiki drinks. Add ¼ cup peeled, coarsely chopped fresh ginger to the saucepan with the sugar and water and bring to a boil. Let cool. Strain, pressing hard on the solids. Store in refrigerator for up to 3 weeks.*

Honey Syrup: *For a more subtle sweetness, use this syrup. Don't use a strong honey, such as chestnut, or its flavor may overpower the cocktail. Simply shake ⅔ c. mild honey and ⅓ c. water together in a covered jar until the honey dissolves. Store in refrigerator for up to 2 months.*

BASICS

Lavender Syrup: *Be sure to use edible culinary lavender, now available in the spice section of many supermarkets, and not lavender intended for potpourri. Add 3 tablespoons edible dried lavender to the saucepan with the sugar and water and bring to a boil. Let cool. Strain and store in refrigerator for up to 3 weeks.*

Lemongrass Syrup: *Cut off the woody tops from 5 lemongrass stalks and peel off and discard the outer layers. Coarsely chop the tender bulbous bottoms. Add to the hot syrup in the saucepan and let cool. Strain, pressing hard on solids. Store in refrigerator for up to 3 weeks.*

Rhubarb Syrup: *Add ½ c. thinly sliced rhubarb to the saucepan with the sugar and water and bring to a boil. Let cool. Strain and store in refrigerator for up to 3 weeks. Makes about 1¼ c.*

Vanilla Syrup: *Add 3 vanilla beans, split lengthwise, to the hot syrup and let cool. Using the tip of a small knife, scrape the seeds from each vanilla bean half into the syrup. Discard the beans. Store in refrigerator for up to 3 weeks.*

Quick Simple Syrup: *The only difference between this and the cooked syrup is that the cooked version is best for infusing with flavorings. Be sure to use superfine (also called bartenders' or bakers') sugar, available at supermarkets in the baking aisle. Combine 1 cup superfine sugar and 1 cup water in a covered jar. Shake well until the sugar dissolves. Store in refrigerator for up to 2 months.*

☐ HOMEMADE GRENADINE

Makes about ¾ c.
Sure, you can buy the commercial stuff. But with pomegranate juice on every supermarket shelf (look for bargain-priced juice at grocers with Middle Eastern products), why not make your own? The flavor is superior.

½ c. pomegranate juice
½ c. superfine sugar
A few drops orange blossom
    water (optional)

Combine pomegranate juice, sugar, and orange blossom water, if using, in a covered jar and shake well to dissolve sugar. Store in refrigerator for up to 2 months.

COCKTAIL CLASSICS

EING A BARTENDER requires far more than memorizing a few recipes and learning to use some basic tools. Sure, you might be able to mix a drink, but that is no guarantee you will consistently produce truly great drinks.

A bartender is in many ways like a chef—taking individual ingredients and mixing them together to create an artful blending of flavors. The best cocktails are a form of cuisine in their own right.

Just as a great chef must have a command of the foundations of cooking, like a mastery of classic French sauces, the bartender must understand the basic techniques, processes, methods, and products involved in the craft. And this includes an understanding and appreciation of the classic cocktails. These recipes are the foundation for nearly every existing drink and provide the basis for creating new and distinctive drinks.

The following eight cocktails form the basis for most modern cocktails. Understand their histories, variations, and processes, and you'll be well on your way to a better appreciation of your craft as well as being able to create original cocktails that may someday take their place among the greats.

THE OLD-FASHIONED WHISKEY COCKTAIL

Unlike other cuisines of the world, the cocktail is only a few hundred years old. While we don't know precisely when or where the cocktail made its official first appearance, we can trace it back as far as 1806. There, in a popular New York publication called *The Balance, and Columbian Repository*, we find the cocktail defined.

In the May 13 edition, an editor responded to a letter from a devoted reader about the term "cock-tail" as it appeared in the previous week's edition, saying:

As I make it a point, never to publish anything (under my editorial head) but which I can explain, I shall not hesitate to gratify the curiosity of my inquisitive correspondent: Cock tail, then is a stimulating liquor, composed of spirits of any kind, sugar, water and bitters—it is vulgarly called a bittered sling.

At the core of this, you see the definition of the cocktail: "spirits of any kind, sugar, water and bitters." While the term "cocktail" has since been broadened to include far more drinks, and with a far less distinct definition, this original definition is one of which all bartenders should be aware. As the cocktail evolved, this earliest of cocktails became known simply as the Old-Fashioned.

There are many who claim the Old-Fashioned was invented at the Pendennis Club in Louisville, Kentucky. One of the oldest records of a recipe going by the name of Old-Fashioned is from *Modern American Drinks* by George J. Kappeler, published in 1895:

☐ THE OLD-FASHIONED WHISKEY COCKTAIL

Dissolve a small lump of sugar with a little water in a whiskey-glass; add two dashes Angostura bitters, a small piece ice, a piece lemon-peel, one jigger whiskey. Mix with small bar-spoon and serve, leaving spoon in glass.

Remembering the earlier stated definition of a cocktail, what is an Old-Fashioned but "spirits of any kind [whiskey], sugar, water and bitters"? To draw an even closer connection, many recipes of that time would also indicate that other spirits could be used in an Old-Fashioned in order to make an Old-Fashioned Brandy Cocktail, or an Old-Fashioned Rum Cocktail.

In the first known bartender's guide, *How to Mix Drinks* (Dick & Fitzgerald, 1862), Jerry Thomas writes:

♀ WHISKEY COCKTAIL
Use a small bar glass.

3 or 4 dashes of gum syrup
2 do. Bitters (Bogart's)
1 wine-glass of whiskey, and a piece of lemon peel.

Fill one-third full of fine ice; shake and strain in a fancy red-wine glass.

To translate some unfamiliar terminology, gum syrup (sometimes called gomme syrup), is a sugar syrup thickened with gum arabic. The abbreviation "do." stands for "ditto" and refers to the word "dashes" in the line above. Bogart's is a type of bitters that is no longer produced commercially. A wine-glass held 2 ounces.

This is the same cocktail as the Old-Fashioned and leads to the conclusion that the Pendennis Club didn't actually invent the Old-Fashioned, but simply provided their customers with a whiskey cocktail made the old-fashioned way. Many cocktails have far more stories attempting to describe their origins. After all, drinking and storytelling go hand in hand, so treat any tale of cocktail invention with a bit of skepticism.

Here's a contemporary version of the Old-Fashioned.

☐ OLD-FASHIONED WHISKEY COCKTAIL
2 oz. rye or bourbon whiskey
¼ oz. simple syrup
2 dashes Angostura bitters
Garnish: Lemon twist

Pour rye or bourbon, syrup, and bitters into a cracked-ice-filled old-fashioned glass and stir. Add lemon twist.

This Old-Fashioned reflects the way this cocktail should taste. Simple syrup is used because it's easier than muddling the sugar in the glass and also provides a more consistent sweetening. Unlike many modern renditions, there is no cherry or orange muddled in with the bitters and sweetener at the beginning and there is no soda or water at the end. The water melting from the ice is just the right amount to even out the rough edges of the whiskey.

The beauty of this recipe lies in its simplicity and authenticity. Hundreds of years ago, spirits were so rough that sweeteners were needed to mask their flavors. Today, spirits are of much higher quality and don't need to be masked; instead the sweetener is being used to counterbalance the alcoholic bite, as well as fill out the flavor profile in areas where the spirit doesn't touch.

Bitters, as we have seen, are at the very heart of the definition of a cocktail. Prior to around 1900 it was almost unthinkable to have a cocktail that didn't include bitters in some form. Bitters, when added in small amounts, offer complexity to the overall flavor of the drink.

Finally, the water that is added to the Old-Fashioned and other cocktails through the ice serves to tone down and mellow the overall flavors as well as soften the bite typical of a straight spirit. Topping the drink off with additional water, as is often done, only results in a very diluted drink. The ice alone is sufficient.

But what about that cherry and orange? They were not part of the original drink and are in fact relative newcomers to the Old-Fashioned glass. You'll find an orange slice being used instead of a lemon twist in the 1930 printing of *The Savoy Cocktail Book* by Harry Craddock. (Craddock was an American bartender who migrated to the bar at the Savoy Hotel in London during Prohibition. We all can be thankful that he chronicled most of his recipes in his book.) For the next several decades you'll see lemon, pineapple, orange, and cherry all make an appearance, either separately or in various combinations, but always as a garnish. Exactly when the practice of muddling the fruit came into fashion is hard to determine, but it doesn't appear to be referenced in print much before the 1990s.

The modern maraschino cherry didn't come onto the scene until the early 1900s, just before Prohibition. It was intended as a "temperance" replacement for the brandy-soaked marasca cherries, which previously had been in common use. Prohibition made the original version impossible to obtain in the United States, and so maraschino cherries quickly replaced them in baking and garnishing. Muddling them into the drink does little to improve the flavor or the aesthetics of this drink, even if you use imported Marasca cherries.

The orange is a slightly different story. If you glance over many of the historical recipes, you will occasionally see a dash of orange curaçao added. Muddling a slice of orange into the Old-Fashioned extracts similar essential oils to those found in orange liqueurs. Another way to obtain these oils is add an orange twist to the drink. If you wish, slice off a small disk of orange peel, about the size of a half-dollar, point the orange side toward the ice in the glass, and squeeze the peel to release its oils over the ice before adding the whiskey. This will provide an excellent essence of orange to the drink. Garnish the drink with a half orange-wheel and cherry, permitting the fresh fruits to play the ornamental role for which they were intended.

By playing with these techniques and various spirits, you will rediscover this seminal cocktail as it was crafted over two hundred years ago.

THE MANHATTAN COCKTAIL

A hundred years after the Old-Fashioned, near the end of the 1800s, we find the Manhattan. In the second half of the 1800s cocktails began to really catch on, and bartenders were expanding both their repertoire of drinks and the palette of products at their disposal for making them. Simplicity of design, however, was still very much at the core of all drinks.

The Manhattan appears to have come onto the scene about 1882, at which time it was mentioned that a cocktail made from just whiskey, sweet vermouth, and bitters was coming into vogue. It went by not only "Manhattan," but also "Turf Club Cocktail" and "Jockey Club Cocktail." The "Manhattan" moniker almost certainly comes from the Manhattan Club of New York, with the other clubs eager to have their names attached to the drink as well.

Like the Old-Fashioned, the recipe for the Manhattan is deceptively simple—just whiskey, sweet vermouth, and bitters. And likewise, the art of making a great one is in the details.

Here's how to make a Manhattan for today's palates:

ⵧ MANHATTAN
2 oz. rye whiskey
½ oz. sweet vermouth
1 dash Angostura bitters
Garnish: Maraschino cherry, preferably Italian

Stir with ice and strain into chilled cocktail glass. Garnish with cherry.

You'll note two peculiarities in this recipe. The first is the use of rye whiskey; the second is that it is stirred.

As indicated earlier, this drink originated in New York, and in those days the rye whiskey distillers were located in the East, making rye whiskey the spirit of choice. Bourbon, from Kentucky and the surrounding area, was far less common in New York. Today, bourbon may be the default spirit of the Manhattan, but rye has been making a comeback and is worth seeking out. Many people substitute Canadian whisky for rye, but the two are actually quite a bit different. For one thing, rye whiskey must be made from at least 51 percent rye, while Canadian whisky contains far less. This doesn't mean that you can't make a Manhattan with Canadian whisky, or bourbon for that matter, but they will yield vastly different results.

Stirring versus shaking is an age-old debate, and it plays a big role in getting the proper results in many cocktails, specifically a Manhattan. Both shaking and stirring are intended to chill the drink. In addition, as the ice chills the drink it also is melting and therefore contributing water to the drink, an important addition to every cocktail. But because this drink should be clear, and not foamy, stirring is preferred.

Just as the Old-Fashioned could be made with different spirits to create slightly different variations on a theme, there are also variations of the Manhattan. Initially, the Manhattan was designed to use sweet vermouth. But if customers wanted it made with dry vermouth instead, they would ask for a "dry" Manhattan. And asking for a "perfect" Manhattan indicates a 50/50 mixture of sweet and dry vermouth.

Like its progenitor the Old-Fashioned, this recipe contains bitters. And while the vogue for the past decade was to provide bitters on a "by request" basis, this vital ingredient has staged a deserved return to the Manhattan and should be provided as a standard ingredient.

THE MARTINI COCKTAIL

Making its appearance only a few years after the Manhattan, the Martini is a cocktail that has come to be the icon of this genre, so much so that almost any drink in a stemmed cocktail glass is now dubbed a Martini by the drinking public.

There are many stories surrounding the origins of the Martini, but its true origins appear to lie with its forgotten sibling, the Martinez. In *The Bar-Tender's Guide* (1887), "Professor" Jerry Thomas writes:

☍ MARTINEZ COCKTAIL

TAKE:
1 dash of Boker's bitters
2 dashes of Maraschino
1 pony of Old Tom gin
1 wine-glass of vermouth
2 small lumps of ice

Shake up thoroughly, and strain into a large cocktail glass. Put a quarter of a slice of lemon in the glass and serve. If the guest prefers it very sweet, add two dashes of gum syrup.

Again, a bit of translation is required to understand this drink in today's context. Boker's bitters, an aromatic bitters, and Old Tom Gin, a sweetened gin popular in the late 1800s, haven't been made for the past few decades, but are now newly available. A wine-glass usually referred to a 2-ounce pour. The vermouth, while not specified, was probably Italian, what today's drinkers would call sweet or red vermouth. This Martinez was hardly "dry."

In the same book, a recipe for a Manhattan was listed that was essentially the same, except that it used rye whiskey instead of gin. As we previously saw, the Manhattan had also been described five years earlier as being simply whiskey, sweet vermouth, and bitters, so clearly there were some significant variations making the rounds, and it would take a few years for a consensus to settle in on what the proper recipe was. In those days, the art of bartending was in its golden age, with a great deal of competition, experimentation, and advancement of the craft.

By the 1890s recipes for a drink now known as the Martini were appearing. In *Modern American Drinks: How to Mix and Serve All Kinds of Cups and Drinks* (1895), George J. Kappeler writes:

☿ MARTINI COCKTAIL

Half a mixing-glass full of fine ice, three dashes orange bitters, one-half jigger Tom gin, one-half jigger Italian vermouth, a piece lemon peel. Mix, strain into cocktail-glass. Add a maraschino cherry, if desired by customer.

From this we can see that the Martini, containing just gin, sweet vermouth, and bitters, was really a gin version of the Manhattan. And like the Manhattan, when ordered normally it would be made with sweet vermouth, and when ordered "dry" with dry (French) vermouth.

While the Manhattan has pretty much survived to the modern day with its recipe intact, the Martini has not fared so well. It was following Prohibition, when untrained amateurs took to the bar, that the concept of "dry" when applied to the Martini came to mean using less dry vermouth. Today some bartenders use none at all. Orange bitters, once a required component of the Martini, were forgotten, to the point of extinction. They have only resurfaced in the last few years.

One could hardly consider a glass of plain cold gin a cocktail deserving of the name Martini. To rediscover the sophisticated balance and complexity that is possible with the Martini, it is necessary to return to its roots.

☿ TRADITIONAL MARTINI (SWEET)

1 oz. gin
1 oz. sweet vermouth
1 dash orange bitters
Garnish: Lemon twist

Stir with ice and strain into chilled cocktail glass. Add lemon twist.

Y **TRADITIONAL MARTINI (DRY)**
1 oz. gin
1 oz. dry vermouth
1 dash orange bitters
Garnish: Lemon twist

Stir with ice and strain into chilled cocktail glass. Add lemon twist.

Try each of the above exactly as indicated. As with any culinary product, the quality of the ingredients that go into it will greatly affect the outcome, so be sure to use a good gin and good vermouth.

There are several aspects of these recipes that you will notice as being significantly different from what you might be used to. For one thing, there are only 2 ounces total of liquid being used here; this obviously will result in a drink that will look rather lost in today's 5- to 8-ounce cocktail glasses. In the days before Prohibition, the typical cocktail glass was about 4 ounces in size, so the recipes above, with the addition of water from mixing, resulted in a perfectly sized drink.

Another difference you'll see is what appears to be a massive amount of vermouth being used. The result is a drink that bears little resemblance to today's Martini. Push your prejudices aside and instead focus simply on the overall taste of the drink itself, and you'll find the vermouth is not only enjoyable but in perfect balance with the gin.

As noted, the Martini should be stirred, like the Manhattan, to retain its clarity.

And while the olive is the more popular modern garnish, the olive brine affects the delicate balance of the drink. We prefer, at least initially, to get to know this drink with this more understated lemon twist.

Perhaps more than with any other cocktail, the ratios of the ingredients in a Martini require precise balance. No one ingredient should outshine the other, and all ingredients should be playing together in the final product.

The Martini recipes listed here would be inappropriate to serve to a random customer who simply asked for a "Martini." But through the careful understanding of not only the history of this drink but its blending of complex flavors, you'll gain new insights into the mystique of this cocktail. You will find Martini recipes that will be at home in a modern bar in the gin and vodka chapters.

It is also important to recognize how a cocktail recipe can change over time. A few words need to be said about cocktail histories. Like any recipe, it can be difficult or impossible to establish the details of a cocktail's invention. There are often a few claims on a single drink. Knowing a fact or two about a drink may help a bartender keep the huge catalog straight.

Some cocktail titles are actually numbered to differentiate between the various versions. For example, the Alexander No. 1 identifies the original formula for the creamy drink with crème de cacao, which was made with gin. Alexander No. 2 is actually a Brandy Alexander. The Corpse Reviver is another drink that has had a number of incarnations. In this book, we have included our favorite versions of a cocktail, but haven't listed an entire sequence if one of them isn't up to our standards.

Regardless of the well-established history of morphing cocktails, some artisan bartenders, whose goal is to create perfectly crafted, tasty drinks, take the attitude that the Vodka Martini simply does not exist. The reasoning is that if a Vodka Martini is made in the manner that most people order it (very dry), the drink is essentially flavorless. When a bartender is doing his or her job right, the goal should also be to give the customers what they want, regardless of personal likes and dislikes. Even the Very Dry Vodka Martini, the drink that craft bartenders love to hate, can be improved upon by using a small-batch vermouth or a "blond" aperitivo (such as Cocchi Americano). Make the Martini lover a Vesper (page 116) according to James Bond's original recipe, and get ready for some interesting conversation on how to really make a Martini.

MARGARITA, DAIQUIRI, AND SIDECAR

As we've seen through the Old-Fashioned, Manhattan, and even Martini, drinks in the mixed drink category known as "cocktail" always included bitters as one of their ingredients. In those days, there were many different categories of mixed drinks, with the category itself defining much of the recipe. Forgotten monikers like Daisy, Fizz, Cobbler, Crusta, and the still-surviving Sour were each categories of their own. And many of them are coming back as bartenders stretch their talents.

Mixed drinks reached both their apogee and their nadir during Prohibition. To disguise the flavor of so-called bathtub gin and other ill-prepared spirits, more and more ingredients were added to drinks. The term "cocktail" grew to such popularity that it eventually came to encompass many of the drinks that were previously from other categories. The "Sour" is one such category, and it even has vestiges in many modern cocktail names, like the Whiskey Sour.

The traditional sour was made using a spirit of any kind, a sweetening ingredient, and a souring ingredient. The sweetener could be as simple as just sugar or syrup, or it could be a sweet liqueur or cordial. The souring ingredient was normally lemon juice, but it could also be lime juice or grapefruit juice, or some combination of these.

Today, the Margarita is the reigning sour. Like most cocktails, the history of the Margarita is often debated and never resolved. A commonly repeated story has it being invented in 1948 by Margarita Sames for a large party she was holding in Acapulco, Mexico. There is a competing story that claims it was created in 1942 by Francisco Morales, who called this drink a "Daisy," which in Spanish is "Margarita." Another tale insists it was created in the early 1930s at the Caliente Race Track in Tijuana. These and many other conflicting stories all claim to recount the origins of the most popular tequila-based cocktail. But one thing that all of them agree upon is that the original recipe consists of tequila, Cointreau, and lime juice, which clearly follows the classic recipe for a sour.

The Daiquiri is a rum version of the traditional sour, although these days many people will unfortunately confuse it with the blended frozen version, which, unless properly made, can be too reminiscent of "slushee" drinks from childhood.

It is fairly certain that the name of this drink comes from the similarly named town on the east coast of Cuba. While the commonly told story says that it was an American by the name of Jennings Cox who was living in Daiquiri who invented the drink, it is more likely that this was just a commonly served drink and that Americans who came to visit Mr. Cox and were served this drink began referring to it as "that Daiquiri drink." While the Margarita uses Cointreau as its sweetening ingredient, the Daiquiri uses just plain sugar or simple syrup for the task. However, it too is a sour.

The first appearance of the Sidecar recipe is found in *Cocktails: How to Mix Them*, by Robert Vermeire, published in 1922. Here, the recipe was listed as "⅙ gill of fresh Lemon Juice, ⅙ gill of Cointreau, ⅙ gill of Cognac Brandy." The use of "gill" here might be confusing (a gill is 4 ounces), but the important thing to note is the equal proportions. It is debated whether this drink originated in Paris or London, but it is generally accepted that it was created in Europe at just about the same time that American Prohibition began. Over the years, the proportions have changed a bit to make a less tart drink.

For all of these cocktails it has become overly common for bars to use a "sour mix" to make them, often just combining a premade sour mix with the base spirit in order to quickly and efficiently churn out drinks. This approach, however, is not one that should be followed by a quality bar, any more than a quality restaurant would premake all of their meals and simply reheat them in the microwave.

In achieving balance, these drinks should be neither overly sour nor overly sweet. And the base spirit, while not dominant, should be present in flavor.

☐ MARGARITA
For glass: Lime wedge, coarse (kosher) salt
1½ oz. blanco tequila
¾ oz. Cointreau or triple sec
¾ oz. fresh lime juice

Rim chilled cocktail glass with lime and salt. Shake remaining ingredients with ice and strain into glass.

☐ DAIQUIRI
2 oz. light rum
¾ oz. fresh lime juice
¾ oz. simple syrup

Shake with ice and strain into a chilled cocktail glass.

☐ SIDECAR
1 oz. Cognac
1 oz. triple sec
½ oz. fresh lemon juice

Shake with ice and strain into a chilled cocktail glass.

While each of these cocktails follows the same basic approach of spirit plus sweet plus sour, the actual ratios being used for each of them are listed differently. Because of the variation among spirits brands and the even greater variation in things like natural citrus, you should be prepared to adjust your recipes for balance. These recipes are merely a starting point.

A mastery of these principles can help you to improve the way you make drinks like the Lemon Drop, Kamikaze, Cosmopolitan, Between the Sheets, and Aviation, all of which owe their origins to the sour.

THE MAI-TAI

Just as America was coming out of Prohibition, Donn Beach was setting up shop with his Polynesian-themed restaurants, which became known as "Don the Beachcomber." In the 1940s Victor Bergeron threw his hat in the ring and started the Trader Vic's chain. These two franchises specifically ushered in a new era, not only in restaurant culture, but in the cocktails they produced as well. This was the time of the "tiki craze," and there were many similarly themed restaurants that sprang up during this time in order to provide the American public with a much-needed vacation, one sip at a time. Rum was the prominent spirit, with various, often exotic, juices and syrups being used as flavoring agents. Actually, rum is Caribbean, not Polynesian, but when something tastes as good as well-made tiki drink, why split hairs?

Competition between these restaurants was often fierce, with their various cocktail recipes being so closely guarded that even the bartenders themselves did not know how to make them. They would use custom-made flavored syrups and mixes labeled "Don's Mix #1," "Don's Mix #2," and so forth. The bartenders wouldn't know precisely what was in the mix and therefore couldn't reveal the recipes even if they wanted to.

This caused a problem, however, for the customers. After having a particularly fine drink at one bar, they would innocently attempt to order it at some other bar and be faced with an apologetic bartender who had no idea how to make it. Often, these bartenders would attempt to come up with a close approximation. If they felt that their result was a fine-tasting drink, it would then become a new incarnation of the drink.

With the casual proliferation of such a variety of different recipes for a drink with a single name, it is difficult to identify which is the original drink. One of the most popular drinks during this time was the Mai-Tai, and because of this it probably ended up with the highest number of variations. Fortunately, the version that started its popularity, which is referred to as the original Mai-Tai, was recorded by Victor "Trader Vic" Bergeron in 1944. There was apparently a similarly named drink listed on an earlier "Don the Beachcomber" menu, but its recipe was so radically different (and unpopular) that the Trader Vic recipe is clearly a different drink entirely.

As recorded by Mr. Bergeron himself, the original recipe for the Mai-Tai was as follows:

☐ MAI-TAI (TRADER VIC'S)
2 oz. 17-year-old J. Wray and Nephew Ltd. rum
½ oz. French Garnier orgeat
½ oz. Holland DeKuyper orange Curaçao
¼ oz. rock candy syrup
Juice from one fresh lime
Garnish: ½ lime shell, fresh mint sprig

Hand shake and garnish with half of the lime shell inside the drink and float a sprig of fresh mint at the edge of the glass.

J. Wray and Nephew Ltd. now make a 21-year-old rum, but any aged Jamaican rum will be fine. Garnier is no longer in business, so use the oregeat of your choice. You can make a good Mai-Tai with any brand of curaçao. Rock candy syrup is made from crystallized sugar, but simple syrup is a fine stand-in.

Over time, this recipe went through a number of changes, often to accommodate changes in product brands, with the final (and present-day) version served at Trader Vic's being one that turns to a custom-made Mai-Tai mix to be added to rum and lime juice. Those in the know, however, will order their Mai-Tais at one of the many Trader Vic's around the world by requesting a "San Francisco Mai-Tai," a drink made from scratch, without the mix.

This drink is served at other bars across the country with ingredients as far-reaching as pineapple juice, grenadine, passion fruit syrup, orange juice, amaretto, and even cherry brandy. Sometimes the resultant drink may be quite good indeed, but technically it is not a Mai-Tai and would be better to take an original name than to wear the guise of this classic.

A variation of the original Mai-Tai that holds up well without worrying about specific branded products is this one:

☐ **MAI-TAI**
2 oz. dark rum, preferably Jamaican
½ oz. orange curaçao
1 oz. fresh lime juice
½ oz. orgeat syrup
¼ oz. simple syrup
Garnish: Fresh pineapple wedge skewered with maraschino cherry, fresh mint sprig

Shake without ice. Strain into an ice-filled old-fashioned glass. Garnish with skewered pineapple, cherry, and mint.

Another variation is to include super-premium or exotic rums.

BLOODY MARY

The Bloody Mary is an interesting cocktail, with ingredients more commonly found in the kitchen than behind the bar. The most credible story is that it was invented by Fernand Petiot of Harry's American Bar in Paris in the 1920s. When it traveled to America, for many years it was known as a Red Snapper. Its storied past has even inspired drinks-expert Jeff Pogash (full disclosure: father of editor) to write a book titled *The Quest for the Bloody Mary* (2011, Thorn Willow Press).

A vodka-based cocktail, the Bloody Mary owes its flavor to the other ingredients, as vodka does not impart much taste on its own.

The basic Bloody Mary recipe:

☐ BLOODY MARY
1½ oz. vodka
3 oz. tomato juice
¼ oz. fresh lemon juice
4 dashes Worcestershire sauce
2–3 drops hot red pepper sauce
Freshly ground black pepper
Garnish: Lime wedge, 3 green olives

Roll with ice between both halves of Boston shaker. Strain into ice-filled old-fashioned glass. Garnish with lime and olives.

Something interesting has happened with the Bloody Mary that sets it apart from other drinks. While it is often easy to get into a debate over the "correctness" of one recipe or the other, the Bloody Mary has become a drink in which the differences between personal renditions are celebrated.

The above is essentially the "mother" recipe from which different offspring arise. The vodka and tomato juice are the core ingredients, but as for the rest, anything goes as long as you arrive at a spicy and savory drink with a rich and robust flavor.

Among the creative ingredients that have found their way into the Bloody Mary are celery salt, soy sauce, wasabi, horseradish, cumin, chili powder, curry powder, cayenne pepper, ginger, liquid smoke, steak sauce, Angostura bitters, sherry, beef broth, clam juice, and countless others. The Bloody Mary has essentially become the "meat loaf" of cocktails. Almost anything goes as long as it's recognizable in the end.

And while originally the garnish of a wedge of lemon or lime was relatively unassuming, such a modest appointment is almost an insult today. The choices for garnishing a Bloody Mary can range from a simple selection of olives or a long, crisp celery stick with its leaves still attached to cooked appetizers that are specifically designed to be a value-added accompaniment. Bloody Marys have appeared with sautéed peppers, roasted baby onions, spicy shrimp, chicken satay, cubes of beef, and even whole raw oysters. It's the drink that drinks like a meal, where a little ostentation is welcome.

Historical Cocktail Names

Throughout this book, you will see the same cocktail names appear again and again—Bishop, Cobbler, Rickey, and more. Knowing the basic characteristics of a given cocktail is one way to keep track of the various recipes. Here are some the most common cocktails, most of which have been in service for decades, if not centuries.

Bishop A red wine–based drink, sweetened with citrus and sugar and sometimes spiced.

Buck Usually made with gin, this is a tall drink with ginger ale and a generous squeeze of fresh lemon juice.

Cobbler Shaved or cracked ice is a key element in a cobbler, with the addition of a base liquor and a generous topping of seasonal fresh fruit.

Collins Originally made with gin, but now most often with vodka, the Collins is a thirst-quenching drink of base liquor, lemon juice, and sugar, topped off with soda water.

Crusta The two identifying marks of a Crusta are a sugar-rimmed serving glass (the "crust" that gives the cocktail its name) and a long spiral of citrus zest to garnish and flavor the drink.

Daisy Similar to a Sour (base spirit, lemon juice, and sugar) but with a dose of grenadine or fruit syrup, and served over ice. Some versions have a splash of soda water.

Fix Another tall, tart drink with base spirit, lemon juice, and sugar, always served over lots of ice, sometimes shaved ice.

Fizz A shaken cocktail comprised of base spirit (usually gin), citrus juice, sugar, and sometimes cream, it gets its bubbles from soda water. Some Fizzes include egg (whole, white, or yolk) to encourage a good froth.

Flip On the sweet side, this rich cocktail is always shaken with an egg.

Highball One of the most popular cocktails, this is simply a base spirit with a carbonated liquid, usually soda. Americans like it with ice, which British drinkers traditionally omit.

Julep A symbol of Southern hospitality, the word comes from the Arabic *julāb* ("rose water"), which originally meant a sweetened medicine. Today, it is a base spirit (almost always bourbon), sweetened with sugar and served with a profusion of fresh mint, traditionally over shaved ice in a silver cup.

Pousse-Café The name of this drink type ("coffee pusher" in French) identifies it as a beverage to be served after dinner or even after dessert. It consists of carefully layered liqueurs (and sometimes other ingredients) in a tall, but small, glass.

Rickey Related to the Collins, but without sugar.

Sangaree The name is derived from the Spanish *sangria*, showing how the original version featured fortified wine from the Mediterranean (such as port). It often has a topping of grated nutmeg.

Sling A tall cocktail along the lines of a Collins, but with fruit brandy as a main flavoring, these drinks are related to the original Singapore Sling (mixed with gin, cherry brandy, Bénédictine, and soda).

Smash A cousin of the Julep, in which flavoring ingredients (fruits, sugar, and/or mint) are muddled (that is, smashed) and mixed with a base liquor.

Sour Actually, this kind of cocktail is more sweet-and-sour, as simple syrup is used to balance the sour ingredient (commonly lemon or lime juice). A sour can be made with just about any base spirit, although whiskey is the most familiar.

Swizzle The drinks in this cocktail family are all mixed with a long stick that is twirled between the bartender's palms.

Toddy These days, a toddy is a warming drink of spirits and hot water (and sometimes spices). In Colonial America, it could have been any alcoholic drink that combined liquor and water of any temperature.

BRANDY

BRANDY TAKES ITS NAME from the Dutch word *brandewijn*, or "burned wine," which refers to the process of heating the wine during distillation. Brandy as a category embodies a dizzying number of subcategories, including fruit brandy, grappa, marc, pomace, and eau de vie, to name only a few. The most generic definition for this spirit is that it is distilled from fermented fruit; it is sometimes aged in oak casks or barrels; and it usually clocks in at around 80 proof. While it is often considered an after-dinner sipping spirit, brandy is also widely used in cocktails.

Generally, fruit brandies and eaux de vie can legally be made from practically any fruit, including apples, pears, apricots, blackberries, and cherries. At the high end of the brandy spectrum, you'll find Calvados from the north of France, cognac and Armagnac from southwest France, and Solera Gran Reserva under the Brandy de Jerez imprimatur from the south of Spain. Artisanal brandies are also being made here in the United States, with many of the best hailing from California and Oregon.

In cocktails, cognac plays a leading role in a number of recipes dating back to the birth of the cocktail in Antoine Peychaud's apothecary shop in New Orleans. Indeed, the original juleps were made with cognac, not whiskey. Armagnac, cognac's rustic cousin, has a distinctly stronger flavor than cognac and is employed as a substitute to enhance the brandy presence in a cocktail. Calvados, made with apples, is naturally used to ratchet up the quality of any cocktail calling for mere apple brandy. New Jersey's applejack gets its due in the Jack Rose and other classics. Pisco, a South American brandy, has found its way into many drinks beyond the Pisco Sour and Pisco Punch.

♈ ACCOUTREMENT

Created by CHRIS HANNAH,
New Orleans, LA.

1½ oz. Calvados
½ oz. Strega
¼ oz. orange-flavored
    liqueur, preferably Creole
    Shrubb
½ oz. fresh lemon juice
2 dashes Peychaud's bitters
Garnish: Italian cherry in syrup

*Shake with ice and strain into
chilled cocktail glass. Add
cherry.*

♈ THE "23"

For glass: Lemon wedge and
    superfine sugar
2½ oz. Armagnac
½ oz. sweet vermouth
½ oz. fresh lemon juice
2 dashes Angostura
    bitters
Garnish: Lemon twist

*Rim chilled cocktail glass
with lemon and sugar.
Shake remaining ingredients
with ice and strain into glass.
Add lemon twist.*

ALABAZAM

2 oz. Armagnac
¾ oz. fresh lemon juice
½ oz. orange curaçao
½ oz. simple syrup
2 dashes Angostura bitters
2 dashes Peychaud's bitters
Garnish: Orange twist, flamed

*Shake with ice and strain into
ice-filled old-fashioned glass.
Flame orange twist and add.*

♈ AMERICAN BEAUTY COCKTAIL

½ oz. brandy
½ oz. dry vermouth
½ oz. fresh orange juice
½ oz. grenadine
1 dash white crème
    de menthe
1 dash port

*Shake first five ingredients
with ice and strain into chilled
cocktail glass. Top with port.*

APPLE BRANDY COCKTAIL

1½ oz. apple brandy
1 tsp. grenadine
1 tsp. fresh lemon juice

Shake with ice and strain into chilled cocktail glass.

APPLE BRANDY HIGHBALL

2 oz. apple brandy
Ginger ale or soda water
Garnish: Lemon twist
   (optional)

Pour brandy into ice-filled highball glass. Fill with ginger ale or soda water. Add lemon twist, if desired, and stir.

APPLE BRANDY RICKEY

1½ oz. apple brandy
½ oz. fresh lime juice
Soda water
Garnish: Lime wedge

Stir brandy and lime juice in highball glass. Add ice, fill with soda water, and stir again. Add lime.

APPLE BRANDY SOUR

2 oz. apple brandy
¾ oz. fresh lemon juice
¾ oz. simple syrup
Garnish: Lemon half-wheel,
   maraschino cherry

Shake with ice and strain into chilled cocktail glass. Garnish with lemon and cherry.

BRANDY

SAY HELLO

Greet all guests as they arrive at the bar. If you are busy with a guest make eye contact with new arrivals. Eye contact and a quick smile or nod of awareness will put a new arrival at ease. It will give them the confidence to enjoy the friend they may be with or their surroundings without monitoring your every move to make that initial contact. If you are really slammed the guest will give you the few extra minutes you need if you just give them a smile and a nod.

—DALE DeGROFF (aka King Cocktail),
author of *The Craft of the Cocktail*

APRICOT BRANDY RICKEY

2 oz. apricot-flavored
    brandy
½ oz. fresh lime juice
Soda water
Garnish: Lime wedge

*Stir brandy and lime juice
in highball glass. Add ice,
fill with soda water, and stir
again. Add lime.*

APRICOT COOLER

Orange and/or lemon zest
    spiral
2 oz. apricot-flavored
    brandy
Soda water or ginger ale

*Insert citrus spiral and dan-
gle end over rim of Collins
glass. Add brandy and ice.
Fill with soda water or ginger ale, and stir.*

APRICOT FIZZ

2 oz. apricot-flavored
    brandy
1 oz. fresh lemon juice
½ oz. fresh lime juice
1 tsp. simple syrup
Soda water

*Shake first four ingredients
with ice. Strain into ice-
filled highball glass. Fill with
soda water and stir.*

B & B

½ oz. brandy
½ oz. Bénédictine

*Combine ingredients in
cordial glass.*

BABBIE'S SPECIAL COCKTAIL

1½ oz. apricot-flavored
    brandy
½ oz. gin
½ oz. half-and-half

*Shake with ice and strain
into chilled cocktail glass.*

BEE STINGER

1½ oz. blackberry brandy
½ oz. white crème de menthe

*Shake with ice and strain
into chilled cocktail glass.*

BETSY ROSS

1½ oz. brandy
1½ oz. tawny port
1 dash triple sec

*Stir with ice and strain into
chilled cocktail glass.*

BISTRO SIDECAR

Created by KATHY CASEY,
Seattle, WA

For glass: Tangerine wedge,
    superfine sugar
1½ oz. brandy
½ oz. Tuaca
½ oz. hazelnut liqueur, such
    as Frangelico
½ oz. fresh tangerine juice
¼ oz. fresh lemon juice
¼ oz. simple syrup
Garnish: Roasted hazelnut

*Rim chilled cocktail glass
with tangerine and sugar.
Shake ingredients with
ice. Strain into glass. Add
hazelnut.*

BLACK FEATHER

1 oz. brandy
1 oz. dry vermouth
½ oz. triple sec
1 dash Angostura bitters
Garnish: Lemon twist

Stir and strain into chilled cocktail glass. Add lemon twist.

BOMBAY COCKTAIL

Harry Craddock, an American bartender who landed at London's Savoy after Prohibition, chronicled many of his creations in his 1930 *Savoy Cocktail Book*. You'll see some of his recipes in this book.

1 oz. brandy
½ oz. dry vermouth
½ oz. sweet vermouth
¼ oz. triple sec
¼ tsp. anisette

Stir with ice and strain into chilled cocktail glass.

BOSOM CARESSER

1 oz. brandy
1 oz. madeira
½ oz. triple sec

Stir with ice and strain into chilled cocktail glass.

BRANDIED MADEIRA

1 oz. brandy
1 oz. madeira
½ oz. dry vermouth
Garnish: Lemon twist

Stir with ice and strain into ice-filled old-fashioned glass. Add lemon twist.

BRANDIED PORT

1 oz. brandy
1 oz. tawny port
½ oz. fresh lemon juice
1 tsp. maraschino liqueur
Garnish: Orange wheel

Shake with ice and strain into ice-filled old-fashioned glass. Garnish with orange.

BRANDY ALEXANDER NO. 1

¾ oz. brandy
¾ oz. dark crème de cacao
¾ oz. heavy cream
Garnish: Freshly grated nutmeg

Shake well with ice and strain into chilled cocktail glass. Top with nutmeg.

BRANDY ALEXANDER NO. 2

1 oz. brandy
1 oz. white crème de cacao
1 oz. half-and-half
Garnish: Freshly grated nutmeg

Shake with ice and strain into chilled cocktail glass. Top with nutmeg.

BRANDY CASSIS

1½ oz. brandy
1 oz. fresh lemon juice
½ oz. crème de cassis
Garnish: Lemon twist

Shake with ice and strain into chilled cocktail glass. Add lemon twist.

BRANDY

BRANDY COBBLER

2 oz. brandy
1 tsp. simple syrup
2 oz. soda water
Garnish: Fresh seasonal fruit

Combine brandy, syrup, and soda water in red-wine glass. Fill glass with shaved ice. Garnish with fruit. Serve with straws.

BRANDY COCKTAIL

2 oz. brandy
1 tsp. simple syrup
2 dashes Angostura bitters
Garnish: Lemon twist

Stir ingredients with ice and strain into chilled cocktail glass. Add lemon twist.

BRANDY COLLINS

2 oz. brandy
¾ oz. fresh lemon juice
¾ oz. simple syrup
Soda water
Garnish: Orange or lemon wheel, maraschino cherry

Shake brandy, lemon juice, and syrup and strain into ice-filled Collins glass. Fill with soda water and stir. Garnish with citrus and cherry. Serve with straws.

BRANDY CRUSTA

One of the oldest cocktails, appearing in the first bartenders' guide by "Professor" Jerry Thomas in 1862, this drink is distinguished by its sugared rim and a curled lemon zest almost filling the glass.

For glass: Lemon wedge, superfine sugar
Long, wide spiral of lemon zest
2 oz. brandy
½ oz. triple sec
1 tsp. maraschino liqueur
1 tsp. fresh lemon juice
1 dash Angostura bitters
Garnish: Orange wheel

Rim chilled cocktail glass with lemon and sugar. Curl the zest spiral on its side in glass. Stir ingredients with ice and strain into glass. Garnish with orange.

BRANDY DAISY

2 oz. brandy
1 oz. fresh lemon juice
1 tsp. simple syrup
¼ oz. raspberry syrup or grenadine
Garnish: Fresh seasonal fruit

Shake with ice and strain into beer mug or 8-oz. metal cup. Add ice. Garnish with fruit.

BRANDY FIX

2½ oz. brandy
¾ oz. fresh lemon juice
¾ oz. simple syrup
Garnish: Lemon wheel

Stir brandy, lemon juice, and syrup in shaved ice–filled highball glass. Add lemon. Serve with straws.

BRANDY FIZZ

2 oz. brandy
¾ oz. fresh lemon juice
¾ oz. simple syrup
Soda water

Shake brandy, lemon juice, and syrup with ice and strain into ice-filled highball glass. Fill with soda water and stir.

BRANDY GUMP COCKTAIL

1½ oz. brandy
¾ oz. fresh lemon juice
¼ oz. grenadine

Shake with ice and strain into chilled cocktail glass.

BRANDY HIGHBALL

2 oz. brandy
Ginger ale or soda water
Garnish: Lemon twist

Pour brandy into ice-filled highball glass. Fill with ginger ale or soda water. Add lemon twist and stir gently.

BRANDY JULEP

2½ oz. brandy
½ oz. simple syrup
5–6 fresh mint leaves
Garnishes: Pineapple, orange, or lemon slice; maraschino cherry

Stir brandy, syrup, and mint in Collins glass. Fill with shaved ice and stir until mint rises to top, being careful not to bruise leaves. (Do not hold sides of glass while stirring to frost exterior.) Garnish with fruit. Serve with straws.

BRANDY

BRANDY SANGAREE

2 oz. brandy
½ oz. simple syrup
Soda water
½ oz. port
Garnish: Freshly grated nutmeg

Add brandy and syrup to highball glass. Add ice, fill with soda water, and stir. Float port (see page 18) on top and top with nutmeg.

BRANDY SLING

2 oz. brandy
¾ oz. fresh lemon juice
¾ oz. cherry-flavored brandy
Garnish: Lemon twist

Stir in old-fashioned glass. Fill with ice and stir again. Add lemon twist.

BRANDY SMASH

1 sugar cube
1 oz. soda water
4 fresh mint leaves
2 oz. brandy
Garnish: Lemon twist,
    orange wheel, maraschino
    cherry

*Muddle sugar with soda
water and mint in old-
fashioned glass. Add brandy
and ice. Stir and add lemon
twist. Garnish with orange
and cherry.*

BRANDY SOUR

2 oz. brandy
¾ oz. fresh lemon juice
¾ oz. simple syrup
Garnish: Lemon half-wheel,
    maraschino cherry

*Shake with ice and strain
into chilled cocktail glass.
Garnish with lemon and
cherry.*

BRANDY SWIZZLE

2 oz. brandy
¾ oz. fresh lime juice
¾ oz. simple syrup
2 dashes Angostura bitters
Soda water

*Stir brandy, lime juice,
syrup, and bitters in Collins
glass. Add ice and enough
soda to fill glass ¾ full.
Swizzle with barspoon to
frost glass. Add more ice and
soda as needed. Serve with
swizzle stick.*

BRANDY TODDY

2 oz. brandy
1 tsp. simple syrup
Garnish: Lemon twist

*Stir brandy and syrup in
old-fashioned glass. Add
1 ice cube and lemon twist.*

BRANDY VERMOUTH COCKTAIL

2 oz. brandy
½ oz. sweet vermouth
1 dash Angostura bitters

*Stir with ice and strain into
chilled cocktail glass.*

BRUNSWICK STREET COCKTAIL

1½ oz. cognac
1½ oz. sweet sherry,
    preferably Pedro Ximénez
1 egg yolk
Garnish: Freshly grated
    nutmeg

*Shake without ice. Add ice
and shake again. Strain into
chilled cocktail glass. Top
with nutmeg.*

BULLDOG COCKTAIL

1½ oz. cherry-flavored brandy
¾ oz. gin
½ oz. fresh lime juice

*Shake with ice and strain
into chilled cocktail glass.*

BRANDY

BULL'S EYE

1 oz. brandy
2 oz. hard cider
Ginger ale

Stir brandy and hard cider in highball glass. Add ice, fill with ginger ale, and stir again.

BULL'S MILK

1½ oz. brandy
1 oz. light rum
¼ oz. simple syrup
3 oz. milk
Garnish: Freshly grated nutmeg, ground cinnamon

Shake with ice and strain into chilled Collins glass. Top with nutmeg and cinnamon.

CADIZ

¼ oz. blackberry-flavored brandy
¼ oz. dry sherry
½ oz. triple sec
½ oz. half-and-half

Shake with ice and strain into ice-filled old-fashioned glass.

CALVADOS COCKTAIL

1½ oz. Calvados
1½ oz. fresh orange juice
¾ oz. triple sec
1 dash orange bitters

Shake with ice and strain into chilled cocktail glass.

CARA SPOSA

1 oz. coffee-flavored brandy
¾ oz. triple sec
½ oz. half-and-half

Shake with ice and strain into chilled cocktail glass.

CARROLL COCKTAIL

1½ oz. brandy
¾ oz. sweet vermouth
Garnish: Maraschino cherry

Stir with ice and strain into chilled cocktail glass. Add cherry.

CHAMPS ÉLYSÉES COCKTAIL

Here's another contribution from Harry Craddock's *Savoy Cocktail Book*.

1 oz. brandy
½ oz. yellow Chartreuse
½ oz. fresh lemon juice
1 tsp. simple syrup
1 dash Angostura bitters

Shake with ice and strain into chilled cocktail glass.

CHARLES COCKTAIL

1½ oz. brandy
1½ oz. sweet vermouth
1 dash Angostura bitters

Stir with ice and strain into chilled cocktail glass.

CHERRY BLOSSOM

For glass: Cherry-flavored
    brandy, superfine sugar
1½ oz. brandy
½ oz. cherry-flavored
    brandy
½ oz. fresh lemon juice
¼ oz. triple sec
¼ oz. grenadine
Garnish: Maraschino cherry

*Rim chilled cocktail glass
with brandy and sugar.
Shake ingredients with ice
and strain into glass. Add
cherry.*

CHICAGO COCKTAIL

For glass: Lemon wedge,
    superfine sugar
2 oz. brandy
¼ oz. triple sec
1 dash Angostura bitters

*Rim chilled old-fashioned
glass with lemon and sugar.
Stir remaining ingredients
with ice and strain into
glass.*

CLASSIC COCKTAIL

For glass: Lemon wedge,
    superfine sugar
1 oz. brandy
½ oz. fresh lemon juice
¼ oz. orange curaçao
¼ oz. maraschino liqueur

*Rim chilled old-fashioned
glass with lemon and sugar.
Shake remaining ingredients
with ice and strain into
glass.*

COFFEE GRASSHOPPER

¾ oz. coffee-flavored brandy
¾ oz. white crème de menthe
¾ oz. half-and-half

*Shake with ice and strain
into ice-filled old-fashioned
glass.*

COGNAC HIGHBALL

2 oz. cognac
Ginger ale or soda water
Garnish: Lemon twist
    (optional)

*Pour Cognac into ice-filled
highball glass and fill with
ginger ale or soda water.
Add lemon twist, if desired,
and stir.*

COLD DECK COCKTAIL

1 oz. brandy
½ oz. sweet vermouth
1 tsp. white crème de menthe

*Stir with ice and strain into
chilled cocktail glass.*

CORPSE REVIVER NO. 1

The Corpse Reviver No. 2 is a
gin drink, but Cognac fans like
this one, which is sure to bring
you around.

2 oz. cognac
1 oz. Calvados, apple brandy,
    or applejack
1 oz. sweet vermouth

*Stir with ice and strain into
a chilled cocktail glass.*

BISTRO SIDECAR

BRANDY CRUSTA

AVIATION

EARL GREY MAR-TEA-NI

HARVEST NECTAR

ZOMBIE

JINX

SIDEWINDER

CRÈME DE CAFÉ

1 oz. coffee-flavored brandy
½ oz. light rum
½ oz. anisette
1 oz. half-and-half

Shake with ice and strain into chilled old-fashioned glass.

THE CRUX

¾ oz. Dubonnet
¾ oz. triple sec
¾ oz. brandy
¾ oz. fresh lemon juice
Garnish: Orange twist

Stir with ice and strain into chilled cocktail glass. Add orange twist.

CUBAN COCKTAIL NO. 2

1½ oz. brandy
½ oz. light rum
½ oz. apricot-flavored brandy
½ oz fresh lime juice

Shake with ice and strain into chilled cocktail glass.

D'ARTAGNAN

1 tsp. Armagnac
1 tsp. Grand Marnier
1 tsp. simple syrup
½ oz. fresh orange juice
3 oz. chilled Champagne
Garnish: 3 long, thin strips of orange zest (use channel tool)

Shake first four ingredients with ice and strain into champagne flute. Top with Champagne and insert orange zest strips to extend the length of the glass.

DEAUVILLE COCKTAIL

½ oz. brandy
½ oz. apple brandy
½ oz. triple sec
½ oz. fresh lemon juice

Shake with ice and strain into chilled cocktail glass.

DEPTH BOMB

1 oz. apple brandy
1 oz. brandy
1 dash fresh lemon juice
1 dash grenadine

Shake with ice and strain into ice-filled old-fashioned glass.

DOLORES

1 oz. brandy, preferably Spanish
1 oz. cherry liqueur
1 oz. white or dark crème de cacao
1 egg white
Garnish: Freshly grated nutmeg

Shake without ice. shake with ice and strain into a chilled champagne flute. Top with nutmeg.

DREAM COCKTAIL

1½ oz. brandy
¾ oz. triple sec
1 dash anisette

Shake with ice and strain into chilled cocktail glass.

BRANDY

Y EAST INDIA COCKTAIL NO. 1

1½ oz. brandy
½ oz. Jamaican rum
½ oz. triple sec
½ oz. pineapple juice
1 dash Angostura bitters
Garnish: Lemon twist,
    maraschino cherry

Shake with ice and strain into chilled cocktail glass. Add lemon twist and cherry.

☐ EL PROFESOR

Created by ENRIQUE SANCHEZ,
San Francisco, CA

1 oz. pisco
½ oz. Punt e Mes
½ oz. Bénédictine
2 dashes aromatic bitters,
    such as Fee's
Garnish: Lemon twist

Stir with ice and strain into chilled old-fashioned glass. Add lemon twist.

Y ETHEL DUFFY COCKTAIL

¾ oz. apricot-flavored brandy
¾ oz. white crème de menthe
¾ oz. triple sec

Shake with ice and strain into chilled cocktail glass.

Y FALLEN LEAVES

¾ oz. Calvados
¾ oz. sweet vermouth
¼ oz. dry vermouth
1 dash brandy
Garnish: Lemon twist

Stir with ice and strain into chilled cocktail glass. Add lemon twist.

Y FANCY BRANDY

2 oz. brandy
¼ oz. triple sec
¼ oz. simple syrup
1 dash Angostura bitters
Garnish: Lemon twist

Shake with ice and strain into chilled cocktail glass. Add lemon twist.

Y FANTASIO COCKTAIL

1 oz. brandy
¾ oz. dry vermouth
1 tsp. white crème de menthe
1 tsp. maraschino liqueur

Stir with ice and strain into chilled cocktail glass.

Y FONTAINEBLEAU SPECIAL

1 oz. brandy
1 oz. anisette
½ oz. dry vermouth

Shake with ice and strain into chilled cocktail glass.

▽ FRENCH QUARTER

2½ oz. brandy
¾ oz. Lillet Blanc
Garnish: Lemon quarter-
    wheel

*Stir with ice and strain
into chilled cocktail glass.
Garnish with lemon.*

▽ FROUPE COCKTAIL

1½ oz. brandy
1½ oz. sweet vermouth
1 tsp. Bénédictine

*Stir with ice and strain into
chilled cocktail glass.*

▢ GEORGIA MINT JULEP

2 mint sprigs
¼ oz. simple syrup
1½ oz. brandy
1 oz. peach-flavored
    brandy
Garnish: Additional
    mint sprigs

*Muddle mint and syrup in
Collins glass. Fill with ice.
Add brandy and peach-
flavored brandy. Stir and
garnish with additional
mint.*

▽ GILROY COCKTAIL

¾ oz. cherry-flavored
    brandy
¾ oz. gin
½ oz. dry vermouth
½ oz. fresh lemon juice
1 dash orange bitters

*Shake with ice and strain
into chilled cocktail glass.*

▽ GOAT'S DELIGHT

1½ oz. brandy
1½ oz. kirschwasser
¼ oz. half-and-half
1 dash orgeat or almond syrup
1 dash absinthe or pastis

*Shake with ice and strain
into chilled cocktail glass.*

▢ GOLDEN DAWN

1 oz. apple brandy
½ oz. apricot-flavored brandy
½ oz. gin
1 oz. fresh orange juice
1 tsp. grenadine

*Shake first four ingredients
with ice and strain into ice-
filled old-fashioned glass.
Add grenadine.*

▢ GOTHAM

1 splash absinthe or pastis
3 oz. brandy
3 dashes peach bitters
Garnish: Lemon twist

*Pour absinthe into chilled
old-fashioned glass and
swirl to coat. Shake
brandy and bitters with ice
and strain into glass. Add
lemon twist.*

▽ HARVARD COCKTAIL

1½ oz. brandy
¾ oz. sweet vermouth
½ oz fresh lemon juice
1 tsp. grenadine
1 dash Angostura bitters

*Shake with ice and strain
into chilled cocktail glass.*

BRANDY

HARVARD COOLER

2 oz. apple brandy
½ oz. simple syrup
Soda water or ginger ale
Garnish: Orange and/or lemon
    zest spiral

*Stir brandy and syrup in
Collins glass. Add ice cubes
and fill with soda water or
ginger ale. Insert spiral
of orange or lemon zest (or
both) and dangle end(s) over
rim of glass.*

HONEYMOON
COCKTAIL

¾ oz. apple brandy
¾ oz. Bénédictine
¾ oz. fresh lemon juice
½ oz. triple sec

*Shake with ice and strain
into chilled cocktail glass.*

JACK-IN-THE-BOX

1 oz. applejack
1 oz. pineapple juice
1 dash Angostura bitters

*Shake with ice and strain
into chilled cocktail glass.*

JACK MAPLES

2 oz. applejack
1 tsp. maple syrup (grade B
    or medium-amber)
1 dash aromatic bitters, such
    as Fee's
Garnish: Cinnamon stick

*Stir with ice and strain into
cocktail glass. Garnish with
cinnamon stick.*

JACK ROSE COCKTAIL

Was this drink named for a
notorious gangster? Probably
not. Jack is a nickname for New
Jersey applejack, and grenadine
gives the drink a pink tinge, so
that may provide the simplest,
if dullest, answer.

1½ oz. applejack
½ oz. fresh lime juice
¼ oz. grenadine

*Shake with ice and strain
into chilled cocktail glass.*

JAMAICA GRANITO

1½ oz. brandy
1 oz. triple sec
1 small scoop lemon or
    orange sherbet
Soda water
Garnish: Freshly grated nutmeg

*Add first three ingredients
to Collins glass. Add soda
water. Top with nutmeg.*

JAPANESE

2 oz. brandy
½ oz. orgeat or almond
    syrup
2 dashes Angostura bitters
Garnish: Lemon twist

*Stir with ice and strain into
chilled cocktail glass. Add
lemon twist.*

JERSEY LIGHTNING

1½ oz. applejack
½ oz. sweet vermouth
1 oz. fresh lime juice

*Shake with ice and strain
into chilled cocktail glass.*

JOHNNY APPLESEED

Created by JONATHAN POGASH,
New York, NY

2 slices Fuji apple, chopped
½ oz. fresh lemon juice
½ oz. simple syrup
1 oz. cognac
½ oz. cherry-flavored brandy
1 oz. unfiltered apple juice
Garnish: 1 Fuji apple slice

Muddle first 3 ingredients in mixing glass. Add remaining ingredients and shake with ice. Strain through wire sieve into ice-filled wine glass. Garnish with apple slice.

JACK RABBIT PUNCH

Created by JONATHAN POGASH,
New York, NY

1½ oz. applejack
¾ oz. pear liqueur
¼ oz. allspice liqueur
   (pimento dram)
¾ oz. fresh lemon juice
½ oz. maple syrup
2 oz. sparkling wine
Garnish: Freshly grated
   nutmeg, cinnamon stick,
   sliced pear

Shake ingredients, except for sparkling wine, with ice and strain into ice-filled brandy snifter. Top with sparkling wine. Add garnishes.

KUMQUAT COOLER

Created by JIM MEEHAN,
New York, NY

3 kumquats, sliced
1½ oz. cognac
½ oz. Strega
½ oz. fresh lemon juice
¼ oz. dark rum
¼ oz. simple syrup
Garnish: Kumquat slice and
   lemon wheel, speared on
   toothpick

Muddle kumquats in mixing glass. Add remaining ingredients and ice and shake. Strain into crushed ice–filled Collins glass. Garnish with kumquat and lemon.

LADY BE GOOD

1½ oz. brandy
½ oz. white crème de menthe
½ oz. sweet vermouth

Shake with ice and strain into chilled cocktail glass.

LA JOLLA

1½ oz. brandy
½ oz. crème de banana
½ oz. fresh lemon juice
1 tsp. fresh orange juice

Shake with ice and strain into chilled cocktail glass.

LIBERTY COCKTAIL

1½ oz. apple brandy
¾ oz. light rum
1 tsp. simple syrup

Stir with ice and strain into chilled cocktail glass.

BRANDY

LUXURY COCKTAIL

1 oz. brandy
2 dashes orange bitters
3 oz. chilled Champagne

Gently fold ingredients with ice, so as not to remove bubbles, then strain into chilled champagne flute.

METROPOLE

1½ oz. brandy
1½ oz. dry vermouth
2 dashes orange bitters
1 dash Peychaud's bitters
Garnish: Maraschino cherry

Stir with ice and strain into chilled cocktail glass. Garnish with cherry.

METROPOLITAN COCKTAIL

1¼ oz. brandy
1¼ oz. sweet vermouth
¼ oz. simple syrup
1 dash Angostura bitters

Stir with ice and strain into chilled cocktail glass.

MIDNIGHT COCKTAIL

1 oz. apricot-flavored brandy
½ oz. triple sec
½ oz. fresh lemon juice

Shake with ice and strain into chilled cocktail glass.

MIKADO COCKTAIL

1 oz. brandy
1 dash triple sec
1 dash grenadine
1 dash crème de noyaux
1 dash Angostura bitters

Stir in ice-filled old-fashioned glass.

MON SHERRY

Created by HAL WOLIN, New York, NY

1½ oz. cognac
¾ oz. pear liqueur
½ oz. medium-dry sherry, such as amontillado
2 dashes orange bitters
Garnish: Italian preserved cherry, freshly grated nutmeg

Shake with ice and strain into chilled cocktail glass. Add cherry and top with nutmeg.

MONTANA

1½ oz. brandy
1 oz. tawny port
½ oz. dry vermouth

Stir in ice-filled old-fashioned glass.

MOONLIGHT

2 oz. apple brandy
¾ oz. fresh lemon juice
¾ oz. simple syrup

Shake with ice and strain into ice-filled old-fashioned glass.

☐ MORNING COCKTAIL

1 oz. brandy
1 oz. dry vermouth
1 dash triple sec
1 dash maraschino liqueur
1 dash anisette
2 dashes orange bitters
Garnish: Maraschino cherry

Stir with ice and strain into chilled cocktail glass. Garnish with cherry.

☐ NETHERLAND

1 oz. brandy
1 oz. triple sec
1 dash orange bitters

Stir in ice-filled old-fashioned glass.

☐ NICKY FINN

1 oz. brandy
1 oz. triple sec
1 oz. fresh lemon juice
1 dash absinthe or pastis
Garnish: Maraschino cherry
   or lemon twist

Shake with ice and strain into chilled cocktail glass. Garnish with cherry or lemon twist.

☐ NIGHT & DAY

Created by PETER CHASE,
New York, NY

¾ oz. cognac
¾ oz. overproof rye whiskey
¾ oz. sweet vermouth
½ oz. maple syrup
1 dash Peychaud's bitters
1 dash Angostura bitters
Garnish: Orange and lemon
   twists

Stir with ice and strain into ice-filled old-fashioned glass. Add orange and lemon twists.

☐ THE NORMANDY

1½ oz. Calvados
1½ oz. Dubonnet
1 oz. apple cider
¼ oz. fresh lime juice
Garnish: Red apple slice

Shake with ice and strain into chilled cocktail glass. Garnish with apple slice.

☐ OLYMPIC COCKTAIL

¾ oz. brandy
¾ oz. triple sec
¾ oz. fresh orange juice

Shake with ice and strain into chilled cocktail glass.

☐ PARADISE COCKTAIL

1 oz. apricot-flavored
   brandy
¾ oz. gin
1 oz. fresh orange juice

Shake with ice and strain into chilled cocktail glass.

BRANDY

PEACH SANGAREE

1 oz. peach-flavored brandy
1 oz. tawny port
Soda water
Garnish: Freshly grated
    nutmeg

*Add brandy and port to
ice-filled highball glass.
Add soda water. Top with
nutmeg.*

PISCO PUNCH

The drink of the Gold Rush
in San Francisco, as the
most readily available brandy
was Peruvian. This is an
adaptation of the original,
invented at The Bank
Exchange bar.

2 oz. pisco
¾ oz. pineapple juice
½ oz. simple syrup
½ oz. fresh lemon juice

*Shake with ice and strain
into ice-filled old-fashioned
glass.*

PISCO SOUR

2 oz. pisco
¾ oz. fresh lime juice
¼ oz. simple syrup
½ oz. egg white
Garnish: 1 dash Angostura
    bitters

*Shake without ice. Add ice
and shake again. Strain
into chilled champagne flute
or cocktail glass. Top with
bitters.*

PLAZA PUNCH

Created by JONATHAN POGASH,
New York, NY

1½ oz. pisco
¾ oz. orange liqueur
¼ oz. amaro
¾ oz. pineapple juice
½ oz. fresh lime juice
1 tsp. agave nectar
2 dashes Peychaud's bitters
Garnish: Freshly grated
    nutmeg

*Shake with ice and strain
into ice-filled brandy snifter.
Top with nutmeg.*

POOP DECK
COCKTAIL

1 oz. brandy
1 oz. tawny port
½ oz. blackberry-flavored
    brandy

*Shake with ice and strain
into chilled cocktail glass.*

PRESTO COCKTAIL

1 splash anisette
1½ oz. brandy
½ oz. sweet vermouth
½ oz. fresh orange juice

*Pour anisette into chilled
cocktail glass, swirl to coat
inside; discard remaining
anisette. Shake remaining
ingredients with ice and
strain into glass.*

PRINCE OF WALES

¾ oz. madeira
¾ oz. brandy
¼ oz. triple sec
1 dash Angostura bitters
3 oz. chilled Champagne

Gently fold ingredients with ice, so as not to remove bubbles. Strain into chilled champagne flute.

PRINCESS POUSSE-CAFÉ

¾ oz. apricot-flavored brandy
½ oz. half-and-half

Pour brandy into pousse-café glass. Carefully float cream (see page 18) on top.

RENAISSANCE

2 oz. brandy
1 oz. sweet vermouth
½ oz. limoncello
2 dashes peach bitters
Garnish: Lemon twist

Stir with ice and strain into chilled cocktail glass. Add lemon twist.

ROYAL SMILE COCKTAIL

1 oz. apple brandy
½ oz. gin
½ oz. fresh lemon juice
1 tsp. grenadine

Stir with ice and strain into chilled cocktail glass.

ST. CHARLES PUNCH

"Professor" Jerry Thomas spent some time bartending in New Orleans. This drink appears in his book, and could be named for the St. Charles Hotel in that city.

1 oz. brandy
½ oz. triple sec
1 oz. fresh lemon juice
½ oz. simple syrup
3 oz. tawny port
Garnish: Lemon wheel, maraschino cherry

Shake first four ingredients with ice. Strain into ice-filled Collins glass. Top with port. Garnish with lemon and cherry.

SARATOGA COCKTAIL (JOHNSON VERSION)

Harry Johnson was another superstar of bartending's Golden Age during the late nineteenth century. His salute to New York State's horse-crazy resort town has fruity flavors.

2 oz. brandy
1 tsp. fresh lemon juice
1 tsp. pineapple juice
½ tsp. maraschino liqueur
2 dashes Angostura bitters

Shake with ice and strain into chilled cocktail glass.

BRANDY

SARATOGA COCKTAIL (THOMAS VERSION)

Saratoga Springs also inspired Professor Jerry Thomas to create a cocktail, but his has more alcohol heft.

¾ oz. brandy
¾ oz. rye whiskey
¾ oz. dry vermouth
2 dashes Angostura bitters
Garnish: Lemon wedge

Shake with ice and strain into chilled cocktail glass. Garnish with lemon.

SAUCY SUE COCKTAIL

2 oz. apple brandy
½ tsp. apricot-flavored brandy
½ tsp. absinthe or pastis

Stir with ice and strain into chilled cocktail glass.

SEVILLA 75

1 oz. Spanish brandy
½ oz. fresh lemon juice
1 tsp. simple syrup
2 oz. Spanish sparkling wine (cava)

Shake first three ingredients and strain into chilled red-wine glass. Top with sparkling wine.

SHRINER COCKTAIL

1½ oz. brandy
1½ oz. sloe gin
1 tsp. simple syrup
2 dashes Angostura bitters
Garnish: Lemon twist

Stir with ice and strain into chilled cocktail glass. Add lemon twist.

SIDECAR COCKTAIL

An American military officer, who arrived at his favorite Parisian bar in a motorcycle sidecar, loved this drink, and soon everyone in Paris was drinking it.

For glass: Lemon wedge, superfine sugar
1 oz. brandy
1 oz. triple sec
½ oz. fresh lemon juice

Rim chilled cocktail glass with lemon and sugar. Shake remaining ingredients with ice and strain into glass.

SLOPPY JOE'S COCKTAIL NO. 2

¾ oz. brandy
¾ oz. tawny port
¾ oz. pineapple juice
¼ oz. triple sec
¼ oz. grenadine

Shake with ice and strain into chilled cocktail glass.

SMART ALEC

2 oz. cognac
1 oz. triple sec
1 oz. yellow Chartreuse
1 dash orange bitters

Stir and strain into chilled champagne coupe or cocktail glass.

SOMBRERO

1½ oz. coffee-flavored brandy
1 oz. half-and-half

Pour brandy into ice-filled old-fashioned glass. Float half-and-half on top.

SOOTHER COCKTAIL

½ oz. brandy
½ oz. apple brandy
½ oz. triple sec
½ oz. fresh lemon juice
½ oz. simple syrup

Shake with ice and strain into chilled cocktail glass.

STAR COCKTAIL

1 oz. apple brandy
1 oz. sweet vermouth
1 dash Angostura bitters
Garnish: Lemon twist

Stir with ice and strain into chilled cocktail glass. Add lemon twist.

STINGER

Reginald Claypool Vanderbilt, the millionaire equestrian, loved his brandy stingers.

1½ oz. brandy
½ oz. white crème de menthe

Shake with ice and strain into chilled cocktail glass.

STIRRUP CUP

1 oz. cherry-flavored brandy
1 oz. brandy
1 oz. fresh lemon juice
½ oz. simple syrup

Shake with ice and strain into ice-filled old-fashioned glass.

THE TANTRIS SIDECAR

Created by AUDREY SAUNDERS, New York, NY

For glass: Lemon wedge, superfine sugar
1 oz. VS cognac
½ oz. Calvados or apple brandy
½ oz. triple sec
½ oz. fresh lemon juice
½ oz. simple syrup
¼ oz. pineapple juice
¼ oz. green Chartreuse
Garnish: Lemon twist

Rim chilled cocktail glass with lemon and sugar. Shake remaining ingredients with ice and strain into glass. Add lemon twist.

TEMPER COCKTAIL

1 oz. tawny port
1 oz. apricot-flavored brandy

Stir with ice and strain into chilled cocktail glass.

THANKSGIVING SPECIAL

¾ oz. apricot-flavored brandy
¾ oz. gin
¾ oz. dry vermouth
¼ oz. fresh lemon juice
Garnish: Marachino cherry

Shake with ice and strain into chilled cocktail glass. Garnish with cherry.

BRANDY

TULIP COCKTAIL

¾ oz. apple brandy
¾ oz. sweet vermouth
¼ oz. fresh lemon juice
¼ oz. apricot-flavored brandy

Shake with ice and strain into chilled cocktail glass.

VALENCIA COCKTAIL

1½ oz. apricot-flavored brandy
½ oz. fresh orange juice
2 dashes orange bitters

Shake with ice and strain into chilled cocktail glass.

VANDERBILT COCKTAIL

1½ oz. brandy
¾ oz. cherry-flavored brandy
½ oz. simple syrup
2 dashes Angostura bitters

Stir with ice and strain into chilled cocktail glass.

WHIP COCKTAIL

1 splash anisette
1½ oz. brandy
¾ oz. dry vermouth
½ oz. sweet vermouth
1 tsp. triple sec

Swirl anisette in chilled cocktail glass to coat inside; discard excess anisette. Stir remaining ingredients with ice and strain into glass.

WIDOW'S KISS

The Hoffman House ran one of the premier bars during New York's Gaslight Era, and this ladylike drink probably debuted there.

1½ oz. Calvados or apple brandy
¾ oz. yellow Chartreuse
¾ oz. Bénédictine
1 dash Angostura bitters

Stir with ice and strain into chilled cocktail glass.

WINDY CORNER COCKTAIL

2 oz. blackberry-flavored brandy
Garnish: Freshly grated nutmeg

Stir brandy with ice and strain into chilled cocktail glass. Top with nutmeg.

GIN

GIN WAS CREATED OVER 300 years ago by a Dutch chemist named Dr. Franciscus Sylvius in an attempt to enhance the therapeutic properties of juniper in a medicinal beverage. He called it *genièvre*, French for "juniper," a term that was anglicized by English soldiers fighting in the Netherlands, who also nicknamed it "Dutch courage." The popularity of gin in England became such that the "London dry" style evolved into the benchmark of quality. The clear spirit is made from a mash of cereal grain (primarily corn, rye, barley, and wheat) that is flavored with botanicals (primarily juniper), which gives it its unique taste. Other botanicals employed in top-secret recipes include coriander, lemon and orange peel, cassia root, anise, and fennel seeds, to name only a few.

Gin, like many other spirits, changed in character in the early nineteenth century, when advances made in distilling equipment revolutionized the way it was made. Today, it's changing again. A new international style called "New Western dry" has emerged in the past decade; it's lighter and more balanced, meant to be sipped as well as mixed into cocktails. Historical styles of gin are making a comeback too, such as "Old Tom" (a sweeter version of London dry) and the lower-proof Dutch original genever, which is distilled from malted grain mash similar

to whiskey and aged in oak casks. Unless otherwise designated, the recipes in this book use London dry gin.

Regardless of the classification, probably the best way
to compare gins is to mix them with tonic or vermouth and
imagine the myriad possibilities.

ABBEY COCKTAIL

1½ oz. gin
1 oz. fresh orange juice
1 dash orange bitters
Garnish: Maraschino cherry

*Shake with ice and strain into
chilled cocktail glass. Add
cherry.*

A CURRANT AFFAIR

Created by ERYN REECE,
New York, NY

1½ oz. gin
½ oz. crème de cassis
½ oz. cream sherry
Garnish: Lemon wheel wrapped
   around 3 fresh black
   currants and skewered

*Shake with ice and strain
through wire sieve into chilled
cocktail glass. Garnish with
lemon and currants.*

ALABAMA FIZZ

2 oz. gin
¾ oz. fresh lemon juice
¾ oz. simple syrup
Soda water
Garnish: 2 mint sprigs

*Shake gin, lemon juice, and
syrup with ice. Strain into ice-
filled highball glass and fill with
soda water. Garnish with mint.*

ALASKA COCKTAIL

1½ oz. gin
¾ oz. yellow Chartreuse
2 dashes orange bitters

*Stir with ice and strain into
chilled cocktail glass.*

ALBEMARLE FIZZ

2 oz. gin
¾ oz. fresh lemon juice
1 tsp. raspberry syrup
¼ oz. simple syrup
Soda water

*Shake first four ingredients
with ice and strain into ice-
filled highball glass. Fill with
soda water.*

ALEXANDER COCKTAIL NO. 1 (GIN)

Creamy and lush, the Brandy
Alexander is a now-familiar after-
dinner drink. However, you might
want to get to know the original
version, made with gin.

1 oz. gin
1 oz. white crème de cacao
1 oz. half-and-half
Garnish: Freshly grated nutmeg

*Shake with ice and strain into
chilled cocktail glass. Top with
nutmeg.*

ALLEN COCKTAIL

1½ oz. gin
¾ oz. maraschino liqueur
½ oz. fresh lemon juice

Shake with ice and strain into chilled cocktail glass.

ANGLER'S COCKTAIL

1½ oz. gin
½ oz. grenadine
1 dash Angostura bitters
1 dash orange bitters

Shake with ice and pour into ice-filled old-fashioned glass.

THE APOLLO

Created by MOSES LABOY,
New York, NY

1 (1-inch) piece fresh ginger, sliced
7 fresh sage leaves
1½ oz. gin
1 egg white
¾ oz. simple syrup
½ oz. fresh lemon juice
Garnish: 1 dash Angostura bitters, fresh sage leaf

Muddle ginger and 7 sage leaves in mixing glass. Add remaining ingredients and shake without ice. Add ice and shake again. Strain into chilled cocktail glass. Top with bitters and single sage leaf.

ARCHANGEL

1 cucumber slice
2¼ oz. gin
¾ oz. Aperol
Garnish: Lemon twist

Muddle cucumber in mixing glass. Add gin and Aperol with ice, stir, and strain into chilled cocktail glass. Add lemon twist.

ARTILLERY

1½ oz. gin
1½ tsp. sweet vermouth
2 dashes Angostura bitters

Stir with ice and strain into chilled cocktail glass.

ASTORIA BIANCO

Created by JIM MEEHAN,
New York, NY

2 oz. gin
¾ oz. dry vermouth
2 dashes orange bitters
Garnish: Orange twist

Stir with ice and strain into chilled cocktail glass. Add orange twist.

AUDREY FANNING

2½ oz. gin
1 oz. sweet vermouth
½ oz. Cherry Heering
2 dashes Peychaud's bitters

Stir with ice and strain into chilled cocktail glass.

GIN

▽ AVIATION

The crème de violette will turn the cocktail a color similar to the wild blue yonder, but if you don't have a bottle in your collection, leave it out.

2 oz. gin
½ oz. maraschino liqueur
¼ oz. fresh lemon juice
¼ oz. crème de violette or Crème Yvette (optional)
Garnish: Fresh or maraschino cherry

Shake with ice and strain into chilled cocktail glass. Garnish with cherry.

▢ BAD-HUMORED OLD-FASHIONED

2 oz. genever
¼ oz. maple syrup
2 dashes Angostura bitters
Garnish: Lemon twist

Stir with ice and strain into chilled old-fashioned glass. Add lemon twist.

▽ BARBARY COAST

Once the epicenter of San Francisco's nightlife, the Barbary Coast well deserves to have a drink named after it.

¾ oz. gin
¾ oz. Scotch
¾ oz. white crème de cacao
¾ oz. half-and-half

Shake with ice and strain into chilled cocktail glass.

▽ BARON COCKTAIL

1½ oz. gin
½ oz. dry vermouth
½ oz. triple sec
¼ oz. sweet vermouth
Garnish: Lemon twist

Stir with ice and strain into chilled cocktail glass. Add lemon twist.

▽ BASIL'S BITE

3 fresh basil leaves
2 oz. gin
1 tsp. Cynar
¾ oz. Aperol
Garnish: Small fresh basil leaf

Muddle basil leaves in mixing glass. Shake with remaining ingredients and ice. Strain into chilled cocktail glass. Garnish with basil leaf.

▽ BEAUTY-SPOT COCKTAIL

1 dash grenadine
1 oz. gin
½ oz. sweet vermouth
½ oz. dry vermouth
½ oz. fresh orange juice

Dash grenadine into bottom of chilled cocktail glass. Shake remaining ingredients with ice. Strain into glass.

BEE'S KNEES

This cocktail has "Prohibition era" written all over it. "Bee's knees" is a phrase from the Jazz Age meaning "the best," and the use of honey would sweeten and mask the rough taste of the gin.

2 oz. gin
½ oz. fresh lemon juice
¾ oz. Honey Syrup
    (page 25)

Shake with ice and strain into chilled champagne coupe.

BEE STING

2 oz. gin
¾ oz. fresh lemon juice
¾ oz. Honey Syrup
    (page 25)
1 tsp. absinthe or pastis
Garnish: Star anise pod

Shake with ice and strain into chilled cocktail glass. Garnish with star anise.

BELMONT COCKTAIL

2 oz. gin
¾ oz. half-and-half
¼ oz. raspberry syrup

Shake with ice and strain into chilled cocktail glass.

BENNETT COCKTAIL

1½ oz. gin
½ oz. fresh lime juice
½ oz. simple syrup
2 dashes orange bitters

Shake with ice and strain into chilled cocktail glass.

BERLINER

For glass: Superfine sugar, coarsely ground caraway seed, lemon wedge
1½ oz. gin
½ oz. dry vermouth
½ oz. kümmel
½ oz. fresh lemon juice
Garnish: Lemon twist

Mix sugar and caraway seed. Rim chilled cocktail glass with lemon and sugar mixture. Shake next four ingredients with ice and pour into glass. Add lemon twist.

BERMUDA BOUQUET

1½ oz. gin
¾ oz. apricot-flavored brandy
¾ oz. fresh orange juice
¾ oz. fresh lemon juice
¼ oz. simple syrup
1 tsp. grenadine
1 tsp. triple sec

Shake with ice and strain into ice-filled highball glass.

BERMUDA HIGHBALL

¾ oz. gin
¾ oz. brandy
¾ oz. dry vermouth
Ginger ale or soda water
Garnish: Lemon twist

Pour gin, brandy, and vermouth into ice-filled highball glass. Fill with ginger ale or soda water. Add lemon twist and stir.

GIN

▽ BLACK CAT

Created by NICHOLAS JARRETT,
New York, NY

1 grapefruit twist
1 tsp. simple syrup
1 oz. Old Tom gin
1 oz. mezcal
¾ oz. Punt e Mes
¾ oz. amontillado sherry
Garnish: Grapefruit twist

*Muddle grapefruit twist and
syrup in mixing glass. Add
other ingredients and stir
with ice. Strain into chilled
cocktail glass. Add grapefruit twist.*

▽ BLOOD ORANGE

1½ oz. gin
½ oz. Campari
½ oz. amaro, such as
    Ramazzotti or Averna
1 oz. fresh orange juice

*Shake with ice and strain
into chilled cocktail glass.*

▽ BLOOMSBURY

2 oz. gin
½ oz. Licor 43
½ oz. Lillet Blanc
2 dashes Peychaud's bitters
Garnish: Lemon twist

*Stir with ice and strain into
chilled cocktail glass. Add
lemon twist.*

▽ BLUE MOON COCKTAIL

1½ oz. gin
¾ oz. blue curaçao
Garnish: Lemon twist

*Stir with ice and strain into
chilled cocktail glass. Add
lemon twist.*

▽ BOBBO'S BRIDE

1 oz. gin
1 oz. vodka
½ oz. peach liqueur
½ oz. Campari
Garnish: Fresh peach slice

*Stir with ice and strain
into chilled cocktail glass.
Garnish with peach.*

▽ BOOMERANG

1½ oz. gin
1 oz. dry vermouth
1 tsp. maraschino liqueur
1 dash Angostura bitters
Garnish: Lemon twist

*Stir with ice and strain into
chilled cocktail glass. Add
lemon twist.*

▽ BOSTON COCKTAIL

¾ oz. gin
¾ oz. apricot-flavored
    brandy
½ oz. fresh lemon juice
¼ oz. grenadine

*Shake with ice and strain
into chilled cocktail glass.*

BRIDAL

2 oz. gin
1 oz. sweet vermouth
¼ oz. maraschino liqueur
1 dash orange bitters
Garnish: Maraschino cherry

Stir with ice and strain into chilled cocktail glass. Add cherry.

BRONX COCKTAIL

It is clear that this is a Perfect Martini with some orange juice in it. The drink's history is not so apparent, and it may be another creation of the Waldorf-Astoria, or the invention of a homesick Bronx-born restaurateur who lived in Philadelphia.

1 oz. gin
½ oz. dry vermouth
½ oz. sweet vermouth
1 oz. fresh orange juice
Garnish: Orange wheel

Shake with ice and strain into chilled cocktail glass. Add orange wheel.

BROOKLYN WANDERER

Created by HAL WOLIN, New York, NY

2 oz. genever
½ oz. allspice liqueur (pimento dram)
½ oz. mezcal
½ oz. pineapple juice
½ oz. orgeat syrup
½ oz. fresh lime juice
½ oz. Cinnamon Syrup (page 25)
2 dashes Angostura bitters
Garnish: Fresh mint leaf

Shake without ice. Strain into ice-filled pilsner glass. Swizzle with barspoon. Garnish with mint.

THE BROTHERS PERRYMAN

Created by RYAN MAYBEE, Kansas City, MO

1½ oz. Plymouth gin
¾ oz. Campari
¾ oz. elderflower liqueur
Garnish: Orange twist, flamed

Stir well with ice and strain into ice-filled old-fashioned glass. Flame orange twist and add.

CABARET

1½ oz. gin
½ oz. dry vermouth
¼ oz. Bénédictine
2 dashes Angostura bitters
Garnish: Maraschino cherry

Stir with ice and strain into chilled cocktail glass. Add cherry.

GIN

☿ CANDIED APPLE MARTINI

Created by JONATHAN POGASH, New York, NY

1 oz. Plymouth gin
½ oz. Grand Marnier
¼ oz. Cinnamon Syrup (page 25)
½ oz. fresh lemon juice
¾ oz. apple cider
Garnish: Red apple slice

Shake with ice and strain into chilled cocktail glass. Garnish with apple.

☿ CAPRICIOUS

1½ oz. gin
½ oz. dry vermouth
½ oz. elderflower liqueur
2 dashes Peychaud's bitters

Stir with ice and strain into chilled cocktail glass.

☿ THE CARICATURE COCKTAIL

1½ oz. gin
¾ oz. triple sec
½ oz. sweet vermouth
½ oz. Campari
½ oz. fresh grapefruit juice
Garnish: Orange twist

Shake with ice and strain into chilled cocktail glass. Add orange twist.

☿ CASINO COCKTAIL

2 oz. gin
¼ tsp. maraschino liqueur
¼ tsp. fresh lemon juice
2 dashes orange bitters
Garnish: Maraschino cherry

Shake with ice and strain into chilled cocktail glass. Add cherry.

☿ CHELSEA SIDECAR

¾ oz. gin
¾ oz. triple sec
½ oz. fresh lemon juice

Shake with ice and strain into chilled cocktail glass.

☿ CHIN UP

1 (½-inch-thick) cucumber slice, peeled
2 oz. gin
½ oz. Cynar
½ oz. dry vermouth
1 small pinch salt
Garnish: Paper-thin cucumber slice

Muddle thick cucumber slice in mixing glass. Add remaining ingredients and ice, and stir well. Strain into chilled cocktail glass. Garnish with thin cucumber slice.

☐ CHOCOLATE ITALIAN

1½ oz. gin
¾ oz. Campari
¾ oz. Punt e Mes
¾ oz. white crème de cacao
Garnish: Orange twist

Stir with ice and strain into ice-filled old-fashioned glass. Add orange twist.

CLARIDGE COCKTAIL

Dating back to Harry McElhone's 1927 *Barflies and Cocktails* (he was the Harry of Harry's New York Bar in Paris), this cocktail is an artful blend of herbal and fruit flavors.

1 oz. gin
¾ oz. dry vermouth
½ oz. apricot-flavored brandy
¼ oz. triple sec

Stir with ice and strain into chilled cocktail glass.

CLOISTER

1½ oz. gin
½ oz. yellow Chartreuse
½ oz. fresh grapefruit juice
¼ oz. fresh lemon juice
¼ oz. simple syrup
Garnish: Grapefruit twist

Shake with ice and strain into chilled cocktail glass. Add grapefruit twist.

CLOVER CLUB

The Clover Club is an august business organization in Philadelphia, but the drink that bears its name is a frothy, pink diversion.

1½ oz. gin
¾ oz. fresh lemon juice
½ oz. sweet vermouth
¼ oz. grenadine or raspberry syrup
1 egg white

Shake without ice. Add ice and shake again. Strain into chilled red-wine glass.

CLUB COCKTAIL

1½ oz. gin
¾ oz. sweet vermouth
Garnish: Maraschino cherry or green olive

Stir with ice and strain into chilled cocktail glass. Add cherry or olive.

COLONIAL COCKTAIL

1½ oz. gin
½ oz. fresh grapefruit juice
1 tsp. maraschino liqueur
Garnish: Green olive

Shake with ice and strain into chilled cocktail glass. Add olive.

THE COLONIAL COOLER

1½ oz. gin
1½ oz. sweet vermouth
¼ oz. triple sec
1 dash Angostura bitters
Soda water
Garnish: Mint sprig, pineapple wedge

Pour first four ingredients into ice-filled Collins glass. Fill with soda water. Garnish with mint and pineapple.

CONFIDENTIAL COCKTAIL

¾ oz. gin
¾ oz. dry vermouth
½ oz. Strega
½ oz. Cherry Marnier

Stir with ice and strain into chilled cocktail glass.

GIN

COOPERSTOWN COCKTAIL

1 oz. gin
½ oz. dry vermouth
½ oz. sweet vermouth
Garnish: Mint sprig

Shake with ice and strain into chilled cocktail glass. Add mint.

CORNWALL NEGRONI

2 oz. gin
½ oz. Punt e Mes
½ oz. sweet vermouth
½ oz. Campari
Garnish: Orange twist, flamed

Stir with ice and strain into chilled cocktail glass. Flame orange twist and add.

CORPSE REVIVER NO. 2

There was an entire group of "morning-after" drinks, each called a Corpse Reviver. See page 58 for the cognac version.

¾ oz. gin
¾ oz. fresh lemon juice
¾ oz. triple sec
¾ oz. Lillet Blance
1 dash absinthe or pastis

Shake with ice and strain into chilled cocktail glass.

THE CORRECT COCKTAIL

1½ oz. gin
½ oz. ginger liqueur
½ oz. triple sec
½ oz. fresh lemon juice
2 dashes orange bitters
Garnish: Lemon twist

Shake with ice and strain into chilled champagne flute. Add lemon twist.

COUNT CURREY

1½ oz. gin
¼ oz. simple syrup
Chilled Champagne

Shake gin and syrup with ice and strain into chilled champagne flute. Fill with Champagne.

CREAM FIZZ

2 oz. gin
¾ oz. fresh lemon juice
¾ oz. simple syrup
¾ oz. half-and-half
Soda water

Shake first four ingredients with ice and strain into ice-filled highball glass. Fill with soda water and stir.

CRIMSON COCKTAIL

1½ oz. gin
½ oz. fresh lemon juice
¼ oz. grenadine
¾ oz. tawny port

Shake first three ingredients with ice and strain into chilled cocktail glass. Float port (see page 18) on top.

CRYSTAL SLIPPER COCKTAIL

1½ oz. gin
½ oz. blue curaçao
2 dashes orange bitters

Stir with ice and strain into chilled cocktail glass.

CUCUMBER-APPLE FIZZ

Created by KENTA GOTA, New York, NY

1 apple slice
1 cucumber slice
¾ oz. fresh lemon juice
¾ oz. simple syrup
1½ oz. gin
¾ oz. Cynar
Soda water
Garnish: Apple and cucumber slices

Muddle apple and cucumber with lemon juice and syrup in mixing glass. Add gin and Cynar and shake with ice. Strain into ice-filled highball glass. Top with soda water. Garnish with apple and cucumber slices.

CUCUMBER CANTALOUPE SOUR

2 cucumber slices, chopped
2 oz. Cantaloupe Juice (recipe follows)
1½ oz. gin
¾ oz. fresh lemon juice
½ oz. Honey Syrup (page 25)
Garnish: Cucumber slice

Muddle chopped cucumber in mixing glass. Add remaining ingredients and shake with ice. Strain into chilled cocktail glass. Garnish with cucumber slice.

CANTALOUPE JUICE

Puree about ½ cup peeled, diced, and seeded cantaloupe in blender. Strain through cheesecloth-lined sieve.

DAISY MAE

2 oz. gin
1 oz. fresh lime juice
¾ oz. green Chartreuse
¾ oz. simple syrup
Garnish: Mint sprig

Shake with ice and strain into red-wine glass with ice. Add mint.

DAMN-THE-WEATHER COCKTAIL

1 oz. gin
½ oz. fresh orange juice
¼ oz. sweet vermouth
¼ oz. triple sec

Shake with ice and strain into chilled cocktail glass.

GIN

✧ DARB COCKTAIL

¾ oz. gin
¾ oz. dry vermouth
¾ oz. apricot-flavored
  brandy
¾ oz. fresh lemon juice

*Shake with ice and strain
into chilled cocktail glass.*

✧ THE DEEP BLUE SEA

2 oz. gin
¾ oz. Lillet Blanc
¼ oz. crème de violette
1 dash orange bitters
Garnish: Lemon twist

*Stir with ice and strain into
chilled cocktail glass. Add
lemon twist.*

✧ DEEP SEA COCKTAIL

1 splash anisette
1 oz. gin
1 oz. dry vermouth
1 dash orange bitters

*Swirl anisette in chilled
cocktail glass to coat
inside; discard excess anisette. Stir remaining ingredients with ice and strain
into glass.*

✧ DELMONICO NO. 1

¾ oz. gin
½ oz. brandy
½ oz. dry vermouth
½ oz. sweet vermouth
Garnish: Lemon twist

*Stir with ice and strain into
chilled cocktail glass. Add
lemon twist.*

✧ DEMPSEY COCKTAIL

1 oz. gin
1 oz. apple brandy
¼ oz. grenadine
1 tsp. anisette

*Stir with ice and strain into
chilled cocktail glass.*

🥃 DIAMOND FIZZ

2 oz. gin
¾ oz. fresh lemon juice
¾ oz. simple syrup
Chilled Champagne

*Shake first three ingredients
with ice and strain into ice-
filled highball glass. Fill with
Champagne and stir.*

✧ DIVA QUARANTA

1½ oz. gin
1 oz. pomegranate juice
½ oz. simple syrup
½ oz. Campari
Garnish: Orange twist

*Shake first three ingredients
with ice and strain into
chilled cocktail glass. Top with
Campari. Add orange twist.*

✧ DOC DANEEKA ROYALE

2 oz. gin
½ oz. fresh lemon juice
½ oz. maple syrup
Chilled Champagne
Garnish: Grapefruit twist

*Shake first three ingredi-
ents and strain into chilled
cocktail glass. Top with
Champagne. Add grapefruit
twist.*

⅄ DOFF YOUR HAT

Created by DAVID WILLHITE,
Chicago, IL

1 oz. genever
¾ oz. Cynar
¾ oz. sweet vermouth
½ oz. Grand Marnier
1 dash orange bitters
Garnish: Orange twist

*Stir with ice and strain
into chilled cocktail glass.
Twist orange twist over
drink, then discard zest.*

⅄ DUTCH AND BUTTERSCOTCH

1½ oz. genever
½ oz. butterscotch liqueur
2 dashes Angostura bitters
Garnish: Orange twist,
    flamed

*Stir with ice and strain into
chilled cocktail glass. Flame
orange twist and add.*

⅄ EARL GREY MAR-TEA-NI

Created by AUDREY SAUNDERS,
New York, NY

For glass: Lemon wedge,
    superfine sugar
1½ oz. Earl Grey Gin (recipe
    follows)
1 oz. simple syrup
¾ oz. fresh lemon juice
1 egg white
Garnish: Freshly grated lemon
    zest, lemon twist

*Rim chilled cocktail glass
with lemon and sugar. Shake
remaining ingredients
without ice. Add ice and
shake again. Strain into
glass. Grate lemon zest on
top and add lemon twist.*

EARL GREY GIN

*Shake 1 Tbs. loose-leaf
Earl Grey tea with 8 oz.
gin in jar and let stand
2 hours. Stir and strain.*

⅄ EASTSIDE

3 slices cucumber
6–8 fresh mint leaves
1 oz. fresh lime juice
¾ oz. simple syrup
2 oz. gin
Garnish: Cucumber slice

*Muddle 3 cucumber slices
and mint with lime juice
and syrup. Add gin
and ice and shake. Strain
into chilled cocktail
glass. Garnish with
cucumber.*

GIN

EASY LIKE SUNDAY MORNING COCKTAIL

1½ oz. gin
1¼ oz. pineapple juice
¾ oz. simple syrup
½ oz. fresh lemon juice
1 dash Angostura bitters

Shake first four ingredients with ice and strain into ice-filled Collins glass. Add bitters and stir.

EDEN

2 oz. gin
½ oz. fresh lemon juice
½ oz. rose syrup
¼ oz. Campari
Garnish: Lemon twist

Shake with ice and strain into ice-filled old-fashioned glass. Add lemon twist.

THE ELDER STATESMAN

Created by RICK RODGERS, Maplewood, NJ.

1 lime wedge
4 raspberries
1½ ounces gin
½ oz. elderberry liqueur
Garnish: Lime twist

Rim chilled cocktail glass with lime wedge. Muddle raspberries and lime wedge in mixer glass. Add gin and elderberry liqueur and shake with ice. Double-strain into glass. Add lime twist.

EMERSON

1½ oz. gin
1 oz. sweet vermouth
½ oz. fresh lime juice
1 tsp. maraschino liqueur

Shake with ice and strain into chilled cocktail glass.

THE ENGLISH CHANNEL

Created by JONATHAN POGASH, New York, NY

The gin is British, and the ginger liqueur is French, and they are symbolically separated by the English Channel, hence this cocktail's name.

2 large fresh basil leaves
1½ oz. gin
½ oz. ginger liqueur
½ oz. simple syrup
½ oz. fresh lemon juice
1 oz. peach puree
1 bay leaf
Garnish: Fresh basil leaf

Smack 2 basil leaves between the palms of your hands to release the aroma, then add to mixing glass. Add remaining ingredients with ice and shake. Strain into chilled cocktail glass. Garnish with basil.

ENGLISH HIGHBALL

¾ oz. gin
¾ oz. brandy
¾ oz. sweet vermouth
Ginger ale or soda water
Garnish: Lemon twist

Pour gin, brandy, and vermouth into ice-filled highball glass. Fill with ginger ale or soda water and stir. Add lemon twist.

ENGLISH ROSE COCKTAIL

For glass: Lemon wedge, granulated sugar
1½ oz. gin
¾ oz. apricot-flavored brandy
¾ oz. dry vermouth
½ oz. fresh lemon juice
¼ oz. grenadine
Garnish: Maraschino cherry

Rim chilled cocktail glass with lemon and sugar. Shake next five ingredients with ice and strain into glass. Add cherry.

FALLEN ANGEL

1½ oz. gin
½ oz. fresh lime juice
½ oz. white crème de menthe
1 dash Angostura bitters
Garnish: Maraschino cherry

Shake with ice and strain into chilled cocktail glass. Add cherry.

FANCY GIN

2 oz. gin
½ oz. simple syrup
¼ oz. triple sec
1 dash Angostura bitters
Garnish: Lemon twist

Shake with ice and strain into chilled cocktail glass. Add lemon twist.

FARE THEE WELL

1½ oz. gin
1 tsp. dry vermouth
1 tsp. sweet vermouth
1 tsp. triple sec

Shake with ice and strain into chilled cocktail glass.

FIFTY-FIFTY MARTINI

1½ oz. gin
1½ oz. dry vermouth

Stir with ice and strain into chilled cocktail glass.

FINE-AND-DANDY COCKTAIL

1½ oz. gin
½ oz. triple sec
½ oz. fresh lemon juice
1 dash Angostura bitters
Garnish: Maraschino cherry

Shake with ice and strain into chilled cocktail glass. Add cherry.

GIN

♈ FINO MARTINI

2 oz. gin
½ oz. fino sherry
Garnish: Lemon twist

Stir gin and sherry with ice in mixing glass. Strain into chilled cocktail glass. Add lemon twist.

▢ FITZGERALD

1½ oz. gin
1 oz. simple syrup
¾ oz. fresh lemon juice
2 dashes Angostura bitters
Garnish: Lemon wedge

Shake with ice and strain into chilled old-fashioned glass. Add lemon wedge.

♈ FLAMINGO COCKTAIL

1½ oz. gin
½ oz. apricot-flavored brandy
½ oz. fresh lime juice
¼ oz. grenadine

Shake with ice and strain into chilled cocktail glass.

▢ FLORADORA COOLER

¾ oz. fresh lime juice
½ oz. simple syrup
¼ oz. grenadine
2 oz. gin
2 oz. soda water or ginger ale

Stir first three ingredients in Collins glass. Add ice and pour in gin. Fill with soda water or ginger ale and stir again.

♈ FLORIDA

1½ oz. gin
1 tsp. kirschwasser
1 tsp. triple sec
¾ oz. fresh orange juice
¼ oz. fresh lemon juice

Shake with ice and strain into chilled cocktail glass.

♈ FRENCH "75"

The 75mm French howitzer model 1897 was a small but powerful gun. Harry's New York Bar felt that this drink packed a similar punch, and christened the cocktail after the artillery in 1915.

1½ oz. gin
¾ oz. fresh lemon juice
½ oz. simple syrup
Chilled Champagne

Shake first three ingredients with ice. Strain into chilled champagne flute and top with Champagne.

♈ GARNET

1½ oz. gin
¾ oz. triple sec
¾ oz. pomegranate juice
¾ oz. fresh grapefruit juice
Garnish: Orange twist, flamed

Shake with ice and strain into chilled cocktail glass. Flame orange twist and add.

♈ GERSHWIN

2 oz. gin
½ oz. ginger liqueur
½ oz. simple syrup
¾ oz. fresh lemon juice
3 drops rose water

Shake with ice and strain into chilled cocktail glass.

GIBSON (GIN)

2½ oz. gin
½ oz. dry vermouth
Garnish: Cocktail onion

Stir with ice and strain into chilled cocktail glass. Add onion.

GIMLET (GIN)

2 oz. gin
¾ oz. fresh lime juice
¾ oz. simple syrup

Shake with ice and strain into chilled cocktail glass.

Note: *If desired, substitute 1 oz. Rose's Sweetened Lime Juice for the fresh lime juice and simple syrup.*

GIN ALOHA

2 oz. gin
½ oz. triple sec
¾ oz. pineapple juice
1 dash orange bitters

Shake with ice and strain into chilled cocktail glass.

GIN AND BITTERS

½ tsp. Angostura bitters
3 oz. gin

Pour bitters into cocktail glass and swirl the glass until it is entirely coated with the bitters. Add gin. (No ice is used in this drink.)

GIN BUCK

1½ oz. gin
1 oz. fresh lemon juice
Ginger ale

Pour gin and lemon juice into ice-filled old-fashioned glass. Fill with ginger ale and stir.

GIN COBBLER

2 tsp. simple syrup
2 oz. soda water
2 oz. gin
Garnish: Generous amount of fresh seasonal fruit

Stir syrup and soda water in red-wine glass. Fill with ice and add gin. Stir and top with fruit. Serve with straws.

GIN COOLER

2 oz. gin
1 tsp. simple syrup
Soda water or ginger ale
Garnish: Lemon and/or orange zest spiral

Stir gin and syrup in Collins glass. Add ice, fill with soda water or ginger ale, and stir again. Insert citrus spiral(s) and dangle end(s) over rim of glass.

GIN DAISY

2 oz. gin
¾ oz. fresh lemon juice
½ oz. simple syrup
¼ tsp. grenadine
Garnish: Seasonal fresh fruit

Shake with ice. Strain into chilled beer mug or metal cup. Add ice and garnish with fruit.

GIN

GIN FIX

2½ oz. gin
1 oz. fresh lemon juice
1 oz. simple syrup
Garnish: Lemon wheel

Stir gin, lemon juice, and syrup in ice-filled highball glass. Garnish with lemon wheel. Serve with straws.

GIN FIZZ

2 oz. gin
1 oz. fresh lemon juice
2 tsp. simple syrup
Soda water

Shake first three ingredients with ice. Pour with ice into highball glass. Fill with soda water and stir.

GIN GIN MULE

An antecedent to the Moscow Mule (page 183). Audrey Saunders, owner of Pegu Club in New York City, makes this version with gin and refreshing notes of mint and lime.

6–8 mint sprigs
1 oz. simple syrup
¾ oz. fresh lime juice
1½ oz. gin
Ginger beer

Muddle mint with syrup and lime juice in mixing glass. Add gin and ice and shake well. Strain into ice-filled highball glass. Fill with ginger beer.

GIN HIGHBALL

2 oz. gin
Ginger ale or soda water
Garnish: Lemon twist

Pour gin into ice-filled high-ball glass. Fill with ginger ale or soda water and stir. Add lemon twist.

GIN RICKEY

1½ oz. gin
½ oz. fresh lime juice
Soda water
Garnish: Lime wedge

Pour gin and lime juice into ice-filled highball glass and fill with soda water. Stir. Add lime wedge.

GIN SANGAREE

2 oz. gin
¾ oz. simple syrup
Soda water
¾ oz. tawny port
Garnish: Freshly grated nutmeg

Stir gin and syrup in high-ball glass. Add ice. Fill with soda water and stir. Float port (see page 18) on top. Top with nutmeg.

GIN AND SIN

1½ oz. gin
½ oz. fresh lemon juice
½ oz. fresh orange juice
¼ oz. grenadine

Shake with ice and strain into chilled cocktail glass.

GIN AND SIP

1 splash absinthe
2½ oz. gin
½ oz. amaro, such as
    Ramazzotti or Averna

*Swirl absinthe in chilled
old-fashioned glass to
coat inside; discard excess
absinthe. Stir gin and amaro
with ice and strain into
glass.*

GIN SMASH

8 fresh mint leaves
1 sugar cube
1 oz. soda water
2 oz. gin
Garnish: Orange wheel and/or
    maraschino cherry, lemon
    twist

*Muddle mint and sugar
cube in old-fashioned glass.
Add soda water and mix to
dissolve sugar. Add gin
and ice and stir. Garnish
with orange wheel and/or
cherry and the lemon
twist.*

GIN SOUR

2 oz. gin
¾ oz. fresh lemon juice
¾ oz. simple syrup
Garnish: Lemon half-wheel,
    maraschino cherry

*Shake with ice and strain
into chilled sour glass. Add
lemon and cherry.*

GIN SQUIRT

1½ oz. gin
1 tsp. simple syrup
1 tsp. grenadine
Soda water
Garnish: Pineapple cubes,
    whole strawberries

*Stir first three ingredients
with ice and strain into
ice-filled highball glass. Fill
with soda water and stir.
Garnish with pineapple
and strawberries.*

GIN SWIZZLE

2 oz. gin
¾ oz. fresh lime juice
¾ oz. simple syrup
2 oz. soda water
2 dashes Angostura bitters

*Pour ingredients into ice-
filled highball glass. With
barspoon between your
palms, move hands back
and forth and up and down
to quickly rotate and lift
spoon, until glass is frosted.*

GIN THING

1½ oz. gin
½ oz. fresh lime juice
Ginger ale

*Pour gin and lime juice into
ice-filled highball glass and
fill with ginger ale.*

GIN

GIN TODDY

2 oz. gin
½ oz. simple syrup
Garnish: Lemon twist

Stir gin and syrup in old-fashioned glass. Add 1 ice cube and stir again. Add lemon twist.

GIN AND TONIC

2 oz. gin
Tonic water
Garnish: Lime wedge (optional)

Pour gin into ice-filled highball glass and fill with tonic water. Stir. Add lime wedge, if desired.

GIRL FROM CADIZ

Created by RYAN MAYBEE, Kansas City, MO

1 tsp. dried juniper berries
½ oz. simple syrup
1½ oz. gin
1½ oz. fino sherry
½ oz. fresh lemon juice
4 fresh mint leaves
Garnish: Lemongrass stalk

Muddle juniper berries with simple syrup in mixing glass. Add gin, sherry, lemon juice, and mint and shake well with ice. Strain through wire sieve into ice-filled Collins glass. Garnish with lemongrass.

GOLDEN DAZE

1½ oz. gin
½ oz. peach-flavored brandy
1 oz. fresh orange juice

Shake with ice and strain into chilled cocktail glass.

GOLF COCKTAIL

1½ oz. gin
¾ oz. dry vermouth
2 dashes Angostura bitters

Stir with ice and strain into chilled cocktail glass.

GRAND ROYAL FIZZ

2 oz. gin
¾ oz. fresh orange juice
½ oz. fresh lemon juice
½ oz. half-and-half
½ oz. simple syrup
1 tsp. maraschino liqueur
Soda water

Shake first six ingredients with ice. Strain into ice-filled highball glass. Fill with soda water and stir.

GREEN DRAGON

1½ oz. gin
1 oz. fresh lemon juice
½ oz. kümmel
½ oz. green crème de menthe
4 dashes orange bitters

Shake with ice and strain into chilled cocktail glass.

GREYHOUND (GIN)

1½ oz. gin
5 oz. fresh grapefruit juice

Pour into ice-filled highball glass. Stir well.

GYPSY COCKTAIL

1½ oz. gin
1½ oz. sweet vermouth
Garnish: Maraschino cherry

Stir with ice and strain into chilled cocktail glass. Add cherry.

HARLEM COCKTAIL

1½ oz. gin
¾ oz. pineapple juice
½ tsp. maraschino liqueur
Garnish: 2 pineapple chunks

Shake with ice and strain into chilled cocktail glass. Garnish with pineapple chunks on rim of glass.

HASTY COCKTAIL

1½ oz. gin
¾ oz. dry vermouth
¼ oz. grenadine
1 tsp. anisette

Stir with ice and strain into chilled cocktail glass.

HAWAIIAN COCKTAIL

2 oz. gin
½ oz. pineapple juice
½ oz. triple sec

Shake with ice and strain into chilled cocktail glass.

HAYS FIZZ

½ tsp. absinthe or pastis
2 oz. gin
¾ oz. fresh lemon juice
¾ oz. simple syrup
Soda water
Garnish: Cherry/orange flag

Add pastis to Collins glass and swirl to coat inside of glass. Shake remaining ingredients with ice. Strain into ice-filled glass. Fill with soda water. Garnish with cherry/orange flag.

HOFFMAN HOUSE MARTINI

This venerable hotel, demolished in 1915, served a drink that is a dead ringer for a wet Martini.

1½ oz. gin
¾ oz. dry vermouth
2 dashes orange bitters
Garnish: Orange twist

Stir with ice and strain into chilled cocktail glass. Add orange twist.

HOKKAIDO COCKTAIL

1½ oz. gin
1 oz. sake
½ oz. triple sec

Shake with ice and strain into chilled cocktail glass.

HOMESTEAD COCKTAIL

1½ oz. gin
¾ oz. sweet vermouth
Garnish: Orange wheel

Stir with ice and strain into chilled cocktail glass. Garnish with orange wheel.

GIN

HONOLULU COCKTAIL NO. 1

1½ oz. gin
½ oz. simple syrup
¼ oz. fresh orange juice
¼ oz. pineapple juice
¼ oz. fresh lemon juice
1 dash orange bitters

Shake with ice and strain into chilled cocktail glass.

HONOLULU COCKTAIL NO. 2

¾ oz. gin
¾ oz. maraschino liqueur
¾ oz. Bénédictine

Stir with ice and strain into chilled cocktail glass.

HOSKINS

2 oz. gin
¾ oz. Amer Picon or Torani Amer
¾ oz. maraschino liqueur
¼ oz. triple sec
1 dash orange bitters
Garnish: Orange twist, flamed

Stir with ice and strain into chilled cocktail glass. Flame orange twist and add.

HUDSON BAY

1 oz. gin
½ oz. cherry-flavored brandy
½ oz. fresh orange juice
¼ oz. 151-proof rum
¼ oz. fresh lime juice

Shake with ice and strain into chilled cocktail glass.

HULA-HULA COCKTAIL

1½ oz. gin
¾ oz. fresh orange juice
½ oz. simple syrup

Shake with ice and strain into chilled cocktail glass.

HUMMINGBIRD DOWN

2 oz. gin
¾ oz. fresh lemon juice
¾ oz. Honey Syrup (page 25)
¼ oz. green Chartreuse
Garnish: Fresh mint leaf

Shake with ice and strain into chilled cocktail glass. Add mint leaf.

IDEAL COCKTAIL

1 oz. gin
1 oz. dry vermouth
¼ oz. maraschino liqueur
¼ oz. fresh grapefruit or fresh lemon juice
Garnish: Maraschino cherry

Shake with ice and strain into chilled cocktail glass. Add cherry.

IMPERIAL COCKTAIL

1½ oz. gin
1½ oz. dry vermouth
1 tsp. maraschino liqueur
1 dash Angostura bitters
Garnish: Maraschino cherry

Stir with ice and strain into chilled cocktail glass. Add cherry.

INCOME TAX COCKTAIL

An obvious cousin to the Bronx, with bitters.

1 oz. gin
¼ oz. dry vermouth
¼ oz. sweet vermouth
1 oz. fresh orange juice
1 dash Angostura bitters

Shake with ice and strain into chilled cocktail glass.

THE INSCRIPTION

Created by TED HENWOOD, New York, NY.

Dash of absinthe
2½ oz. gin
1 oz. elderflower liqueur
Garnish: Orange twist

Swirl absinthe in chilled cocktail glass to coat inside; discard excess absinthe. Stir gin and elderflower liqueur with ice and strain into glass. Add orange twist.

JABBERWOCKY FIZZ

1½ oz. gin
1 oz. Drambuie
½ oz. fresh lemon juice
½ oz. fresh lime juice
Soda water

Shake first four ingredients with ice and strain into ice-filled Collins glass. Fill with soda water.

JAMAICA GLOW

1 oz. gin
½ oz. Jamaican rum
¾ oz. fresh orange juice
½ oz. red wine

Shake with ice and strain into chilled cocktail glass.

JASMINE

¾ oz. Campari
1½ oz. gin
1 oz. triple sec
½ oz. fresh lemon juice

Shake with ice and strain into chilled cocktail glass.

JEWEL COCKTAIL

¾ oz. gin
¾ oz. green Chartreuse
¾ oz. sweet vermouth
1 dash orange bitters
Garnish: Maraschino cherry

Stir with ice and strain into chilled cocktail glass. Add cherry.

JOCKEY CLUB COCKTAIL

1½ oz. gin
½ oz. fresh lemon juice
½ oz. white crème de cacao
1 dash Angostura bitters

Shake with ice and strain into chilled cocktail glass.

THE JOLLITY BUILDING

1½ oz. gin
½ oz. amaro, such as
    Ramazzotti or Averna
¼ oz. maraschino liqueur
1 dash orange bitters
Garnish: Orange twist

Stir with ice and strain into chilled cocktail glass. Add orange twist.

JOULOUVILLE

1 oz. gin
½ oz. apple brandy
½ oz. fresh lemon juice
¼ oz. sweet vermouth
¼ oz. grenadine

Shake with ice and strain into chilled cocktail glass.

JOURNALIST COCKTAIL

1½ oz. gin
¼ oz. dry vermouth
¼ oz. sweet vermouth
¼ oz. fresh lemon juice
¼ oz. triple sec
1 dash Angostura bitters

Shake with ice and strain into chilled cocktail glass.

JUDGE JR. COCKTAIL

¾ oz. gin
¾ oz. light rum
½ oz. fresh lemon juice
¼ oz. simple syrup
¼ oz. grenadine

Shake with ice and strain into chilled cocktail glass.

JUDGETTE COCKTAIL

¾ oz. peach-flavored brandy
¾ oz. gin
¾ oz. dry vermouth
¼ oz. fresh lime juice
Garnish: Maraschino cherry

Shake with ice and strain into chilled cocktail glass. Add cherry.

JUNIPER BREEZE NO. 1

Created by JULIE REINER, New York, NY

Use nonalcoholic elderflower cordial, not liqueur, for this cocktail.

1½ oz. gin
¾ oz. fresh grapefruit juice
½ oz. cranberry juice
½ oz. elderflower cordial
¼ oz. fresh lime juice
Garnish: Orange twist

Roll with ice in shaker. Pour into chilled cocktail glass. Add orange twist.

JUPITER

2 oz. gin
1 oz. dry vermouth
1 tsp. fresh orange juice
1 tsp. crème de violette, Crème Yvette, or Grand Marnier

Shake with ice and strain into chilled cocktail glass.

KISS IN THE DARK

¾ oz. gin
¾ oz. cherry-flavored brandy
¾ oz. dry vermouth

Stir with ice and strain into chilled cocktail glass.

KNICKERBOCKER COCKTAIL

1½ oz. gin
¾ oz. dry vermouth
1 tsp. sweet vermouth
Garnish: Lemon twist

Stir with ice and strain into chilled cocktail glass. Add lemon twist.

KNOCKOUT COCKTAIL

¾ oz. gin
¾ oz. dry vermouth
½ oz. anisette
1 tsp. white crème de menthe
Garnish: Maraschino cherry

Stir with ice and strain into chilled cocktail glass. Add cherry.

LA BICYCLETTE

2 oz. gin
¾ oz. sweet vermouth
½ oz. elderflower liqueur
2 dashes peach bitters

Stir with ice and strain into chilled cocktail glass.

LA CAMPANILE COCKTAIL

Created by CHRIS PATINO, New York, NY

2 oz. Plymouth gin
¾ oz. ruby port
1 oz. fresh orange juice
¼ oz. Fernet-Branca
Garnish: Orange twist

Shake with ice and strain into chilled cocktail glass. Add orange twist.

LA LOUCHE

1½ oz. gin
½ oz. Lillet Rouge
¼ oz. yellow Chartreuse
¼ oz. fresh lime juice
Garnish: Lime twist

Shake with ice and strain into chilled cocktail glass. Add lime twist.

GIN

LA TAZZA D'EVA

6 fresh mint leaves
1 oz. amaro, such as Ramazzotti or Averna
1 oz. gin
1 oz. apple juice
1 oz. tonic water
Garnish: Apple slice, rosemary sprig

Muddle mint in highball glass. Add ice and remaining ingredients and stir. Garnish with apple and rosemary.

LADY FINGER

1 oz. gin
1 oz. cherry-flavored brandy
½ oz. kirschwasser

Shake with ice and strain into chilled cocktail glass.

LAST WORD

¾ oz. gin
¾ oz. green Chartreuse
¼ oz. maraschino liqueur
¾ oz. fresh lime juice

Shake with ice and strain into chilled cocktail glass.

LEAPFROG HIGHBALL

2 oz. gin
1 oz. fresh lemon juice
Ginger ale

*Pour gin and lemon juice
into ice-filled highball glass
and fill with ginger ale. Stir.*

LEAPYEAR

2 oz. gin
½ oz. sweet vermouth
½ oz. Grand Marnier
¼ oz. fresh lemon juice

*Shake with ice and strain
into chilled cocktail glass.*

LEAVE-IT-TO-ME COCKTAIL NO. 1

1 oz. gin
½ oz. apricot-flavored brandy
½ oz. dry vermouth
¼ oz. fresh lemon juice
¼ oz. grenadine

*Shake with ice and strain
into chilled cocktail glass.*

LEAVE-IT-TO-ME COCKTAIL NO. 2

1½ oz. gin
1 tsp. raspberry syrup
1 tsp. fresh lemon juice
1 tsp. maraschino liqueur

*Stir with ice and strain into
chilled cocktail glass.*

THE LEMONY SNICKET COCKTAIL

2½ oz. gin
½ oz. limoncello
½ oz. yellow Chartreuse
½ oz. fresh lemon juice
Garnish: Maraschino cherry

*Shake with ice and
strain into chilled cock-
tail glass. Garnish with
the cherry.*

LEO DE JANEIRO

2 oz. gin
2 oz. pineapple juice
4 dashes Angostura bitters
Garnish: Pineapple wedge

*Shake with ice and
strain into ice-filled
Collins glass. Garnish with
the pineapple wedge on the
glass rim.*

LIGHT AND DAY

2 oz. gin
½ oz. yellow Chartreuse
¼ oz. maraschino liqueur
¼ oz. fresh orange juice
3 dashes Peychaud's bitters

*Stir with ice and strain into
chilled cocktail glass.*

LONDON COCKTAIL

2 oz. gin
½ oz. simple syrup
1 tsp. maraschino liqueur
2 dashes orange bitters
Garnish: Lemon twist

Stir with ice and strain into chilled cocktail glass. Add lemon twist.

THE LONDONER

2 oz. gin
½ oz. Grand Marnier
½ oz. sweet vermouth
1 dash orange bitters
Garnish: Orange twist, flamed

Shake with ice and strain into chilled cocktail glass. Flame orange twist and add.

LONE TREE COOLER

2 oz. gin
½ oz. dry vermouth
½ oz. simple syrup
Soda water or ginger ale
Garnish: Orange and/or lemon zest spiral

Stir gin, vermouth, and syrup in Collins glass. Add ice and fill with soda water or ginger ale. Add orange and/or lemon spiral(s) and dangle end(s) over glass rim.

MAIDEN'S BLUSH COCKTAIL

1½ oz. gin
1 tsp. triple sec
1 tsp. grenadine
¼ tsp. fresh lemon juice

Shake with ice and strain into chilled cocktail glass.

MAIDEN'S PLEA

1½ oz. gin
1 oz. fresh lemon juice
½ oz. triple sec

Shake with ice and strain into chilled cocktail glass.

MAJOR BAILEY

12 fresh mint leaves
¼ oz. fresh lime juice
¼ oz. fresh lemon juice
½ oz. simple syrup
2 oz. gin
Garnish: Mint sprig

Muddle first four ingredients in Collins glass. Add gin and ice and stir until glass is frosted. Add mint sprig and serve with straws.

MARLOWE

Raymond Chandler's iconic detective, Philip Marlowe, liked his Gimlets heavy on the Rose's.

1½ oz. gin
1½ oz. Rose's Sweetened Lime Juice

Shake with ice and strain into chilled cocktail glass.

MARTINEZ COCKTAIL

This is a modern-day version of the cocktail that may or may not have become the Martini. Read more on the subject on page 34.

1½ oz. Old Tom gin
½ oz. sweet vermouth
1 tsp. maraschino liqueur
1 dash orange bitters

Stir with ice and strain into chilled cocktail glass.

GIN

♈ MARTINI (TRADITIONAL 2-TO-1)

1½ oz. gin
¾ oz. dry vermouth
Garnish: Lemon twist or
    green olive

*Stir with ice and strain into
chilled cocktail glass. Add
lemon twist or olive.*

♈ MARTINI (DRY 4-TO-1)

2 oz. gin
½ oz. dry vermouth
Garnish: Lemon twist or
    green olive

*Stir with ice and strain into
chilled cocktail glass. Add
lemon twist or olive.*

♈ MARTINI (EXTRA DRY 8-TO-1)

1 splash dry vermouth
2 oz. gin
Garnish: Lemon twist or
    green olive

*Swirl vermouth in chilled
cocktail glass to coat inside;
discard excess vermouth.
Stir gin with ice and strain
into glass. Add lemon twist
or olive.*

♈ MARTINI (PERFECT)

1½ oz. gin
½ oz. dry vermouth
½ oz. sweet vermouth
Garnish: Lemon twist or
    green olive

*Stir with ice and strain into
chilled cocktail glass. Add
lemon twist or olive.*

♈ MARTINI (SWEET)

1 oz. gin
1 oz. sweet vermouth
Garnish: Lemon twist

*Stir with ice and strain into
chilled cocktail glass. Add
lemon twist.*

♈ MAURICE COCKTAIL

1 oz. gin
1 oz. fresh orange juice
½ oz. sweet vermouth
½ oz. dry vermouth
1 dash Angostura bitters

*Shake with ice and strain
into chilled cocktail glass.*

♈ MAXIM

1½ oz. gin
¾ oz. dry vermouth
¼ oz. white crème de cacao
Garnish: Maraschino cherry

*Shake with ice and strain
into chilled cocktail glass.
Add cherry.*

☐ MAXWELL'S RETURN

15 fresh rosemary leaves
2 oz. gin
1 oz. pineapple juice
½ oz. simple syrup
½ oz. fresh lime juice
¼ oz. green Chartreuse
Garnish: Rosemary sprig

*Muddle rosemary leaves in
mixing glass. Add remain-
ing ingredients. Shake with
ice and double-strain into
ice-filled old-fashioned glass.
Garnish with rosemary
sprig.*

MELON STAND

4 (1-inch) chunks peeled
   watermelon
2 oz. gin
½ oz. Aperol
½ oz. simple syrup
¾ oz. fresh lemon juice
Garnish: Watermelon cube
   or ball

*Muddle melon chunks in
mixing glass. Add remain-
ing ingredients. Shake with
ice and strain into Collins
glass filled with crushed ice.
Garnish with watermelon.*

MERCY, MERCY

2 oz. gin
½ oz. Aperol
½ oz. Lillet Blanc
1 dash Angostura bitters
Garnish: Orange twist

*Stir with ice and strain into
chilled cocktail glass. Add
orange twist.*

MERRY WIDOW
COCKTAIL NO. 1

1¼ oz. gin
1¼ oz. dry vermouth
1 tsp. Bénédictine
1 tsp. anisette
1 dash orange bitters
Garnish: Lemon twist

*Stir with ice and strain into
chilled cocktail glass. Add
lemon twist.*

MR. MANHATTAN
COCKTAIL

4 fresh mint sprigs
1 sugar cube
½ oz. fresh orange juice
¼ oz. fresh lemon juice
1½ oz. gin

*Strip leaves from sprigs
into mixing glass. Add sugar
and juices and muddle. Add
gin and shake with ice.
Strain into chilled cocktail
glass.*

MONARCH

7 fresh mint leaves
2 oz. gin
¾ oz. fresh lemon juice
¾ oz. elderflower liqueur
½ oz. simple syrup
Garnish: Grapefruit twist

*Smack mint leaves between
palms and drop into mixing
glass. Add remaining ingredients and ice. Shake and
double-strain into chilled
cocktail glass. Add grapefruit twist.*

GIN

THE MONEYPENNY

For glass: Lemon wedge,
    Demerara sugar
1 oz. gin
1 oz. fresh grapefruit juice
½ oz. Lillet Blanc
½ oz. fresh lemon juice
1 dash grapefruit bitters
Garnish: Grapefruit twist

*Rim chilled cocktail glass
with lemon and sugar. Shake
remaining ingredients with
ice and strain into glass. Add
grapefruit twist.*

MONKEY GLAND

In the 1920s, there was a
popular youth rejuvenation
process that involved monkey
hormones, which lent its name
to this invigorating cocktail.

2 oz. gin
1 oz. fresh orange juice
¼ oz. grenadine
1 dash absinthe
Garnish: Orange twist

*Shake with ice and strain
into chilled cocktail glass. Add
orange twist.*

MONTE CARLO
IMPERIAL COCKTAIL

2 oz. gin
½ oz. white crème de menthe
½ oz. fresh lemon juice
Chilled Champagne

*Shake first three ingredients
with ice and strain into
ice-filled highball glass. Fill
glass with Champagne
and stir.*

MONTMARTRE
COCKTAIL

1¼ oz. dry gin
½ oz. sweet vermouth
½ oz. triple sec
Garnish: Maraschino cherry

*Stir with ice and strain into
chilled cocktail glass. Add
cherry.*

MOONDREAM

1½ oz. gin
1 oz. manzanilla sherry
¼ oz. crème de pêche

*Stir with ice and strain into
chilled cocktail glass.*

MORRO

For glass: Lemon wedge,
    superfine sugar
1 oz. gin
½ oz. dark rum
½ oz. pineapple juice
½ oz. fresh lime juice
1 tsp. simple syrup

*Rim chilled cocktail glass
with lemon and sugar. Shake
remaining ingredients with
ice and strain into glass.*

NEGRONI

The story goes that bartender Fosco Scarselli of Florence, Italy, concocted this *molto Italiano* cocktail for Count Camillo Negroni in 1919.

¾ oz. gin
¾ oz. Campari
¾ oz. sweet vermouth
Garnish: Orange twist

Stir with ice and strain into chilled cocktail glass or ice-filled old-fashioned glass. Add orange twist.

NEW AMSTERDAM

2 oz. genever
1 oz. kirschwasser
1 tsp. simple syrup
2 dashes Peychaud's bitters
Garnish: Lemon twist

Stir with ice and strain into chilled cocktail glass. Add lemon twist.

NIGHTMARE

1½ oz. gin
½ oz. madeira
½ oz. cherry-flavored brandy
1 tsp. fresh orange juice

Shake with ice and strain into chilled cocktail glass.

NON CI CREDO

2 oz. gin
¾ oz. Aperol
¾ oz. fresh lemon juice
¼ oz. simple syrup
1 egg white
3 dashes peach bitters

Shake without ice. Add ice, shake again, and strain into chilled cocktail glass.

GIN

NOVARA

1½ oz. gin
½ oz. Campari
½ oz. passion fruit juice
½ oz. fresh lemon juice

Shake with ice and strain into chilled cocktail glass.

OBITUARY COCKTAIL

2 oz. gin
¼ oz. dry vermouth
¼ oz. absinthe

Stir with ice and strain into chilled cocktail glass.

THE OLD GOAT

1½ oz. genever
¾ oz. crème de cassis
Ginger ale
Garnish: Lime wedge

Combine gin and crème de cassis in ice-filled Collins glass. Top with ginger ale and stir. Squeeze and add lime wedge.

❖ OPAL COCKTAIL

1 oz. gin
½ oz. triple sec
½ oz. fresh orange juice
¼ oz. simple syrup

*Shake with ice and strain
into chilled cocktail glass.*

❖ OPERA

2 oz. gin
½ oz. Dubonnet
¼ oz. maraschino liqueur
1 dash orange bitters
Garnish: Lemon twist

*Stir with ice and strain into
chilled cocktail glass. Add
lemon twist.*

❖ ORANGE BLOSSOM

1½ oz. gin
¾ oz. fresh orange juice
¼ oz. simple syrup

*Shake with ice and strain
into chilled cocktail glass.*

❖ ORANGE BUCK

1½ oz. gin
1 oz. fresh orange juice
¼ oz. fresh lime juice
Ginger ale

*Shake first three ingredients
with ice and strain into ice-
filled highball glass. Fill with
ginger ale and stir.*

❖ ORANGE OASIS

1½ oz. gin
½ oz. cherry-flavored brandy
4 oz. fresh orange juice
Ginger ale

*Shake first three ingredients
with ice and strain into ice-
filled highball glass. Fill with
ginger ale and stir.*

POUR IN VIEW

Make drinks in front of the guest whenever possible.
This was a tradition that started in the nineteenth century
when a patron wanted to be sure he was getting the
genuine product, but the whole cocktail experience is
incomplete if the visual and the interaction with the
bartender are missing.

—DALE DeGROFF (aka King Cocktail),
author of *The Craft of the Cocktail*

ORIENT EXPRESS

2 oz. gin
1 oz. sake
½ oz. Lemongrass Syrup
   (page 26)
Garnish: Thin green apple
   slice

*Stir with ice and strain
into chilled cocktail glass.
Garnish with apple.*

THE OUTSIDER

2 oz. gin
1 oz. apple cider
1 oz. fresh lemon juice
¾ oz. simple syrup
1 splash ginger ale
Garnish: Thin red apple slice

*Shake first four ingredients
with ice and strain into
ice-filled Collins glass. Add
ginger ale. Garnish with
apple slice.*

PAISLEY MARTINI

2 oz. gin
½ oz. dry vermouth
1 tsp. Scotch
Garnish: Lemon twist

*Stir with ice and strain into
chilled cocktail glass. Add
lemon twist.*

PALL MALL

1½ oz. gin
½ oz. dry vermouth
½ oz. sweet vermouth
½ oz. white crème de menthe

*Stir in ice-filled old-
fashioned glass.*

PALM BEACH COCKTAIL

1½ oz. gin
¼ oz. sweet vermouth
¼ oz. fresh grapefruit juice

*Shake with ice and strain into
chilled cocktail glass.*

PAPAYA SLING

1½ oz. gin
1 oz. fresh lime juice
½ oz. papaya-flavored syrup
1 dash Angostura bitters
Soda water
Garnish: Skewered pineapple
   chunks

*Shake first four ingredients
with ice and strain into
ice-filled Collins glass. Fill
with soda water and stir.
Garnish with skewered
pineapple.*

PARCHMENT FIZZ

Created by DAMON DYER,
New York, NY

1½ oz. Plymouth gin
¾ oz. fresh lime juice
½ oz. dry vermouth
½ oz. simple syrup
½ oz. pear eau-de-vie
2 dashes Peychaud's
   bitters
1 dash absinthe
Soda water
Garnish: Pear slice

*Shake first seven ingredients
with ice. Strain into ice-filled
highball glass. Top with soda
water. Garnish with pear.*

GIN

PARISIAN

1 oz. gin
1 oz. dry vermouth
¼ oz. crème de cassis

Shake with ice and strain into chilled cocktail glass.

PARK AVENUE

1½ oz. gin
½ oz. pineapple juice
¼ oz. sweet vermouth

Stir with ice and strain into chilled cocktail glass.

PEARL WHITE

Ms. White was the star of the classic silent movie serials that kept her character in constant peril from an assortment of moustache-twisting bad guys.

6 fresh mint leaves
2 oz. gin
½ oz. Lillet Blanc
½ oz. fresh lemon juice
¼ oz. simple syrup

Muddle mint in mixing glass. Add remaining ingredients and ice. Shake and double-strain into chilled cocktail glass.

PEGU CLUB

This drink hails from the 1920s. The Pegu Club in New York City pays homage to the original in Rangoon, Burma.

2 oz. gin
½ oz. orange curaçao
½ oz. fresh lime juice
1 dash Angostura bitters

Stir with ice and strain into chilled cocktail glass.

PERFECT COCKTAIL

1½ oz. gin
¼ oz. dry vermouth
¼ oz. sweet vermouth
1 dash Angostura bitters

Stir with ice and strain into chilled cocktail glass.

PERFECT 10

1 oz. gin
½ oz. triple sec
½ oz. Campari
¼ oz. fresh lemon juice
¼ oz. simple syrup
Garnish: Lemon twist

Shake with ice and strain into chilled cocktail glass. Add lemon twist.

PETER PAN COCKTAIL

¾ oz. fresh orange juice
¾ oz. dry vermouth
¾ oz. gin
2 dashes Angostura bitters

Shake with ice and strain into chilled cocktail glass.

PICCADILLY COCKTAIL

1½ oz. gin
¾ oz. dry vermouth
¼ oz. anisette
¼ oz. grenadine

Stir with ice and strain into chilled cocktail glass.

PINK GIN

1½ oz. gin
3–4 dashes Angostura bitters

Stir with ice and strain into chilled cocktail glass.

PINK LADY

1½ oz. gin
¾ oz. fresh lemon juice
½ oz. applejack
¼ oz. grenadine
1 egg white

Shake without ice. Add ice and shake again. Strain into chilled red-wine glass.

POLLYANNA

3 orange wheels
3 pineapple chunks
2 oz. gin
½ oz. sweet vermouth
¼ oz. grenadine

Muddle orange and pineapple. Add remaining ingredients, shake with ice, and strain into chilled cocktail glass.

POLO COCKTAIL

1½ oz. gin
½ oz. fresh lemon juice
½ oz. fresh orange juice

Shake with ice and strain into chilled cocktail glass.

POMPANO

1 oz. gin
1 oz. fresh grapefruit juice
½ oz. dry vermouth

Shake with ice and strain into chilled cocktail glass.

POPPY COCKTAIL

1½ oz. gin
¾ oz. white crème de cacao

Stir with ice and strain into chilled cocktail glass.

PRINCE'S SMILE

1 oz. gin
½ oz. apricot-flavored brandy
½ oz. apple brandy
¼ oz. fresh lemon juice

Shake with ice and strain into chilled cocktail glass.

PRINCETON COCKTAIL

1 oz. gin
1 oz. dry vermouth
½ oz. fresh lime juice

Shake with ice and strain into chilled cocktail glass.

PROHIBITION COCKTAIL

1½ oz. gin
1½ oz. Lillet Blanc
¼ oz. apricot-flavored brandy
¼ oz. fresh orange juice
Garnish: Lemon twist

Shake and strain into cocktail glass. Add lemon twist.

GIN

⅄ THE PULITZER

Created by JONATHAN POGASH,
New York, NY.

1¼ oz. Plymouth gin
½ oz. elderflower liqueur
¼ oz. Fernet-Branca
¼ oz. fresh lemon juice
1 tsp. agave nectar
Garnish: Fresh mint sprig

*Shake with ice and strain
into chilled cocktail glass.
Garnish with mint.*

⅄ QUEEN ELIZABETH

1½ oz. gin
½ oz. dry vermouth
¼ oz. Bénédictine

*Stir with ice and strain into
chilled cocktail glass.*

⍍ RAMOS GIN FIZZ

The invention of Harry Ramos, a
nineteenth-century New Orleans
bartender, this drink is still a
de rigueur brunch cocktail in
the Crescent City as well as in
San Francisco. For a while, the
cocktail was so popular that
Ramos had to hire an entire
battalion of bartenders to keep
up with the shaking.

1½ oz. gin
1 oz. heavy cream
½ oz. simple syrup
½ oz. fresh lemon juice
½ oz. fresh lime juice
1 egg white
3–4 dashes orange blossom
    water
1 oz. soda water

*Shake all ingredients except
soda water without ice well
until foamy. Add ice and
shake well until chilled.
Strain into chilled highball
glass. Top with soda water
and stir.*

⅄ RED BARON

1½ oz. gin
½ oz. sweet vermouth
½ oz. amaro, such as
    Ramazzotti or Averna
¼ oz. maraschino liqueur
Garnish: Lemon twist

*Stir with ice and strain into
chilled cocktail glass. Add
lemon twist.*

RED CLOUD

1½ oz. gin
½ oz. apricot-flavored brandy
¼ oz. fresh lemon juice
½ oz. grenadine

*Shake with ice and
strain into chilled
cocktail glass.*

REMSEN COOLER

Similar to a Gin Cooler, but a
bit sweeter, thanks to the Old
Tom gin.

2 oz. Old Tom gin
1 tsp. simple syrup
Soda water or ginger ale
Garnish: Lemon and/or
    orange zest spiral

*Stir gin and syrup in
Collins glass. Add ice,
fill with soda water or
ginger ale, and stir again.
Insert citrus spiral(s) and
dangle end(s) over rim
of glass.*

RENAISSANCE
COCKTAIL

1½ oz. gin
½ oz. dry sherry
½ oz. light cream or half-
    and-half
Garnish: Freshly grated nutmeg

*Shake with ice and strain
into chilled cocktail glass.
Top with nutmeg.*

ROBERT E. LEE
COOLER

2 oz. gin
2 oz. soda water
½ oz. fresh lime juice
1 tsp. simple syrup
¼ tsp. anisette
Ginger ale
Garnish: Orange and/or lemon
    zest spiral

*Pour first five ingredients
into ice-filled Collins
glass. Top with ginger
ale and stir. Add citrus
spiral(s) and dangle end(s)
over rim.*

ROLLS-ROYCE

1½ oz. gin
½ oz. dry vermouth
½ oz. sweet vermouth
1 tsp. Bénédictine

*Stir with ice and strain
into chilled cocktail glass.*

GIN

ROSE COCKTAIL (ENGLISH)

For glass: Lemon wedge, superfine sugar
1 oz. gin
½ oz. apricot-flavored brandy
½ oz. dry vermouth
¼ oz. fresh lemon juice
¼ oz. grenadine

Rim chilled cocktail glass with lemon and sugar. Shake remaining ingredients with ice and strain into glass.

ROSE COCKTAIL (FRENCH)

1½ oz. gin
½ oz. cherry-flavored brandy
½ oz. dry vermouth

Stir with ice and strain into chilled cocktail glass.

RUSTY MONK

2 oz. gin
1 oz. Dubonnet
½ oz. yellow Chartreuse
2 dashes orange bitters
Garnish: Orange twist

Stir and strain into chilled cocktail glass. Add orange twist.

SALTY DOG (GIN)

One could substitute vodka for the gin, but this is the most flavorful version.

For glass: Lemon wedge, kosher salt
1½ oz. gin
5 oz. fresh grapefruit juice

Rim highball glass with lemon and salt. Fill with ice. Pour in gin and grapefruit juice and stir well.

SAN MARTIN COCKTAIL

Another cocktail named for a person, this one is probably an eponym for José de San Martín, the Latin American patriot.

1½ oz. gin
1½ oz. sweet vermouth
1 tsp. green or yellow Chartreuse

Stir with ice and strain into chilled cocktail glass.

SAN SEBASTIAN

1 oz. gin
½ oz. fresh grapefruit juice
½ oz. fresh lemon juice
¼ oz. light rum
¼ oz. triple sec

Shake with ice and strain into chilled cocktail glass.

GIN

⅂ SATAN'S WHISKERS

¾ oz. gin
¾ oz. dry vermouth
¾ oz. sweet vermouth
½ oz. Grand Marnier
½ oz. fresh orange juice
1 dash orange bitters

Shake with ice and strain into chilled cocktail glass.

⅂ SENSATION COCKTAIL

1½ oz. gin
½ oz. fresh lemon juice
1 tsp. maraschino liqueur
Garnish: 2 mint sprigs

Shake with ice and strain into chilled cocktail glass. Garnish with mint.

⅂ SEVENTH HEAVEN COCKTAIL

1½ oz. gin
½ oz. maraschino liqueur
¼ oz. fresh grapefruit juice
Garnish: Mint sprig

Shake with ice and strain into chilled cocktail glass. Garnish with mint.

⅂ SHADY GROVE

1½ oz. gin
1 oz. fresh lemon juice
2 tsp. simple syrup
Ginger beer

Shake first three ingredients with ice and strain into ice-filled highball glass. Fill with ginger beer.

⅂ THE SHIPROCK

Created by TED HENWOOD, New York, NY

3 fresh sage leaves
2½ oz. Plymouth gin
½ oz. Ginger Syrup (page 25)
½ oz. fresh lemon juice
1 drop orange blossom water
Garnish: Orange twist

Muddle sage leaves in mixing glass. Add gin, ginger syrup, lemon juice, and orange blossom water and shake with ice. Strain into chilled cocktail glass. Add orange twist.

⅂ SILVER BULLET

1 oz. gin
1 oz. kümmel
½ oz. fresh lemon juice

Shake with ice and strain into chilled cocktail glass.

⅂ SILVER COCKTAIL

1 oz. dry vermouth
1 oz. gin
1 tsp. maraschino liqueur
1 tsp. simple syrup
2 dashes orange bitters
Garnish: Lemon twist

Stir with ice and strain into chilled cocktail glass. Add lemon twist.

SILVER KING FIZZ

2 oz. gin
¾ oz. fresh lemon juice
¾ oz. simple syrup
1 egg white
4 dashes orange bitters
Soda water
Garnish: Orange wheel

*Shake first five ingredients
very well without ice until
foamy. Add ice and shake
again. Strain into ice-filled
highball glass. Top with soda
water. Garnish with orange.*

SILVER STAR DAISY

1 oz. gin
1 oz. fresh lemon juice
½ oz. apple brandy
½ oz. orange curaçao
½ oz. simple syrup
1 egg white
Soda water
1 dash orange bitters

*Shake all but bitters very
well without ice. Add ice and
shake again. Strain into ice-
filled highball glass. Top with
soda, then dash with bitters.*

SILVER STREAK

1½ oz. gin
1 oz. kümmel

*Shake with ice and strain
into chilled cocktail glass.*

SMOKEY HOLLANDER

Created by CHRIS HANNAH,
New Orleans, LA

1½ oz. genever
½ oz. mezcal
½ oz. fresh lemon juice
½ oz. agave nectar
Garnish: Lemon twist

*Shake with ice and strain
into chilled cocktail glass.
Add lemon twist.*

SNOWBALL

1½ oz. gin
½ oz. anisette
½ oz. half-and-half

*Shake with ice and strain
into chilled cocktail glass.*

SO CUE

1 oz. gin
1 oz. soju (Korean
   liqueur)
1 oz. dry vermouth
¾ oz. simple syrup
½ oz. fresh lime juice
Garnish: Cucumber slice

*Stir with ice and strain
into chilled cocktail glass.
Garnish with cucumber
slice.*

SOLOMON

1½ oz. gin
¾ oz. fresh lemon juice
½ oz. simple syrup
½ oz. kirschwasser
¼ oz. Cherry Heering
1 dash Angostura bitters
Garnish: 2 maraschino
cherries, each skewered
onto a straw, with the
cherry near the bottom of
the straw

*Shake with ice and strain
into Collins glass filled
with ice. Insert the cherry-
skewered straws.*

SORRISO

Created by FRANCESCO
LAFRANCONI, Las Vegas, NV

1 oz. Plymouth gin
1 oz. pear-flavored vodka
½ oz. oloroso sherry
½ oz. cherry-flavored brandy
2 dashes Angostura bitters
Garnish: Orange and lemon
twists, Italian preserved
cherry

*Stir with ice and strain
into chilled cocktail glass.
Garnish with lemon and
orange twists and cherry.*

SOUTHERN BRIDE

1½ oz. gin
1 oz. fresh grapefruit juice
1 dash maraschino liqueur

*Shake with ice and strain
into chilled cocktail glass.*

SOUTH-SIDE COCKTAIL

8–10 fresh mint leaves
1½ oz. gin
¾ oz. fresh lemon juice
¾ oz. simple syrup
Garnish: Fresh mint sprig

*Muddle mint leaves gently
in mixing glass. Add remaining ingredients and shake
with ice. Strain into chilled
cocktail glass. Add the mint
sprig.*

SOUTH-SIDE FIZZ

8–10 fresh mint leaves
2 oz. gin
¾ oz. fresh lemon juice
¾ oz. simple syrup
Soda water
Garnish: Fresh mint sprig

*Muddle mint leaves gently
in mixing glass. Add gin,
lemon juice, and syrup and
shake with ice. Strain into
ice-filled highball glass. Fill
with soda water and stir.
Add mint sprig.*

SPENCER COCKTAIL

1½ oz. gin
¾ oz. apricot-flavored brandy
¼ oz. fresh orange juice
1 dash Angostura bitters
Garnish: Maraschino cherry,
orange twist

*Shake with ice and strain
into chilled cocktail glass.
Add the cherry and orange
twist.*

GIN

▽ THE STANDARD

Created by JAMES MENITE,
New York City, NY

1¼ oz. gin
½ oz. yellow Chartreuse
1¼ oz. fresh ruby red
    grapefruit juice
¾ oz. fresh lemon juice
Garnish: Orange twist,
    flamed

*Shake with ice and strain
into cocktail glass. Flame
orange twist and add.*

▽ STANLEY COCKTAIL

1 oz. gin
¼ oz. light rum
½ oz. fresh lemon juice
¼ oz. grenadine

*Shake with ice and strain
into chilled cocktail glass.*

▣ STAR DAISY

1 oz. gin
1 oz. apple brandy
1 oz. fresh lemon juice
1 tsp. grenadine
1 tsp. simple syrup
Garnish: Fresh seasonal fruit

*Shake with ice. Strain
into ice-filled beer mug or
metal cup. Garnish with
fruit.*

▽ STRAIGHT LAW
COCKTAIL

1½ oz. dry sherry
¾ oz. gin

*Stir with ice and strain into
chilled cocktail glass.*

▯ STRAITS SLING

2 oz. gin
1 oz. fresh lemon juice
½ oz. Cherry Heering
½ oz. Bénédictine
2 dashes orange bitters
2 dashes Angostura bitters
Soda water

*Shake first six ingredients
with ice. Strain into
ice-filled Collins glass. Fill
with soda water and stir.*

▽ SUMMER CABINET

1 oz. gin
¾ oz. oloroso sherry
½ oz. fresh lemon juice
½ oz. apricot liqueur, such as
    barack pálinka
1 dash lemon bitters

*Shake with ice and
strain into chilled cocktail
glass.*

THE SUN ALSO RISES

Created by JONATHAN POGASH,
New York, NY

4 raspberries
¼ oz. fresh lime juice
¼ oz. fresh lemon juice
½ oz. simple syrup
1¼ oz. Peach Tea–Infused
  Gin (recipe follows)
¼ oz. Grand Marnier
Garnish: Fresh mint sprig

*Muddle raspberries with
lime and lemon juices and
syrup. Add gin and Grand
Marnier and shake with ice.
Strain through wire sieve
into ice-filled old-fashioned
glass. Garnish with mint.*

PEACH TEA–INFUSED GIN

*Pour 1 cup gin into bowl.
Add 1 peach tea bag. Let
stand for 20 minutes. Strain
into another bowl, pressing
hard on tea bag. Funnel into
covered jar, pressing hard on
peach bag. Store, refrigerated, for up to 3 weeks.*

SWEET BASIL MARTINI

3 fresh basil leaves
1 lemon wedge
1½ oz. gin
¾ oz. Lillet Blanc
½ oz. simple syrup
Garnish: Lemon wheel

*Muddle the basil and lemon
wedge in mixing glass.
Add remaining ingredients
and shake with ice. Strain
into chilled cocktail glass.
Garnish with lemon.*

T & T

2 oz. Tanqueray gin
Tonic water
Garnish: Lime wedge

*Pour gin into ice-filled
highball glass and fill with
tonic water. Stir. Add lime
wedge.*

TAILSPIN

¾ oz. gin
¾ oz. sweet vermouth
¾ oz. green Chartreuse
¼ oz. Campari
Garnish: Lemon twist,
  maraschino cherry

*Stir with ice and strain
into chilled cocktail glass.
Add lemon twist and
cherry.*

TANGO COCKTAIL

1 oz. gin
½ oz. fresh orange juice
½ oz. dry vermouth
½ oz. sweet vermouth
½ tsp. triple sec

*Shake with ice and
strain into chilled cocktail
glass.*

THE TART GIN
COOLER

2 oz. gin
2 oz. fresh pink grapefruit juice
2 oz. tonic water
1 dash Peychaud's bitters

*Pour first three ingredients
into ice-filled Collins glass.
Top with bitters.*

GIN

Y THIRD-DEGREE COCKTAIL

Similar to the Obituary, but this one has an olive.

1½ oz. gin
¾ oz. dry vermouth
1 tsp. anisette
Garnish: Green olive

Stir with ice and strain into chilled cocktail glass. Add olive.

Y THREE CARD MONTY

1 oz. gin
1 oz. Campari
1 oz. tawny port

Stir with ice and strain into chilled cocktail glass.

Y THUNDERCLAP

¾ oz. gin
¾ oz. blended whiskey
¾ oz. brandy

Stir with ice and strain into chilled cocktail glass.

Y TILLICUM

Robert Hess (www.drinkboy.com) is the creator of this smoked salmon–garnished variation on the Martini theme.

2¼ oz. gin
¾ oz. dry vermouth
2 dashes Peychaud's bitters
Garnish: 1 slice smoked salmon, skewered on a toothpick

Stir with ice and strain into chilled cocktail glass. Garnish with salmon.

TOM COLLINS

In the 1870s, a practical joke made the rounds where the instigator insisted that the victim knew their mutual (and fictional) good friend "Tom Collins" to the point that fisticuffs often occurred. That is just one tale of how this cocktail was named.

2 oz. gin
1 oz. fresh lemon juice
1 oz. simple syrup
Soda water
Garnish: Orange and lemon wheels, maraschino cherry

Shake gin, lemon juice, and syrup with ice and strain into Collins glass. Add several ice cubes, fill with soda water, and stir. Garnish with orange, lemon, and cherry. Serve with a straw.

TROPICAL SPECIAL

2 oz. fresh grapefruit juice
1½ oz. gin
1 oz. fresh orange juice
1 oz. fresh lime juice
½ oz. triple sec
Garnish: Fresh tropical fruit slices, maraschino cherry

Shake with ice and strain into ice-filled highball glass. Garnish with tropical fruits and cherry.

TURF COCKTAIL

There are three distinct cocktails named for a horse lover's hangout. Our favorite version hails from the old Waldorf-Astoria Hotel's bar of the late nineteenth century.

2 oz. genever
1 oz. sweet vermouth
1 dash Angostura bitters
Garnish: Lemon twist

Stir with ice and strain into chilled cocktail glass. Add lemon twist.

TUXEDO COCKTAIL

Again, we owe thanks to Harry Johnson's 1882 *Bartender's Manual* for a timeless libation.

1 oz. Old Tom gin
1 oz. dry vermouth
1 tsp. absinthe
1 tsp. maraschino liqueur
2 dashes orange bitters
Garnish: Maraschino
   cherry

Stir with ice and strain into chilled cocktail glass. Add the cherry.

TWENTIETH-CENTURY COCKTAIL

1½ oz. gin
¾ oz. Lillet Blanc
¾ oz. fresh lemon juice
½ oz. white crème
   de cacao

Shake with ice and strain into chilled cocktail glass.

TYPHOON

1 oz. gin
1 oz. fresh lime juice
½ oz. anisette
Chilled Champagne

Shake first three ingredients with ice and strain into ice-filled Collins glass. Top with Champagne.

UNION COCKTAIL

1½ oz. gin
¾ oz. sloe gin
1 tsp. grenadine

Shake with ice and strain into chilled cocktail glass.

UNION JACK

2 oz. gin
½ oz. Pimm's No. 1
½ oz. crème de violette or
   Crème Yvette
2 dashes orange bitters
Garnish: Orange twist

Stir with ice and strain into chilled cocktail glass. Add orange twist.

THE VALENTINO

2 oz. gin
½ oz. Campari
½ oz. sweet vermouth
Garnish: Orange twist

Stir with ice and strain into chilled cocktail glass. Add orange twist.

GIN

VESPER

James Bond's favorite cocktail, as described in Ian Fleming's book *Casino Royale*, named for Vesper Lynd, the novel's female character. We suggest stirring, not shaking, the drink, but it's hard to argue with 007.

3 oz. gin
1 oz. vodka
½ oz. Cocchi Americano
Garnish: Large lemon twist

Shake with ice. Strain into chilled Champagne or cocktail glass. Add lemon twist.

VICTOR

1½ oz. gin
½ oz. brandy
½ oz. sweet vermouth

Stir with ice and strain into chilled cocktail glass.

VIEUX MOT

1½ oz. gin
¾ oz. fresh lemon juice
½ oz. elderflower liqueur
½ oz. simple syrup

Shake with ice and strain into chilled cocktail glass.

VOW OF SILENCE

1½ oz. gin
¾ oz. fresh grapefruit juice
½ oz. fresh lime juice
½ oz. yellow Chartreuse
¼ oz. amaro, such as Averna
¼ oz. simple syrup

Shake with ice and strain into chilled cocktail glass.

WAIKIKI BEACHCOMBER

¾ oz. gin
¾ oz. triple sec
½ oz. pineapple juice

Shake with ice and strain into chilled cocktail glass.

WALLICK COCKTAIL

The Hotel Wallick was another old-time New York hostelry with a famous bar. This cocktail consists of a recognizable blend of gin, vermouth, and a sweetener.

1½ oz. gin
1½ oz. dry vermouth
1 tsp. triple sec

Stir with ice and strain into chilled cocktail glass.

WALLIS BLUE COCKTAIL

To color this cocktail blue, substitute blue curaçao for the triple sec.

For glass: Lime wedge, superfine sugar
1 oz. gin
1 oz. triple sec
1 oz. fresh lime juice

Rim old-fashioned glass with lime and sugar. Fill with ice. Shake remaining ingredients with ice and strain into glass.

GIN

☐ WATER LILY

¾ oz. gin
¾ oz. triple sec
¾ oz. crème de violette
¾ oz. fresh lemon juice
Garnish: Orange twist

*Shake with ice and strain
into chilled cocktail glass.
Add orange twist.*

☐ WEMBLY COCKTAIL

1½ oz. gin
¾ oz. dry vermouth
½ oz. apple brandy
½ oz. apricot-flavored brandy

*Stir with ice and strain into
chilled cocktail glass.*

☐ WESTERN ROSE

1 oz. gin
½ oz. dry vermouth
½ oz. apricot-flavored brandy
1 tsp. fresh lemon juice

*Shake with ice and strain
into chilled cocktail glass.*

☐ WHITE LADY

1½ oz. gin
¾ oz. triple sec
½ oz. fresh lemon juice

*Shake with ice and strain
into chilled cocktail glass.*

☐ WHITE SPIDER

1 oz. gin
¾ oz. fresh lemon juice
½ oz. triple sec
¼ oz. simple syrup

*Shake with ice and strain
into chilled cocktail glass.*

☐ WHITE WAY COCKTAIL

1½ oz. gin
¾ oz. white crème de
menthe

*Shake with ice and strain
into chilled cocktail glass.*

☐ WILL ROGERS

Another drink named for a show
business personality, Rogers
starred in vaudeville, Broadway,
and movies until his 1935
death in a plane crash.

1½ oz. gin
½ oz. dry vermouth
½ oz. fresh orange juice
1 dash triple sec

*Shake with ice and strain
into chilled cocktail glass.*

☐ THE WINK

1 splash absinthe
2 oz. gin
¼ oz. triple sec
¼ oz. simple syrup
2 dashes Peychaud's bitters

*Rinse a chilled old-
fashioned glass with
absinthe and pour out
excess absinthe. Stir
remaining ingredients with
ice and strain into glass.
Garnish with a wink.*

THE WINKLE

3 fresh sage leaves
2 oz. gin
1 oz. fresh lime juice
½ oz. limoncello
½ oz. simple syrup
4 raspberries
Garnish: Lemon twist

Muddle sage in mixing glass. Add remaining ingredients. Shake with ice and double-strain into chilled cocktail glass. Add lemon twist.

WOLF'S BITE

1½ oz. gin
1 oz. fresh grapefruit juice
½ oz. green Chartreuse

Shake with ice and strain into chilled cocktail glass.

WOODSTOCK

1½ oz. gin
1 oz. fresh lemon juice
1½ tsp. maple syrup
1 dash orange bitters

Shake with ice and strain into chilled cocktail glass.

XANTHIA COCKTAIL

¾ oz. gin
¾ oz. cherry-flavored brandy
¾ oz. yellow Chartreuse

Stir with ice and strain into chilled cocktail glass.

EDUCATE THE CUSTOMER

Too often a customer walks into a bar and orders the same cocktail they always do. This is generally out of habit, or for lack of a better idea. A well-informed bartender will have a selection of great cocktails to recommend to their patrons. By turning the customer on to a new cocktail, whether it is an original creation or a classic, you are both educating your guest and making sure to create repeat business. Get them addicted to your special cocktails, and let them have that vodka tonic at any other bar; I guarantee you will see their faces again.

—JULIE REINER, owner, Flatiron Lounge,
New York City

⅄ YALE COCKTAIL

1½ oz. gin
½ oz. dry vermouth
1 tsp. blue curaçao
1 dash Angostura bitters

Stir with ice and strain into chilled cocktail glass.

⅄ YOKAHAMA ROMANCE

2½ oz. sake
1 oz. gin
¼ oz. maraschino liqueur
Garnish: 1 unsprayed rose petal

Stir with ice and strain into chilled cocktail glass. Add rose petal.

GIN

RUM

RUM WAS FIRST PRODUCED in Brazil, Barbados, and Jamaica after Columbus introduced sugarcane to the West Indies in the late fifteenth century; within two centuries it was the favorite spirit of New England. Today this spirit, created from molasses, sugarcane juice, or syrup made by reducing the free-run juice of sugarcane, is among the most popular in the United States.

Rums can be divided into three stylistic types: Light rums, sometimes called white or silver, are traditionally produced in southern Caribbean islands (like Puerto Rico, Trinidad, and Barbados) and aged up to a year in barrels. Medium rums, sometimes called gold or amber, are smoother as a result of either congeners (organic compounds produced during fermentation), the addition of caramel, or occasionally through aging in wood barrels. Dark rums, which take their color from being aged anywhere from 3 to 12 years (and in some cases from the addition of caramel), are produced in the tropics: Jamaica, Haiti, and Martinique. And speaking of the French island of Martinique, if you see the words "rhum agricole" on a bottle or menu it refers to how pure-cane rum is known there. Brazilians call their pure-cane spirit "cachaça," which is synonymous with Caipirinha cocktails.

Subcategories of rum include spiced or flavored rums, which are infused with spices or aromatics while being distilled. There are also 151-proof rums, also called high-proof rums, which are often added to complete a mixed drink, or used in desserts or dessert cocktails that call for flaming—literally igniting the spirit. (Obviously, one should be very careful when playing with fire and high-proof rum!)

A DAY AT THE BEACH

1 oz. coconut-flavored rum
½ oz. amaretto
4 oz. fresh orange juice
½ oz. grenadine
Garnish: Pineapple wedge, strawberry

Shake rum, amaretto, and orange juice with ice and pour into ice-filled highball glass. Top with grenadine. Garnish with pineapple and strawberry.

AGRICOLE RUM PUNCH

2 oz. aged rhum agricole
1 oz. fresh lime juice
1 oz. simple syrup
2 dashes Angostura bitters
¼ oz. allspice liqueur (pimento dram)
Garnish: Freshly ground nutmeg

Shake with ice and strain into ice-filled Collins glass. Top with nutmeg.

AIR MAIL

1 oz. light rum
½ oz. fresh lime juice
½ oz. Honey Syrup (page 25)
1 splash chilled Champagne

Shake rum, lime juice, and syrup with ice. Strain into chilled champagne flute. Top with Champagne.

ANCIENT MARINER

1 oz. aged rum
1 oz. dark rum
¾ oz. fresh lime juice
½ oz. fresh grapefruit juice
½ oz. simple syrup
¼ oz. allspice liqueur (pimento dram)
Garnish: Lime wedge, fresh mint sprig

Shake with ice and strain into old-fashioned glass filled with crushed ice. Garnish with lime and mint.

BAHAMA MAMA

½ oz. dark rum
½ oz. coconut liqueur
¼ oz. 151-proof rum
¼ oz. coffee liqueur
½ oz. fresh lemon juice
4 oz. pineapple juice
Garnish: Strawberry or maraschino cherry

Shake with ice and strain into ice-filled highball glass. Garnish with strawberry or cherry.

□ BAJITO

4 fresh mint leaves
4 fresh basil leaves
5 slices fresh lime
1 oz. simple syrup
3 oz. dark rum
Garnish: 1 fresh basil leaf

Muddle mint, 4 basil leaves, and lime with syrup in mixing glass. Add ice and rum. Shake well and strain into ice-filled old-fashioned glass. Garnish with basil leaf.

▽ BANANA COW

1 oz. light rum
1 oz. crème de banana
1½ oz. heavy cream
1 dash grenadine
Garnish: Banana slice, freshly grated nutmeg

Shake with crushed ice and strain into chilled cocktail glass. Garnish with banana slice on glass rim and top with nutmeg.

□ THE BEACHBUM

1 oz. light rum
1 oz. dark rum
½ oz. apricot-flavored brandy
1 oz. pineapple juice
¾ oz. fresh lime juice
½ oz. almond or orgeat syrup
Garnish: Orange/cherry flag

Shake with ice and strain into ice-filled Collins glass. Garnish with orange/cherry flag.

▽ BEACHCOMBER

For glass: Lime wheel, superfine sugar
1½ oz. light rum
½ oz. triple sec
½ oz. grenadine
½ oz. simple syrup
½ oz. fresh lemon juice

Rim chilled cocktail glass with lime and sugar; reserve lime. Shake remaining ingredients with ice and strain into glass. Garnish with reserved lime.

▽ THE BEAUTY BENEATH

2 oz. dark rum
½ oz. sweet vermouth
½ oz. Campari
½ oz. triple sec
1 dash Angostura bitters
Garnish: Orange twist

Shake with ice and strain into chilled cocktail glass. Add orange twist.

▽ BEE'S KISS

1½ oz. light rum
1 oz. heavy cream
¾ oz. Honey Syrup (page 25)

Shake and strain into a chilled champagne flute.

▽ BENJAMIN BARKER DAIQUIRI

2 oz. dark rum
½ oz. fresh lime juice
½ oz. simple syrup
½ oz. Campari
2 dashes absinthe
Garnish: Lime wedge

Shake with ice and strain into chilled cocktail glass. Garnish with lime wedge.

RUM

BERMUDA RUM SWIZZLE

2 oz. dark rum
1 oz. fresh lime juice
1 oz. pineapple juice
1 oz. fresh orange juice
¼ oz. falernum
Soda water
Garnish: Orange wheel,
    maraschino cherry

Combine first five ingredients in ice-filled Collins glass. With barspoon between your palms, move hands back and forth and up and down to quickly rotate and lift spoon, until glass is frosted. Top with soda water. Garnish with orange and cherry. Serve with a swizzle stick.

BERMUDA TRIANGLE

1 oz. peach schnapps
½ oz. spiced rum
3 oz. fresh orange juice

Pour ingredients into ice-filled old-fashioned glass.

BITCHES' BREW

1 oz. dark rum
1 oz. rhum agricole
1 oz. fresh lime juice
½ oz. simple syrup
½ oz. allspice liqueur
    (pimento dram)
1 egg
Garnish: Freshly grated
    nutmeg

Shake without ice. Shake with ice and strain into highball glass. Top with nutmeg.

THE BITTER, DARK & STORMY

Created by TED HENWOOD,
New York, NY

2½ oz. dark rum
5 dashes orange bitters
Ginger beer
Garnish: Lime wedge

Pour rum and bitters into ice-filled highball glass. Top with ginger beer and stir. Squeeze lime into glass and add wedge.

BITTERLY DARK

1½ oz. dark rum
1 oz. amaro, such as
    Ramazzotti or Averna
1 oz. fresh blood orange juice
¼ oz. crème de cassis
Garnish: Blood orange wheel

Shake and strain into chilled cocktail glass. Garnish with orange wheel.

BLACK DEVIL

2 oz. light rum
½ oz. dry vermouth
Garnish: Black olive

Stir with ice and strain into chilled cocktail glass. Add olive.

BLACK MARIA

2 oz. light rum
2 oz. coffee-flavored brandy
½ oz. simple syrup
4 oz. hot strong brewed coffee

Stir in prewarmed Irish coffee glass.

BLACK WIDOW

3 oz. dark rum
1 oz. white crème de menthe

Shake with ice and strain into ice-filled old-fashioned glass.

BLOOD AND SAMBA

¾ oz. cachaça
¾ oz. sweet vermouth
¾ oz. Cherry Heering
¾ oz. fresh orange juice
2 dashes Peychaud's bitters
Garnish: Orange twist, flamed

Shake with ice and strain into chilled cocktail glass. Flame orange twist and add.

BLUE HAWAIIAN

A tiki drink with impeccable heritage, it was created in 1957 by Harry Yee, head bartender at the Hilton Hawaiian Village, in Waikiki, Hawaii.

1 oz. light rum
1 oz. blue curaçao
1 oz. cream of coconut
2 oz. pineapple juice
Garnish: Pineapple wedge, maraschino cherry

Combine ingredients with 1 cup crushed ice in blender on high speed. Pour into chilled highball glass. Garnish with pineapple and cherry.

BOLERO

1½ oz. light rum
¼ oz. brandy
¼ tsp. sweet vermouth

Stir with ice and strain into chilled cocktail glass.

BORINQUEN

1½ oz. light rum
1 oz. fresh lime juice
1 oz. fresh orange juice
½ oz. passion fruit syrup
1 tsp. 151-proof rum

Process with ½ cup crushed ice in blender on low speed. Pour into chilled old-fashioned glass.

RUM

BOSSA NOVA SPECIAL COCKTAIL

1 oz. dark rum
1 oz. Galliano
¼ oz. apricot-flavored brandy
2 oz. pineapple juice
¼ oz. fresh lemon juice
1 egg white
Garnish: Maraschino cherry

Shake without ice. Shake with ice and strain into ice-filled highball glass. Garnish with cherry.

BOSTON COOLER

2 oz. light rum
1 oz. fresh lemon juice
2 tsp. simple syrup
Soda water or ginger ale
Garnish: Orange or lemon zest spiral

Stir rum, lemon juice, and syrup in Collins glass. Add ice, fill with soda water or ginger ale, and stir again. Add citrus spiral and dangle end over glass rim.

Y BOSTON SIDECAR

¾ oz. light rum
¾ oz. brandy
¾ oz. triple sec
½ oz. fresh lime juice

Shake with ice and strain into chilled cocktail glass.

Y BUCCANEER

1½ oz. spiced rum
½ oz. white crème de cacao
¾ oz. fresh lime juice
¾ oz. pineapple juice
½ oz. falernum
1 dash Angostura bitters
Garnish: Freshly grated
   nutmeg

Shake with ice and strain into chilled cocktail glass. Top with nutmeg.

☐ BUCK JONES

1½ oz. light rum
1 oz. sweet sherry
½ oz. fresh lime juice
Ginger ale

Pour rum, sherry, and lime juice into ice-filled highball glass and stir. Fill with ginger ale.

Y BULL'S BLOOD

¾ oz. dark rum
¾ oz. orange curaçao
¾ oz. Spanish brandy
1½ oz. fresh orange juice
Garnish: Orange twist, flamed

Shake with ice and strain into chilled cocktail glass. Flame orange zest and add.

☐ BURGUNDY BISHOP

1 oz. light rum
½ oz. fresh lemon juice
2 tsp. simple syrup
Red wine
Garnish: Fresh seasonal fruit

Shake rum, lemon juice, and syrup with ice. Strain into ice-filled highball glass. Fill with red wine and stir. Garnish with fruit.

Y CABLE CAR

This drink is a specialty of star mixologist Tony Abou-Ganim.

For glass: Lemon wedge,
   Cinnamon Sugar (recipe
   follows)
2 oz. spiced rum
¾ oz. triple sec
¾ oz. fresh lemon juice
½ oz. simple syrup
Garnish: Lemon twist, ground
   cinnamon

Rim chilled cocktail glass with lemon wedge and cinnamon sugar. Shake remaining ingredients with ice and strain into glass. Add lemon twist and top with a sprinkle of cinnamon.

CINNAMON SUGAR

Mix equal parts superfine sugar and ground cinnamon.

CAIPIRINHA

The national drink of Brazil, the name means "country bumpkin."

1 whole lime, cut into quarters
½ oz. simple syrup
2 oz. cachaça

Muddle lime and syrup in old-fashioned glass. Add cachaça and stir. Fill with ice and stir again.

CANADO SALUDO

1½ oz. light rum
1 oz. fresh orange juice
1 oz. pineapple juice
½ oz. fresh lemon juice
½ oz. grenadine
5 dashes Angostura bitters
Garnish: Pineapple wedge, orange wheel, maraschino cherry

Pour ingredients into ice-filled highball glass and stir well. Garnish with pineapple, orange, and cherry.

CAPTAIN'S BLOOD

1½ oz. dark rum
¼ oz. fresh lime juice
¼ oz. simple syrup
¼ oz. falernum
2 dashes Angostura bitters
Garnish: Lemon zest spiral

Shake with ice and strain into chilled cocktail glass. Add lemon spiral.

CARIBBEAN GINGER

Created by Raphael Reyes, New York, NY

To obtain fresh ginger juice, shred fresh ginger (no need to peel) on the large holes of a box grater, wrap in a clean bar towel, and wring into a bowl.

2 oz. dark rum
1 oz. pineapple juice
½ oz. Demerara Syrup (page 25)
½ oz. fresh lime juice
½ oz. fresh ginger juice
Garnish: Ground cinnamon

Shake well with ice and strain into chilled cocktail glass. Top with cinnamon.

RUM

CARIBBEAN ROMANCE

1½ oz. light rum
1 oz. amaretto
1½ oz. fresh orange juice
1½ oz. pineapple juice
¼ oz. grenadine
Garnish: Orange, lemon, or lime wheel

Shake rum, amaretto, and juices with ice and strain into ice-filled highball glass. Float grenadine on top. Garnish with citrus.

CASTAWAY

1½ oz. dark rum
¾ oz. coffee liqueur
3 oz. pineapple juice
Garnish: Maraschino cherry
speared to pineapple wedge

*Shake with ice and strain
into hurricane or highball
glass filled with crushed ice.
Garnish with cherry-
pineapple spear.*

CHANTILLY COCKTAIL

For glass: Lemon wedge,
Cinnamon Sugar
(page 126)
1½ oz. dark rum
¾ oz. apricot-flavored brandy
1 oz. fresh lemon juice
1 oz. simple syrup
2 dashes peach bitters
Garnish: Cinnamon stick
wrapped with orange zest
spiral

*Rim chilled cocktail glass
with lemon and cinnamon
sugar. Shake remaining
ingredients with ice and
strain into glass. Add
cinnamon-orange garnish.*

CHERIE

1 oz. light rum
½ oz. triple sec
½ oz. cherry-flavored
brandy
1 oz. fresh lime juice
Garnish: Maraschino cherry

*Shake with ice and strain
into chilled cocktail glass.
Add cherry.*

CHET BAKER

1 sugar cube
2 dashes Angostura bitters
2 oz. dark rum
¼ oz. Punt e Mes
¼ oz. Honey Syrup (page 25)
Garnish: Lemon twist

*Muddle sugar cube with
bitters in mixing glass. Add
ice, then other ingredients,
and stir briefly. Strain into
ice-filled old-fashioned glass.
Garnish with lemon twist.*

CHINESE COCKTAIL

1½ oz. dark rum
½ oz. grenadine
1 tsp. maraschino liqueur
1 tsp. triple sec
1 dash Angostura bitters

*Shake with ice and strain
into chilled cocktail glass.*

CHOCOLATE RUM

1 oz. light rum
½ oz. dark crème de cacao
½ oz. white crème de menthe
1 tsp. 151-proof rum
¼ oz. half-and-half

*Shake with ice and strain into
ice-filled old-fashioned glass.*

COCOMACOQUE

2 oz. pineapple juice
2 oz. fresh orange juice
1½ oz. light rum
1 oz. fresh lemon juice
2 oz. red wine
Garnish: Pineapple wedge

*Shake first four ingredients.
Strain into ice-filled Collins
glass and top with wine. Add
pineapple.*

COFFEY PARK SWIZZLE

1 oz. dark rum
1 oz. amontillado sherry
¾ oz. ginger liqueur
¾ oz. fresh lime juice
¼ oz. falernum
4 dashes Angostura bitters
Garnish: Mint sprig

Pour ingredients into crushed ice-filled Collins glass. With barspoon between your palms, move hands back and forth and up and down to quickly rotate and lift spoon until glass is frosted. Add mint.

COLADAS

LEMON-COCONUT COLADA

1½ oz. citrus-flavored rum
1½ oz. coconut-flavored rum
2 oz. cream of coconut
1 oz. heavy cream
4 oz. pineapple juice
½ oz. fresh lemon juice
Garnish: Freshly grated lemon zest or toasted coconut

Shake with ice and strain into ice-filled hurricane glass. Top with lemon zest or coconut.

PIÑA COLADA

Another rum drink with a murky history, it was probably the invention of Ramon "Monchito" Marrero at the Caribe Hilton's Beachcomber Bar in San Juan, PR, in 1954, at the time when cream of coconut was just hitting the marketplace.

3 oz. light rum
3 oz. pineapple juice
1½ oz. cream of coconut
Garnish: Pineapple wedge, maraschino cherry

Combine ingredients with 2 cups of crushed ice in blender on high speed. Pour into chilled Collins glass. Garnish with pineapple and cherry and serve with a straw.

RUM

CONCRETE JUNGLE

Created by HAL WOLIN, New York, NY

1½ oz. dark rum
½ oz. Calvados
½ oz. Amaro Nonino
½ oz. sweet vermouth
1 dash absinthe
1 dash orange bitters

Stir with ice and strain into chilled cocktail glass.

CONTINENTAL

1¾ oz. light rum
½ oz. fresh lime juice
¼ oz. green crème de menthe
1 tsp. simple syrup
Garnish: Lemon twist

Shake with ice and strain into chilled cocktail glass. Add lemon twist.

CORKSCREW

1½ oz. light rum
½ oz. dry vermouth
½ oz. peach-flavored brandy
Garnish: Lime wheel

*Shake with ice and strain
into chilled cocktail glass.
Garnish with lime.*

CREAM PUFF

2 oz. light rum
1 oz. half-and-half
1 tsp. simple syrup
Soda water

*Shake first three ingredients
with ice and strain into
chilled highball glass over
2 ice cubes. Fill with soda
water and stir.*

CREOLE

1½ oz. rhum agricole
1½ oz. cold beef bouillon
1 tsp. fresh lemon juice
1 dash hot red pepper sauce
Salt and freshly ground
   pepper

*Shake with ice and strain into
ice-filled old-fashioned glass.*

CREOLE CLUB COCKTAIL

2 oz. aged rhum agricole
1 oz. Creole Shrubb
   (rum-based orange liqueur)
¾ oz. fresh lime juice
1 dash Angostura bitters
1 dash orange bitters
Garnish: Freshly grated
   nutmeg, star anise pod

*Shake with ice and strain into
chilled cocktail glass. Top with
nutmeg and add star anise.*

CUBA LIBRE

Coca-Cola was introduced
to Cuba in 1900, and this
cocktail was born almost
immediately thereafter. "*¡Cuba
libre!* (Free Cuba!)" was a battle
cry during the Cuban War of
Independence, which ended
just two years before.

2 oz. rum
Cola
Garnish: Lime wedge

*Pour rum into ice-filled high-
ball glass. Fill with cola and
stir. Squeeze lime into glass
and add wedge.*

CUBAN SPECIAL

1 oz. light rum
½ oz. pineapple juice
½ oz. fresh lime juice
¼ oz. triple sec
Garnish: Pineapple wedge,
   maraschino cherry

*Shake with ice and strain
into chilled cocktail glass.
Garnish with pineapple and
cherry.*

THE CURE AND THE CAUSE

Created by ANDRES SANCHEZ, Philadelphia, PA.

You will find jars of wild hibiscus flowers in rose syrup at specialty stores. See page 320 for online resources.

12 blueberries
½ oz. syrup from wild hibiscus flowers in rose syrup
1½ oz. cachaça
¾ oz. açai berry liqueur
1 oz. fresh lime juice
Garnish: Fresh blueberries

Muddle 12 blueberries and syrup in mixing glass. Add remaining ingredients and shake with ice. Strain into ice-filled highball glass. Garnish with blueberries.

DAIQUIRIS

CLASSIC DAIQUIRI

This is the original cocktail and not the frozen version, which can be found on page 261.

2 oz. light rum
¾ oz. fresh lime juice
¾ oz. simple syrup

Shake with ice and strain into chilled cocktail glass.

DERBY DAIQUIRI

1½ oz. light rum
1 oz. fresh orange juice
½ oz. fresh lime juice
½ oz. simple syrup

Combine ingredients with ½ cup cracked ice in blender and blend on low speed until smooth. Pour into champagne flute.

HEMINGWAY DAIQUIRI

Papa liked his Daiquiris with grapefruit juice and sweetness provided by maraschino. A double of this drink is called a Papa Doble, and Hemingway was certainly a two-fisted drinker.

2 oz. light rum
¾ oz. fresh grapefruit juice
½ oz. fresh lime juice
¼ oz. maraschino liqueur

Shake with ice and strain into ice-filled cocktail glass.

PASSION DAIQUIRI

1½ oz. light rum
1 oz. fresh lime juice
½ oz. passion fruit juice or puree
½ oz. simple syrup

Shake with ice and strain into chilled cocktail glass.

RUM

☐ STRAWBERRY DAIQUIRI

2 strawberries, chopped
1 oz. fresh lime juice
½ oz. simple syrup
1 oz. light rum
½ oz. strawberry schnapps

Muddle strawberries, lime juice, and syrup in mixing glass. Add rum and schnapps. Shake with ice and strain into chilled cocktail glass.

☐ DAISY DE SANTIAGO

2 oz. dark rum
¾ oz. fresh lime juice
¾ oz. simple syrup
1 oz. yellow Chartreuse
Garnish: Fresh mint sprig

Shake first three ingredients with ice and strain into ice-filled red-wine glass. Carefully float Chartreuse (see page 18) on top. Add mint.

☐ DARK 'N STORMY

The national drink of Bermuda requires just two Bermudian products, ginger beer and dark rum. Dark 'n Stormy® is a registered trademark of Gosling Brothers Limited, Hamilton, Bermuda.

Ginger beer
2 oz. Gosling's dark rum

Pour ginger beer into an ice-filled old-fashioned glass. Float rum (see page 18) on top.

☐ DIABOLO

2 oz. light rum
½ oz. triple sec
½ oz. dry vermouth
2 dashes Angostura bitters
Garnish: Orange twist

Stir with ice and strain into chilled cocktail glass. Add orange twist.

☐ DINGO

½ oz. light rum
½ oz. Tennessee sour mash whiskey
½ oz. amaretto
2 oz. fresh orange juice
1 oz. fresh lemon juice
1 oz. simple syrup
1 splash grenadine
Garnish: Orange wheel

Shake with ice and pour into ice-filled highball glass. Garnish with orange.

☐ DOCTOR FUNK NO. 2

The real Doctor Funk was Robert Louis Stevenson's physician in the South Seas. Some versions of this drink go heavy on the absinthe, so add more if you wish.

1½ oz. dark rum
½ oz. falernum
½ oz. grenadine
¾ oz. fresh lime juice
1 dash absinthe
1 dash Angostura bitters
Soda water
Garnish: Lime wedge

Shake first six ingredients with ice and strain into hurricane glass. Fill with soda water. Add lime.

EL PRESIDENTE COCKTAIL NO. 1

It is said that this was the drink that Cuban president Carmen Menocal tried to serve to President Calvin Coolidge during a state visit. As the meeting occurred during Prohibition, Coolidge reportedly declined.

1½ oz. light rum
¾ oz. fresh lime juice
1 tsp. pineapple juice
1 tsp. grenadine

Shake with ice and strain into chilled cocktail glass.

EL PRESIDENTE COCKTAIL NO. 2

1½ oz. light rum
¾ oz. dry vermouth
1 dash Angostura bitters

Stir with ice and strain into chilled cocktail glass.

FAIR-AND-WARMER COCKTAIL

1½ oz. light rum
¾ oz. sweet vermouth
½ tsp. triple sec

Stir with ice and strain into chilled cocktail glass.

RUM

GET IN THEIR HEADS

If a bartender has time, it's always good to try to get "inside the head" of his or her customer, to try to discern their individual tastes. For instance, if somebody orders a Negroni, the bartender might ask, "Traditional gin Negroni?" since many people in the 21st century seem to prefer vodka (some people might not condone this, but facts are facts). This can lead to asking which brand of gin the customer prefers, and in turn, when the guest returns to the bar, the bartender might suggest another cocktail made with the same gin. Thus the bartender better understands the customer, and the customer enjoys the bar more.

—GARY REGAN, copublisher,
ArdentSpirits.com

☐ FAT LIKE BUDDHA

2 oz. dark rum
¾ oz. Dubonnet Rouge
¼ oz. Bénédictine
¼ oz. triple sec
Garnish: Orange twist, flamed

Stir with ice and strain into chilled cocktail glass. Flame orange twist and add.

☐ FIREMAN'S SOUR

2 oz. light rum
2 oz. fresh lime juice
¼ oz. simple syrup
¼ oz. grenadine
Soda water (optional)
Garnish: Lemon half-wheel,
   maraschino cherry

Shake first four ingredients with ice and strain into chilled old-fashioned glass. Fill with soda water, if desired. Garnish with lemon and cherry.

☐ FLORIDITA NO. 1

1½ oz. light rum
½ oz. fresh lime juice
½ oz. sweet vermouth
1 tsp. white crème de cacao
1 tsp. grenadine
Garnish: Lime twist

Shake with ice and strain into chilled cocktail glass. Add lime twist.

☐ FLORIDITA NO. 3

2 oz. light rum
¾ oz. fresh lime juice
½ oz. fresh grapefruit juice
½ oz. maraschino liqueur
½ oz. simple syrup
Garnish: Lime wheel

Shake with ice and strain into chilled champagne flute. Garnish with lime wheel.

☐ FOG CUTTER

1½ oz. light rum
½ oz. brandy
½ oz. gin
1½ oz. fresh lemon juice
1 oz. fresh orange juice
1½ tsp. almond or orgeat
   syrup
1 tsp. sweet sherry

Shake first six ingredients with ice and strain into ice-filled Collins glass. Top with sherry.

☐ GAUGIN

2 oz. light rum
½ oz. fresh lemon juice
½ oz. fresh lime juice
½ oz. passion fruit syrup
Garnish: Maraschino
   cherry

Combine ingredients with 1 cup crushed ice in blender on low speed. Serve in chilled old-fashioned glass. Add cherry.

GINGER GRAPEFRUIT RICKEY

2 oz. light rum
2 oz. fresh grapefruit juice
1 oz. ginger liqueur
½ oz. fresh lime juice
Soda water

Shake first four ingredients with ice. Strain into ice-filled highball glass and top with soda water.

GOLDEN ECLIPSE

Created by CHARLES H. STEADMAN, Palm Beach, FL

1½ oz. dark rum
¼ oz. amaro, such as Ramazzotti or Averna
½ oz. fresh lemon juice
1 dash orange bitters
3 oz. sparkling apple cider
Garnish: Golden Delicious apple wedge

Shake first four ingredients with ice. Strain into chilled cocktail glass. Top with cider. Garnish with apple wedge perched on glass rim.

GOLDEN FRIENDSHIP

1 oz. light rum
1 oz. sweet vermouth
1 oz. amaretto
Ginger ale
Garnish: Orange zest spiral, maraschino cherry

Stir first three ingredients in ice-filled Collins glass with ice, then fill with ginger ale. Garnish with orange and cherry.

GRANDE GUIGNOL

1½ oz. dark rum
¾ oz. yellow Chartreuse
¾ oz. Cherry Heering
¾ oz. fresh lime juice
Garnish: Lime wheel

Shake with ice and strain into chilled cocktail glass. Garnish with lime.

HAI KARATE

2 oz. dark rum
1 oz. fresh lime juice
1 oz. pineapple juice
1 oz. fresh orange juice
1 tsp. maple syrup
1 dash Angostura bitters
Garnish: Cherry/orange flag

Shake with ice and strain into ice-filled Collins glass. Garnish with cherry/orange flag.

HARVEST NECTAR

1½ oz. light rum
1 oz. pineapple juice
1 oz. cranberry juice
1 oz. fresh orange juice
1 oz. lemon-lime soda

Shake with ice and strain into ice-filled beer mug.

HAVANA COCKTAIL

¾ oz. light rum
1½ oz. pineapple juice
¼ oz. fresh lemon juice

Shake with ice and strain into chilled cocktail glass.

RUM

Y HEMINGWAY'S NOG

Created by ALEX STRAUS,
Hollywood, CA

1½ oz. dark rum
¾ oz. vanilla liqueur
¼ oz simple syrup
1 oz. crème fraîche
3 dashes tiki bitters, such as
    Bittermen's 'Elemakule
Garnish: Freshly grated
    nutmeg

*Shake with ice and strain
into chilled cocktail glass.
Top with nutmeg.*

Y THE HOLY ROLLER

Created by TREVOR EASTER,
San Francisco, CA

1½ oz. cachaça
¾ oz. fresh lime juice
½ oz. Honey Syrup
    (page 25)
6–8 fresh mint leaves
2 dashes Angostura bitters
½ oz. Champagne or
    sparkling wine
Garnish: Fresh mint sprig

*Shake first five ingredients
with ice. Strain into chilled
cocktail glass. Top with
Champagne or sparkling
wine. Garnish with mint.*

Y HOP TOAD

¾ oz. light rum
¾ oz. apricot-flavored
    brandy
½ oz. fresh lime juice

*Shake with ice and strain
into chilled cocktail glass.*

HURRICANE

The specialty cocktail of Pat
O'Brien's in New Orleans. You
can buy Hurricane mix, but this
from-scratch version is even
better.

1½ oz. dark rum
1½ oz. light rum
1 oz. passion fruit syrup
1 oz. lime juice
¾ oz. fresh orange juice
½ oz. simple syrup
½ oz. grenadine
Garnish: Orange half-wheel,
    maraschino cherry

*Shake with ice and strain
into ice-filled hurricane
glass. Garnish with orange
and cherry.*

HURRICANE LEAH

¼ oz. light rum
¼ oz. gin
¼ oz. vodka
¼ oz. blanco tequila
¼ oz. blue curaçao
1 dash cherry-flavored brandy
1½ oz. simple syrup
1½ oz. fresh lemon juice
3 oz. fresh orange juice
Garnish: Orange wheel

*Pour ingredients, in order
given, into ice-filled hurricane glass and stir. Garnish
with orange wheel.*

☐ HUSH AND WONDER

1 splash crème de violette
2 oz. light rum
¾ oz. fresh lime juice
¾ oz. simple syrup
3 dashes grapefruit bitters

Pour crème de violette into chilled cocktail glass and swirl to coat; discard excess liqueur. Shake remaining ingredients with ice and strain into glass.

☐ IRRESISTIBLE

1½ oz. light rum
½ oz. sweet vermouth
¼ oz. Bénédictine
¼ oz. fresh lemon juice
Garnish: Lemon twist

Shake and strain into cocktail glass. Add lemon twist.

☐ JACK SPARROW FLIP

2 oz. dark rum
¾ oz. madeira
¾ oz. simple syrup
1 egg
2 dashes Angostura bitters
Garnish: Freshly grated nutmeg

Shake without ice. Then shake with ice and strain into highball glass. Top with nutmeg.

☐ JACQUELINE

2 oz. dark rum
1 oz. triple sec
1 oz. fresh lime juice
1 dash simple syrup

Shake with ice and strain into chilled cocktail glass.

☐ JADE

1½ oz. light rum
½ oz. fresh lime juice
½ tsp. green crème de menthe
½ tsp. triple sec
Scant ½ oz. simple syrup
Garnish: Lime wheel

Shake with ice and strain into chilled cocktail glass. Garnish with lime.

☐ JAMAICAN CRAWLER

1 oz. light rum
1 oz. melon liqueur
3 oz. pineapple juice
1 splash grenadine

Shake first three ingredients with ice and pour into Collins glass. Add grenadine and stir.

☐ JAMAICAN GINGER

1½ oz. light rum
1 oz. dark rum
½ oz. falernum
½ oz. fresh lime juice
4 dashes Angostura bitters
Ginger ale
Garnish: Lime wheel

Stir first five ingredients in ice-filled Collins glass. Top with ginger ale. Garnish with lime.

RUM

KNICKERBOCKER SPECIAL COCKTAIL

2 oz. light rum
½ tsp. triple sec
1 tsp. fresh lemon juice
1 tsp. fresh orange juice
1 tsp. raspberry syrup
Garnish: Small pineapple slice

Shake with ice and strain into chilled cocktail glass. Garnish with pineapple.

KO ADANG

2 oz. dark rum
1 oz. coconut rum
½ oz. ginger liqueur
½ oz. mango nectar
½ oz. cream of coconut
½ oz. fresh lime juice
Garnish: Lime wheel

Shake with ice and strain into ice-filled Collins glass. Garnish with lime.

LA VITA DULCE

Created by ABIGAIL GULLO, New York City, NY

1½ oz. spiced rum
¾ oz. mezcal
¾ oz. fresh lime juice
¾ oz. simple syrup
Garnish: Ground cinnamon

Shake with ice and strain into chilled cocktail glass. Top with cinnamon.

LEVELHEADED COCKTAIL

1½ oz. aged rhum agricole
1 oz. cold brewed coffee
½ oz. allspice liqueur (pimento dram)
¼ oz. simple syrup
2 dashes Angostura bitters

Shake with ice and strain into snifter.

LITTLE DEVIL COCKTAIL

¾ oz. light rum
¾ oz. gin
½ oz. fresh lemon juice
¼ oz. triple sec

Shake with ice and strain into chilled cocktail glass.

LITTLE PRINCESS COCKTAIL

1½ oz. light rum
1½ oz. sweet vermouth

Shake with ice and strain into chilled cocktail glass.

LOOK OUT BELOW

1½ oz. 151-proof rum
½ oz. fresh lime juice
¼ oz. grenadine

Shake with ice and strain into ice-filled old-fashioned glass.

LOUNGE LIZARD

1 oz. dark rum
½ oz. amaretto
Cola
Garnish: Lime wedge

Pour rum and amaretto into ice-filled Collins glass. Fill with cola and stir. Garnish with lime.

LUMINATION

2 slices fresh ginger
1 oz. simple syrup
2 oz. dark rum
1 oz. VS Cognac
1 oz. fresh lemon juice
1 dash Angostura bitters
Garnish: Lemon twist

Muddle ginger in syrup in mixing glass. Add remaining ingredients and ice and shake. Strain into chilled champagne flute. Add lemon twist.

MAI-TAI (TRADER VIC VERSION)

2 oz. dark rum, preferably Jamaican
½ oz. orange curaçao
1 oz. fresh lime juice (reserve ½ lime shell for garnish)
½ oz. orgeat syrup
¼ oz. rock candy syrup or simple syrup
Garnish: Fresh mint sprig; pineapple wedge skewered with maraschino cherry

Shake ingredients without ice. Strain into ice-filled old-fashioned glass. Garnish with lime shell, mint, and skewered pineapple and cherry.

MALMAISON

For glass: Anisette
1 oz. light rum
½ oz. cream sherry
1 oz. fresh lemon juice

Rim chilled cocktail glass with anisette. Shake remaining ingredients with ice. Strain into glass.

MANDEVILLE

1½ oz. light rum
1 oz. dark rum
½ oz. fresh lemon juice
1 tsp. anisette
1 tsp. grenadine
Cola

Shake first five ingredients with ice and strain into ice-filled old-fashioned glass. Top with cola.

MARIPOSA

1 oz. light rum
½ oz. brandy
½ oz. fresh lemon juice
½ oz. fresh orange juice
1 dash grenadine

Shake with ice and strain into chilled cocktail glass.

MARTINIQUE ROSE

2 oz. aged rhum agricole
½ oz. amaretto
¾ oz. fresh lime juice
¾ oz. fresh grapefruit juice
½ oz. orgeat or almond syrup

Shake with ice and strain into chilled cocktail glass.

MARY PICKFORD COCKTAIL

Mary Pickford was a star of the silent film era who also became known as an astute businesswoman.

1½ oz. light rum
¾ oz. pineapple juice
¼ oz. maraschino liqueur
¼ oz. grenadine

Shake with ice and strain into chilled cocktail glass.

RUM

MIDNIGHT EXPRESS

1½ oz. dark rum
½ oz. triple sec
¾ oz. fresh lime juice
¼ oz. fresh lemon juice
¼ oz. simple syrup

Shake with ice and pour into ice-filled old-fashioned glass.

MOJITO

This Cuban drink has attained cocktail immortality. Some believe that its history is as long as rum itself, even if it has only recently gained popularity in the U.S.

3 lime wedges
8–10 fresh mint leaves
¾ oz. simple syrup
2 oz. light rum
Soda water
Garnish: Fresh mint sprig

Muddle the limes, mint, and syrup in a Collins glass. Add the rum with ice and stir well. Top with soda water. Garnish with mint.

MONKEY WRENCH

1½ oz. light rum
Fresh grapefruit juice

Pour rum into ice-filled Collins glass. Fill with grapefruit juice and stir.

MOONQUAKE SHAKE

1½ oz. dark rum
1 oz. coffee-flavored brandy
¼ oz. fresh lemon juice

Shake with ice and strain into chilled cocktail glass.

NEVADA COCKTAIL

1½ oz. light rum
1 oz. fresh grapefruit juice
¾ oz. fresh lime juice
¾ oz. simple syrup
1 dash Angostura bitters

Shake with ice and strain into chilled cocktail glass.

NEW ORLEANS BUCK

1½ oz. light rum
1 oz. fresh orange juice
½ oz. fresh lemon juice
Ginger ale

Shake first three ingredients with ice and strain into ice-filled Collins glass. Fill with ginger ale and stir.

NIGHT CAP

2 oz. light rum
½ oz. simple syrup
Warm milk
Garnish: Freshly grated nutmeg

Pour rum and syrup in pre-warmed Irish coffee glass, fill with warm milk, and stir. Top with nutmeg.

OH, GOSH!

1½ oz. light rum
1½ oz. triple sec
1 oz. fresh lime juice
Garnish: Lemon twist

Shake with ice and strain into chilled cocktail glass. Add lemon twist.

THE OLD CUBAN

This recipe is a specialty of Audrey Saunders, owner of Pegu Club, New York, NY.

6 fresh mint leaves
1 oz. simple syrup
¾ oz. fresh lime juice
1½ oz. dark rum
2 dashes Angostura bitters
2 oz. Champagne
Garnish: Chopped fresh mint

Muddle mint leaves, syrup, and lime juice in mixing glass. Add rum, bitters, and ice and shake well. Strain into chilled cocktail glass and top with Champagne. Garnish with chopped mint.

PADDINGTON

1 splash absinthe
1½ oz. light rum
½ oz. Lillet Blanc
½ oz. fresh grapefruit juice
½ oz. fresh lemon juice
1 tsp. orange marmalade
Garnish: Grapefruit twist

Pour absinthe into chilled cocktail glass, swirl to coat inside, and discard excess. Shake remaining ingredients with ice and strain into glass. Add grapefruit twist.

PALMETTO COCKTAIL

1½ oz. light rum
1½ oz. dry vermouth
2 dashes Angostura
    bitters

Stir with ice and strain into chilled cocktail glass.

PARIS WHEN IT SIZZLES

2 oz. dark rum
¾ oz. elderflower liqueur
½ oz. fresh lime juice
1 dash Angostura bitters
Garnish: Lime wedge

Shake with ice and strain into chilled cocktail glass. Garnish with lime.

PEARL BUTTON

2 oz. cachaça (Brazilian rum)
¾ oz. Lillet Blanc
½ oz. fresh lime juice
Lemon-lime soda
Garnish: Pineapple wedge,
    maraschino cherry

Shake first three ingredients with ice and strain into ice-filled Collins glass. Top with soda. Garnish with pineapple and cherry.

PINEAPPLE COCKTAIL

1½ oz. light rum
¾ oz. pineapple juice
½ tsp. fresh lemon juice

Shake with ice and strain into chilled cocktail glass.

PINEAPPLE FIZZ

2 oz. light rum
1 oz. pineapple juice
1 tsp. simple syrup
Soda water

Shake rum, pineapple juice, and syrup with ice and strain into chilled highball glass over 2 ice cubes. Fill with soda water and stir.

PINK CREOLE

1½ oz. light rum
½ oz. fresh lime juice
¼ oz. grenadine
¼ oz. half-and-half
Garnish: Rum-soaked black cherry

Shake with ice and strain into chilled cocktail glass. Add cherry.

PINK PARADISE

1½ oz. coconut-flavored rum
1 oz. amaretto
3 oz. cranberry juice
1½ oz. pineapple juice
Garnish: Pineapple wedge, maraschino cherry

Stir ingredients in ice-filled hurricane glass. Garnish with pineapple and cherry.

PLANTER'S COCKTAIL

1½ oz. Jamaican rum
½ oz. fresh lemon juice
1 tsp. simple syrup

Shake with ice and strain into chilled cocktail glass.

TEND TO PEOPLE

As bartenders, we are there to tend to peoples' needs. Mixing up a great drink, although very important, is only a part of that equation. Being considered a great bartender should be as important as being a talented mixologist. They call it the hospitality industry for a reason: You need to be able to tune into people, and then follow through with them. Folks who choose to sit at your bar rather than at a floor table are doing so for a reason—often they are looking for interaction.

—AUDREY SAUNDERS (aka Libation Goddess),
owner, Pegu Club, New York City

PLANTER'S PUNCH NO. 1

2½ oz. light rum
2 oz. fresh lime juice
½ oz. simple syrup
2 oz. soda water
1 dash grenadine
Garnish: Lemon, orange, and pineapple slices; maraschino cherry

Stir rum, lime juice, syrup, and bitters in ice-filled Collins glass until glass is frosted. Fill with soda water and top with grenadine. Garnish with the fruit. Serve with a straw.

PLANTER'S PUNCH NO. 2

2 oz. light rum
2 oz. fresh orange juice
1 oz. fresh lime juice
½ oz. pineapple juice
¼ oz. fresh lemon juice
1 oz. Jamaican rum
¼ oz. triple sec
1 dash grenadine
Garnish: Lemon, orange, and pineapple slices; maraschino cherry; fresh mint sprig dipped in sugar

Stir first five ingredients in ice-filled Collins glass until glass is frosted. Add Jamaican rum, stir, and top with triple sec and grenadine. Garnish with fruit and mint. Serve with a straw.

POKER COCKTAIL

1½ oz. light rum
1½ oz. sweet vermouth

Stir with ice and strain into chilled cocktail glass.

PROHIBITION PUNCH

Created by Hospitality Holdings, New York, NY

1½ oz. dark rum
¾ oz. Grand Marnier
1 oz. passion fruit juice
1 oz. cranberry juice
¼ oz. fresh lemon juice
2 oz. Champagne

Shake first five ingredients with ice. Strain into ice-filled snifter. Top with Champagne.

PUERTO RICAN RUM DAISY

1½ oz. dark rum
¼ oz. orange curaçao
¾ oz. fresh lemon juice
½ oz. fresh orange juice
½ oz. simple syrup
1 dash Angostura bitters
Garnish: Freshly grated nutmeg, orange wheel

Shake with ice and strain into chilled cocktail glass. Top with nutmeg and garnish with orange.

QUAKER'S COCKTAIL

¾ oz. light rum
¾ oz. brandy
½ oz. fresh lemon juice
¼ oz. raspberry syrup

Shake with ice and strain into chilled cocktail glass.

RUM

☙ QUARTER DECK COCKTAIL

1½ oz. light rum
½ oz. cream sherry
½ oz. fresh lime juice

Stir with ice and strain into chilled cocktail glass.

☙ RESTLESS NATIVE

2 oz. coconut rum
¾ oz. white crème de cacao
1½ oz. fresh lime juice
Garnish: Lime zest spiral

Shake with ice and strain into chilled cocktail glass. Garnish with lime spiral.

☐ RINGO STARR

3 red grapes
½ lemon
6 fresh mint leaves
1 sugar cube
2 oz. African rum, such as Starr

Muddle grapes, lemon, mint, and sugar in shaker. Add rum and ice and shake briefly. Strain into chilled old-fashioned glass.

☙ RIO FIX

1 splash absinthe or pastis
1½ oz. cachaça
½ oz. maraschino liqueur
¾ oz. fresh lime juice
½ oz. pineapple juice

Pour pastis into chilled champagne flute and swirl to coat inside. Shake remaining ingredients with ice and strain into glass.

☙ ROBSON COCKTAIL

1½ oz. Jamaican rum
½ oz. fresh lemon juice
½ oz. fresh orange juice
¼ oz. grenadine

Shake with ice and strain into chilled cocktail glass.

☙ RUM COBBLER

2 oz. light rum
¼ oz. simple syrup
Soda water
Garnish: Generous amount of fresh seasonal fruit

In red-wine glass, stir rum and syrup. Top with soda water. Garnish with fruit and serve with a straw.

☐ RUM COLLINS

2 oz. light rum
1 oz. fresh lime juice
½ oz. simple syrup
Soda water
Garnish: Lemon wheel, maraschino cherry

Shake rum, lime juice, and syrup with ice and strain into chilled Collins glass. Add several ice cubes, fill with soda water, and stir. Add lemon and cherry. Serve with a straw.

RUM COOLER

2 oz. light rum
½ oz. simple syrup
2 oz. soda water
Soda water or ginger ale
Garnish: Orange and/or
    lemon zest

*Stir rum and syrup in
Collins glass. Fill with
ice, add soda water or ginger
ale, and stir again. Insert
citrus spiral(s) and dangle
end(s) over glass rim.*

RUM DAISY

2 oz. light rum
½ oz. fresh lemon juice
1 tsp. simple syrup
1 tsp. grenadine
Garnish: Fresh seasonal fruit

*Shake with ice and strain
into chilled beer mug or
metal cup. Add 1 large ice
cube. Garnish with fruit.*

RUM FIX

2½ oz. light rum
1 oz. fresh lemon or lime juice
½ oz. simple syrup
Garnish: Lemon wheel

*Pour ingredients into ice-filled
highball glass and stir. Add
lemon. Serve with a straw.*

RUM HIGHBALL

2 oz. light or dark rum
Ginger ale or soda water
Garnish: Lemon twist

*Pour rum into highball glass
over ice cubes. Fill with
ginger ale or soda water and
stir. Add lemon twist.*

RUM MARTINI

2 oz. light rum
1 dash dry vermouth
Garnish: Lemon twist

*Stir rum and vermouth with
ice in mixing glass. Strain
into ice-filled cocktail glass.
Add lemon twist.*

RUM OLD-FASHIONED

1½ oz. light rum
1 tsp. 151-proof rum
1 tsp. simple syrup
1 dash Angostura bitters
Garnish: Lemon twist

*Stir in ice-filled old-
fashioned glass. Add lemon
twist.*

RUM RELAXER

1½ oz. light rum
1 oz. pineapple juice
½ oz. grenadine
Lemon-lime soda
Garnish: Orange wheel,
    maraschino cherry

*Shake first three ingredients
with ice and pour with ice
into hurricane or parfait
glass. Fill glass with lemon-
lime soda. Garnish with
orange and cherry.*

RUM RICKEY

1½ oz. light rum
½ oz. fresh lime juice
Soda water
Garnish: Lime wedge

*Pour rum and lime juice into
ice-filled highball glass. Fill
with soda water and stir.
Add lime.*

RUM

RUM SCREWDRIVER

1½ oz. light rum
5 oz. fresh orange juice

Stir rum and orange juice in ice-filled highball glass.

RUM SOUR

2 oz. light rum
¾ oz. fresh lemon juice
¾ oz. simple syrup
Garnish: Lemon half-wheel, maraschino cherry

Shake with ice and strain into chilled sour glass. Garnish with lemon and cherry.

RUM SWIZZLE

2 oz. light or dark rum
1 oz. fresh lime juice
½ oz. simple syrup
2 dashes Angostura bitters
Soda water

Combine first four ingredients in ice-filled Collins glass. With bar spoon between your palms, move hands back and forth and up and down to quickly rotate and lift spoon, until glass is frosted. Top with soda water. Serve with a swizzle stick.

RUM TODDY (COLD)

These days, a toddy is a hot drink, but originally, it referred to a mixture of sweetened rum and water.

2 oz. light or dark rum
½ oz. water
1 tsp. simple syrup
Garnish: Lemon twist

Stir rum, water, and syrup in old-fashioned glass. Add large cube of ice. Add lemon twist.

S & V

1½ oz. light rum
½ oz. Creole Shrubb (rum-based orange liqueur)
½ oz. ruby port
½ oz. fresh lime juice
Garnish: Lime wheel

Shake with ice and strain into chilled cocktail glass. Garnish with lime.

SAINT LUCY BRACER

2 oz. dark rum
½ oz. butterscotch schnapps
½ oz. sweet vermouth
2 dashes Angostura bitters
Garnish: Edible flower, such as nasturtium

Stir with ice and strain into chilled cocktail glass. Garnish with flower.

SANTIAGO COCKTAIL

1½ oz. light rum
1 oz. fresh lime juice
½ oz. simple syrup
½ oz. grenadine

Shake with ice and strain into chilled cocktail glass.

SARGASSO

2 oz. aged rhum agricole
¾ oz. dry sherry
½ oz. Aperol
2 dashes Angostura
   bitters
Garnish: Orange twist

Stir with ice and strain into chilled cocktail glass. Garnish with orange twist.

SAXON COCKTAIL

1¾ oz. light rum
½ oz. fresh lime juice
½ tsp. grenadine
Garnish: Orange twist

Shake with ice and strain into chilled cocktail glass. Add orange twist.

SIR WALTER COCKTAIL

¾ oz. light rum
¾ oz. brandy
1 tsp. grenadine
1 tsp. triple sec
1 tsp. fresh lemon juice

Shake with ice and strain into chilled cocktail glass.

SLOPPY JOE'S COCKTAIL NO. 1

¾ oz. light rum
¾ oz. dry vermouth
½ oz. triple sec
1 oz. fresh lime juice
½ oz. grenadine

Shake with ice and strain into chilled cocktail glass.

SPANISH TOWN COCKTAIL

2 oz. light rum
½ oz. triple sec

Stir with ice and strain into chilled cocktail glass.

STONE COCKTAIL

1 oz. dry sherry
½ oz. light rum
½ oz. sweet vermouth

Stir with ice and strain into chilled cocktail glass.

STONE WALL

3 thin slices peeled fresh
   ginger
¾ oz. Demerara Syrup
   (page 25)
1½ oz. fresh apple cider
1½ oz. light rum
Jamaican ginger beer
Garnish: Green apple slice,
   lime wedge

Muddle ginger and syrup in mixing glass. Add cider and rum and shake with ice. Strain into ice-filled old-fashioned glass and fill with ginger beer. Add apple and lime.

STORMY COLADA

2 oz. dark rum
2 oz. pineapple juice
Ginger beer
Garnish: Skewered pineapple
   wedge, mint sprig, candied
   ginger slice

Add rum and pineapple juice to ice-filled highball glass. Fill with ginger beer and stir. Add skewered garnish.

RUM

▽ SUNSET AT GOWANUS

2 oz. dark rum
¾ oz. fresh lime juice
½ oz. maple syrup
¼ oz. brandy
¼ oz. yellow Chartreuse

*Shake with ice and strain
into chilled cocktail glass.*

▯ SUSIE TAYLOR

2 oz. light rum
½ oz. fresh lime juice
Ginger ale

*Pour rum and lime juice
into ice-filled Collins glass.
Fill with ginger ale and stir.*

▯ TAHITI CLUB

2 oz. light rum
½ oz. fresh lemon juice
½ oz. fresh lime juice
½ oz. pineapple juice
¼ oz. maraschino liqueur
Garnish: Lemon wheel

*Shake with ice and strain
into ice-filled old-fashioned
glass. Add lemon.*

▽ THIRD-RAIL COCKTAIL

¾ oz. light rum
¾ oz. apple brandy
¾ oz. brandy
¼ tsp. anisette

*Shake with ice and strain
into chilled cocktail glass.*

▽ THREE MILLER COCKTAIL

1½ oz. light rum
¾ oz. brandy
¼ oz. grenadine
¼ oz. fresh lemon juice

*Shake with ice and strain
into chilled cocktail glass.*

▽ TOMATO DAIQUIRI

3 fresh cherry tomatoes
2 oz. dark rum
1 oz. fresh lime juice
1 oz. simple syrup
1 dash Angostura bitters

*Muddle tomatoes in mixing
glass. Add remaining ingredients. Shake with ice and
strain into chilled cocktail
glass.*

BE PITHY (BUT HOLD THE PITH)

When a recipe calls for a twist of lemon or lime, you want the skin, not the pith. This can be hard to do with a knife, but easy with a sharp vegetable peeler, especially the small, plastic-handled Swiss one made by Kuhn Rikon.

—WILLIAM GRIMES, author of *Straight Up or On the Rocks: The Story of the American Cocktail*

TORRIDORA COCKTAIL

1½ oz. light rum
½ oz. coffee-flavored brandy
1½ tsp. half-and-half
1 tsp. 151-proof rum

Shake first three ingredients with ice and strain into chilled cocktail glass. Float 151-proof rum (see page 18) on top.

TROPICA COCKTAIL

2 oz. light rum
3 oz. pineapple juice
1 oz. fresh grapefruit juice
1 dash grenadine
Garnish: Pineapple wedge

Mix ingredients in ice-filled Collins glass. Add pineapple wedge.

URBAN ANXIETY

Created by AARON DEFEO, Tucson, AZ.

1 oz. cachaça
1 oz. sweet vermouth
¾ oz. Cynar
2 dashes Angostura bitters
Garnish: Grapefruit twist, flamed

Stir with ice and strain into chilled cocktail glass. Flame grapefruit twist and add.

THE VACATION COCKTAIL

1 tsp. peeled and chopped fresh ginger
¾ oz. fresh lime juice
Scant ½ oz. simple syrup
½ oz. light rum
½ oz. dark rum
1 oz. mango juice
½ oz. cranberry juice
½ oz. fresh orange juice
½ oz. spiced rum
Garnish: Mango slice

Muddle ginger, lime juice, and syrup in mixing glass. Add all but spiced rum. Shake with ice. Strain into chilled cocktail glass and float spiced rum (see page 18) on top. Garnish with mango.

VAN VLEET

3 oz. light rum
1 oz. maple syrup
1 oz. fresh lemon juice

Shake with ice and strain into ice-filled old-fashioned glass.

VIRGINIA DARE

2 slices ripe pear
2 oz. dark rum
½ oz. Bénédictine
2 dashes Angostura bitters

Muddle 1 pear slice in mixing glass. Add remaining ingredients. Shake with ice and strain through a fine wire sieve into chilled cocktail glass. Garnish with remaining pear slice.

RUM

🍸 WHITE LILY COCKTAIL

¾ oz. light rum
¾ oz. triple sec
¾ oz. gin
1 dash anisette

Shake with ice and strain into chilled cocktail glass.

🍸 WHITE LION COCKTAIL

1½ oz. light rum
1 oz. fresh lemon juice
½ oz. simple syrup
1 tsp. grenadine
2 dashes Angostura bitters

Shake with ice and strain into chilled cocktail glass.

🥤 WIKI WAKI WOO

½ oz. light rum
½ oz. 151-proof rum
½ oz. vodka
½ oz. blanco tequila
½ oz. triple sec
1 oz. amaretto
1 oz. fresh orange juice
1 oz. pineapple juice
1 oz. cranberry juice
Garnish: Orange wheel, maraschino cherry

Stir all ingredients with ice. Pour, with ice, into hurricane or parfait glass. Add orange and cherry.

🍸 X.Y.Z. COCKTAIL

1 oz. light rum
½ oz. triple sec
½ oz. fresh lemon juice

Shake with ice and strain into chilled cocktail glass.

🥤 ZOMBIE

Another addition to the Polynesian drink canon by Donn (Don the Beachcomber) Beach. Here is a mash-up of the many circulating recipes for this fully loaded tiki classic. The constants are copious amounts of rum and fruit juices.

1 oz. gold rum
1 oz. 151-proof rum
1 oz. light rum
1 oz. fresh lemon juice
1 oz. fresh lime juice
1 oz. pineapple juice
1 oz. passion fruit syrup
2 tsp. Demerara Syrup (page 25)
1 dash tiki (such as Bittermen's 'Elemakule) or Angostura bitters (optional)
Garnish: Fresh mint sprig

Shake with ice and pour into chilled Collins glass. Garnish with mint.

TEQUILA

TEQUILA IS MADE FROM the blue agave plant, an aloe vera–like plant that takes between eight and ten years to mature. Then it can only be harvested once by stripping away its leaves and cooking what's left: a core that weighs on average forty to seventy pounds (and it takes fifteen pounds of core to produce only one quart of tequila). The cooked cores are fermented with yeast (which converts the sugar to alcohol), then distilled twice—the second time yielding what will become tequila.

Like Scotch and bourbon, tequila takes its name from its place of origin, in this case the town of Tequila in Mexico's state of Jalisco. By Mexican law, it can only be produced in this region under strict guidelines—though that doesn't stop less scrupulous producers from making it outside those boundaries with whatever they want. There are two kinds of tequila: 100 percent blue agave and *mixto*, the former made purely from agave, the latter distilled with a mixture of 60 percent blue agave plus "other sugars." Just look for "100 percent agave" and you're safe. Mezcal, similar to tequila but with a richer, smokier flavor, is made mostly in Oaxaca, from the maguey plant.

Finally, there are four official classifications for tequila, though some have confusing subtitles. At the first rung is *blanco* (also called "silver" or "white"), which is clear, transparent, and bottled immediately after distillation. Next comes *oro* ("gold," or "*joven*"), which is blanco blended with caramel and other additives to impart an aged appearance; then *reposado*, which is blanco actually aged in white oak barrels for up to one year. At the top there's *añejo*, which is blanco aged in white oak barrels for at least one year, though often much longer.

ALAMO SPLASH

1½ oz. blanco tequila
1 oz. fresh orange juice
½ oz. pineapple juice
1 splash lemon-lime soda

Pour first three ingredients into ice-filled Collins glass. Top with lemon-lime soda and stir.

AMANTE PICANTE

2 cucumber slices
2 fresh cilantro sprigs
2 oz. blanco tequila
1 oz. fresh lime juice
1 oz. simple syrup
2 dashes jalapeño hot pepper
    sauce
Garnish: Cucumber slice

Muddle 2 cucumber slices and cilantro in mixing glass. Add remaining ingredients. Shake with ice and double-strain into chilled cocktail glass. Garnish with cucumber.

BRAVO

2 oz. añejo tequila
¼ oz. agave nectar
2 dashes Angostura bitters
1 dash orange bitters
Garnish: Grapefruit twist

Stir with ice and strain into chilled old-fashioned glass. Add grapefruit twist.

BIG RED HOOTER

1 oz. blanco tequila
¾ oz. amaretto
2 oz. pineapple juice
½ oz. grenadine
Garnish: Maraschino cherry

Pour tequila and amaretto into ice-filled Collins glass. Fill with pineapple juice and top with grenadine. Add cherry. Serve with straw.

BLOODY MARIA

1 oz. blanco tequila
2 oz. tomato juice
¼ oz. fresh lemon juice
1 dash hot red pepper sauce
1 pinch celery salt
Garnish: Lemon wheel

Stir with ice. Strain into ice-filled old-fashioned glass. Add lemon wheel.

▽ BLUE MARGARITA

For glass: Lime juice, coarse salt
1½ oz. blanco tequila
½ oz. blue curaçao
1 oz. fresh lime juice

Rim chilled cocktail glass with lime juice and salt. Shake remaining ingredients with ice and strain into glass.

☐ BRAVE BULL

1½ oz. blanco tequila
1 oz. coffee liqueur
Garnish: Lemon twist

Pour into ice-filled old-fashioned glass and stir. Add lemon twist.

☐ BUM'S RUSH

1½ oz. blanco tequila
¾ oz. triple sec
¾ oz. honey liqueur
1 oz. fresh lime juice
1 oz. fresh apple cider
Garnish: Lime wedge

Shake with ice and strain into ice-filled Collins glass. Garnish with lime.

▽ CACTUS BERRY

For glass: Lime wedge, coarse salt
1¼ oz. blanco tequila
1¼ oz. red wine
½ oz. triple sec
½ oz. simple syrup
¼ oz. fresh lemon juice
¼ oz. fresh lime juice
1 splash lemon-lime soda

Rim chilled cocktail glass with lime and salt. Shake remaining ingredients with ice and pour into glass.

▽ CAMINO DEL RAY

Created by TED HENWOOD, New York, NY

1¾ oz. añejo tequila
1 oz. oloroso sherry
½ oz. Drambuie
1 dash rhubarb bitters
Garnish: Lemon twist

Stir with ice and strain into chilled cocktail glass. Add lemon twist.

▽ CATALINA MARGARITA

1½ oz. blanco tequila
1 oz. peach schnapps
1 oz. blue curaçao
2 oz. simple syrup
2 oz. fresh lemon juice

Shake with ice and strain into chilled cocktail glass.

TEQUILA

CHAPALA

1½ oz. reposado tequila
1½ oz. fresh orange juice
¾ oz. fresh lemon juice
¼ oz. grenadine
Garnish: Orange blossoms
(optional); orange wedge

Shake and strain into hurricane glass. Fill glass with crushed ice. Garnish with orange blossoms, if using, and orange wedge.

CHINCHONA

1½ oz. añejo tequila
¾ oz. Lillet Rouge
½ oz. orange curaçao
2 dashes orange bitters
Garnish: Orange twist

Stir with ice and strain into chilled cocktail glass. Add orange twist.

CHUPA CABRA

2 oz. blanco tequila
¾ oz. fresh grapefruit juice
½ oz. fresh lime juice
½ oz. Campari
½ oz. simple syrup
1 dash Angostura bitters
Garnish: Lime wheel

Shake with ice and strain into chilled cocktail glass. Garnish with lime.

COMPANY B

1 whole strawberry, hulled
1½ oz. blanco tequila
½ oz. Campari
½ oz. triple sec
½ oz. fresh lemon juice
¼ oz. agave nectar
Garnish: Strawberry slice

Muddle whole strawberry in mixing glass. Add remaining ingredients. Shake with ice and strain through fine wire sieve into chilled cocktail glass. Garnish with strawberry slice.

COUNT CAMILLO'S PALOMA

Think of this as a tequila Negroni, just the way Count Camillo Negroni, the supposed namesake of the Italian cocktail, would have liked it—if he were Mexican instead of Italian.

¾ oz. blanco tequila
¾ oz. sweet vermouth
¾ oz. Campari
2 oz. grapefruit soda
Garnish: Rosemary sprig

Pour ingredients into Collins glass and stir briefly. Fill with ice. Garnish with rosemary.

DIABLO

1½ oz. blanco tequila
¾ oz. crème de cassis
½ oz. fresh lime juice
Ginger ale
Garnish: Lime wheel

Shake first three ingredients with ice. Strain into ice-filled Collins glass. Top with ginger ale. Garnish with lime.

JACKIE O

TOASTED DROP

EASTERN SOUR

HORSE'S NECK

COFFEE NUDGE

PIMM'S CUP

B-52

PICKLEBACK

DIRTY DAISY

Created by BLAIR FRODELIUS,
Syracuse, NY

1½ oz. reposado tequila
1 oz. white curaçao
½ oz. olive brine
1 tsp. balsamic vinegar
1 tsp. fresh lime juice
Garnish: Lime wheel

*Shake well with ice and
strain into chilled cocktail
glass. Garnish with lime
wheel.*

EL MOLINO

Created by JIM MEEHAN,
New York, NY.

1½ oz. mezcal
¾ oz. palo cortado or oloroso
    sherry
¼ oz. allspice liqueur
    (pimento dram)
¼ oz. white crème de cacao

*Stir with ice and strain into
chilled cocktail glass.*

EL NIÑO

6 lime wedges
1 whole strawberry
¾ oz. simple syrup
2 oz. blanco tequila
5 drops rose water

*Muddle lime, strawberry, and
syrup in mixing glass. Add
tequila and rose water and ice.
Shake briefly and strain into
ice-filled old-fashioned glass.*

EL OSO (THE BEAR)

Created by BRENDAN DORR,
Washington, DC

1¾ oz. añejo tequila
¾ oz. honey liqueur
½ oz. maraschino liqueur
2 dashes The Bitter Truth's
    Jerry Thomas' Own
    Decanter Bitters
Garnish: Dehydrated Orange
    Wheel (recipe follows)

*Stir with ice. Drop dehy-
drated orange wheel into old-
fashioned glass and add ice.
Strain cocktail into glass.*

DEHYDRATED ORANGE WHEEL

*Slice 1 large navel orange
into ¹/₁₆-inch-thick rounds.
Arrange on baking sheet lined
with silicone baking mat.
Sift 3 Tbs. confectioners'
sugar over oranges. Bake in
preheated 225°F oven until
dried, about 2¼ hours. Let
cool completely. Store in air-
tight container at room temperature for up to 1 month.
Makes about 1½ dozen.*

FLOWER POWER

2 oz. blanco tequila
1 oz. fresh grapefruit juice
½ oz. agave nectar
1 egg white
3 drops orange blossom water
2 dashes Peychaud's bitters

*Shake without ice. Then
shake with ice and strain
into chilled cocktail glass.*

TEQUILA

▽ FROSTBITE

1 oz. blanco tequila
¾ oz. white crème de cacao
¾ oz. heavy cream
Garnish: Freshly grated nutmeg

*Shake with ice and strain
into chilled cocktail glass.
Top with nutmeg.*

▽ GUADALAJARA

2 oz. blanco tequila
1 oz. dry vermouth
½ oz. Bénédictine
Garnish: Lemon twist

*Stir with ice and strain into
chilled cocktail glass. Add
lemon twist.*

⬚ HAIRY SUNRISE

¾ oz. blanco tequila
¾ oz. vodka
½ oz. triple sec
3 oz. fresh orange juice
1 tsp. fresh grenadine
Garnish: Lime wedge

*Shake first four ingredients
with ice. Strain into ice-
filled Collins glass. Float
grenadine (see page 18) on
top. Garnish with lime.*

▽ HIGH PLAINS DRIFTER NO. 1

1 splash Campari
2 oz. blanco tequila
¾ oz. fresh lime juice
¾ oz. Honey Syrup
   (page 25)
1 dash Angostura bitters

*Swirl Campari in chilled
cocktail glass to coat inside;
discard excess Campari.
Shake remaining ingredients
with ice and strain into
glass.*

⬚ HOT PANTS

For glass: Lime wedge, coarse
   salt
1½ oz. blanco tequila
½ oz. peppermint schnapps
½ oz. fresh grapefruit juice
2 tsp. simple syrup

*Rim old-fashioned glass
with lime and salt. Fill
with ice. Shake remaining
ingredients with ice. Strain
into glass.*

▽ THE INTERESTING COCKTAIL

2 oz. blanco tequila
½ oz. Aperol
½ oz. dark crème de
   cacao
¾ oz. fresh lemon juice
Garnish: Grapefruit twist

*Shake with ice and strain
into chilled cocktail glass.
Add grapefruit twist.*

JINX COCKTAIL

Created by JAKE SHER,
White Plains, NY

1 oz. blanco tequila
¾ oz. blood orange
   liqueur
¾ oz. Becherovka (Czech
   digestif)
1 oz. fresh grapefruit juice
Garnish: Grapefruit twist,
   flamed

*Shake with ice and strain
into chilled cocktail glass.
Flame grapefruit twist
and add.*

LA BOMBA

For glass: Lime wedge,
   superfine sugar
1¼ oz. gold tequila
¾ oz. triple sec
1½ oz. pineapple juice
1½ oz. fresh orange juice
2 dashes grenadine
Garnish: Lime wheel

*Rim chilled cocktail glass
with lime wedge and sugar.
Combine next four ingre-
dients with ice and shake
briefly. Pour with ice into
glass. Add grenadine and
garnish with lime wheel.*

LA PERLA

1½ oz. reposado tequila
1½ oz. manzanilla sherry
¾ oz. pear liqueur
Garnish: Lemon twist

*Stir with ice and strain into
chilled cocktail glass. Add
lemon twist.*

LA ULTIMA PALABRA

¾ oz. blanco tequila
¾ oz. fresh grapefruit juice
¾ oz. fresh lime juice
¾ oz. yellow Chartreuse
¾ oz. maraschino liqueur
Garnish: Grapefruit twist

*Shake with ice and strain
into chilled cocktail glass.
Add grapefruit twist.*

LILLYPAD

1½ oz. blanco tequila
½ oz. Lillet Blanc
½ oz. Lillet Rouge
1½ oz. apple juice
¾ oz. fresh lime juice
¼ oz. agave nectar
Garnish: Blood orange wheel

*Shake with ice and strain
into chilled cocktail glass.
Garnish with blood orange
wheel.*

MARGARITA

The story behind the Margarita
is on page 38. The rimming of
the glass is optional.

For glass: Lime wedge, coarse
   salt
1½ oz. blanco tequila
¾ oz. Cointreau triple sec
¾ oz. fresh lime juice

*Rim chilled cocktail glass
with lime and salt. Shake
remaining ingredients and
ice and strain into glass.*

Note: *To serve on-the-
rocks, strain into ice-filled,
rimmed old-fashioned glass.*

TEQUILA

MEXICANA

1½ oz. blanco tequila
1 oz. fresh lemon juice
½ oz. pineapple juice
1 tsp. grenadine

Shake with ice and strain into chilled cocktail glass.

MEXICAN FIRING SQUAD

2 oz. blanco tequila
1 oz. simple syrup
¾ oz. fresh lime juice
1 tsp. pomegranate molasses (available at Middle Eastern grocers)
2 dashes Angostura bitters
Garnish: Lime wheel

Shake and strain into ice-filled highball glass. Garnish with lime.

MEXICAN MADRAS

1½ oz. blanco tequila
2 oz. cranberry juice
1 oz. fresh orange juice
¼ oz. fresh lime juice
Garnish: Orange wheel

Shake with ice and strain into old-fashioned glass. Garnish with orange.

MEXICAN MONK

Created by ERIC ALPERIN, Los Angeles, CA

2 oz. reposado tequila
½ oz. dry sherry
¼ oz. coffee liqueur
¼ oz. Bénédictine
Garnish: Lemon twist

Stir well with ice and strain into chilled cocktail glass. Add lemon twist.

MEXICOLA

2 oz. blanco tequila
½ oz. fresh lime juice
Cola

Pour tequila and lime juice into ice-filled Collins glass. Fill with cola and stir.

NO. 8

2 oz. reposado tequila
¾ oz. palo cortado or oloroso sherry
½ oz. honey liqueur
2 dashes orange bitters
Garnish: Lemon twist

Stir with ice and strain into chilled cocktail glass. Garnish with lemon twist.

THE NOMAD SOUTH

Created by TED HENWOOD, New York, NY

2 oz. blanco tequila
1 oz. fresh orange juice
½ oz. blood orange juice
½ oz. agave nectar
½ oz. fresh lime juice
1 dash whiskey barrel bitters

Shake well with ice and strain into ice-filled old-fashioned glass.

THE OAXACA OLD-FASHIONED

A modern-day classic, this drink was invented by New York bartender Phil Ward.

1½ oz. reposado tequila
½ oz. mezcal
¼ oz. agave nectar
2 dashes Angostura bitters
Garnish: Orange twist, flamed

Stir with ice and strain into chilled old-fashioned glass. Flame orange twist and add.

OLDEST TEMPTATION

2 oz. añejo tequila
1 oz. apple juice
½ oz. fresh lemon juice
½ oz. triple sec
¼ oz. simple syrup
1 dash Angostura bitters
Garnish: Lemon twist, flamed

Shake with ice and strain into chilled cocktail glass. Flame lemon twist and add.

PACIFIC SUNSHINE

For glass: Lemon wheel, coarse salt
1½ oz. blanco tequila
1½ oz. blue curaçao
¾ oz. simple syrup
¾ oz. fresh lemon juice
1 dash Angostura bitters

Rim chilled hurricane or parfait glass with lemon and salt; reserve lemon. Shake remaining ingredients with ice in mixing glass. Pour with ice into glass. Garnish with reserved lemon wheel.

PALOMA

2 oz. blanco tequila
Grapefruit-flavored soda
Garnish: Lime wedge

Pour tequila into ice-filled Collins glass. Fill glass with soda and stir briefly. Garnish with lime wedge.

PALOMA (NATURAL)

2 oz. blanco tequila
2 oz. fresh white or ruby red grapefruit juice
Soda water
Garnish: Lime wedge

Pour tequila and grapefruit juice into ice-filled Collins glass. Fill with soda water and stir briefly. Garnish with lime wedge.

PANCHO VILLA

1 oz. añejo tequila
¾ oz. Aperol
¾ oz. sweet vermouth
1 dash peach bitters
Garnish: Grapefruit twist

Stir with ice and strain into chilled cocktail glass. Garnish with grapefruit twist.

TEQUILA

Y PIÑA AGAVE

2 cucumber slices
1½ oz. blanco tequila
1 oz. pineapple juice
¾ oz. fresh lemon juice
½ oz. agave nectar
Lemon-lime soda
Garnish: Cucumber slice

Muddle 2 cucumber slices in mixing glass. Add the next four ingredients. Shake with ice and strain into chilled cocktail glass. Top with soda and garnish with cucumber slice.

Y THE PONCHO

2 oz. reposado tequila
½ oz. dry vermouth
½ oz. maraschino liqueur
2 dashes Peychaud's bitters
Garnish: Maraschino cherry

Stir with ice and strain into chilled cocktail glass. Add cherry.

Y PURPLE PANCHO

For glass: Lime wedge,
  superfine sugar
1 oz. blanco tequila
½ oz. blue curaçao
½ oz. sloe gin
2 oz. fresh lime juice
1 oz. fresh lemon juice
1 oz. simple syrup
Garnish: Lime wheel

Rim chilled cocktail or margarita glass with lime wedge and sugar. Shake remaining ingredients with ice and pour with ice into glass. Garnish with lime wheel.

Y QUETZALCOATL

Created by JAKE SHER,
White Plains, NY.

1 oz. blanco tequila
¾ oz. mezcal
½ oz. crème de pêche
½ oz. guava puree
½ oz. fresh grapefruit juice
Garnish: Grapefruit twist

Shake with ice and strain into cocktail glass. Add grapefruit twist.

Y THE REFUGE

1½ oz. blanco tequila
½ oz. Aperol
¼ oz. fresh lime juice
¼ oz. fresh grapefruit juice
¼ oz. agave nectar

Shake with ice. Strain into chilled cocktail glass.

☐ ROSITA

1½ oz. blanco tequila
½ oz. sweet vermouth
½ oz. dry vermouth
½ oz. Campari
1 dash Angostura bitters
Garnish: Lemon twist

Stir with ice. Strain into ice-filled old-fashioned glass. Add lemon twist.

☐ SANTANA SLING

1½ oz. reposado tequila
½ oz. Cherry Heering
¼ oz. Batavia arrack or
  light rum
½ oz. fresh lime juice
3 oz. ginger beer

Pour first four ingredients into ice-filled Collins glass and stir. Add ginger beer and stir again.

SATIN SHEETS

1½ oz. blanco tequila
½ oz. falernum
½ oz. simple syrup
¾ oz. fresh lime juice
Garnish: Lime wheel

*Shake with ice and strain
into chilled cocktail glass.
Garnish with lime.*

SEA OF CORTEZ

1½ oz. blanco tequila
1 oz. fresh lime juice
¾ oz. crème de cassis
¼ oz. orange curaçao

*Shake with ice and strain
into chilled cocktail glass.*

THE SFOZANDO

Created by ERYN REECE,
New York, NY.

1 oz. mezcal
¾ oz. rye whiskey
½ oz. dry vermouth
½ oz. Bénédictine
1 dash chocolate bitters
Garnish: Orange twist

*Stir with ice and strain into
cocktail glass. Add orange
twist.*

SHADY LADY

1 oz. blanco tequila
1 oz. melon liqueur
4 oz. fresh grapefruit juice
Garnish: Lime wedge;
    honeydew melon wedge or
    maraschino cherry

*Combine all ingredients in
ice-filled highball glass and
stir. Garnish with lime and
melon or cherry.*

SIDEWINDER

Created by BRENT BUTLER,
San Francisco, CA

1½ oz. reposado tequila
½ oz. Campari
½ oz. vanilla syrup,
    preferably B.A. Reynold's
½ oz. fresh lime juice
¼ oz. mezcal
2 oz. ginger beer
1 pinch sea salt
Garnish: Fresh mint sprig

*Fill Collins glass ¾ full with
crushed ice. Add all ingredients. Swizzle with barspoon
until glass is frosted. Fill to
brim with additional ice.
Garnish with mint.*

SILK STOCKINGS

1½ oz. blanco tequila
1 oz. white crème de cacao
1½ oz. heavy cream
1 dash grenadine
Garnish: Ground cinnamon

*Shake ingredients with
ice and strain into chilled
cocktail glass. Top with
cinnamon.*

SLOE TEQUILA

1 oz. blanco tequila
½ oz. sloe gin
½ oz. fresh lime juice
Garnish: Cucumber peel twist

*Combine ingredients with
½ cup crushed ice in blender
on low speed. Pour into old-
fashioned glass. Add cucumber twist.*

TEQUILA

SMOKED MARGARITA

½ tsp. smoky Scotch
  whisky, such as Islay
  or Skye
1 oz. reposado tequila
1 oz. triple sec
½ oz. fresh lemon juice
½ oz. fresh lime juice
Garnish: Lime wedge

*Pour Scotch into old-
fashioned glass and swirl
to coat. Add ice. Shake
remaining ingredients with
ice and strain into glass.
Add lime wedge.*

SOUTH OF THE BORDER

1 oz. blanco tequila
¾ oz. coffee-flavored
  brandy
½ oz. fresh lime juice
Garnish: Lime wheel

*Shake with ice and strain
into chilled sour glass.
Garnish with lime.*

SPICE OF LIFE

Created by ADAM FRAGER,
St. Louis, MO

3 cucumber slices
12 fresh mint leaves
¾ oz. simple syrup
2 oz. Jalapeño-Infused
  Tequila (recipe follows)
¾ oz. fresh lime juice
Garnish: Cucumber slice,
  fresh mint sprig

*Muddle 3 cucumber slices,
mint leaves, and syrup in
mixing glass. Add tequila and
lime juice with ice and shake.
Double-strain into ice-filled
old-fashioned glass. Garnish
with cucumber slice and
mint sprig.*

JALAPEÑO-INFUSED TEQUILA

*Combine 1 cup reposado
tequila with ½ seeded and
chopped jalapeño in bowl.
Let stand at room temperature for 30 minutes. Strain
to remove jalapeño, then
funnel into bottle. Store in
refrigerator for up to
2 weeks.*

☐ STRAWBERRY MARGARITA

For glass: Lime wedge, superfine sugar or coarse salt (optional)
3 fresh strawberries, cut in half
¾ oz. strawberry schnapps
1½ oz. blanco tequila
¾ oz. triple sec
¾ oz. fresh lime juice
Garnish: Whole strawberry

If desired, rim chilled cocktail glass with lime and sugar or salt. Muddle strawberries with schnapps in mixing glass. Add remaining ingredients and shake with ice. Strain through fine wire sieve into glass. Add strawberry.

☐ SUNDAY CONFESSION

1 oz. blanco tequila
1 oz. limoncello
½ oz. fresh lemon juice
Ginger beer
Garnish: Lemon wedge

Pour the first three ingredients into Collins glass and stir briefly. Add ice and top with ginger beer. Add lemon.

☐ TEQUILA CANYON

1½ oz. blanco tequila
¼ oz. triple sec
1 oz. cranberry juice
1 oz. pineapple juice
1 oz. fresh orange juice
Garnish: Lime wheel

Pour into Collins glass and stir. Add ice. Garnish with lime. Serve with straw.

☐ TEQUILA COLLINS

2 oz. blanco tequila
½ oz. fresh lemon juice
½ oz. simple syrup
Soda water
Garnish: Lemon wheel, orange wheel, maraschino cherry

Shake first three ingredients with ice and strain into chilled Collins glass. Add several ice cubes, fill with soda water, and stir. Garnish with lemon, orange, and cherry. Serve with straw.

☐ TEQUILA MANHATTAN

2 oz. blanco tequila
1 oz. sweet vermouth
1 dash Angostura bitters
Garnish: Maraschino cherry

Shake with ice and strain into ice-filled old-fashioned glass. Add cherry.

☐ TEQUILA MATADOR

1½ oz. blanco tequila
2 oz. pineapple juice
½ oz. fresh lime juice

Shake with ice and strain into chilled champagne flute.

TEQUILA

Y TEQUILA MOCKINGBIRD

Created by JONATHAN POGASH,
New York, NY

For glass: Lime wedge,
    coarse salt
¼ tsp. minced ginger
1¾ oz. blanco tequila
1½ tsp. agave nectar
1 oz. fresh lime juice
Garnish: Lime wheel

*Rim one half of a chilled
cocktail glass with lime and
salt. Muddle ginger in mixing glass. Add remaining
ingredients with ice and
shake. Strain into glass.
Garnish with lime wheel.*

☐ TEQUILA OLD-
FASHIONED

1½ oz. blanco tequila
1 tsp. simple syrup
1 dash Angostura bitters
1 splash soda water
Garnish: Lemon twist

*Pour tequila, syrup, and bit-
ters in ice-filled old-fashioned
glass and stir. Add soda. Add
lemon twist.*

Y TEQUILA PINK

1½ oz. blanco tequila
1 oz. dry vermouth
¼ oz. grenadine

*Shake with ice and strain
into chilled cocktail glass.*

KEEP TRACK

Make a check immediately after serving a drink or a
round of drinks. The bar can get away from you quickly
if you're not organized and methodical about all your
tasks—especially billing. No matter how busy the bar
gets, keep your tasks ordered and handle one job at a
time. Keep the rest of the bar happy with your grace,
confidence, and sparkling dialogue.

—DALE DeGROFF (aka King Cocktail), author of
The Craft of the Cocktail

TEQUILA SMASH

4 blueberries
4 Bing cherries
2 oz. blanco tequila
½ oz. maraschino liqueur
½ oz. fresh lime juice
Garnish: Lime wheel
    skewered with blueberry
    and Bing cherry

*Muddle blueberries and
cherries in mixing glass.
Add remaining ingredients
and shake. Double-strain
into ice-filled old-fashioned
glass. Garnish with skew-
ered fruit.*

TEQUILA SOUR

2 oz. blanco tequila
¾ oz. fresh lemon juice
¾ oz. simple syrup
Garnish: Lemon half-wheel,
    maraschino cherry

*Shake with ice and strain
into chilled sour glass.
Garnish with lemon and
cherry.*

TEQUILA STRAIGHT

1 pinch coarse salt
1½ oz. blanco tequila
1 lime wedge

*Put salt between thumb
and index finger on back of
one hand. Hold shot glass
of tequila in same hand and
lime wedge in other hand.
Taste the salt, drink the
tequila, and then suck
the lime.*

TEQUILA SUNRISE

2 oz. blanco tequila
4 oz. fresh orange juice
¾ oz. grenadine

*Pour tequila and orange
juice into ice-filled highball
glass. Stir and add ice.
Slowly pour in grenadine
and allow to settle at
glass bottom. Before
drinking, stir to create the
"sunrise."*

TEQUINI

1½ oz. blanco tequila
½ oz. dry vermouth
1 dash Angostura bitters
    (optional)
Garnish: Lemon twist

*Stir with ice and strain into
chilled cocktail glass. Add
lemon twist.*

TEQUONIC

2 oz. blanco tequila
¼ oz. fresh lemon or lime
    juice
Tonic water
Garnish: Lemon or lime
    wedge

*Pour tequila into ice-filled
old-fashioned glass. Add
juice, fill with tonic water,
and stir. Garnish with citrus
wedge.*

TEQUILA

TÍA JUANATHAN

1½ oz. blanco tequila
½ oz. fresh lime juice
½ oz. Aperol
½ oz. yellow Chartreuse
Soda water
Garnish: Orange half-wheel

Shake first four ingredients with ice and strain into ice-filled highball glass. Top with soda water. Garnish with orange.

TIJUANA TAXI

2 oz. gold tequila
1 oz. blue curaçao
1 oz. tropical fruit schnapps
Lemon-lime soda
Garnish: Orange wheel, maraschino cherry

Pour first three ingredients into ice-filled large highball glass. Fill with lemon-lime soda. Garnish with orange and cherry.

TOREADOR

1½ oz. blanco tequila
½ oz. dark crème de cacao
½ oz. half-and-half
Garnish: Whipped cream, cocoa

Shake with ice. Strain into chilled cocktail glass. Top with whipped cream, sprinkle with cocoa.

KEEP IT SIMPLE

A simple drink that's perfectly executed is far, far more satisfying than a complex, creative one that isn't. If a patron's drink is too warm, too sweet, too weak, or too strong (yes, such a thing is theoretically possible), he or she won't be impressed by its clever name and its innovative use of infusions. On the other hand, strain a subzero-cold mixture of gin and vermouth into a chilled glass and twist a swatch of fresh lemon peel over the top and that patron won't care in the slightest that you're out of shiso-infused vodka and fresh lemongrass juice.

—DAVE WONDRICH, drinks correspondent, *Esquire* magazine

THE 21ST CENTURY

1 splash absinthe
1½ oz. blanco tequila
¾ oz. fresh lime juice
¾ oz. white crème de cacao

*Swirl absinthe in chilled
cocktail glass to coat inside;
discard excess absinthe.
Shake remaining ingredients
with ice and strain into glass.*

VAGABUNDO

You'll need fresh celery juice to
make this cocktail.

2 oz. reposado blanco tequila
1½ oz. pineapple juice
1½ oz. fresh celery juice
½ oz. fresh lime juice
Garnish: Lime wheel

*Shake ingredients with ice.
Strain into ice-filled hurricane glass. Garnish with
lime wheel.*

VENIAL SIN

1½ oz. blanco tequila
½ oz. mezcal
½ oz. yellow Chartreuse
¼ oz. elderflower liqueur
¼ oz. maraschino liqueur

*Stir with ice and strain into
chilled cocktail glass.*

VIVA VILLA

For glass: Lime wedge, coarse
salt
1½ oz. blanco tequila
1 oz. fresh lime juice
½ oz. simple syrup

*Rim old-fashioned glass
with lime and salt. Fill with
ice. Shake remaining ingredients with ice and strain
into glass.*

WAITING ON SUMMER

Created by DANIEL BAUTISTA,
Chicago, IL

3 cucumber slices
3 fresh sage leaves
½ oz. fresh lime juice
1½ oz. blanco tequila
¾ oz. simple syrup
3 oz. ginger ale
Garnish: Strawberry slice

*Muddle cucumber, sage, and
lime juice in mixing glass.
Add tequila and syrup with
ice and shake. Double-strain
into ice-filled Collins glass.
Top with ginger ale. Garnish
with strawberry.*

YELLOW ROSE OF TEXAS

2 oz. blanco tequila
¾ oz. fresh lemon juice
½ oz. simple syrup
¼ oz. yellow Chartreuse
3 drops rose water

*Shake first four ingredients
with ice and strain into
chilled cocktail glass. Top
with rose water.*

TEQUILA

VODKA

ACCORDING TO U.S. LAW, vodkas produced in the country must be pure spirits with no additives except water; nonaged; and basically colorless, tasteless, and odorless. This description may sound lackluster, but it explains why vodka is one of today's most popular spirits: Because of its purity, vodka graciously assumes the characteristics of whatever it's mixed with.

Vodka is generally made from grain (corn, rye, or wheat) or potatoes, with grain accounting for nearly all the vodka available on the international market. It is a rectified spirit, meaning it's distilled at least three times, and then filtered—the most important step—typically through charcoal, although some distillers claim to employ diamond dust and even quartz crystals.

Stylistic differences between one vodka and another are subtle, even at the very high end, given that discernible flavor isn't a factor. Vodka is often described by its texture on the tongue or mouthfeel, ranging from clean and crisp to viscous and silky. Subtle sensations in the finish—after it's swallowed—can range from slightly sweet to medicinal. The finish could also reveal if a vodka is hot, rough, and raw (usually the mark of an inexpensive bulk vodka, or perhaps one with higher-than-normal

80 proof) or, conversely, if it is smooth, round, and rich (one made by a master distiller).

That said, the very best vodkas, the so-called super-premium brands (priced higher than $30 per bottle), are perfect when unadorned, say in a Martini, or for a chilled straight shot to accompany caviar. Flavored vodkas are used in many drinks, but they work best in tandem with actual fruit and other ingredients, as some of these vodkas can taste artificial.

ADMIRAL PERRY

Created by BLAIR FRODELIUS, Syracuse, NY

2 oz. pear-flavored vodka
1 oz. cinnamon schnapps
1 oz. dry vermouth
1 dash white crème de cacao
Garnish: Thin pear slice

Stir with ice and shake into chilled cocktail glass. Garnish with pear slice.

ALFIE COCKTAIL

1½ oz. lemon-flavored vodka
¾ oz. pineapple juice
½ oz. triple sec

Shake with ice and strain into chilled cocktail glass.

AQUEDUCT

1½ oz. vodka
¾ oz. fresh lime juice
½ oz. white curaçao or triple sec
½ oz. apricot-flavored brandy
Garnish: Orange twist

Shake with ice and strain into chilled cocktail glass. Add orange twist.

BASIL 8

3 fresh basil leaves
5 white grapes
1½ oz. vodka
¾ oz. fresh lime juice
1 oz. simple syrup
1 dash Angostura bitters
Ginger ale
Garnish: Fresh basil sprig, white grape

Muddle basil and 5 grapes in Collins glass. Add next four ingredients and stir. Add ice and top with ginger ale. Garnish with basil sprig and 1 white grape.

BEER BUSTER

1½ oz. 100-proof vodka
Chilled beer or ale
2 dashes hot red pepper sauce

Pour vodka into highball glass and fill with beer or ale. Add hot sauce and stir lightly.

☐ BELLA FRAGOLIA

Created by ERICK CASTRO,
San Francisco, CA

1 strawberry, chopped
4 fresh basil leaves
2 oz. vodka
1 oz. fresh lemon juice
1 oz. simple syrup
Soda water
Garnish: Strawberry slice,
   fresh basil leaf

*Muddle chopped strawberry
and 4 basil leaves in mixing
glass. Add vodka, lemon
juice, and syrup with ice
and shake well. Double-
strain into ice-filled
old-fashioned glass and
top with soda water.
Garnish with strawberry
and basil.*

☐ BIANCA

For glass: Lime wedge,
   superfine sugar
1½ oz. citrus-flavored
   vodka
2 oz. pomegranate juice
¼ oz. fresh lime juice
1 splash simple syrup
1 splash fresh lemon juice
Garnish: Lemon twist, fresh
   pomegranate seeds

*Rim chilled cocktail glass
with lime and sugar. Shake
remaining ingredients
with ice and strain into
glass. Add lemon twist and
pomegranate seeds.*

☐ THE BIG CRUSH

1 oz. raspberry-flavored vodka
½ oz. triple sec
½ oz. raspberry-flavored
   liqueur
½ oz. fresh lime juice
Chilled Champagne
Garnish: Fresh blackberries
   and raspberries

*Shake first four ingredients
with ice. Strain into chilled
cocktail glass and top with
Champagne. Garnish with
berries.*

☐ BIKINI

1 oz. vodka
½ oz. light rum
½ oz. fresh lemon juice
½ oz. milk
½ oz. simple syrup
Garnish: Lemon twist

*Shake with ice and strain
into chilled cocktail glass.
Add lemon twist.*

☐ BLACK CHERRY CHOCOLATE

1¼ oz. black cherry–flavored
   vodka
¾ oz. white chocolate liqueur
¾ oz. black cherry juice

*Shake with ice and strain
into chilled cocktail glass.*

☐ BLACK MAGIC

1½ oz. vodka
¾ oz. coffee liqueur
¼ oz. fresh lemon juice
Garnish: Lemon twist

*Shake with ice and strain
into ice-filled old-fashioned
glass. Add lemon twist.*

VODKA

BLACK RUSSIAN

1½ oz. vodka
¾ oz. coffee liqueur

Pour into ice-filled old-fashioned glass and stir.

THE BLOOD ORANGE

2 oz. orange-flavored
    vodka
1 oz. Campari
Garnish: Blood or navel
    orange half-wheel

Stir with ice and strain into chilled cocktail glass. Garnish with orange.

BLOODY BULL

1 oz. vodka
2 oz. tomato juice
2 oz. cold beef bouillon
Garnish: Lemon wedge, lime
    wheel

Pour into ice-filled highball glass. Stir. Squeeze and add lemon. Garnish with lime wheel.

BLOODY MARY

Entertainer Geroge Jessel claimed to be the inventor of this beloved morning cocktail.

1½ oz. vodka
3 oz. tomato juice
¼ oz. fresh lime juice
4 dashes Worcestershire
    sauce
2–3 drops hot red pepper
    sauce
Freshly ground black pepper
    to taste
Garnish: Lime wedge, celery
    stalk

Roll with ice between both halves of Boston shaker. Strain into ice-filled old-fashioned glass. Garnish with lime and celery.

BLUE LAGOON

1 oz. vodka
1 oz. blue curaçao
½ oz. fresh lemon juice
½ oz. simple syrup
Garnish: Maraschino cherry

Shake with ice and strain into ice-filled highball glass. Garnish with cherry.

BOLSHOI PUNCH

1 oz. vodka
¾ oz. fresh lemon juice
½ oz. simple syrup
½ oz. light rum
½ oz. oz. crème de cassis

Shake and pour into ice-filled old-fashioned glass.

VODKA

BORDEAUX COCKTAIL

1½ oz. citrus-flavored vodka
½ oz. Lillet Blanc
Garnish: Lemon twist

Stir with ice and strain into chilled cocktail glass. Add lemon twist.

BOSTON GOLD

1½ oz. vodka
½ oz. crème de banana
2 oz. fresh orange juice

Shake with ice and strain into ice-filled highball glass.

BULLFROG

1½ oz. vodka
5 oz. lemonade
Garnish: Lime wheel

Pour into ice-filled Collins glass and stir. Garnish with lime.

BULL SHOT

1½ oz. vodka
3 oz. cold beef bouillon
1 dash Worcestershire sauce
1 pinch salt
1 pinch freshly ground black pepper

Shake with ice and strain into chilled old-fashioned glass.

CAESAR

For glass: Lemon wedge, celery salt
1½ oz. vodka
4 oz. tomato-clam juice
½ tsp. prepared horseradish
1 dash Worcestershire sauce
1 pinch salt
1 pinch freshly ground black pepper
Garnish: Celery stalk, lemon wedge

Rim highball glass with lemon and celery salt, and then fill with ice. Shake ingredients with ice and strain into glass. Garnish with celery and lemon.

CAPE CODDER

1½ oz. vodka
5 oz. cranberry juice
Garnish: Lime wedge

Pour into ice-filled highball glass. Stir well. Garnish with lime.

CAPPUCCINO COCKTAIL

¾ oz. vodka
¾ oz. coffee-flavored brandy
¾ oz. half-and-half

Shake with ice and strain into chilled cocktail glass.

CARIBBEAN CRUISE

1 oz. vodka
¼ oz. light rum
¼ oz. coconut-flavored rum
1 splash grenadine
4 oz. pineapple juice
Garnish: Pineapple wedge,
   maraschino cherry

*Shake first four ingredients
with ice and pour into
ice-filled Collins glass.
Fill with pineapple juice.
Garnish with pineapple
and cherry.*

CASCO BAY
LEMONADE

1½ oz. citrus-flavored
   vodka
2 oz. ㅡle syrup
2 oz. ㅡ lemon juice
1 splash ㅡranberry juice
Lemon-liㅡe soda
Garnish: Lemon wheel

*Shake first four ingredients
with ice. Pour into ice-filled
Collins glass. Fill glass with
lemon-lime soda. Float
lemon wheel on top.*

CHAMPAGNE
FLAMINGO

¾ oz. vodka
¾ oz. Campari
5 oz. chilled Champagne
Garnish: Orange twist

*Shake vodka and Campari
with ice. Strain into chilled
champagne flute and top
with Champagne. Add
orange twist.*

THE CINQUECENTO

Created by FREDO CERASO,
Los Angeles, CA

1½ oz. bison grass vodka
   (Zubrowka)
½ oz. Bénédictine
½ oz. Campari
¾ oz. fresh grapefruit juice
1 dash Angostura bitters
Garnish: Grapefruit twist

*Shake with ice. Strain through
wire sieve into chilled cocktail
glass. Add grapefruit twist.*

CITRONELLA COOLER

1 oz. citrus-flavored vodka
1 dash fresh lime juice
2 oz. lemonade
1 oz. cranberry juice
Garnish: Lime wedge

*Stir in Collins glass. Add ice
and stir again. Squeeze and
add lime.*

COSMOPOLITAN

The invention of the Cosmo,
which has passed the lips of many
a sophisticated lady (and quite a
few men, too), is often credited to
Cheryl Cook, a bartender in South
Beach, FL. But it really took off
when master mixologist Dale
DeGroff served one to Madonna
at New York's late and lamented
Rainbow Room.

1½ oz. vodka
½ oz. fresh lime juice
½ oz. triple sec
½ oz. cranberry juice
Garnish: Lime wheel

*Shake well with ice and
strain into chilled cocktail
glass. Garnish with lime.*

CROCODILE COOLER

1½ oz. citrus-flavored vodka
1 oz. melon liqueur
¾ oz. triple sec
¾ oz. simple syrup
1 oz. fresh lemon juice
Lemon-lime soda
Garnish: Pineapple wedge,
    maraschino cherry or lime
    wheel

*Stir first five ingredients in
hurricane glass. Add ice,
fill with lemon-lime soda,
and stir again. Garnish
with pineapple and cherry
or lime wheel. Serve with
a straw.*

CUBELTINI

3 cucumber slices
5–7 fresh mint leaves
1½ oz. simple syrup
2 oz. vodka
1 oz. fresh lime juice
Garnish: Fresh mint sprig

*Muddle the cucumber, mint
leaves, and syrup. Add
vodka and lime juice. Shake
and strain into chilled cocktail glass. Garnish with mint
sprig.*

DESERT SUNRISE

1¼ oz. vodka
1½ oz. fresh orange juice
1½ oz. pineapple juice
1 dash grenadine

*Pour first three ingredients
over crushed ice in Collins
glass. Do not stir. Top with
grenadine.*

DREAMY DORINI SMOKING MARTINI

Created by AUDREY SAUNDERS,
New York City, NY

2 oz. vodka
½ oz. smoky Scotch, such as
    Laphroaig
4 drops pastis
Garnish: Lemon twist

*Stir with ice and strain into
a chilled cocktail glass. Add
lemon twist.*

ELECTRIC JAM

1¼ oz. vodka
½ oz. blue curaçao
1 oz. simple syrup
1 oz. fresh lemon juice
Lemon-lime soda

*Pour first four ingredients
into ice-filled Collins glass.
Fill with lemon-lime soda
and stir.*

FLATIRON MARTINI

Created by JULIE REINER,
owner of Flatiron Lounge,
New York, NY

1 splash triple sec
1½ oz. orange-flavored
    vodka
1½ oz. Lillet Blanc
Garnish: Orange wheel

*Swirl triple sec in
chilled cocktail glass to
coat inside; discard excess
triple sec. Stir vodka and
Lillet with ice and strain
into glass. Garnish with
orange.*

VODKA

♇ FRENCH MARTINI

1½ oz. vodka
¾ oz. black raspberry liqueur
¾ oz. pineapple juice

*Shake with ice and strain
into chilled cocktail glass.*

☐ FRISKY WITCH

1 oz. vodka
1 oz. Sambuca
Garnish: Black licorice stick

*Stir in old-fashioned glass.
Add ice and stir again.
Garnish with licorice.*

☐ GABLES COLLINS

1½ oz. vodka
1 oz. crème de noyaux
½ oz. fresh lemon juice
½ oz. pineapple juice
Soda water
Garnish: Lemon wheel,
    pineapple chunk

*Shake first four ingredients
with ice and strain into ice-
filled Collins glass. Fill with
soda water. Garnish with
lemon and pineapple.*

☐ GENTLE BEN

1 oz. vodka
1 oz. gin
1 oz. blanco tequila
Fresh orange juice
Garnish: Orange wheel,
    maraschino cherry

*Shake first three ingredients
with ice and pour into ice-
filled Collins glass. Fill with
orange juice and stir. Garnish
with orange and cherry.*

☐ GEORGIA MULE

1 peach slice, skinned
1½ oz. vodka
½ oz. fresh lemon juice
2 dashes peach bitters
Ginger beer
Garnish: Peach slice

*Muddle 1 peach slice
in Collins glass. Add
vodka, lemon juice, and
bitters, then stir. Fill with
ice and ginger beer; stir
again. Garnish with peach
slice.*

☐ GEORGIA PEACH

1½ oz. vodka
½ oz. peach schnapps
1 dash grenadine
Lemonade

*Stir first three ingredients
in Collins glass. Add ice
and stir again. Fill with
lemonade.*

☐ GLASS TOWER

1 oz. vodka
1 oz. peach schnapps
1 oz. white rum
1 oz. triple sec
½ oz. sambuca
Lemon-lime soda
Garnish: Orange wheel,
    maraschino cherry

*Pour first five ingredients
into Collins glass. Add ice,
then fill with lemon-lime
soda and stir. Garnish with
orange and cherry.*

GODCHILD

1 oz. vodka
1 oz. amaretto
1 oz. heavy cream

Shake well with ice and strain into chilled cocktail glass.

GODMOTHER

1½ oz. vodka
¾ oz. amaretto

Combine in ice-filled old-fashioned glass.

GRAPEFRUIT GIMLET ROYALE

1½ oz. vodka
1 oz. fresh grapefruit juice
¼ oz. fresh lime juice
¼ oz. simple syrup
2 oz. chilled Champagne

Shake first four ingredients with ice and strain into chilled cocktail glass. Top with Champagne.

GRAPE NEHI

1 oz. vodka
1 oz. raspberry-flavored liqueur
1 oz. fresh lemon juice

Shake with ice and strain into chilled cocktail glass.

VODKA

MAKE PEOPLE HAPPY

Bartenders should never lose sight of the primary mission of their job: to make people happy. This can be done by serving a great cocktail, but it can also be achieved by telling a good joke, commiserating with some unhappy soul, or introducing like-minded people to each other, and in a million other different ways. Some of my favorite bartenders have worked in shot-and-a-beer joints, and wouldn't know how to fix a decent Margarita to save their lives. If a bartender makes the customers happy, he or she is doing a good job.

—GARY REGAN, copublisher,
ArdentSpirits.com

THE GROUPIE

Created by ERIC TECOSKY,
Los Angeles, CA

3 lemon wedges
½ tsp. superfine sugar
2 oz. citrus-flavored vodka
Ginger beer

*Muddle lemons and sugar in
mixing glass. Add vodka and
ice and shake. Strain into
ice-filled old-fashioned glass
and top with ginger beer.*

HANDBALL COOLER

1½ oz. vodka
Soda water
½ oz. fresh orange juice
Garnish: Lime wedge

*Pour vodka into ice-filled
highball glass. Fill almost
to top with soda water. Top
with orange juice and stir.
Add lime.*

HARRINGTON

1½ oz. vodka
¼ oz. triple sec
1 tsp. green Chartreuse
Garnish: Orange zest

*Stir with ice and strain into
chilled cocktail glass. Add
orange zest.*

HARVEY WALLBANGER

In the 1970s, this golden-hued
cocktail fueled virtually every
Sunday brunch in America. The
distinctive tall bottle of Galliano
graced many a knotty pine–
paneled home bar.

1 oz. vodka
4 oz. fresh orange juice
½ oz. Galliano

*Stir vodka and orange
juice in Collins glass. Add
ice and stir again. Float
Galliano (see page 18) on
top.*

HEADLESS HORSEMAN

2 oz. vodka
3 dashes Angostura
   bitters
Ginger ale
Garnish: Orange wheel

*Pour vodka and bitters into
Collins glass. Add ice, fill
with ginger ale, and stir.
Garnish with orange.*

HUMPTY DUMPTY

2 oz. vodka
1 oz. fresh fresh orange juice
½ oz. Galliano
1 whole egg
3 dashes Peychaud's
   bitters

*Shake without ice. Shake
with ice and strain into
chilled cocktail glass.*

HUNTSMAN COCKTAIL

1½ oz. vodka
½ oz. Jamaican rum
½ oz. fresh lime juice
½ oz. simple syrup

Shake with ice and strain into chilled cocktail glass.

IBIZA

1 oz. orange-flavored vodka
½ oz. Campari
1 oz. fresh grapefruit juice
1 tsp. pomegranate molasses
1 dash peach schnapps
1 dash apple schnapps
Garnish: Grapefruit twist

Shake with ice and strain into chilled cocktail glass. Add grapefruit twist.

ITALIAN SCREWDRIVER

For glass: Lime wedge, superfine sugar
1½ oz. citrus-flavored vodka
3 oz. fresh orange juice
2 oz. fresh grapefruit juice
1 splash ginger ale
Garnish: Lime wheel

Rim hurricane glass with lime wedge and sugar; fill with ice. Shake remaining ingredients with ice. Strain into glass. Garnish with lime.

JACKIE-O

You'll find pink sanding sugar at cake decorating and specialty food stores (page 320).

For glass: Lime wedge, pink sanding sugar (page 320)
½ oz. citrus-flavored vodka
½ oz. orange-flavored vodka
½ oz. crème de cassis
1 oz. apricot nectar
½ oz. fresh lemon juice
½ oz. cranberry juice
Chilled Champagne
Garnish: Orange half-wheel, lime wheel

Rim chilled large cocktail glass with lime wedge and pink sugar. Shake first six ingredients with ice and strain into glass. Top with Champagne. Garnish with orange and lime.

THE JAMAICAN TEN SPEED

1 oz. vodka
¾ oz. melon liqueur
¼ oz. crème de banana
¼ oz. coconut-flavored rum
½ oz. half-and-half

Shake with ice and strain into chilled cocktail glass.

VODKA

JUNGLE JUICE

1 oz. vodka
1 oz. light rum
½ oz. triple sec
1 oz. cranberry juice
1 oz. fresh orange juice
1 oz. pineapple juice
1 splash simple syrup
1 splash fresh lemon juice
Garnish: Orange wheel,
    maraschino cherry

*Shake with ice and pour
with ice into ice-filled Collins
glass. Garnish with orange
and cherry.*

KATANA

3 cucumber slices
1½ oz. vodka
½ oz. sake
¾ oz. fresh lime juice
¾ oz. simple syrup
Garnish: 1 cucumber slice

*Muddle 3 cucumber slices
in mixing glass. Add
remaining ingredients.
Shake with ice. Double-
strain into chilled cocktail
glass. Garnish with cucumber slice.*

KRETCHMA COCKTAIL

1 oz. vodka
1 oz. white crème de cacao
¼ oz. fresh lemon juice
¼ oz. grenadine

*Shake with ice and
strain into chilled cocktail
glass.*

L.A. SUNRISE

1 oz. vodka
½ oz. crème de banana
2 oz. fresh orange juice
2 oz. pineapple juice
¼ oz. dark rum
Garnish: Lime wheel,
    maraschino cherry

*Shake first four ingredients
with ice. Strain into ice-
filled hurricane or parfait
glass. Float rum (see page
18) on top. Garnish with
lime and cherry.*

LEAVES OF GRASS

Created by NATASHA DAVID,
New York, NY

1½ oz. aquavit
½ oz. Old Tom gin
¼ oz. Demerara Syrup
    (page 25)
2 dashes orange bitters
1 dash absinthe
Garnish: Celery stick

*Stir with ice and strain into
ice-filled old-fashioned glass.
Add celery stick.*

LEMON CRUSH

For glass: Lemon wedge,
    superfine sugar
1½ oz. citrus-flavored vodka
½ oz. crema di limoncello
½ oz. triple sec
1 oz. fresh lemon juice

*Rim chilled cocktail glass
with lemon and sugar. Shake
ingredients with ice and
strain into glass.*

LEMON DROP

Thanks to the arrival of lemon-flavored vodka on the scene, the Lemon Drop has become a modern classic.

For glass: Lemon wedge, superfine sugar
1½ oz. lemon-flavored vodka
¾ oz. fresh lemon juice
¼ oz. simple syrup
Garnish: Lemon wedge

Rim chilled cocktail glass with lemon and sugar. Shake ingredients with ice. Strain into glass. Squeeze lemon wedge and add.

LE PARADINI

1½ oz. vodka
½ oz. raspberry-flavored liqueur
½ oz. Grand Marnier
1 oz. chilled Champagne

Shake first three ingredients with ice and strain into chilled cocktail glass. Top with Champagne.

LIGHTS ON THE PLAZA

Created by JONATHAN POGASH, New York, NY

2 (½-inch-thick) cucumber slices, chopped
½ oz. fresh lemon juice
½ oz. simple syrup
1½ oz. açai berry–flavored vodka
½ oz. black raspberry liqueur
1 oz. sparkling wine
Garnish: 1 raspberry sandwiched between 2 thin cucumber slices, skewered

Muddle cucumbers, lemon juice, and syrup in mixing glass. Add vodka, raspberry liqueur, and ice and shake. Double-strain into chilled cocktail glass. Top with sparkling wine. Garnish with raspberry-cucumber skewer.

LIMONCELLO MANZANILLA MARMALADE SOUR

1½ oz. citrus-flavored vodka
¾ oz. limoncello
¾ oz. manzanilla sherry
¾ oz. fresh lemon juice
1 tsp. grapefruit marmalade
Garnish: Orange twist

Shake with ice and double-strain into chilled cocktail glass. Add orange twist.

L'ITALIENNE

2 oz. vodka
¼ oz. Lillet Blanc
¼ oz. Ramazzotti Amaro
1 dash orange bitters

Stir and strain into chilled cocktail glass.

VODKA

LONG ISLAND ICED TEA

If this drink makes you think of hot summer days in the Hamptons, you should know that it may have been invented in the 1920s in a community called Long Island near Kingsport, TN.

¾ oz. vodka
¾ oz. blanco tequila
¾ oz. gin
¾ oz. light rum
¾ oz. triple sec
½ oz. simple syrup
½ oz. fresh lemon juice
Cola, as needed
Garnish: Lemon wedge

Shake ingredients, except cola, with ice and pour with ice into highball glass. Add cola for color. Add lemon.

THE LOOP

2 oz. black cherry–flavored vodka
½ oz. white crème de cacao
½ oz. Chile Syrup (page 25)
Garnish: Grated bittersweet chocolate

Shake ingredients with ice. Pour into chilled old-fashioned glass. Garnish with chocolate grated on top.

LYCHEE LUCY

1½ oz. vodka
½ oz. lychee liqueur
½ oz. fresh orange juice
½ oz. pineapple juice
2 dashes Angostura bitters
Garnish: Canned pitted lychee nut stuffed with a small pineapple leaf

Shake with ice and strain into chilled cocktail glass. Add lychee-pineapple garnish.

MADRAS

1½ oz. vodka
4 oz. cranberry juice
1 oz. fresh orange juice
Garnish: Lime wedge

Build in order given into ice-filled highball glass. Squeeze lime and add.

MARACUYA MOSQUITO

4 fresh basil leaves
1½ oz. vodka
½ oz. green Chartreuse
½ oz. fresh lime juice
½ oz. simple syrup
1 oz. passion fruit juice
Garnish: Basil leaf

Muddle 4 basil leaves in mixing glass. Add remaining ingredients. Shake with ice. Double-strain through wire sieve into crushed ice–filled Collins glass. Garnish with a basil leaf.

MARTINI (VODKA)

If you insist on making your Martini with vodka, see the gin versions on page 98 and substitute the former for the latter.

⅂ MISS JONES

1½ oz. vanilla-flavored vodka
1 oz. fresh lemon juice
½ oz. butterscotch schnapps
½ oz. limoncello
Garnish: Star anise pod

Shake with ice and strain into chilled cocktail glass. Garnish with star anise.

⅂ MR. 404

1½ oz. vodka
¾ oz. elderflower liqueur
¾ oz. fresh lemon juice
½ oz. simple syrup
½ oz. Aperol
Garnish: Orange twist

Shake with ice and strain into chilled cocktail glass. Add orange twist.

⅂ MOCHA EXPRESS

1½ oz. vodka
¾ oz. Irish cream liqueur
¾ oz. coffee liqueur
¾ oz. cold brewed espresso coffee

Shake with ice and strain into chilled cocktail glass.

MOSCOW MULE

Many historians trace the popularity of vodka in America to this drink, invented in Los Angeles in the early 1940s. See Resources (page 316) for where to purchase authentic Moscow Mule mugs.

1½ oz. vodka
½ oz. fresh lime juice
Ginger beer
Garnish: Lime wedge

Pour vodka and lime juice into copper Moscow Mule mug or standard beer mug. Add ice cubes and fill with ginger beer. Squeeze lime wedge and add to glass.

NIJINKSY BLINI

1 oz. vodka
1 oz. peach schnapps
1 oz. peach puree
¼ oz. fresh lemon juice
Chilled Champagne

Shake first four ingredients with ice. Strain into chilled champagne flute and top with Champagne.

⅂ NINOTCHKA COCKTAIL

1½ oz. vodka
½ oz. white crème de cacao
¼ oz. fresh lemon juice

Shake with ice and strain into chilled cocktail glass.

VODKA

PEACH ICED TEA

1½ oz. peach-flavored vodka
½ oz. orange curaçao
¾ oz. fresh lemon juice
½ oz. Honey Syrup (page 25)
2 oz. iced tea
Garnish: Peach slice, lemon
    wheel

Shake with ice and strain into ice-filled Collins glass. Garnish with peach and lemon.

PETIT ZINC

1 oz. vodka
½ oz. triple sec
½ oz. sweet vermouth
½ oz. fresh orange juice
Garnish: Orange wedge

Shake with ice and strain into chilled cocktail glass. Garnish with orange.

PICKLED MARTINI

2 oz. vodka
¼ oz. dry vermouth
¾ oz. sweet pickle brine
Garnish: Sweet pickle slice

Stir with ice and strain into chilled cocktail glass. Garnish with pickle.

PICKLED PINK

Created by CHRIS PATINO,
New York, NY

2 oz. vodka
1 oz. aquavit
½ oz. dill pickle brine
2 dashes Angostura bitters
Garnish: Dill sprig

Shake with ice and strain into cocktail glass. Garnish with dill.

PINK LEMONADE

1½ oz. citrus-flavored vodka
¼ oz. triple sec
¼ oz. fresh lime juice
¼ oz. fresh lemon juice
¼ oz. simple syrup
2 oz. cranberry juice
Garnish: Lemon wheel

Shake with ice and strain into ice-filled Collins glass. Garnish with lemon.

PINK PUSSYCAT

1½ oz. vodka
2 oz. pineapple or
    fresh grapefruit juice
½ oz. grenadine

Pour ingredients into ice-filled highball glass and stir.

POLYNESIAN COCKTAIL

For glass: Lime wedge,
    superfine sugar
1½ oz. vodka
¾ oz. cherry-flavored brandy
¾ oz. fresh lime juice

Rim chilled cocktail glass with lime and sugar. Shake ingredients with ice and strain into glass.

PRETTY IN PINK

2 oz. vodka
½ oz. cranberry juice
¾ oz. crème de noyaux
¾ oz. fresh lemon juice
Soda water

Shake first four ingredients and strain into ice-filled Collins glass. Top with soda water.

PRIORITY COCKTAIL

2 oz. vodka
½ oz. Calvados
½ oz. coffee liqueur
Garnish: Lemon twist

Stir with ice and strain into chilled cocktail glass. Add lemon twist.

PURPLE MASK

1 oz. vodka
1 oz. Concord grape juice
½ oz. white crème de cacao

Shake with ice and strain into chilled cocktail glass.

PURPLE PASSION

1½ oz. vodka
2 oz. fresh grapefruit juice
2 oz. Concord grape juice
½ oz. simple syrup

Shake with ice. Pour with ice into Collins glass.

PURPLE PASSION ICED TEA

½ oz. vodka
½ oz. light rum
½ oz. gin
½ oz. black raspberry liqueur
½ oz. simple syrup
¾ oz. fresh lemon juice
3 oz. lemon-lime soda
Garnish: Lemon twist

Pour ingredients into ice-filled highball glass in order listed and stir. Add lemon twist.

PURPLE RUBY

1½ oz. vodka
1½ oz. pomegranate juice
½ oz. fresh grapefruit juice
¼ oz. fresh lime juice
¼ oz. Honey Syrup (page 25)
Garnish: Grapefruit twist

Shake with ice and strain into chilled cocktail glass. Add grapefruit twist.

RED APPLE

1½ oz. 100-proof vodka
1 oz. apple juice
½ oz. fresh lemon juice
1 tsp. grenadine

Shake with ice and strain into chilled cocktail glass.

REDHEAD MARTINI

4 strawberries, cut into halves
¾ oz. fresh lemon juice
¾ oz. simple syrup
1½ oz. citrus-flavored vodka
1 splash chilled moscato d'Asti or sweet sparkling wine
Garnish: Strawberry

Muddle halved strawberries in mixing glass with lemon juice and syrup. Add vodka and ice and shake well. Strain into chilled cocktail glass. Add sparkling wine. Garnish with the strawberry.

ROBIN'S NEST

1 oz. vodka
1 oz. cranberry juice
½ oz. white crème de cacao

Shake with ice and strain into chilled cocktail glass.

VODKA

ROSEMARY CLEMENTINE SPARKLE

Created by KATHY CASEY,
Seattle, WA

¼ clementine or mandarin
    orange
1½ oz. vodka
¾ oz. fresh lemon juice
¾ oz. Honey Syrup
    (page 25)
1 fresh rosemary sprig
1 splash chilled sparkling
    wine or Champagne
Garnish: Fresh rosemary
    sprig

Squeeze clementine into mixing glass. Twist rind and add to glass. Add vodka, lemon juice, syrup, and rosemary sprig. Add ice and shake. Strain into chilled cocktail glass. Top with sparkling wine or Champagne. Garnish with remaining rosemary sprig.

ROUXBY RED

For glass: Lemon wedge,
    coarse salt
1½ oz. grapefruit-flavored
    vodka
¼ oz. fresh lemon juice
¾ oz. fresh grapefruit juice
½ oz. Campari
½ oz. simple syrup

Rim chilled cocktail glass with lemon and salt. Shake remaining ingredients with ice and strain into glass.

RUBY RED

2 oz. grapefruit-flavored
    vodka
1½ oz. triple sec
1½ oz. fresh ruby red
    grapefruit juice
1 splash fresh orange
    juice
Garnish: Grapefruit twist

Shake with ice and strain into chilled cocktail glass. Add grapefruit twist.

RUSSIAN BEAR COCKTAIL

1 oz. vodka
½ oz. white crème de
    cacao
½ oz. half-and-half

Stir with ice and strain into chilled cocktail glass.

SAMPAN SHIPWRECK A

Created by JAKE SHER,
White Plains, NY

1½ oz. vodka
½ oz. orange liqueur
½ oz. canned coconut
    milk
½ oz. cold brewed
    chai tea
½ oz. orgeat or almond
    syrup
Garnish: Pineapple
    wedge

Shake well with ice. Double-strain into chilled cocktail glass. Perch pineapple on rim of glass.

SALTY DOG (VODKA)

For glass: Lemon wedge,
coarse salt
1½ oz. vodka
5 oz. fresh grapefruit juice

*Rim highball glass with
lemon and salt. Fill with ice.
Add vodka and grapefruit
juice and stir.*

SCREWDRIVER

1½ oz. vodka
5 oz. fresh orange juice

*Pour into ice-filled highball
glass. Stir well.*

SEA BREEZE

1½ oz. vodka
4 oz. cranberry juice
1 oz. fresh grapefruit juice
Garnish: Lime wedge

*Pour into ice-filled highball
glass. Garnish with lime.*

SHALOM

1½ oz. 100-proof vodka
1 oz. madeira
½ oz. fresh orange juice
Garnish: Orange wheel

*Shake with ice and strain
into ice-filled old-fashioned
glass. Add orange wheel.*

SIBERIAN SLEIGHRIDE

1¼ oz. vodka
¾ oz. white crème de cacao
½ oz. white crème de menthe
3 oz. half-and-half
Garnish: Shaved bittersweet
chocolate

*Shake with ice and strain
into chilled snifter. Sprinkle
with chocolate shavings.*

SONIC BLASTER

½ oz. vodka
½ oz. light rum
½ oz. crème de banana
1 oz. pineapple juice
1 oz. fresh orange juice
1 oz. cranberry juice
Garnish: Orange and lime
wheels

*Shake and pour into ice-
filled Collins glass. Garnish
with orange and lime.*

SOVIET

1½ oz. vodka
½ oz. amontillado sherry
½ oz. dry vermouth
Garnish: Lemon twist

*Shake with ice and strain
into ice-filled old-fashioned
glass. Add lemon twist.*

SPUTNIK

1¼ oz. vodka
1¼ oz. peach schnapps
3 oz. fresh orange juice
3 oz. half-and-half
Garnish: Peach slice

*Shake with ice until frothy
and pour into red-wine glass.
Garnish with peach.*

VODKA

Y STOCKHOLM 75

For glass: Lemon wedge,
    superfine sugar
¾ oz. citrus-flavored vodka
¾ oz. simple syrup
¾ oz. fresh lemon juice
3 oz. chilled Champagne

*Rim chilled cocktail glass
with lemon and sugar.
Shake vodka, syrup, and
lemon juice with ice.
Strain into glass. Fill with
Champagne.*

Y STUPID CUPID

2 oz. citrus-flavored vodka
½ oz. sloe gin
1 splash simple syrup
1 splash fresh lemon juice
Garnish: Maraschino cherry

*Shake with ice and strain
into chilled cocktail glass.
Garnish with cherry.*

Y THE SUMMER OF LOVE

2 oz. orange-flavored vodka
2 drops rose water
1 oz. Lillet Blanc
¼ oz. black raspberry liqueur
Garnish: Lemon twist

*Shake with ice and strain
into chilled cocktail glass.
Add lemon twist.*

SURF RIDER

2 oz. vodka
½ oz. sweet vermouth
2 oz. fresh orange
    juice
½ oz. fresh lemon
    juice
¼ oz. grenadine
Garnish: Orange half-wheel,
    maraschino cherry

*Shake with ice and strain
into ice-filled highball glass.
Garnish with orange and
cherry.*

Y SWEET MARIA

1 oz. vodka
½ oz. amaretto
½ oz. half-and-half

*Shake with ice and strain
into chilled cocktail glass.*

Y TABBY CAT

2 oz. Dubonnet Rouge
1 oz. orange-flavored
    vodka
2 dashes orange bitters
Garnish: Lemon twist

*Stir with ice and strain into
chilled cocktail glass. Add
lemon twist.*

THYME COLLINS

Created by JOSHUA PEKAR,
Fairfield, CT

2 oz. citrus-flavored vodka
1 oz. mint syrup
1 oz. fresh lemon juice
1 thyme sprig
3 oz. bitter lemon soda
Garnish: 2 long thyme
    sprigs

*Put first four ingredients in
mixing glass, add ice, and
shake well. Strain into ice-
filled Collins glass. Top with
bitter lemon soda and stir
briefly. Garnish with long
thyme sprigs.*

TIGER TANAKA

3 fresh cilantro leaves
1 (¼-inch-thick) slice peeled
    fresh ginger
2 oz. citrus-flavored vodka
½ oz. limoncello
¾ oz. pineapple juice

*Muddle cilantro and ginger
in mixing glass. Add remaining ingredients and shake.
Double-strain into chilled
cocktail glass.*

THE TITIAN

1 oz. orange-flavored vodka
½ oz. Grand Marnier
1 oz. passion fruit juice
½ oz. fresh lime juice
½ oz. pomegranate syrup
Garnish: Fresh raspberry

*Shake with ice and strain
into chilled cocktail glass.
Garnish with raspberry.*

TOASTED DROP

For glass: Lemon wedge,
    Cinnamon Sugar (page 126)
1½ oz. citrus-flavored vodka
¾ oz. limoncello
¼ oz. amaretto
¾ oz. fresh lemon juice
1 egg white
Garnish: Lemon twist

*Rim chilled cocktail glass
with lemon and cinnamon
sugar. Shake ingredients
without ice. Add ice and
shake again. Strain into
glass. Add lemon twist.*

TOP BANANA

1 oz. vodka
1 oz. crème de banana
2 oz. fresh orange juice

*Shake with ice and strain into
ice-filled old-fashioned glass.*

TRIDENT

1 oz. aquavit or vodka
½ oz. Cynar
1 oz. dry sherry
2 dashes peach bitters
Garnish: Lemon twist

*Stir and strain into cocktail
glass. Garnish with lemon
twist.*

TWISTER

2 oz. vodka
½ oz. fresh lime juice
Lime wedge
Lemon-lime soda

*Pour vodka and lime juice
into Collins glass. Add several ice cubes. Squeeze lime
into glass and add. Fill with
lemon-lime soda and stir.*

VODKA

UNDERNEATH THE MANGO TREE

Created by JONATHAN POGASH, New York, NY

For glass: Lime wedge, Sweet Chili Powder (recipe follows)
1 oz. mango-flavored vodka
½ oz. peach liqueur
¾ oz. fresh lime juice
½ oz simple syrup
2 oz. ginger ale

Rim Collins glass with lime and sweet chili powder. Fill glass with ice. Shake next four ingredients with ice. Strain into glass. Top with ginger ale.

SWEET CHILI POWDER

Combine 2 Tbs. chili powder with 2 Tbs. superfine sugar.

VELVET PEACH HAMMER

1¾ oz. vodka
¾ oz. peach schnapps
¼ oz. simple syrup
½ oz. fresh lemon juice
Garnish: Peach slice

Pour vodka and schnapps into ice-filled old-fashioned glass. Stir and top with syrup and lemon juice. Garnish with peach.

VICTORY COLLINS

1½ oz. vodka
2 oz. unsweetened grape juice
1 oz. fresh lemon juice
½ oz. simple syrup
Garnish: Orange half-wheel

Shake with ice and strain into ice-filled Collins glass. Garnish with orange.

VODKA AND APPLE JUICE

2 oz. vodka
Apple juice

Pour vodka into ice-filled highball glass. Fill with apple juice and stir.

VODKA AND TONIC

2 oz. vodka
Tonic water
Garnish: Lemon or lime wedge

Pour vodka into highball glass over ice. Add tonic and stir. Garnish with lemon or lime wedge.

VODKA COLLINS

2 oz. vodka
¾ oz. fresh lemon juice
¾ oz. simple syrup
Soda water
Garnish: Lemon and orange wheels, maraschino cherry

Shake vodka, lemon juice, and syrup and strain into ice-filled Collins glass. Fill with soda water and stir. Garnish with citrus and cherry. Serve with a straw.

VODKA COOLER

2 oz. vodka
½ oz. simple syrup
Soda water or ginger ale
Garnish: Orange and/or lemon
   zest spiral

*Stir vodka and syrup in
Collins glass. Add ice cubes
and fill with soda water or
ginger ale. Insert a spiral
of orange or lemon zest (or
both) and dangle end(s) over
rim of glass.*

VODKA DAISY

2 oz. vodka
1 oz. fresh lemon juice
½ oz. simple syrup
1 tsp. grenadine
Garnish: Fresh seasonal
   fruit

*Shake with ice. Strain into
ice-filled beer mug or metal
cup. Garnish with fruit.*

VODKA GIMLET

If you are used to Gimlets made
with bottled lime juice, you
owe it to yourself to try one
with fresh lime juice and simple
syrup.

1½ oz. vodka
1 oz. fresh lime juice
½ oz. simple syrup

*Shake with ice and strain
into chilled cocktail glass.*

Note: *If desired, substitute
1 oz. Rose's Sweetened
Lime Juice for the fresh lime
juice and simple syrup.*

VODKA GRASSHOPPER

¾ oz. vodka
¾ oz. green crème de menthe
¾ oz. white crème de cacao
¾ oz. half-and-half

*Shake with ice and strain
into chilled cocktail glass.*

VODKA SLING

2 oz. vodka
1 oz. fresh lemon juice
½ oz. simple syrup
Garnish: Orange twist

*Pour vodka, lemon juice,
and syrup into ice-filled old-
fashioned glass and stir. Add
orange twist.*

VODKA SOUR

2 oz. vodka
¾ oz. fresh lemon juice
¾ oz. simple syrup
Garnish: Lemon half-wheel,
   maraschino cherry

*Shake with ice and strain into
chilled cocktail glass. Garnish
with lemon and cherry.*

VODKA STINGER

1 oz. vodka
1 oz. white crème de menthe

*Shake with ice and strain
into chilled cocktail glass.*

WARSAW COCKTAIL

1½ oz. vodka
½ oz. blackberry-flavored
   brandy
½ oz. dry vermouth
1 tsp. fresh lemon juice

*Shake with ice and strain
into chilled cocktail glass.*

VODKA

⏣ WEST SIDE

1½ oz. lemon-flavored
    vodka
¾ oz. fresh lemon juice
½ oz. simple syrup
6 fresh mint leaves
Soda water

*Shake first four ingredients
with ice and double-strain
into chilled cocktail glass.
Top with a splash of soda
water.*

▢ WHITE RUSSIAN

2 oz. vodka
1 oz. coffee liqueur
Milk or half-and-half

*Pour vodka and coffee
liqueur into ice-filled old-
fashioned glass. Fill with
milk or half-and-half.*

BEND YOUR SPOON

This trick will improve your stirring skills: Put a slight
bend in the long handle of a stainless-steel barspoon.
Now slide the back of the bowl down the inside of
the mixing glass to the bottom. The top end of the
spoon should be directly over the center of the mixing
glass. The bend will allow the spoon to rotate over the
center of the glass with almost no circular movement
of the hand. The back of the spoon will rotate around
the inside of the mixing glass—pushing the ice ahead
so that liquid and cubes rotate gracefully as a unit in
a clockwise direction. Graceful stirring will not only
insure a heavy, silky texture, but is essential in achieving the style and ceremony with which these drinks
should be prepared.

—DALE DeGROFF (aka King Cocktail), author of
The Craft of the Cocktail

WHISKIES

WHISKEY IS AN UMBRELLA term for four distinct spirits—Irish, Scotch, bourbon, and rye—distilled from a fermented mash of grain and aged in oak barrels. In Ireland and the United States, it's spelled with an "e"; in Scotland and Canada it's spelled without one.

Irish whiskey comprises corn-based grain whiskey, barley, and barley malt. In Scotch whisky production, a peat-fueled fire is used to flavor the final product. The whiskeys of Islay and Skye are especially smoky. American whiskey falls into two categories: straight whiskey, which is made from at least 51 percent of a grain, and blended whiskey, a combination of at least two 100-proof straight whiskies blended with neutral spirits, grain spirits, or light whiskies. Straight whiskey is made in three styles: bourbon, Tennessee, and rye. Bourbon can be made with one of two types of mash: sweet, which employs fresh yeast to start fermentation, or sour, which combines a new batch of sweet mash with residual mash from the previous fermentation.

Tennessee whiskey is similar to bourbon, except that before the whiskey goes into charred barrels to mature, it is painstakingly filtered through ten feet of sugar maple charcoal.

Rye (aka straight rye), once the leading brown spirit before Prohibition, is making a comeback. Though wheat and barley are commonly used to make rye whiskey, by U.S. law it must be made with a minimum of 51 percent rye, whereas in Canada anything goes.

The following recipes list a specific whiskey if it's traditional or integral to the drink. Where simply "whiskey" is listed, feel free to experiment.

1626

Created by BLAIR FRODELIUS, Syracuse, NY

2½ oz. bourbon whiskey
¾ oz. gingerbread liqueur
½ tsp. cherry-flavored brandy
2 dashes Angostura bitters
Garnish: Italian preserved cherry

Shake well with ice and strain into chilled cocktail glass. Garnish with cherry.

19TH CENTURY

1½ oz. bourbon whiskey
¾ oz. fresh lemon juice
¾ oz. white crème de cacao
¾ oz. Lillet Rouge

Shake with ice and strain into chilled cocktail glass.

ACADEMIC REVIEW

Created by HAL WOLIN, New York, NY

1½ oz. Irish whiskey
½ oz. applejack
½ oz. Amaro Nonino
½ oz. rye whiskey
¼ oz. Demerara Syrup (page 25)
2 dashes mole bitters
1 dash orange bitters
Garnish: Orange twist

Stir with ice and strain into ice-filled old-fashioned glass. Add orange twist.

ADDERLY COCKTAIL

2 oz. straight rye whiskey
¾ oz. maraschino liqueur
¾ oz. fresh lemon juice
2 dashes orange bitters
Garnish: Orange twist, flamed

Shake with ice and strain into cocktail glass. Flame orange twist and add.

WHISKIES

⅄ AFFINITY COCKTAIL

1 oz. blended Scotch whisky
1 oz. dry vermouth
1 oz. sweet vermouth
3 dashes orange bitters

Stir with ice and strain into chilled cocktail glass.

⅄ AKOGARE

Created by MICHAEL GRONFORS
and JYRI PYLKKANEN,
Helsinki, Finland

1½ oz. straight rye whiskey
¾ oz. Ginger Syrup
    (page 25)
¾ oz. cold brewed black tea,
    preferably Japanese
¾ oz. fresh lemon juice
Garnish: Orange twist

Shake with ice and strain into chilled cocktail glass. Add orange twist.

⅄ ALGONQUIN

1½ oz. straight rye whiskey
1 oz. dry vermouth
1 oz. pineapple juice

Shake with ice and strain into chilled cocktail glass.

⅄ ALLEGHENY

1 oz. bourbon whiskey
1 oz. dry vermouth
½ oz. blackberry-flavored
    brandy
½ oz. fresh lemon juice
Garnish: Lemon twist

Shake with ice and strain into chilled cocktail glass. Add lemon twist.

☐ AMERICANA

1 oz. Tennessee whiskey
½ oz. simple syrup
2 dashes Angostura bitters
Chilled American sparkling
    wine
Garnish: Peach slice

Stir first three ingredients in ice-filled Collins glass. Fill with sparkling wine. Garnish with peach.

☐ AMERICAN TRILOGY

1 brown sugar cube, such as
    Demerara
1 oz. straight rye whiskey
1 oz. applejack
Garnish: Orange twist

Muddle sugar cube in mixer glass. Add whiskey, apple-jack, and ice. Stir and strain into chilled old-fashioned glass. Add orange twist.

⅄ ANGEL'S SHARE

1½ oz. bourbon whiskey
½ oz. amaro, such as
    Ramazzotti or Averna
¼ oz. crème de cassis
1 dash orange bitters
Garnish: Lemon twist

Stir with ice and strain into chilled cocktail glass. Add lemon twist.

☐ AQUARIUS

1½ oz. blended Scotch whisky
½ oz. cherry-flavored brandy
1 oz. cranberry juice

Shake with ice and strain into old-fashioned glass over ice.

☐ AUTUMN LEAVES

¾ oz. straight rye whiskey
¾ oz. apple brandy
¾ oz. sweet vermouth
¼ oz. Strega
2 dashes Angostura bitters
Garnish: Orange twist

Stir with ice and strain into ice-filled old-fashioned glass. Add orange twist.

☐ AZTEC'S MARK

1½ oz. bourbon whiskey
½ oz. white crème de cacao
¼ oz. Bénédictine
2 dashes hot red pepper sauce
Garnish: Orange twist

Stir with ice and strain into chilled cocktail glass. Add orange twist.

☐ BACK PORCH SWIZZLE

1½ oz. bourbon whiskey
½ oz. dry vermouth
1 oz. pineapple juice
1 oz. ginger beer
Green Chartreuse
Garnish: Fresh mint sprig

Pour first four ingredients in crushed ice–filled high-ball glass. With barspoon between your palms, move hands back and forth and up and down to quickly rotate and lift spoon, until glass is frosted. Float Chartreuse (see page 18) on top, and garnish with mint.

☐ BASIN STREET

2 oz. bourbon whiskey
¾ oz. triple sec
¾ oz. fresh lemon juice

Shake well with ice and strain into chilled cocktail glass.

☐ BEALS COCKTAIL

1½ oz. blended Scotch whisky
½ oz. dry vermouth
½ oz. sweet vermouth

Stir with ice and strain into chilled cocktail glass.

☐ THE BEAUTIFUL DAY

Created by TED HENWOOD, New York, NY

More and more bartenders are paying attention to the sustainable agriculture movement with seasonal drinks. When spring comes around and rhurbarb is at its peak, offer this cocktail.

1¼ oz. Irish whiskey
¾ oz. Rhubarb Syrup (page 26)
2 oz. cold brewed green tea
Garnish: Edible flowers

Shake with ice and strain into ice-filled old-fashioned glass. Garnish with edible flowers.

WHISKIES

BENSONHURST

Created by CHAD SOLOMON,
New York, NY

1 splash Cynar
2 oz. straight rye whiskey
1 oz. dry vermouth
¼ oz. maraschino liqueur

*Swirl Cynar in chilled
cocktail glass to coat inside;
discard excess Cynar. Stir
remaining ingredients with
ice and strain into glass.*

BLACK HAWK

1½ oz. bourbon whiskey
1½ oz. sloe gin
Garnish: Maraschino cherry

*Stir with ice and strain
into chilled cocktail glass.
Garnish with cherry.*

BLARNEY STONE
COCKTAIL

2 oz. Irish whiskey
½ oz. anisette
½ oz. triple sec
½ oz. maraschino liqueur
1 dash Angostura bitters
Garnish: Orange twist, green
olive

*Shake with ice and strain
into chilled cocktail glass.
Add orange twist and olive.*

THE BLINKER

The original recipe, published in
1934, used grenadine, but the
raspberry syrup complements
the grapefruit better. In this
recipe, a thick ice-cream
topping syrup is preferable
to the thin beverage flavoring
syrup.

2 oz. straight rye whisky
1½ oz. fresh grapefruit juice
1 tsp. raspberry syrup
Garnish: Grapefruit twist or
skewered raspberry

*Shake and strain into
cocktail glass. Garnish
with grapefruit twist or
raspberry.*

BLOOD AND SAND

Blood and Sand, the iconic
bullfighter movie, was made
first in 1922 with Rudolph
Valentino. The cocktail's color
will give you a hint to how the
drink got its name.

½ oz. blended Scotch
whisky
½ oz. cherry-flavored
brandy
½ oz. sweet vermouth
½ oz. fresh orange juice

*Shake with ice and strain
into chilled cocktail glass.*

BLOODY SCOTSMAN

Created by JONATHAN
POGASH, New York, NY

A busy barkeeper (or organized
home bartender serving a big
brunch) will make up large
batches of morning cocktails to
get a head start on serving. This
great variation on the Bloody
Mary theme uses Scotch to give
it a smoky note.

Makes 14 to 16 servings

24 oz. smoky Scotch whisky,
   such as Laphroaig
24. oz. tomato juice
24 oz. V8 cocktail juice
1 c. ketchup
3 oz. fresh lime juice
3 oz. simple syrup
¾ oz. Worcestershire sauce
1 tsp. freshly ground white
   pepper
1 tsp. freshly ground black
   pepper
⅛ tsp. cayenne pepper
Fine sea salt

*Mix ingredients together,
stirring often, in a large container, adding salt to taste.
Chill for at least 24 hours
before serving. Serve in ice-
filled old-fashioned glasses.*

BOBBY BURNS
COCKTAIL

Mr. Burns, a cigar salesman,
was such a good customer at
the old Waldorf bar in the late
nineteenth century that the
establishment named this drink
after him . . . probably.

1½ oz. blended Scotch whisky
1½ oz. sweet vermouth
1 tsp. Bénédictine
Garnish: Lemon twist

*Stir with ice and strain into
chilled cocktail glass. Add
lemon twist.*

THE BONE

2 oz. bourbon whiskey
½ oz. fresh lime juice
½ oz. simple syrup
3 dashes hot red pepper sauce

*Shake with ice and strain
into chilled shot glass.*

BOURBON À LA CRÈME

2 oz. bourbon whiskey
1 oz. dark crème de cacao
½ oz. vanilla liqueur

*Stir ingredients with ice.
Strain into chilled old-
fashioned glass.*

BOURBON COOLER

2½ oz. bourbon whiskey
½ oz. fresh lemon juice
½ oz. fresh grapefruit juice
½ oz. orgeat syrup
Garnish: Peach slice

*Shake with ice in mixing
glass. Pour with ice into
old-fashioned glass. Garnish
with peach.*

▽ BOURBON CRUSTA

For glass: Lemon wedge,
 superfine sugar
Long, wide spiral of orange
 zest (see page 10)
2 oz. bourbon whiskey
½ oz. triple sec
1 tsp. maraschino liqueur
1 tsp. fresh lemon juice
2 dashes orange bitters

*Rim chilled cocktail glass
with lemon and sugar. Curl
the zest spiral in glass. Stir
remaining ingredients with
ice and strain into glass.*

▢ BOURBON AND ELDER

2 oz. bourbon whiskey
¾ oz. elderflower liqueur
1 dash Angostura bitters
Garnish: Lemon twist

*Stir with ice and strain into
chilled old-fashioned glass.
Add lemon twist.*

▢ BOURBON HIGHBALL

2 oz. bourbon whiskey
Ginger ale or soda water
Garnish: Lemon twist

*Pour whiskey into ice-filled
highball glass. Fill with
ginger ale or soda water and
stir. Add lemon twist.*

▢ BOURBON RENEWAL

2 oz. bourbon whiskey
1 oz. fresh lemon juice
½ oz. crème de cassis
½ oz. simple syrup
1 dash Angostura bitters

*Shake with ice. Strain into
ice-filled old-fashioned glass.*

▢ BRIGHTON PUNCH

¾ oz. bourbon whiskey
¾ oz. brandy
¾ oz. Bénédictine
2 oz. fresh orange juice
1 oz. fresh lemon juice
Soda water
Garnish: Orange and lemon
 wheels

*Shake first five ingredients
with ice and pour with
ice into Collins glass. Fill
with soda water and stir
gently. Garnish with orange
and lemon and serve with
a straw.*

▽ BROOKLYN

1½ oz. rye or bourbon
 whiskey
½ oz. sweet vermouth
1 dash Amer Picon or Torani
 Amer
1 dash maraschino liqueur

*Stir with ice and strain into
chilled cocktail glass.*

▽ BULL AND BEAR

1½ oz. bourbon whiskey
¾ oz. orange curaçao
1 oz. fresh lemon juice
¼ oz. grenadine
Garnish: Maraschino cherry,
 orange half-wheel

*Shake with ice and strain
into chilled cocktail glass.
Garnish with cherry and
orange.*

...LGRAM

.. bourbon whiskey
1 oz. fresh lemon juice
½ oz. simple syrup
Ginger ale

Stir first three ingredients in ice-filled highball glass. Fill with ginger ale.

CALIFORNIA LEMONADE

2 oz. bourbon whiskey
1 oz. fresh lemon juice
1 oz. fresh lime juice
1 oz. simple syrup
¼ oz. grenadine
Soda water
Garnish: Orange and lemon wheels, maraschino cherry

Shake first five ingredients with ice. Strain into shaved ice–filled Collins glass. Fill with soda water and garnish with orange, lemon, and cherry. Serve with straws.

CAMERON'S KICK COCKTAIL

¾ oz. blended Scotch whisky
¾ oz. Irish whiskey
½ oz. fresh lemon juice
2 dashes orange bitters

Shake with ice and strain into chilled cocktail glass.

CANADIAN BREEZE

1½ oz. Canadian whisky
¾ oz. pineapple juice
½ oz. fresh lemon juice
¼ oz. maraschino liqueur
Garnish: Pineapple wedge, maraschino cherry

Shake with ice. Strain into ice-filled old-fashioned glass. Garnish with pineapple and cherry.

YOU'RE IN CHARGE

Ignore absolutes, as well as recipes that say this is the "only" way to make this drink. The best way is the way that works best for you. This also means that just because somebody passes on a tip, rule, or recipe to you, doesn't mean you should assume it is really the right way to do it. As the bartender, you should be the one to decide what really works.

—ROBERT HESS (aka DrinkBoy),
Mixology Research Engineer

CANADIAN CHERRY

For glass: Maraschino liqueur
1½ oz. Canadian whisky
½ oz. maraschino liqueur
½ oz. fresh lemon juice
½ oz. fresh orange juice

Moisten rim of old-fashioned glass with maraschino liqueur. Fill with ice. Shake ingredients with ice and strain into glass.

CANADIAN COCKTAIL

1½ oz. Canadian whisky
½ oz. triple sec
½ oz. simple syrup
1 dash Angostura bitters

Shake with ice and strain into chilled cocktail glass.

CANAL STREET DAISY

1 oz. blended Scotch whisky
1 oz. fresh orange juice
¾ oz. fresh lemon juice
Soda water
Garnish: Orange wheel

Add Scotch and juices to ice-filled Collins glass and stir. Fill with soda water and stir again. Garnish with orange.

CARRÉ REPRISE

1 oz. straight rye whiskey
1 oz. Cognac
1 oz. sweet vermouth
½ oz. elderflower liqueur
1 dash Angostura bitters
1 dash Peychaud's bitters
Garnish: Lemon twist

Stir with ice. Strain into ice-filled old-fashioned glass. Add lemon twist.

CHANCELLOR COCKTAIL

1½ oz. blended Scotch whisky
½ oz. dry vermouth
½ oz. tawny port
1 dash Peychaud's bitters
Garnish: Lemon twist

Stir with ice and strain into chilled cocktail glass. Add lemon twist.

CHAPEL HILL

2 oz. bourbon whiskey
½ oz. triple sec
½ oz. fresh lemon juice
Garnish: Orange twist

Shake with ice and strain into chilled cocktail glass. Add orange twist.

CHAPLIN

¾ oz. bourbon whiskey
¾ oz. dry sherry
¾ oz. Ramazzotti Amaro
1 tsp. triple sec
2 dashes orange bitters
Garnish: Lemon twist

Stir with ice and strain into chilled cocktail glass. Add lemon twist.

CHARACTER DEVELOPMENT

Created by HAL WOLIN, New York, NY

2 oz. Scotch whiskey
½ oz. coconut liqueur
½ oz. dry sherry
2 dashes grapefruit bitters
Garnish: Grapefruit twist

Stir with ice and strain into chilled cocktail glass. Add grapefruit twist.

▽ CHAS

1½ oz. bourbon whiskey
¼ oz. amaretto
¼ oz. Bénédictine
¼ oz. triple sec
¼ oz. orange curaçao
Garnish: Orange twist

Stir with ice and strain into chilled cocktail glass. Add orange twist.

▽ CHEF'S PAIN

2 oz. bourbon whiskey
¾ oz. fresh lime juice
½ oz. blackberry liqueur
½ oz. B & B

Shake with ice and strain into chilled cocktail glass.

▢ CHI-TOWN FLIP

2 oz. bourbon whiskey
¾ oz. tawny port
¾ oz. fresh lemon juice
¾ oz. vanilla liqueur
¼ oz. simple syrup
1 whole egg
3 drops Angostura bitters
Garnish: Freshly grated nutmeg

Shake first six ingredients without ice. Add ice and shake again. Strain into ice-filled Collins glass. Add bitters and top with nutmeg.

▢ COFFEE OLD-FASHIONED

2 oz. bourbon whiskey
¾ oz. simple syrup
2 dashes Angostura bitters
½ cup cold brewed coffee
2 oz. soda water
Garnish: Orange wheel, maraschino cherry

Pour bourbon, syrup, bitters, and coffee into ice-filled old-fashioned glass and stir. Add soda water and stir again. Garnish with orange and cherry.

COMMODORE COCKTAIL

The whiskey used in this recipe has a higher-than-average proportion of rye than usual bourbons, but any rye or bourbon will do.

2 oz. 1792 Ridgemont Reserve Bourbon Whiskey
¾ oz. white crème de cacao
½ oz. fresh lemon juice
1 dash grenadine

Shake with ice and strain into chilled champagne flute.

☐ COTTON CLUB FLIP

Created by DUANE FERNANDEZ,
Jr., New York, NY

Buy some packaged cotton
candy for this cocktail's garnish,
or skip the candy and garnish
with an edible flower.

2 oz. Vanilla-Infused Bourbon
  (recipe follows)
½ oz. Honey-Currant Syrup
  (recipe follows)
¾ oz. fresh lime juice
1 egg white
2 dashes rhubarb bitters
Garnish: Stick of cotton candy

*Shake first four ingredients
without ice. Add ice and
shake again. Strain into ice-
filled old-fashioned glass. Top
with bitters. Garnish with
cotton candy.*

VANILLA-INFUSED BOURBON

*Split 3 Tahitian vanilla
beans lengthwise. Insert into
750-ml bottle of bourbon.
Close bottle and let stand at
room temperature for 3 to 5
days. Remove vanilla beans.
Store bourbon at room temperature for up to 1 month.*

HONEY-CURRANT SYRUP

*Bring 1 cup honey, ½
cup dried currants, and
¼ cup water to a simmer
over medium heat in small
saucepan, stirring to dissolve
honey. Simmer over low
heat for 10 minutes. Remove
from heat and let cool.
Strain into jar, cover, and
refrigerate for up to 3 weeks.*

☖ CREOLE LADY

1½ oz. bourbon whiskey
1½ oz. madeira
1 tsp. grenadine
Garnish: Maraschino cherry

*Stir with ice and strain
into chilled cocktail glass.
Garnish with cherry.*

☐ DAISY DUELLER

2 oz. Tennessee whiskey
¾ oz. fresh lemon juice
¾ oz. simple syrup
½ oz. triple sec
Soda water
Garnish: Orange and lemon
  wheels

*Shake first four ingredients
with ice. Strain into chilled
highball glass. Add ice and
fill with soda. Garnish with
orange and lemon.*

☖ THE DEBONAIR

2½ oz. single-malt Scotch
  whisky
1 oz. ginger liqueur
Garnish: Lemon twist

*Stir and strain into chilled
cocktail glass. Add lemon
twist.*

☖ DE LA LOUISIANE

¾ oz. straight rye whiskey
¾ oz. sweet vermouth
¾ oz. Bénédictine
3 dashes absinthe or pastis
3 dashes Peychaud's bitters
Garnish: Maraschino cherry

*Stir with ice and strain
into chilled cocktail glass.
Garnish with cherry.*

☐ THE DELMARVA COCKTAIL

2 oz. straight rye whiskey
½ oz. dry vermouth
½ oz. white crème de menthe
½ oz. fresh lemon juice
Garnish: Fresh mint sprig

Shake with ice and strain into chilled cocktail glass. Garnish with mint.

☐ DERBY

2 oz. bourbon whiskey
¼ oz. Bénédictine
1 dash Angostura bitters
Garnish: Lemon twist

Stir with ice and strain into chilled cocktail glass. Add lemon twist.

☐ DESHLER

1½ oz. straight rye whiskey
½ oz. Dubonnet Rouge
¼ oz. triple sec
2 dashes Angostura bitters
Garnish: Lemon twist

Stir with ice and strain into chilled champagne flute. Add lemon twist.

☐ DEVIL'S SOUL

Created by TED KILGORE,
St. Louis, MO

1½ oz. straight rye whiskey
½ oz. mezcal
½ oz. amaro, such as
   Ramazzotti or Averna
¼ oz. Aperol
¼ oz. elderflower liqueur
Garnish: Orange twist, flamed

Stir with ice and strain into cocktail glass. Flame orange twist and add to glass.

☐ DINAH COCKTAIL

1½ oz. bourbon whiskey
¾ oz. fresh lemon juice
½ oz. simple syrup
Garnish: Fresh mint leaf

Shake well with ice and strain into chilled cocktail glass. Garnish with mint.

☐ DIRTY HARRY

1 splash absinthe
2 oz. straight rye whiskey
½ oz. sweet vermouth
¼ oz. maraschino liqueur
Garnish: Maraschino cherry

Swirl absinthe in chilled cocktail glass to coat inside; discard excess absinthe. Stir remaining ingredients with ice and strain into glass. Garnish with cherry.

☐ DIXIE WHISKEY COCKTAIL

2 oz. bourbon whiskey
½ oz. white crème de menthe
¼ oz, triple sec
¼ oz. simple syrup
1 dash Angostura bitters

Shake with ice and strain into chilled cocktail glass.

DOUBLE STANDARD SOUR

¾ oz. rye or bourbon whiskey
¾ oz. gin
1 oz. fresh lemon juice
½ tsp. white crème de menthe
½ oz. grenadine
¼ oz. simple syrup
Garnish: Lemon half-wheel, maraschino cherry

Shake with ice and strain into chilled cocktail glass. Garnish with lemon and cherry.

DUBLINER

2 oz. Irish whiskey
½ oz. sweet vermouth
½ oz. Grand Marnier
2 dashes orange bitters
Garnish: Orange twist, flamed

Stir with ice and strain into chilled cocktail glass. Flame orange twist and add.

THE DUBOUDREAU COCKTAIL

Created by JIM MEEHAN, New York City, NY, in honor of bartender Jamie Boudreau, Seattle, WA

2 oz. straight rye whiskey
¾ oz. Dubonnet Rouge
¼ oz. Fernet-Branca
¼ oz. elderflower liqueur
Garnish: Lemon twist

Stir with ice and strain into chilled cocktail glass. Add lemon twist.

DUFFTOWN FLIP

2 oz. blended Scotch whisky
½ oz. port
½ oz. Demerara Syrup (page 25)
½ oz. almond milk
1 whole egg
Garnish: Freshly grated nutmeg

Shake without ice. Then shake with ice and strain into snifter. Top with nutmeg.

WHISKIES

EASTER ELCHIES

2 oz. single-malt Scotch whisky
½ oz. Cherry Heering
½ oz. Punt e Mes
1 dash orange bitters
Garnish: Brandied cherry

Stir with ice and strain into chilled cocktail glass. Garnish with brandied cherry.

EASTERN SOUR

2 oz. bourbon whiskey
1½ oz. fresh orange juice
1 oz. fresh lime juice
¼ oz. orgeat or almond syrup
¼ oz. simple syrup
Garnish: Orange and lime wheels

Shake with ice and strain into ice-filled highball glass. Garnish with orange and lime.

♇ EASTERNER

2 oz. straight rye whiskey
1 oz. fresh grapefruit juice
½ oz. maple syrup
Garnish: Grapefruit twist

*Shake with ice and strain
into chilled cocktail glass.
Add grapefruit twist.*

▢ EMPEROR NORTON'S MISTRESS

Emperor Norton was a famous
eccentric of San Francisco's
post–Gold Rush period.

3 fresh strawberries, cut in
   halves
1½ oz. bourbon whiskey
½ oz. vanilla liqueur
¼ oz. triple sec
Garnish: Strawberry slice

*Muddle halved strawber-
ries in mixing glass. Add
remaining ingredients.
Shake with ice and
double-strain into ice-filled
old-fashioned glass. Garnish
with strawberry slice.*

♇ EVERYBODY'S IRISH COCKTAIL

2 oz. Irish whiskey
1 tsp. green crème
   de menthe
1 tsp. green Chartreuse
Garnish: Green olive

*Stir with ice and strain
into chilled cocktail glass.
Garnish with olive.*

♇ FANCY-FREE COCKTAIL

2 oz. bourbon whiskey
½ oz. maraschino liqueur
1 dash Angostura bitters
1 dash orange bitters

*Stir with ice and strain into
chilled cocktail glass.*

♇ FANCY WHISKEY

2 oz. bourbon or rye whiskey
1 dash Angostura bitters
¼ oz. triple sec
¼ oz. simple syrup
Garnish: Lemon twist

*Shake with ice and strain
into chilled cocktail glass.
Add lemon twist.*

♇ THE FINAL WARD

¾ oz. straight rye whiskey
¾ oz. maraschino liqueur
¾ oz. green Chartreuse
¾ oz. fresh lemon juice

*Shake with ice and strain
into chilled cocktail glass.*

♇ FLYING SCOTCHMAN

1 oz. blended Scotch whisky
1 oz. sweet vermouth
1 dash Angostura bitters
¼ oz. simple syrup

*Stir with ice and strain into
chilled cocktail glass.*

♇ FOX RIVER COCKTAIL

2 oz. bourbon or rye whiskey
½ oz. dark crème de cacao
4 dashes Angostura bitters

*Stir with ice and strain into
chilled cocktail glass.*

FRANCIS THE MULE

2 oz. bourbon whiskey
½ oz. coffee liqueur
½ oz. fresh lemon juice
¼ oz. orgeat or almond syrup
2 dashes orange bitters
Garnish: Lemon twist

Shake with ice and strain into chilled cocktail glass. Add lemon twist.

FRATELLI COCKTAIL

2 oz. straight rye whiskey
½ oz. sweet vermouth
½ oz. yellow Chartreuse
¼ oz. Fernet-Branca

Stir with ice and strain into chilled cocktail glass.

FRISCO SOUR

2 oz. bourbon or rye whiskey
¾ oz. fresh lemon juice
½ oz. fresh lime juice
½ oz. Bénédictine
Garnish: Lemon and lime wheels

Shake with ice and strain into chilled sour glass. Garnish with lemon and lime.

GILCHRIST

1¼ oz. blended Scotch whisky
¾ oz. pear brandy
¾ oz. fresh grapefruit juice
½ oz. amaro, such as Averna
2 dashes grapefruit bitters
Garnish: Lemon twist

Shake with ice and strain into chilled cocktail glass. Add lemon twist.

GODFATHER

1½ oz. blended Scotch whisky
¾ oz. amaretto

Pour into ice-filled old-fashioned glass and stir.

GOLDRUSH

2 oz. bourbon whiskey
¾ oz. fresh lemon juice
1 oz. Honey Syrup (page 25)

Shake and strain into ice-filled old-fashioned glass.

GRANDFATHER

1 oz. bourbon whiskey
1 oz. applejack
1 oz. sweet vermouth
1 dash Angostura bitters
1 dash Peychaud's bitters
Garnish: Maraschino cherry

Stir with ice and strain into chilled cocktail glass. Garnish with cherry.

GREENPOINT

Created by MICHAEL McILROY, New York, NY

2 oz. straight rye whiskey
½ oz. yellow Chartreuse
½ oz. sweet vermouth
1 dash Angostura bitters
1 dash orange bitters
Garnish: Lemon twist

Stir with ice and strain into chilled cocktail glass. Add lemon twist.

WHISKIES

♆ GROUNDS FOR DIVORCE

1½ oz. straight rye whiskey
¾ oz. kirschwasser
¼ oz. Cynar
½ oz. amaro, such as Averna
Garnish: Orange twist

Stir and strain into chilled cocktail glass. Add orange twist.

♆ HARVEST MOON

1½ oz. straight rye whiskey
1 oz. Lillet Blanc
½ oz. apple brandy
¼ oz. green Chartreuse
2 dashes Angostura bitters
Garnish: Orange twist

Stir with ice and strain into chilled cocktail glass. Add orange twist.

♆ HEATHER BLUSH

1 oz. blended Scotch whisky
1 oz. strawberry liqueur
3 oz. chilled sparkling wine
Garnish: Whole strawberry

Pour Scotch and liqueur into chilled champagne flute. Top with sparkling wine. Garnish with strawberry.

♆ HEATHER'S KISS

Created by BLAIR FRODELIUS, Syracuse, NY

2¼ oz. blended Scotch whisky
½ oz. fresh lemon juice
¼ oz. agave nectar
1 tsp. absinthe
Garnish: Apple slice

Shake with ice strain into chilled cocktail glass. Garnish with apple slice.

♆ HEAVENLY DRAM

2 oz. single-malt Scotch whisky
½ oz. Pedro Ximénez sherry
¾ oz. fresh lemon juice
¼ oz. Honey Syrup (page 25)
Garnish: Lemon twist

Shake with ice and strain into chilled cocktail glass. Add lemon twist.

♆ HEBRIDES

1½ oz. single-malt Scotch whisky
½ oz. maraschino liqueur
½ oz. triple sec
2 oz. apple juice
½ oz. fresh lemon juice
1 dash Angostura bitters

Pour into ice-filled Collins glass and stir.

♆ HIGH COTTON

2 oz. straight rye whiskey
½ oz. Pimm's No. 1 Cup
½ oz. Dubonnet Rouge
2 dashes peach bitters
Garnish: Lemon twist, fresh mint sprig

Stir with ice and strain into chilled cocktail glass. Garnish with lemon and mint.

HIGHLAND COOLER

2 oz. blended Scotch
  whisky
½ oz. simple syrup
Soda water or ginger ale
Garnish: Lemon and/or
  orange zest spiral(s)

*Stir Scotch and syrup in
Collins glass. Add ice. Fill
with soda and stir again.
Insert citrus spiral(s) and
dangle end(s) over rim of
glass.*

HILL DOG

Created by CARLOS CUERTA,
Chicago, IL

White whiskey is none other
than moonshine or white
lightning, which isn't colored
because it hasn't been aged in
wood.

1½ oz. white whiskey
½ oz. Grand Marnier
½ oz. dry sherry
½ oz. Lavender Syrup
  (page 26)
Garnish: Orange twist

*Stir with ice and strain into
chilled cocktail glass. Add
orange twist.*

HOLE-IN-ONE

1¾ oz. blended Scotch
  whisky
¾ oz. dry vermouth
¼ oz fresh lemon juice
1 dash orange bitters

*Shake with ice and strain
into chilled cocktail glass.*

HOOT MON COCKTAIL

1½ oz. blended Scotch whisky
¾ oz. sweet vermouth
1 tsp. Bénédictine
Garnish: Lemon twist

*Stir with ice and strain into
chilled cocktail glass. Add
lemon twist.*

HORSE'S NECK (WITH A KICK)

The Horse's Neck was originally
a soft drink with iced ginger
ale garnished with lots of
lemon peel. At some point
in its history, an enterprising
bartender added bourbon (or
brandy) to give it a "kick."

1 long, wide spiral of lemon
  zest (see page 10)
2 oz. bourbon whiskey
Ginger ale

*Insert the lemon spiral in
Collins glass with one end
hanging over the rim. Fill
glass with ice cubes. Add
whiskey. Fill with ginger ale
and stir well.*

HOTEL D'ALSACE

1 fresh rosemary sprig
2 oz. Irish whiskey
½ oz. Bénédictine
½ oz. triple sec

*Muddle leaves from half-
sprig of rosemary in mixing
glass and reserve the other
half. Add remaining ingredients. Stir with ice and strain
into ice-filled old-fashioned
glass. Garnish with remaining half-sprig of rosemary.*

WHISKIES

I.A.P.

2 oz. Tennessee whiskey
¼ oz. Fernet-Branca
3 oz. cola

Build in ice-filled Collins glass.

IMPERIAL FIZZ

1½ oz. bourbon or rye
  whiskey
½ oz. light rum
1 oz. fresh lemon juice
½ oz. simple syrup
Soda water

Shake first four ingredients with ice and strain into ice-filled highball glass. Fill with soda water and stir.

INCIDER COCKTAIL

1½ oz. rye or bourbon
  whiskey
4 oz. apple cider
Garnish: Apple slice

Stir whiskey and apple cider in ice-filled old-fashioned glass. Garnish with apple.

IRISH RICKEY

1½ oz. Irish whiskey
½ oz. fresh lime juice
Soda water
Garnish: Lime wedge

Pour whiskey and lime juice into ice-filled highball glass. Fill with soda water and stir. Garnish with lime.

IRISH SHILLELAGH

1½ oz. Irish whiskey
1 oz. light rum
½ oz. sloe gin
1 oz. fresh lemon juice
½ oz. simple syrup
Garnish: Fresh raspberries
  and strawberries, 2 peach
  slices, maraschino
  cherry

Shake with ice and strain into ice-filled Irish coffee glass. Garnish with berries, peach slices, and cherry.

IRISH WHISKEY COCKTAIL

2 oz. Irish whiskey
½ tsp. triple sec
½ tsp. anisette
¼ oz. maraschino liqueur
1 dash Angostura bitters
Garnish: Green olive

Stir with ice and strain into chilled cocktail glass. Garnish with olive.

IRISH WHISKEY HIGHBALL

2 oz. Irish whiskey
Ginger ale or soda water
Garnish: Lemon twist
  (optional)

Pour whiskey into ice-filled highball glass. Fill with ginger ale or soda water. Add lemon twist, if desired, and stir.

WHISKIES

JITTERBUG SOUR

2 oz. straight rye whiskey
½ oz. Bénédictine
¾ oz. fresh lemon juice
½ oz. Honey Syrup
  (page 25)
1 egg white
1 dash Angostura bitters
Garnish: Lemon twist

Shake first five ingredients with ice and strain into chilled cocktail glass. Add bitters and lemon twist.

JOCOSE JULEP

2½ oz. bourbon whiskey
½ oz. green crème
  de menthe
1 oz. fresh lime juice
½ oz. simple syrup
5 fresh mint leaves
Soda water
Garnish: Fresh mint sprig

Combine first five ingredients in blender without ice until smooth. Pour into ice-filled Collins glass. Fill with soda water and stir. Garnish with mint sprig.

THE JOE LEWIS

Created by CHRIS PATINO, New York, NY

1½ oz. Scotch whisky
1 oz. fresh carrot juice
¾ oz. tawny port
½ oz. fresh lemon juice
1 tsp. agave nectar

Shake with ice and strain into chilled cocktail glass.

JOHN COLLINS

2 oz. bourbon whiskey
1 oz. fresh lemon juice
½ oz. simple syrup
Soda water
Garnish: Orange and lemon
  wheels, maraschino cherry

Shake first three ingredients with ice and strain into Collins glass. Add ice, fill with soda water, and stir. Garnish with orange, lemon, and cherry. Serve with straws.

KEEGAN

1 oz. bourbon whiskey
¾ oz. Aperol
½ oz. yellow Chartreuse
¾ oz. fresh lime juice

Shake with ice and strain into chilled cocktail glass.

KENTUCKY BLIZZARD

1½ oz. bourbon whiskey
1½ oz. cranberry juice
½ oz. fresh lime juice
½ oz. grenadine
½ oz simple syrup
Garnish: Orange half-wheel

Shake ingredients with ice. Strain into chilled cocktail (or ice-filled old-fashioned) glass. Garnish with orange.

KENTUCKY COCKTAIL

1½ oz. 1792 Ridgemont
  Reserve Bourbon Whiskey
¾ oz. pineapple juice

Shake with ice and strain into chilled cocktail glass.

KENTUCKY COLONEL COCKTAIL

2 oz. bourbon whiskey
1 oz. Bénédictine
Garnish: Lemon twist

Stir with ice and strain into chilled cocktail glass. Add lemon twist.

THE KENTUCKY LONGSHOT

2 oz. bourbon whiskey
½ oz. ginger liqueur
½ oz. peach-flavored brandy
1 dash Angostura bitters
1 dash Peychaud's bitters
Garnish: Candied ginger slice

Stir with ice and strain into chilled cocktail glass. Garnish with candied ginger perched on the rim of the glass.

KING COLE COCKTAIL

1 orange wheel
1 pineapple wedge, peeled
¼ oz. simple syrup
2 oz. rye or bourbon whiskey

Muddle first three ingredients well in old-fashioned glass. Add whiskey and ice. Stir.

KISS ON THE LIPS

2 oz. bourbon whiskey
6 oz. apricot nectar

Pour into ice-filled Collins glass and stir. Serve with straw.

KLONDIKE COOLER

2 oz. bourbon whiskey
¼ oz simple syrup
Soda water or ginger ale
Garnish: Orange and/or lemon zest spiral(s)

Stir bourbon and syrup in Collins glass. Add ice. Fill with soda and stir again. Insert citrus spiral(s) and dangle end(s) over rim of glass.

LADIES' COCKTAIL

1¾ oz. bourbon whiskey
1 tsp. anisette
2 dashes Angostura bitters
Garnish: Pineapple wedge

Stir with ice and strain into chilled cocktail glass. Garnish with pineapple.

LA TAVOLA ROTONDA

1½ oz. bourbon whiskey
¾ oz. pineapple juice
½ oz. Campari
½ oz. amaro, such as Ramazzotti or Averna
½ oz. maraschino liqueur
2 dashes Peychaud's bitters
Garnish: Maraschino cherry

Shake with ice and strain into chilled cocktail glass. Garnish with cherry.

LAWHILL COCKTAIL

1½ oz. straight rye whiskey
¾ oz. dry vermouth
¼ oz. maraschino liqueur
¼ oz. anisette
1 dash Angostura bitters

Stir with ice and strain into chilled cocktail glass.

☐ LIBERAL

1½ oz. straight rye whiskey
½ oz. sweet vermouth
¼ oz. Amer Picon or Torani
   Amer
1 dash orange bitters
Garnish: Orange twist

*Stir with ice and strain into
chilled cocktail glass. Add
orange twist.*

☐ LIMESTONE COCKTAIL

1½ oz. bourbon whiskey
1 oz. fresh lemon juice
½ oz. simple syrup
Soda water

*Stir first three ingredients in
ice-filled highball glass. Fill
with soda water; stir again.*

☐ LINSTEAD COCKTAIL

1½ oz. bourbon whiskey
¾ oz. pineapple juice
½ oz. simple syrup
1 tsp. anisette
½ tsp. fresh lemon juice

*Shake with ice and strain
into chilled cocktail glass.*

☐ LOCH LOMOND

1 oz. blended Scotch whisky
1 oz. blue curaçao
½ oz. peach schnapps
3 oz. fresh grapefruit juice
½ oz. fresh lemon juice
Garnish: Star fruit slice

*Shake ingredients with ice
and strain into ice-filled
hurricane or parfait glass.
Garnish with star fruit.*

☐ LOUISVILLE COOLER

1½ oz. 1792 Ridgemont
   Reserve Bourbon
   Whiskey
1 oz. fresh orange juice
½ oz. fresh lime juice
½ oz. simple syrup
Garnish: Orange half-wheel

*Shake ingredients with ice.
Strain into old-fashioned
glass over fresh ice. Garnish
with orange.*

WHISKIES

☐ LOUISVILLE LADY

1 oz. bourbon whiskey
¾ oz. white crème de cacao
¾ oz. heavy cream or half-
   and-half

*Shake with ice and strain
into chilled cocktail glass.*

☐ MAGNOLIA MAIDEN

1¼ oz. bourbon whiskey
1¼ oz. Mandarine Napoléon
1 splash simple syrup
1 splash soda water

*Shake bourbon, Mandarine
Napoléon, and syrup with
ice. Strain into ice-filled
old-fashioned glass. Top with
soda water.*

☐ MAMIE GILROY

2 oz. blended Scotch whisky
½ oz. fresh lime juice
Ginger ale

*Stir Scotch and lime juice in
ice-filled Collins glass. Top
with ginger ale and stir.*

∀ MANHASSET

1½ oz. bourbon whiskey
¾ oz. dry vermouth
¾ oz. sweet vermouth
½ oz. fresh lemon juice

*Shake with ice and strain
into chilled cocktail glass.*

∀ MANHATTAN

For more on the Manhattan,
see page 31.

2 oz. rye or bourbon whiskey
½ oz. sweet vermouth
1 dash Angostura bitters
Garnish: Maraschino cherry

*Stir with ice and strain
into chilled cocktail glass.
Garnish with cherry.*

∀ MANHATTAN (DRY)

For a perfect Manhattan, use ¼
oz. each dry and sweet vermouth.

2 oz. rye or bourbon whiskey
½ oz. dry vermouth
1 dash Angostura bitters
Garnish: Maraschino cherry

*Stir with ice and strain
into chilled cocktail glass.
Garnish with cherry.*

∀ THE MANUSCRIPT

Created by CHAD MICHAEL
GEORGE, Clayton, MO

1½ oz. straight rye whiskey
¾ oz. cherry brandy
½ oz. fresh lemon juice
½ oz. simple syrup
1 oz. chilled Champagne
Garnish: Orange twist, flamed

*Shake first four ingredients
with ice. Strain into chilled
cocktail glass. Top with
Champagne. Flame orange
twist and add.*

∀ MCCOY

1½ oz. Irish whiskey
½ oz. dry sherry
¼ oz. Tuaca
2 dashes peach bitters
Garnish: Orange twist

*Stir with ice and strain into
chilled champagne flute. Add
orange twist.*

QUALITY, NOT QUANTITY

There is no substitute for quality. Just as you can't build
a Ferrari out of Ford parts, you only get out of a cocktail
what you put into it.

—TONY ABOU GANIM (aka The Modern
Mixologist), host of the Fine Living Network's
Raising the Bar: America's Best Bar Chefs

MIAMI BEACH COCKTAIL

¾ oz. blended Scotch whisky
¾ oz. dry vermouth
¾ oz. fresh grapefruit juice

Shake with ice and strain into chilled cocktail glass.

MINT JULEP

Follow this advice from Frances Parkinson Keyes: "Never insult a decent woman, never bring a horse into the house, and never crush the mint in a julep."

½ oz. simple syrup
2½ oz. bourbon whiskey
Garnish: 5 fresh mint sprigs

Pour syrup into silver julep cup, silver mug, or Collins glass. Fill with shaved or crushed ice and add bourbon. Stir until glass is heavily frosted, adding more ice if necessary. (Do not hold glass with hand while stirring.) Garnish with mint so that the tops are about 2 inches above rim of glass. Use short straws so that it will be necessary to bury nose in mint, which is intended for scent rather than taste.

MODERN COCKTAIL

1½ oz. blended Scotch whisky
½ tsp. Jamaican rum
¼ oz. anisette
½ tsp. fresh lemon juice
1 dash orange bitters
Garnish: Maraschino cherry

Shake with ice and strain into chilled cocktail glass. Garnish with cherry.

MONTE CARLO

2 oz. straight rye whiskey
½ oz. Bénédictine
2 dashes Angostura bitters

Stir with ice and strain into chilled cocktail glass.

MOTO GUZZI

1½ oz. bourbon whiskey
1½ oz. Punt e Mes

Stir with ice and strain into chilled cocktail glass.

NARRAGANSETT

1 splash anisette
1½ oz. bourbon whiskey
1 oz. sweet vermouth
Garnish: Lemon twist

Swirl anisette in old-fashioned glass to coat inside. Add ice, then whiskey and vermouth and stir. Add lemon twist.

NEVINS

1½ oz. bourbon whiskey
¾ oz. apricot-flavored brandy
½ oz. fresh grapefruit juice
½ oz. fresh lemon juice
1 dash Angostura bitters

Shake with ice and strain into chilled cocktail glass.

WHISKIES

⚗ NEW YORK COCKTAIL

Sometimes called the New Yorker, this is a reminder that rye was once the whiskey of choice in the Big Apple.

1½ oz. straight rye whiskey
¾ oz. fresh lemon juice
¼ oz. simple syrup
¼ oz. grenadine
Garnish: Lemon twist

Shake with ice and strain into chilled cocktail glass. Add lemon twist.

NEW YORK FLIP

2 oz. straight rye whiskey
¾ oz. tawny port
¾ oz. Demerara Syrup (page 25)
1 oz. heavy cream
1 whole egg
Garnish: Freshly grated nutmeg

Shake without ice. Then shake with ice and strain into chilled champagne flute. Top with nutmeg.

NEW YORK SOUR

2 oz. rye or bourbon whiskey
¾ oz. fresh lemon juice
¾ oz. simple syrup
1 oz. red wine
Garnish: Lemon half-wheel, maraschino cherry

Shake first three ingredients with ice. Strain into ice-filled old-fashioned glass. Float red wine (see page 18) on top. Garnish with lemon and cherry.

NUTCRACKER

2 oz. bourbon whiskey
½ oz. hazelnut liqueur
½ oz. amaretto
½ oz. orgeat or almond syrup
¾ oz. fresh lemon juice
1 egg white
Garnish: Freshly grated nutmeg

Shake without ice. Shake with ice and strain into ice-filled old-fashioned glass. Top with nutmeg.

OLD BAY RIDGE

1 oz. straight rye whiskey
1 oz. aquavit
½ oz. Demerara Syrup (page 25)
2 dashes Angostura bitters
Garnish: Lemon twist

Stir with ice and strain into chilled old-fashioned glass. Add lemon twist.

OLD-FASHIONED COCKTAIL

For more information on the Old-Fashioned Cocktail, see page 28.

2 oz. rye or bourbon whiskey
¼ oz. simple syrup
2 dashes orange or Angostura bitters
Garnish: orange wheel, Italian preserved cherry

Pour whiskey, syrup, and bitters into cracked ice–filled old-fashioned glass and stir. Garnish with orange and cherry.

OLD PAL COCKTAIL

1¼ oz. rye whiskey
½ oz. sweet vermouth
½ oz. grenadine

Stir with ice and strain into chilled cocktail glass.

ORIENTAL COCKTAIL

1 oz. rye whiskey
½ oz. sweet vermouth
½ oz. triple sec
½ oz. fresh lime juice

Shake with ice and strain into chilled cocktail glass.

PADDY COCKTAIL

1½ oz. Irish whiskey
1½ oz. sweet vermouth
1 dash Angostura bitters

Stir with ice and strain into chilled cocktail glass.

PENDENNIS TODDY

1 sugar cube
2 oz. bourbon whiskey
Garnish: 2 lemon wheels

Muddle sugar with 1 tsp. water in ice-filled old-fashioned glass. Fill with ice, add bourbon, and stir. Garnish with lemon.

PENICILLIN

Created by SAM ROSS,
New York, NY

1¾ oz. Scotch whisky
¾ oz. fresh lemon juice
½ oz. Honey Syrup (page 25)
½ oz ginger liqueur
¼ oz. smoky Scotch whisky,
    such as Islay
Garnish: Lemon wheel

Shake first four ingredients with ice and strain into ice-filled old-fashioned glass. Float smoky Scotch on top and garnish with lemon.

THE PITBULL

Created by CHRIS CARLSSON,
Rochester, NY

1 oz. white whiskey, preferably
    Buffalo Trace White Dog
¾ oz. fresh lemon juice
1 oz. simple syrup
1 egg white
Garnish: 3 drops Angostura
    bitters

Shake without ice. Then shake with ice and strain into chilled cocktail glass. Top with bitters.

PLUMMED AWAY

¾ oz. Irish whiskey
¾ oz. plum wine
1½ oz. apple juice
½ oz. fresh lemon juice
½ oz. simple syrup
Garnish: Lemon twist

Pour into ice-filled highball glass. Stir, then add lemon twist.

WHISKIES

PREAKNESS COCKTAIL

1½ oz. straight rye whiskey
¾ oz. sweet vermouth
¼ oz. Bénédictine
1 dash Angostura bitters
Garnish: Lemon twist

Stir with ice and strain into chilled cocktail glass. Add lemon twist.

QUEBEC

For glass: Lemon wedge, superfine sugar
1½ oz. Canadian whisky
½ oz. dry vermouth
1 tsp. Amer Picon or Torani Amer
1 tsp. maraschino liqueur

Rim chilled cocktail glass with lemon and sugar. Shake remaining ingredients with ice and strain into glass.

THE RECONCILIATION

Created by RICHARD BOCCATO, New York, NY

¼ tsp. sambuca
1½ oz. straight rye whiskey
½ oz. amaro, such as Ramazzotti or Averna
1 tsp. orgeat syrup
Garnish: Orange twist

Swirl sambuca in old-fashioned glass to coat inside; discard excess sambuca. Add ice to glass. Shake remaining ingredients with ice and strain into prepared glass. Add orange twist.

RED HOOK

Created by ENZO ENRICO, New York, NY.

2 oz. straight rye whiskey
¼ oz. maraschino liqueur
¼ oz. Punt e Mes
Garnish: Maraschino cherry

Stir with ice and strain into chilled cocktail glass. Garnish with cherry.

RED-HOT PASSION

½ oz. bourbon whiskey
½ oz. amaretto
½ oz. Tennessee sour mash whiskey
¼ oz. sloe gin
1 splash triple sec
1 splash fresh orange juice
1 splash pineapple juice
Garnish: Orange half-wheel

Pour ingredients into ice-filled hurricane or parfait glass and stir gently. Garnish with orange.

RED RAIDER

1 oz. bourbon whiskey
½ oz. triple sec
1 oz. fresh lemon juice
1 tsp. grenadine

Shake with ice and strain into chilled cocktail glass.

REMEMBER THE MAINE

2 oz. straight rye whiskey
¾ oz. sweet vermouth
½ oz. Cherry Heering
1 tsp. absinthe or pastis
Garnish: Lemon twist

Stir with ice and strain into chilled cocktail glass. Add lemon twist.

REVOLVER

Created by JON SANTER,
San Francisco, CA.

2 oz. bourbon
½ oz. Tia Maria
2 dashes orange bitters
Garnish: Orange twist, flamed

*Stir with ice and strain into
chilled cocktail glass. Flame
orange twist and add.*

ROBERT BURNS

1½ oz. blended Scotch whisky
½ oz. sweet vermouth
1 dash orange bitters
1 dash absinthe or pastis

*Stir with ice and strain into
chilled cocktail glass.*

ROB ROY

1½ oz. blended Scotch whisky
¾ oz. sweet vermouth

*Stir with ice and strain into
chilled cocktail glass.*

RORY O' MORE

Here is an Irish version of the
Rob Roy, with orange bitters

1½ oz. Irish whiskey
¾ oz. sweet vermouth
1 dash orange bitters

*Stir with ice and strain into
chilled cocktail glass.*

RUSTY NAIL

1½ oz. blended Scotch whisky
½ oz. Drambuie

*Pour Scotch into ice-filled
old-fashioned glass. Float
Drambuie (see page 18) on
top.*

RYE COCKTAIL

An ideal example of the original
"cocktail," with rye, sugar,
water, and bitters and nothing
else except a cherry garnish.

2 oz. straight rye whiskey
½ oz. simple syrup
1 dash Angostura bitters
Garnish: Maraschino cherry

*Shake with ice and strain
into chilled cocktail glass.
Garnish with cherry.*

RYE HIGHBALL

2 oz. rye whiskey
Ginger ale or soda water
Garnish: Lemon twist

*Pour whiskey into ice-filled
highball glass. Fill with ginger ale or soda. Add lemon
twist and stir.*

SANTIAGO SCOTCH PLAID

1½ oz. blended Scotch
   whisky
½ oz. dry vermouth
2 dashes Angostura bitters
Garnish: Lemon twist

*Stir with ice and strain into
chilled cocktail glass. Add
lemon twist.*

WHISKIES

☐ SAZERAC (RYE)

The official cocktail of New Orleans, nowadays made with rye. The original used cognac, which also makes a fine Sazerac.

1 sugar cube
3 dashes Peychaud's bitters
2 oz. rye whiskey, preferably Buffalo Trace or Sazerac
¼ oz. absinthe, Herbsaint, or Pernod
Lemon twist

Fill old-fashioned glass with ice. Muddle sugar and bitters in second old-fashioned glass. Add whiskey and stir. Discard ice from first glass. Add absinthe to chilled glass, swirl to coat inside, and
discard excess absinthe. Pour whiskey mixture from second glass into chilled glass. Twist lemon over drink, but do not add to glass.

☒ SCOFFLAW

1 oz. Canadian whisky
1 oz. dry vermouth
¼ oz. fresh lemon juice
1 dash grenadine
1 dash orange bitters
Garnish: Lemon wedge

Stir with ice and strain into chilled cocktail glass. Garnish with lemon.

☒ SCOTCH BISHOP COCKTAIL

1 oz. blended Scotch whisky
½ oz. fresh orange juice
½ oz. dry vermouth
½ tsp. triple sec
¼ oz simple syrup
Garnish: Lemon twist

Shake with ice and strain into chilled cocktail glass. Add lemon twist.

☒ SCOTCH BONNET

1¼ oz. single-malt Scotch whisky
¼ oz. dry vermouth
¼ oz. Aperol
2 dashes hot red pepper sauce
Garnish: Orange twist, flamed

Stir with ice and strain into chilled cocktail glass. Flame orange twist and add.

☐ SCOTCH BOUNTY

1 oz. blended Scotch whisky
1 oz. coconut-flavored rum
1 oz. white crème de cacao
½ oz. grenadine
4 oz. fresh orange juice
Garnish: Pineapple wedge, maraschino cherry

Shake with ice and pour with ice into hurricane or parfait glass. Garnish with pineapple and cherry. Serve with a straw.

WHISKIES

SCOTCH HIGHBALL

2 oz. blended Scotch whisky
Ginger ale or soda water
Garnish: Lemon twist

Pour Scotch into ice-filled highball glass and fill with ginger ale or soda water. Add lemon twist and stir.

SCOTCH HOLIDAY SOUR

1½ oz. blended Scotch whisky
1 oz. cherry-flavored brandy
½ oz. sweet vermouth
1 oz. fresh lemon juice
Garnish: Lemon half-wheel

Shake with ice and strain into ice-filled old-fashioned glass. Garnish with lemon.

SCOTCH OLD-FASHIONED

2 oz. blended Scotch whisky
½ oz. simple syrup
1 dash Angostura bitters
Garnish: Lemon twist

Pour Scotch, syrup, and bitters into ice-filled old-fashioned glass and stir. Add lemon twist.

SCOTCH RICKEY

1½ oz. blended Scotch whisky
½ oz. fresh lime juice
Soda water
Garnish: Lime twist

Pour Scotch and lime juice ice-filled highball glass. Fill with soda water and stir. Add lime twist.

SCOTCH ROYALE

1 sugar cube
1 dash Angostura bitters
1½ oz. blended Scotch whisky
Chilled Champagne

Place sugar cube and bitters in chilled champagne flute. Stir Scotch with ice in mixing glass and strain into flute. Fill with Champagne.

SCOTCH SOUR

2 oz. blended Scotch whisky
¾ oz. fresh lime juice
¾ oz. simple syrup
Garnish: Lemon half-wheel, maraschino cherry

Shake with ice and strain into chilled cocktail glass. Garnish with lemon and cherry.

SCOTCH STINGER

1½ oz. blended Scotch whisky
½ oz. white crème de menthe

Shake with ice and strain into chilled cocktail glass.

SCOTTISH GUARD

1½ oz. bourbon whiskey
½ oz. fresh lemon juice
½ oz. fresh orange juice
1 tsp. grenadine

Shake with ice and strain into chilled cocktail glass.

⅂ THE SCOTTISH BANDIT

Created by HAL WOLIN,
New York, NY

1¾ oz. blended Scotch whisky
1 tsp. green Chartreuse
¾ oz. fig juice
½ oz. Cinnamon Syrup
    (page 25)
2 dashes whiskey barrel bitters
Garnish: Orange twist

*Shake with ice and strain
into cocktail glass. Add
orange twist.*

⬚ SEABOARD

1 oz. blended Scotch whisky
1 oz. gin
¾ oz. fresh lemon juice
¾ oz. simple syrup
Garnish: Fresh mint leaves

*Shake with ice and strain
into ice-filled old-fashioned
glass. Garnish with mint
leaves.*

⅂ THE SEELBACH COCKTAIL

A namesake of the famous hotel
in Louisville, KY, this cocktail is
loaded with bitters, so decrease
the amount if you wish.

¾ oz. bourbon whiskey
½ oz. triple sec
7 dashes Angostura bitters
7 dashes Peychaud's bitters
4 oz. chilled Champagne
Garnish: Orange twist

*Add, in order given, to
chilled champagne flute. Add
orange twist.*

⅂ SHAMROCK

1½ oz. Irish whiskey
½ oz. dry vermouth
1 tsp. green crème de menthe
Garnish: Green olive

*Stir with ice and strain
into chilled cocktail glass.
Garnish with olive.*

⅂ THE SHOOT

1 oz. blended Scotch whisky
1 oz. dry sherry
¼ oz. simple syrup
1 tsp. fresh orange juice
1 tsp. fresh lemon juice

*Shake with ice and strain
into chilled cocktail glass.*

⬚ SHRUFF'S END

1 oz. Islay or other peaty
    single-malt Scotch whisky
1 oz. apple brandy
½ oz. Bénédictine
2 dashes Peychaud's bitters

*Stir with ice and strain into
chilled old-fashioned glass.*

⅂ SILENT THIRD

2 oz. blended Scotch whisky
1 oz. triple sec
1 oz. fresh lemon juice

*Shake with ice and strain
into chilled cocktail glass.*

SILVER LINING

1½ oz. straight rye
    whiskey
¾ oz. fresh lemon juice
¾ oz. vanilla liqueur
1 egg white
Soda water

*Shake first four ingredients
without ice. Then shake
with ice and strain into ice-
filled Collins glass. Top with
soda water.*

SLEEPING MONK

Created by KENTA GOTA,
New York, NY

2 oz. Chamomile Tea–
    infused Scotch (recipe
    follows)
¼ oz. yellow Chartreuse
¼ oz. Bénédictine
¾ oz. fresh lemon juice
¾ oz. Honey Syrup (page 25)
1 dash orange bitters
Garnish: Apple slice

*Shake with ice and
strain into chilled cocktail
glass. Garnish with apple
slice.*

CHAMOMILE TEA–INFUSED SCOTCH

*Combine 2 chamomile tea
bags with 8 oz. Scotch in
a bowl and let stand for 30
minutes. Strain into a jar or
bottle, pressing hard on the
tea bags. Cover, and store
in the refrigerator for up to
2 weeks.*

THE SLOPE

2 oz. straight rye whiskey
¾ oz. Punt e Mes
½ oz. apricot liqueur
2 dashes Angostura bitters
Garnish: Maraschino cherry

*Stir with ice and strain
into chilled cocktail glass.
Garnish with cherry.*

SOUTHERN BELLE

1½ oz. Tennessee bourbon
    whiskey
½ oz. triple sec
6 oz. pineapple juice
2 oz. fresh orange juice
1 splash grenadine

*Combine whiskey, triple sec,
and juices in ice-filled Collins
glass. Top with grenadine
and stir once.*

SOUTHERN LADY

2 oz. bourbon whiskey
1 oz. Tennessee sour mash
    whiskey
1 oz. crème de noyaux
3 oz. pineapple juice
2 oz. lemon-lime soda
1 oz. fresh lime juice
Garnish: Pineapple wedge,
    maraschino cherry

*Shake first four ingredients
with ice and strain into hurricane glass half-filled with
ice. Fill with soda to within
1 inch of top of glass. Top
with lime juice and more
ice as needed. Garnish with
pineapple and cherry.*

WHISKIES

SOUTHERN PEACH

¼ oz. grenadine
1½ oz. bourbon whiskey
2 oz. fresh orange juice
1 oz. simple syrup
1 oz. lemon juice
1 oz. peach schnapps
Garnish: Peach slice

Fill hurricane or parfait glass with ice. Pour grenadine over ice; add bourbon. Shake remaining ingredients with ice and pour slowly into glass. Garnish with peach.

STILETTO

1½ oz. bourbon whiskey
1 oz. fresh lemon juice
½ oz. amaretto

Pour into ice-filled old-fashioned glass and stir.

STONE FENCE

2 oz. blended Scotch whisky
2 dashes Angostura bitters
Apple cider

Pour Scotch and bitters into ice-filled highball glass. Fill with cider. Stir.

STRAIGHT RYE WITCH

2 oz. straight rye whiskey
¼ oz. Strega
¼ oz. palo cortado sherry
¼ oz. simple syrup
2 dashes orange bitters
Garnish: Orange twist

Stir with ice and strain into chilled cocktail glass. Add orange twist.

SWISS FAMILY COCKTAIL

1½ oz. blended Scotch whiskey
¾ oz. dry vermouth
1 tsp. anisette
2 dashes Angostura bitters

Stir with ice and strain into chilled cocktail glass.

T-BIRD

1½ oz Canadian whisky
¾ oz. amaretto
2 oz. pineapple juice
1 oz. fresh orange juice
2 dashes grenadine
Garnish: Orange half-wheel, maraschino cherry

Shake with ice and strain into ice-filled highball glass. Garnish with orange and cherry. Serve with straw.

THOROUGHBRED COOLER

1 oz. bourbon whiskey
1 oz. fresh orange juice
½ oz. fresh lemon juice
½ oz. simple syrup
Lemon-lime soda
1 dash grenadine
Garnish: Orange wedge

Pour first four ingredients over ice in highball glass. Fill with lemon-lime soda and stir. Add grenadine. Garnish with orange.

TIPPERARY COCKTAIL

¾ oz. Irish whiskey
¾ oz. green Chartreuse
¾ oz. sweet vermouth

Stir with ice and strain into chilled cocktail glass.

TOMBSTONE

2 oz. straight rye whiskey
½ oz. Demerara Syrup
(page 25)
2 dashes Angostura bitters
Garnish: Lemon twist

*Shake with ice and strain
into chilled cocktail glass.
Add lemon twist.*

TRILBY COCKTAIL

Trilby was the heroine of a
well-known novel and play of
the early 20th century. The
villain of the piece, a very
manipulative character, gave us
the term "Svengali."

1½ oz. bourbon whiskey
¾ oz. sweet vermouth
2 dashes orange bitters

*Stir with ice and strain into
chilled cocktail glass.*

TWIN HILLS

1½ oz. bourbon whiskey
¼ oz. Bénédictine
½ oz. fresh lemon juice
½ oz. fresh lime juice
¾ oz. simple syrup
Garnish: Lemon wheel, lime
wheel

*Shake with ice and strain
into chilled cocktail glass.
Garnish with lemon and lime.*

VAGABOND

1½ oz. single-malt Scotch
whisky
¾ oz. Punt e Mes
¾ oz. Sauternes or other
sweet wine
Garnish: Orange twist

*Stir with ice and strain into
chilled cocktail glass. Add
orange twist.*

VERRAZANO

1 splash Campari
2 oz. bourbon whiskey
1 oz. sweet vermouth
¼ oz. apricot liqueur
Garnish: Orange twist

*Swirl Campari in chilled
cocktail glass to coat inside;
discard excess Campari. Stir
remaining ingredients with
ice and strain into glass. Add
orange twist.*

VIEUX CARRÉ

Another contender in the Most
Beloved New Orleans Cocktail
roundup, this has been around
since 1938, when it was
introduced by Walter Bergeron,
head bartender at the Hotel
Monteleone.

¾ oz. straight rye whiskey
¾ oz. brandy
¾ oz. sweet vermouth
¼ oz. Bénédictine
1 dash Peychaud's bitters
1 dash Angostura bitters

*Pour into ice-filled old-
fashioned glass and stir.*

WHISKIES

℣ WALTERS

1½ oz. blended Scotch
    whisky
½ oz. fresh orange juice
½ oz. fresh lemon juice

*Shake with ice and strain
into chilled cocktail glass.*

℣ WARD EIGHT

Of the many stories telling how
this drink got its name, the one
that sticks is its invention at
Locke-Ober restaurant to honor
a local politician from Boston's
Eighth Ward. The clincher? The
honoree became a teetotaler.

2 oz. rye whiskey
¾ oz. fresh lemon juice
½ oz. simple syrup
¼ oz. grenadine
Garnish: Orange and lemon
    half-wheels, maraschino
    cherry

*Shake with ice and strain
into red-wine glass filled with
ice. Garnish with orange,
lemon, and cherry. Serve
with straws.*

⬚ WASHINGTON APPLE

2 oz. Canadian whisky
2 oz. sour apple schnapps
2 oz. cranberry juice

*Pour into ice-filled highball
glass and stir.*

℣ WEESKI

2 oz. Irish whiskey
1 oz. Lillet Blanc
¼ oz. triple sec
2 dashes orange bitters
Garnish: Orange twist

*Stir with ice and strain into
chilled cocktail glass. Add
orange twist.*

℣ THE WELSHMAN

Created by JONATHAN POGASH,
New York, NY

2 oz. Penderyn single-malt
    Welsh whisky
¾ oz. sweet vermouth
1 dash Angostura bitters
1 dash orange bitters
Garnish: Orange twist

*Stir with ice and strain into
chilled cocktail glass. Add
orange twist.*

℣ THE WHIMSY

Created by TED HENWOOD,
New York City, NY

For glass: Lemon wedge,
    orange volcanic
    sea salt
2 oz. bourbon whiskey
1 oz. fresh lemon juice
½ oz. agave nectar
1 tsp. Fernet-Branca

*Rim a chilled cocktail
glass with lemon and salt.
Shake remaining ingredi-
ents with ice and strain
into glass.*

WHISKEY COBBLER

2 oz. rye or bourbon
  whiskey
½ oz. simple syrup
Soda water
Garnish: Fresh seasonal
  fruit

*Stir whiskey and syrup in
red-wine glass. Fill with
shaved ice, top with soda
water, and stir. Garnish with
fruit. Serve with straws.*

WHISKEY COLLINS

2 oz. rye or bourbon
  whiskey
1 oz. fresh lemon juice
½ oz. simple syrup
Soda water
Garnish: Lemon half-wheel,
  orange half-wheel,
  maraschino cherry

*Shake whiskey, lemon juice,
and syrup with ice and
strain into ice-filled Collins
glass. Top with soda water
and stir. Garnish with
lemon, orange, and cherry.
Serve with straw.*

WHISKEY DAISY

2 oz. rye or bourbon
  whiskey
1 oz. fresh lemon juice
½ oz. simple syrup
1 tsp. grenadine
Garnish: Fresh seasonal fruit

*Shake with ice and strain
into chilled beer mug or
metal cup. Add 1 ice cube.
Garnish with fruit.*

WHISKEY FIX

2½ oz. rye or bourbon whiskey
1 oz. fresh lemon juice
½ oz. simple syrup
Garnish: Lemon wheel

*Shake whiskey, juice, and
syrup with ice. Strain into ice-
filled highball glass. Garnish
with lemon. Serve with straws.*

WHISKEY HIGHBALL

2 oz. rye or bourbon whiskey
Ginger ale or soda water
Garnish: Lemon twist

*Pour whiskey into ice-filled
highball glass. Fill with ginger ale or soda water. Add
lemon twist and stir.*

WHISKEY ORANGE

1½ oz. rye or bourbon whiskey
2 oz. fresh orange juice
½ oz. simple syrup
½ tsp. anisette
Garnish: Orange half-wheel,
  lemon half-wheel

*Shake with ice and strain
into ice-filled highball glass.
Garnish with orange and
lemon.*

WHISKEY RICKEY

1 lime
1½ oz. rye or bourbon
  whiskey
Soda water

*Squeeze ½ oz. lime juice from
lime; reserve spent rinds. Pour
whiskey and lime juice into
ice-filled highball glass. Fill
with soda water and stir. Drop
lime rinds into glass.*

WHISKIES

WHISKEY SANGAREE

2 oz. rye or bourbon whiskey
½ oz. simple syrup
1 splash soda water
½ oz. tawny port
Garnish: Freshly grated
    nutmeg

*Stir whiskey, syrup and
soda water in ice-filled old-
fashioned glass. Float port
(see page 18) on top. Top
with nutmeg.*

WHISKEY SLING

2 oz. rye or bourbon whiskey
1 oz. fresh lemon juice
½ oz. simple syrup
Garnish: Lemon twist

*Pour into ice-filled old-
fashioned glass and stir. Add
lemon twist.*

WHISKEY SMASH

1 sugar cube
1 oz. soda water
4 fresh mint sprigs
2 oz. bourbon whiskey
Garnish: Orange wheel,
    maraschino cherry, lemon
    twist

*Muddle sugar with soda
water and mint in old-
fashioned glass. Add whiskey
and then ice cubes. Stir.
Garnish with orange and
cherry, and add lemon twist.*

WHISKEY SOUR

2 oz. rye or bourbon whiskey
¾ oz. fresh lemon juice
¾ oz. simple syrup
Garnish: Lemon half-wheel,
    maraschino cherry

*Shake with ice and strain into
chilled cocktail glass. Garnish
with lemon and cherry.*

WHISKEY SQUIRT

1½ oz. rye or bourbon
    whiskey
¼ oz. simple syrup
¼ oz. grenadine
Soda water
Garnish: Pineapple cubes,
    whole strawberries

*Shake first three ingredients
with ice and strain into
chilled highball glass. Add
ice and fill with soda water.
Garnish with pineapple and
strawberries.*

WHISKEY SWIZZLE

2 oz. rye or bourbon whiskey
¾ oz. fresh lime juice
¾ oz. simple syrup
2 dashes Angostura bitters
Soda water

*Pour whiskey, lime juice,
syrup, and bitters into
Collins glass. Fill glass with
ice and stir. Add ice and fill
with soda. With barspoon
between your palms, move
hands back and forth and
up and down to quickly
rotate and lift spoon, until
glass is frosted.*

WHISPERS-OF-THE-FROST COCKTAIL

¾ oz. bourbon whiskey
¾ oz. cream sherry
¾ oz. tawny port
¼ oz. simple syrup
Garnish: Orange and lemon
    half-wheels

*Stir with ice and strain
into chilled cocktail glass.
Garnish with orange and
lemon.*

WHOA, NELLIE!

1½ oz. straight rye whiskey
¾ oz. dark rum
½ oz. fresh lemon juice
½ oz. fresh grapefruit juice
½ oz. simple syrup
Garnish: Grapefruit twist

*Shake with ice and strain
into chilled cocktail glass.
Add grapefruit twist.*

WOODWARD COCKTAIL

1½ oz. blended Scotch
    whisky
½ oz. dry vermouth
½ oz. fresh grapefruit juice

*Shake with ice and strain
into chilled cocktail glass.*

WOOLWORTH

2 oz. blended Scotch whisky
1 oz. palo cortado or fino
    sherry
½ oz. Bénédictine
2 dashes orange bitters

*Stir with ice and strain into
chilled cocktail glass.*

WHISKIES

CORDIALS AND LIQUEURS

ORDIALS AND LIQUEURS have been around since the Middle Ages, when they were concocted in European monasteries primarily for medicinal purposes. The historical distinction between cordials (fruit based) and liqueurs (herb based) doesn't really exist anymore, and the word "liqueur" is typically used for both. Crèmes, another common designation, are liqueurs with an especially high sugar content, which gives them a creamy texture. In Europe, liqueurs have long been savored as after-dinner drinks, while Americans have tended to enjoy them mixed with other ingredients.

Liqueurs by today's definition are flavored spirits with between 2.5 percent and 40 percent sweetener, which can come from just about anything, including fruits, herbs, roots, spices, and nuts. The alcohol base used to make liqueurs is produced from grain, grapes, other fruits, or vegetables, and must be flavored in one of four ways: distillation, infusion, maceration, or percolation.

Do not confuse liqueur with fruit brandy, which is distilled from a mash of the fruit itself. Some producers mislabel their liqueurs as brandies, such as "blackberry brandy," when they are technically cordials (or liqueurs). Artificial colors and flavors are permitted in liqueurs. Colorless double-distilled fruit brandy is called eau-de-vie.

The best liqueurs come from all over the globe, and many have closely guarded secret recipes and processes, as well as their own proprietary brand names. Some of the most popular include crème de cacao (cacao and vanilla beans); curaçao (made from dried citrus peel); sambuca (licorice-flavored, made from the elderberry bush's white flowers); sloe gin (sloe berries, from the blackthorn bush); and triple sec (orange-flavored, and similar to curaçao).

ABSINTHE SPECIAL COCKTAIL

1½ oz. absinthe
¼ oz. simple syrup
1 dash orange bitters

Shake with ice and strain into chilled cocktail glass.

AMARETTO AND CREAM

1½ oz. amaretto
1½ oz. half-and-half

Shake with ice and strain into chilled cocktail glass.

AMARETTO ROSE

1½ oz. amaretto
½ oz. fresh lemon juice
½ oz. simple syrup
Soda water

Pour first three ingredients into ice-filled Collins glass and fill with soda water. Stir.

AMARETTO SOUR

1½ oz. amaretto
¾ oz. fresh lemon juice
½ oz. simple syrup
Garnish: Orange half-wheel

Shake with ice and strain into chilled sour glass. Garnish with orange.

AMARETTO STINGER

1½ oz. amaretto
¾ oz. white crème de menthe

Shake with ice and strain into chilled cocktail glass.

AMBER AMOUR

1½ oz. amaretto
¼ oz. fresh lemon juice
¼ oz. simple syrup
Soda water
Garnish: Maraschino cherry

Pour amaretto, lemon juice, and syrup into ice-filled Collins glass. Top with soda water and stir. Garnish with cherry.

APPLE PIE

3 oz. apple schnapps
1 splash cinnamon schnapps
Garnish: Apple slice, ground cinnamon

Pour into ice-filled old-fashioned glass. Garnish with apple and top with cinnamon.

ARISE MY LOVE

1 tsp. green crème de menthe
Chilled Champagne

Pour crème de menthe into champagne flute. Fill with Champagne.

BANSHEE

1 oz. crème de banana
½ oz. white crème de cacao
½ oz. half-and-half

Shake with ice and strain into chilled cocktail glass.

BITTER MAI TAI

Created by JEREMY OERTEL, New York, NY

1½ oz. Campari
¾ oz. dark rum
½ oz. orange curaçao
1 oz. fresh lime juice
¾ oz. orgeat syrup
Garnish: Fresh mint sprig

Shake with ice and strain into crushed ice–filled old-fashioned glass. Garnish with mint.

CORDIALS AND LIQUEURS

BLACKJACK

1 oz. cherry-flavored brandy
½ oz. brandy
1 oz. cold brewed coffee

Shake with ice and strain into ice-filled old-fashioned glass.

BLACKTHORN

1½ oz. sloe gin
1 oz. sweet vermouth
Garnish: Lemon twist

Stir with ice and strain into chilled cocktail glass. Add lemon twist.

BLANCHE

1 oz. anisette
1 oz. triple sec
½ oz. white curaçao

Shake with ice and strain into chilled cocktail glass.

BOCCE BALL

1½ oz. amaretto
1½ oz. fresh orange juice
2 oz. soda water

Pour into ice-filled highball glass and stir gently.

BOSTON ICED COFFEE

6 oz. cold brewed coffee
1 oz. white crème
   de menthe
1 oz. white crème de cacao
1 oz. brandy
Garnish: Lemon twist

*Pour into ice-filled highball
glass and stir. Add lemon
twist.*

BURNING SUN

1½ oz. strawberry
   schnapps
4 oz. pineapple juice
Garnish: Whole strawberry

*Pour into ice-filled highball
glass and stir. Garnish with
strawberry.*

BUSHWHACKER

½ oz. coffee liqueur
½ oz. amaretto
½ oz. light rum
½ oz. Irish cream liqueur
2 oz. half-and-half

*Shake with ice. Pour
into ice-filled old-fashioned
glass.*

CAFÉ CABANA

1 oz. coffee liqueur
Soda water
Garnish: Lime wedge

*Pour liqueur into ice-filled
Collins glass. Fill with soda
water and stir. Garnish with
lime.*

CHARTREUSE SWIZZLE

Created by MARCOVALDO
DIONYSOS, San Francisco, CA

1½ oz. green Chartreuse
1 oz. pineapple juice
¾ oz. fresh lime juice
½ oz. Taylor's Velvet
   Falernum
Garnish: Freshly grated
   nutmeg, fresh mint sprig

*Pour ingredients into Collins
glass and add crushed ice.
Swizzle with bar spoon until
glass is frosted. Top with nutmeg and garnish with mint.*

CHOCOLATE-COVERED STRAWBERRY

1 oz. strawberry schnapps
¼ oz. white crème de cacao
½ oz. heavy cream or half-
   and-half
Garnish: Whole strawberry

*Stir with ice and strain into
ice-filled red-wine glass.
Garnish with strawberry.*

COFFEE NUDGE

½ oz. brandy
½ oz. coffee liqueur
½ oz. dark crème de cacao
4½ oz. hot brewed coffee
Garnish: Whipped cream,
   chocolate shavings

*Pour first three ingredients
into preheated Irish coffee
glass. Fill with coffee and
stir. Top with whipped cream
and chocolate.*

CRÈME DE MENTHE FRAPPÉ

2 oz. green crème de menthe

Fill cocktail glass up to brim with shaved ice. Add crème de menthe. Serve with two short straws.

DEPTH CHARGE

Add a shot of any flavor of schnapps to a mug of cold beer.

DIANA COCKTAIL

1½ oz. white crème de menthe
1½ oz. brandy

Fill cocktail glass with ice. Add crème de menthe, then float (see page 18) brandy on top.

FERRARI

2 oz. dry vermouth
1 oz. amaretto
Garnish: Lemon twist

Pour into ice-filled old-fashioned glass and stir. Add lemon twist.

FRENCH CONNECTION

1½ oz. cognac
¾ oz. amaretto

Pour into ice-filled old-fashioned glass, but do not stir.

FRENCH FANTASY

1 oz. black raspberry liqueur
1 oz. Mandarine Napoléon
2 oz. cranberry juice
2 oz. fresh orange juice
Garnish: Orange half-wheel, maraschino cherry

Pour into ice-filled highball glass and stir. Garnish with orange and cherry.

FUZZY NAVEL

2 oz. 48-proof peach schnapps
3 oz. fresh orange juice
Garnish: Orange half-wheel

Pour schnapps and orange juice into ice-filled highball glass. Garnish with orange.

GOLDEN DREAM

1 oz. Galliano
½ oz. triple sec
½ oz. fresh orange juice
½ oz. half-and-half

Shake with ice and strain into chilled cocktail glass.

GOOBER

1 oz. vodka
1 oz. black raspberry liqueur
1 oz. melon liqueur
¾ oz. triple sec
½ oz. grenadine
2 oz. fresh orange juice
2 oz. pineapple juice
Garnish: Orange wheel, maraschino cherry

Shake with ice and strain into ice-filled Collins glass. Garnish with orange and cherry. Serve with a straw.

CORDIALS AND LIQUEURS

GRAPE SOUR

Created by CHARLES VEXENAT,
London, UK

10 white seedless grapes
1 oz. absinthe
1 oz. fresh lemon juice
2 dashes orange bitters
1 egg white
Garnish: Fennel seeds

*Muddle grapes in mixing
glass. Add remaining
ingredients and shake
without ice. Add ice and shake
again. Double-strain into
chilled cocktail glass. Top
with fennel seeds.*

GRASSHOPPER

¾ oz. green crème
    de menthe
¾ oz. white crème
    de cacao
¾ oz. half-and-half

*Shake with ice and strain
into chilled cocktail glass.*

HEAT WAVE

1¼ oz. coconut-flavored
    rum
½ oz. peach schnapps
3 oz. pineapple juice
3 oz. fresh orange juice
½ oz. grenadine
Garnish: Peach slice

*Shake first four ingredients
with ice and strain into
ice-filled hurricane glass.
Top with grenadine. Garnish
with peach.*

ITALIAN SOMBRERO

1½ oz. amaretto
3 oz. half-and-half

*Shake well with ice. Strain,
with or without ice, into
chilled champagne flute.*

ITALIAN SURFER

1 oz. amaretto
1 oz. brandy
3 oz. pineapple juice
Garnish: Pineapple spear,
    maraschino cherry

*Pour amaretto and brandy
into ice-filled Collins glass.
Add pineapple juice and stir.
Garnish with pineapple and
cherry.*

JOHNNIE COCKTAIL

1½ oz. sloe gin
¾ oz. triple sec
1 tsp. anisette

*Shake with ice and strain
into chilled cocktail glass.*

LIMONCELLO
SUNRISE

1 oz. limoncello
3 oz. fresh orange juice
1 dash grenadine

*Shake limoncello and orange
juice with ice and strain into
chilled old-fashioned glass.
Top with grenadine.*

KARMA SUTRA

Created by JONATHAN POGASH,
New York, NY

1 oz. Darjeeling Tea–Infused
Amaro (recipe follows)
1 oz. Plymouth gin
1 tsp. orange marmalade
¼ oz. fresh orange juice
Garnish: Freshly grated
nutmeg

*Shake with ice and strain
through wire sieve into
chilled cocktail glass.*

DARJEELING TEA–INFUSED AMARO

*Combine 8 oz. amaro (such
as Ramazzotti or Averna)
and 1 Darjeeling tea bag in
bowl and let stand at room
temperature for 45 minutes.
Strain into covered jar,
pressing hard on tea bag.
Store in refrigerator for up
to 2 months.*

LOVER'S KISS

½ oz. amaretto
½ oz. cherry-flavored
brandy
½ oz. dark crème de cacao
1 oz. half-and-half
Garnish: Whipped cream,
chocolate shavings,
maraschino cherry

*Shake with ice and pour
with ice into parfait glass.
Top with whipped cream,
sprinkle with chocolate
shavings, and garnish with
cherry.*

MARMALADE

1½ oz. triple sec
Tonic water
Garnish: Orange half-wheel

*Pour triple sec into ice-filled
highball glass. Fill with tonic
water. Garnish with orange.*

MCCELLAND COCKTAIL

1½ oz. sloe gin
¾ oz. triple sec
1 dash orange bitters

*Shake with ice and strain
into chilled cocktail glass.*

MELON COOLER

¾ oz. melon liqueur
½ oz. peach schnapps
½ oz. raspberry schnapps
1 oz. pineapple juice
Garnish: Lime wheel,
maraschino cherry

*Shake with ice and pour into
chilled cocktail glass. Garnish
with lime and cherry.*

MINT HIGHBALL

2 oz. green crème de menthe
Ginger ale or soda water
Garnish: Lemon twist

*Pour crème de menthe into
ice-filled highball glass. Fill
with ginger ale or soda water
and stir. Add lemon twist.*

MOULIN ROUGE

1½ oz. sloe gin
¾ oz. sweet vermouth
1 dash Angostura bitters

*Stir with ice and strain into
chilled cocktail glass.*

CORDIALS AND LIQUEURS

THE OSCAR WILDE

Created by JONATHAN POGASH,
New York, NY

1¼ oz. absinthe
¾ oz. fresh lemon juice
¾ oz. simple syrup
1 egg white
1 oz. chilled Champagne
Garnish: Freshly grated
   nutmeg, orange twist

*Shake first four ingredients
without ice. Add ice and
shake again. Strain into
white-wine glass. Top with
Champagne. Sprinkle with
nutmeg and add orange
twist.*

PEACH MELBA

1 oz. peach schnapps
½ oz. black raspberry liqueur
3 oz. half-and-half
Garnish: Peach slice

*Shake with ice. Strain into
ice-filled old-fashioned glass.
Garnish with peach. Serve
with short straw.*

PEPPERMINT ICEBERG

2 oz. peppermint schnapps
1 peppermint candy stick

*Pour into ice-filled old-
fashioned glass. Add candy.*

PEPPERMINT STICK

1 oz. peppermint schnapps
1½ oz. white crème de cacao
1 oz. half-and-half

*Shake with ice and strain
into chilled cocktail glass.*

PEPPERMINT TWIST

1½ oz. peppermint
   schnapps
½ oz. white crème de cacao
3 scoops vanilla ice cream
Garnish: Fresh mint sprig,
   peppermint candy stick

*Process in blender until
smooth. Pour into large
hurricane or parfait glass.
Garnish with mint and
peppermint stick. Serve with
straw.*

PIMM'S CUP

James Pimm, a London
restaurateur of the early
nineteenth century, originally
had six different flavors of his
Pimm's Cup liqueurs, but only
No. 1, based on gin, is still
easily found.

2 oz. Pimm's No. 1
3 oz. ginger ale or lemon-lime
   soda
Garnish: Cucumber slices
   and/or lemon wheel

*Pour Pimm's into ice-filled
Collins glass. Top with
chilled ginger ale. Garnish
with cucumbers and/or
lemon.*

PINK SQUIRREL

1 oz. crème de noyaux
½ oz. white crème
   de cacao
½ oz. half-and-half

*Shake with ice and strain
into chilled cocktail glass.*

POUSSE-CAFÉ

See the detailed instructions on page 18 on how to float the liqueur layers on each other for a striped effect.

½ oz. grenadine
½ oz. yellow Chartreuse
½ oz. crème de cassis
½ oz. white crème de menthe
½ oz. green Chartreuse
½ oz. brandy

In order given, carefully float liquors over back of barspoon into pousse-café glass, so that each ingredient layers on preceding one.

PRIZEFIGHTER

Created by NICHOLAS JARRETT, New York, NY

8–10 fresh mint leaves
2–3 lemon wedges
¾ oz. simple syrup
1 oz. Fernet-Branca
1 oz. sweet vermouth
¼ oz. fresh lemon juice
Garnish: 2 fresh mint sprigs

Muddle mint leaves, lemon, and syrup in mixing glass. Add remaining ingredients with ice and shake. Double-strain into crushed ice-filled old-fashioned glass. Garnish with mint.

QUAALUDE

1 oz. vodka
1 oz. hazelnut liqueur
1 oz. coffee liqueur
1 splash milk

Shake with ice and pour into ice-filled old-fashioned glass.

RASPBERRY ROMANCE

1¼ oz. Irish cream liqueur
¾ oz. coffee liqueur
¾ oz. black raspberry liqueur
Soda water

Pour liqueurs into ice-filled parfait or hurricane glass. Fill with club soda and stir.

RITZ FIZZ

1 dash fresh lemon juice
1 dash blue curaçao
1 dash amaretto
Chilled Champagne
Garnish: Lemon twist

Add first three ingredients to chilled champagne flute. Fill with Champagne and stir briefly. Add lemon twist.

ROCKY MOUNTAIN COOLER

1½ oz. peach schnapps
4 oz. pineapple juice
2 oz. lemon-lime soda

Pour into ice-filled Collins glass and stir.

ST. PATRICK'S DAY

¼ oz. green crème de menthe
¾ oz. green Chartreuse
¾ oz. Irish whiskey
1 dash Angostura bitters

Stir with ice and strain into chilled cocktail glass.

SAMBUCA CON MOSCA

2 oz. sambuca
3 coffee beans

Pour sambuca into snifter and float coffee beans on top.

CORDIALS AND LIQUEURS

SAN FRANCISCO COCKTAIL

¾ oz. sloe gin
¾ oz. sweet vermouth
¾ oz. dry vermouth
1 dash Angostura bitters
1 dash orange bitters
Garnish: Maraschino
  cherry

*Shake with ice and strain
into chilled cocktail glass.
Garnish with cherry.*

SANTINI'S POUSSE-CAFÉ

½ oz. brandy
½ oz. maraschino liqueur
½ oz. triple sec
½ oz. gold rum

*Pour ingredients, in order
given, into pousse-café glass.
Ingredients should blend,
and not layer.*

SHANGRI-LITA

Created by BLAIR FRODELIUS,
Syracuse, NY

1½ oz. pomegranate
  liqueur
1 oz. fresh orange juice
¾ oz. fresh lime juice
1 tsp. simple syrup
2 dashes hot red pepper
  sauce
½ oz. soda water

*Shake first five ingredients
with ice. Strain into
chilled cocktail glass.
Top with soda water and
stir briefly.*

SHEER ELEGANCE

1½ oz. amaretto
1½ oz. black raspberry liqueur
½ oz. vodka

*Shake with ice and strain
into chilled cocktail glass.*

SLOEBERRY COCKTAIL

2 oz. sloe gin
1 dash Angostura bitters

*Stir with ice and strain into
chilled cocktail glass.*

SLOE DRIVER

1½ oz. sloe gin
5 oz. fresh orange juice

*Pour ingredients into ice-
filled highball glass and stir.*

SLOE GIN COCKTAIL

2 oz. sloe gin
¼ oz. dry vermouth
1 dash orange bitters

*Stir with ice and strain into
chilled cocktail glass.*

SLOE GIN COLLINS

2 oz. sloe gin
1 oz. fresh lemon juice
Soda water
Garnish: Lemon and orange
  half-wheels, maraschino
  cherry

*Shake sloe gin and lemon
juice with ice and strain into
ice-filled Collins glass. Fill
with soda water and stir.
Garnish with lemon, orange,
and cherry. Serve with straws.*

SLOE GIN FIZZ

2 oz. sloe gin
1 oz. fresh lemon juice
½ oz. simple syrup
Soda water
Garnish: Lemon wheel

Pour sloe gin, lemon juice, and syrup into highball glass. Add ice, fill with soda water, and stir. Garnish with lemon.

SLOE GIN RICKEY

1 lime
2 oz. sloe gin
Soda water

Squeeze ½ oz. lime juice from lime; reserve 1 spent rind. Pour lime juice and sloe gin into ice-filled highball glass. Fill with soda water, add lime rind, and stir.

THE SLOE STARTER

Created by RYAN ALVA LAYMAN, Denver, CO

2 oz. sloe gin
¾ oz. green Chartreuse
¾ oz. fresh lemon juice
3 dashes Peychaud's
   bitters
1 splash soda water
Garnish: Lemon wheel

Shake first four ingredients with ice. Strain into ice-filled old fashioned glass. Top with soda water. Garnish with lemon.

SLOE VERMOUTH

1 oz. sloe gin
1 oz. dry vermouth
½ oz. fresh lemon juice

Shake with ice and strain into chilled cocktail glass.

SOMETHING DIFFERENT

1 oz. peach schnapps
1 oz. amaretto
2 oz. pineapple juice
2 oz. cranberry juice

Shake with ice and pour into ice-filled highball glass.

STRAWBERRY FIELDS FOREVER

2 oz. strawberry schnapps
½ oz. brandy
Soda water
Garnish: Whole strawberry

Pour schnapps and brandy into ice-filled highball glass. Fill with soda water. Garnish with strawberry.

STRAWBERRY SUNRISE

2 oz. strawberry schnapps
½ oz. grenadine
3 oz. fresh orange juice
Garnish: Whole strawberry

Pour schnapps and grenadine into ice-filled highball glass. Fill with orange juice. Garnish with strawberry.

CORDIALS AND LIQUEURS

SUN KISS

2 oz. amaretto
4 oz. orange juice
Garnish: Lime wedge

Pour amaretto into ice-filled Collins glass. Add orange juice. Garnish with lime.

TOASTED ALMOND

1½ oz. coffee liqueur
1 oz. amaretto
1½ oz. half-and-half or milk

Shake with ice and strain into ice-filled old-fashioned glass.

TROPICAL COCKTAIL

¾ oz. white crème de cacao
¾ oz. maraschino liqueur
¾ oz. dry vermouth
1 dash Angostura bitters

Stir with ice and strain into chilled cocktail glass.

TWIN PEACH

2 oz. peach schnapps
4 oz. cranberry juice
Garnish: Peach slice or
    orange half-wheel

Pour schnapps into ice-filled highball glass, fill with cranberry juice, and stir. Garnish with peach or orange.

WATERMELON

1 oz. strawberry liqueur
1 oz. vodka
½ oz. simple syrup
½ oz. fresh lemon juice
1 oz. fresh orange juice
Garnish: Orange half-wheel

Pour into ice-filled Collins glass and stir. Garnish with orange. Serve with a straw.

YELLOW PARROT COCKTAIL

¾ oz. anisette
¾ oz. yellow Chartreuse
¾ oz. apricot-flavored
    brandy

Shake with ice and strain into chilled cocktail glass.

ZWACKBERRY FLIP

Created by ROBERT E. GONZALES, San Francisco, CA

1½ oz. Zwack Unicum
    (Hungarian herbal liqueur)
¾ oz. blackberry puree
½ oz. espresso liqueur, such
    as Stirrings
1 tsp. allspice liqueur
    (pimento dram)
2 dashes vanilla extract
1 egg
Garnish: Chocolate shavings

Shake without ice. Add ice and shake again. Double-strain into chilled cocktail glass. Top with chocolate.

SHOOTERS

WHEN THIS BOOK debuted 75 years ago, a "shot" was 2 ounces of straight whiskey knocked back in a single gulp—just like the scenes in those dusty old Westerns. Today, shots are called shooters, slammers, even tooters, usually preceded by fanciful names—B-52, Sex on the Beach, Kamikaze—and concocted with virtually any spirit and mixer handy in a well-stocked bar.

The universal appeal of shooters is partly attributable to the fact that many are fairly low in alcohol content. Frequently made with several juices as well as lower-proof liqueurs, the small size of the shooter limits the amount of spirit contained in a single drink. Some, like the Rattlesnake, are skillfully layered works of art, similar to a Pousse-Café. Others, like the Bloody Caesar, incorporate surprising ingredients such as clams or oysters.

The granddaddy of all shooters—a lick of salt, washed down with a shot of straight tequila, followed by a suck on a wedge of lime and the obligatory shudder—is not only still alive and kicking, it has inspired similar drinks like the Lemon Drop Shot and the Cordless Screwdriver.

The common denominator for the drinks on the following pages is that they were created with a sense of humor and wit, which is how they should be enjoyed. Once you get the hang of making them, you can experiment with bumping up the recipes to make large batches for parties. You might also feel inspired to create your own, which is how every one of these recipes came to fruition. Imagination and creativity can create a great little drink.

AFFAIR

½ oz. strawberry schnapps
½ oz. cranberry juice
½ oz. fresh orange juice

Stir with ice and strain into chilled cordial glass.

ALABAMA SLAMMER

½ oz. amaretto
½ oz. Tennessee sour mash whiskey
¼ oz. sloe gin
½ oz. fresh lemon juice

Stir first three ingredients with ice and strain into chilled shot glass. Add lemon juice.

ANGEL'S DELIGHT

¼ oz. grenadine
¼ oz. triple sec
¼ oz. sloe gin
¼ oz. half-and-half

Float carefully (see page 18), in order given, over back of barspoon into chilled cordial glass, so that each ingredient layers on preceding one.

ANGEL'S KISS

¼ oz. white crème de cacao
¼ oz. sloe gin
¼ oz. brandy
¼ oz. half-and-half

Float carefully (see page 18), in order given, over back of barspoon into chilled cordial glass, so that each ingredient layers on preceding one.

ANGEL'S TIP

¾ oz. white crème de cacao
¾ oz. half-and-half
Garnish: Maraschino cherry on long skewer

Pour crème de cacao into cordial glass. Carefully float cream (see page 18) over back of barspoon on top. Place skewered cherry over mouth of glass.

ANGEL'S WING

½ oz. white crème de cacao
½ oz. brandy
½ oz. half-and-half

Float carefully (see page 18), in order given, over back of barspoon into chilled cordial glass, so that each ingredient layers on preceding one.

B-52

½ oz. coffee liqueur
½ oz. Irish cream liqueur
½ oz. Mandarine Napoléon

Float carefully (see page 18), in order given, over back of barspoon into chilled shot glass, so that each ingredient layers on preceding one.

BANANA BOMBER

1 oz. banana-flavored
    schnapps, preferably
    99 Bananas
¾ oz. triple sec
1 splash grenadine

Shake with ice and strain into chilled shot glass.

BANANA SLIP

¾ oz. crème de banana
¾ oz. Irish cream liqueur

Pour crème de banana into cordial glass. Carefully float Irish cream liqueur (see page 18) over back of barspoon on top.

BETWEEN-THE-SHEETS

½ oz. fresh lemon juice
¼ oz. brandy
¼ oz. triple sec
¼ oz. light rum

Shake with ice and strain into chilled shot glass.

BLOODY CAESAR SHOOTER

1 littleneck clam, shucked
1 oz. vodka
1½ oz. tomato juice
2 drops hot red pepper sauce
2 drops Worcestershire sauce
1 dash prepared horseradish
Garnish: Celery salt, lime
    wedge

Put clam in the bottom of chilled shot glass. Shake vodka, tomato juice, sauces, and horseradish with ice, and strain into glass. Top with celery salt and garnish with lime.

BLUE MARLIN

¾ oz. light rum
¾ oz. blue curaçao
¼ oz. fresh lime juice

Stir with ice and strain into chilled shot glass.

BONZAI PIPELINE

1 oz. tropical fruit schnapps
½ oz. vodka

Stir with ice and strain into chilled shot glass.

☐ BUZZARD'S BREATH

½ oz. amaretto
½ oz. peppermint schnapps
½ oz. coffee liqueur

Stir with ice and strain into chilled shot glass.

☐ CAPRI

¾ oz. white crème de cacao
¾ oz. crème de banana
¾ oz. half-and-half

Shake with ice and strain into chilled cordial glass.

☐ CARAMEL APPLE

1 oz. butterscotch schnapps
½ oz. apple-flavored schnapps, preferably 99 Apples

Shake with ice and strain into chilled shot glass.

☐ C.C. KAZI

¾ oz. blanco tequila
¾ oz. cranberry juice
¼ oz. fresh lime juice

Shake with ice and strain into chilled cordial glass.

☐ CHARLIE CHAPLIN

½ oz. sloe gin
½ oz. apricot-flavored brandy
½ oz. fresh lemon juice

Shake with ice and strain into chilled cordial glass.

☐ CORDLESS SCREWDRIVER

1¾ oz. vodka
Orange wedge
Sugar

Shake vodka with ice and strain into shot glass. Dip orange wedge in sugar. Shoot the vodka and immediately take a draw on the orange.

☐ COSMOS

1½ oz. vodka
½ oz. fresh lime juice

Shake with ice and strain into chilled shot glass.

☐ FIFTH AVENUE

½ oz. dark crème de cacao
½ oz. apricot-flavored brandy
½ oz. half-and-half

Float carefully (see page 18), in order given, over back of barspoon into chilled cordial glass, so that each ingredient layers on preceding one.

☐ FLYING GRASSHOPPER

¾ oz. green crème de menthe
½ oz. white crème de cacao
½ oz. vodka

Stir with ice and strain into chilled cordial glass.

SHOOTERS

4TH OF JULY TOOTER

½ oz. grenadine
½ oz. vodka
½ oz. blue curaçao

Float carefully (see page 18), in order given, over back of barspoon into chilled cordial or shot glass, so that each ingredient layers on preceding one.

FOXY LADY

¾ oz. amaretto
¼ oz. dark crème de cacao
¾ oz. heavy cream

Shake with ice and strain into chilled cordial glass.

GALACTIC ALE

½ oz. vodka
½ oz. blue curaçao
¼ oz. fresh lime juice
¼ oz. black raspberry liqueur

Shake with ice and strain into chilled shot glass.

GREEN DEMON

½ oz. vodka
½ oz. light rum
½ oz. melon liqueur
½ oz. lemonade

Shake with ice and strain into chilled shot glass.

INTERNATIONAL INCIDENT

¼ oz. vodka
¼ oz. coffee liqueur
¼ oz. amaretto
¼ oz. hazelnut liqueur
½ oz. Irish cream liqueur

Shake with ice and strain into chilled shot glass.

IRISH CHARLIE

¾ oz. Irish cream liqueur
¾ oz. white crème de menthe

Shake with ice and strain into chilled cordial glass.

IRISH FLAG

½ oz. green crème de menthe
½ oz. Irish cream liqueur
½ oz. Mandarine Napoléon

Float carefully (see page 18), in order given, over back of barspoon into chilled cordial glass, so that each ingredient layers on preceding one.

JOHNNY ON THE BEACH

¾ oz. vodka
¼ oz. melon liqueur
¼ oz. black raspberry liqueur
¼ oz. pineapple juice
¼ oz. fresh orange juice
¼ oz. fresh grapefruit juice
¼ oz. cranberry juice

Shake with ice and strain into chilled shot glass.

KAMIKAZE

½ oz. vodka
½ oz. triple sec
½ oz. fresh lime juice

Shake with ice and strain into chilled shot glass.

LEMON DROP SHOT

1½ oz. vodka
Lemon wedge
Sugar

Stir vodka with ice. Strain into chilled shot glass. Dip lemon wedge in sugar. Shoot the vodka and immediately take a draw on the lemon.

MELON BALL

½ oz. melon liqueur
½ oz. vodka
½ oz. pineapple juice

Shake with ice and strain into chilled cordial glass.

MOCHA MINT

½ oz. coffee-flavored brandy
½ oz. white crème de cacao
½ oz. white crème de menthe

Shake with ice and strain into chilled cordial glass.

MONKEY SHINE SHOOTER

½ oz. bourbon liqueur
½ oz. crème de banana
½ oz. Irish cream liqueur

Shake with ice and strain into chilled cordial glass.

NUTTY PROFESSOR

½ oz. Mandarine Napoléon
½ oz. hazelnut liqueur
½ oz. Irish cream liqueur

Shake and strain into shot glass.

OH, MY GOSH SHOOTER

¾ oz. amaretto
¾ oz. peach schnapps

Stir with ice and strain into chilled shot glass.

PARISIAN BLONDE

½ oz. light rum
½ oz. triple sec
½ oz. Jamaican rum

Shake with ice and strain into chilled cordial glass.

PEACH BUNNY

½ oz. peach-flavored brandy
½ oz. white crème de cacao
½ oz. half-and-half

Shake with ice and strain into chilled cordial glass.

PEACH TART

1 oz. peach schnapps
½ oz. fresh lime juice

Stir with ice and strain into chilled shot glass.

PEPPERMINT PATTIE

¾ oz. white crème de cacao
¾ oz. white crème de menthe

Shake with ice and strain into chilled cordial glass.

PICKLEBACK

Created at the Bushwick
Country Club, Brooklyn, NY.

1½ oz. Irish whiskey
1½ oz. cold dill pickle brine

*Shoot whiskey, followed by
pickle brine.*

PIGSKIN SHOT

½ oz. vodka
½ oz. melon liqueur
¼ oz. simple syrup
¼ oz. fresh lemon juice

*Shake with ice and strain
into chilled shot glass.*

PINEAPPLE-UPSIDE-DOWN CAKE

½ oz. Irish cream liqueur
½ oz. vodka
½ oz. butterscotch schnapps
½ oz. pineapple Juice

*Shake and strain into shot
glass.*

PORT AND STARBOARD

½ oz. grenadine
½ oz. green crème de menthe

*Pour grenadine into poussecafé glass. Carefully float
crème de menthe (see page 18)
over back of barspoon on top
of grenadine.*

PURPLE HOOTER

1 oz. citrus-flavored vodka
½ oz. triple sec
¼ oz. black raspberry liqueur

*Shake with ice and strain
into chilled shot glass.*

RATTLESNAKE

½ oz. coffee liqueur
½ oz. white crème de cacao
½ oz. Irish cream liqueur

*Float carefully (see page
18), in order given, over
back of barspoon into chilled
cordial or shot glass, so that
each ingredient layers on
preceding one.*

ROCKY MOUNTAIN

¾ oz. Tennessee sour mash
  whiskey
¾ oz. amaretto
¼ oz. fresh lime juice

*Shake with ice and strain
into chilled shot glass.*

SAMBUCA SLIDE

½ oz. sambuca
½ oz. vodka
½ oz. half-and-half

*Stir with ice and strain into
chilled shot glass.*

SCOOTER

½ oz. amaretto
½ oz. brandy
½ oz. half-and-half

*Shake with ice and strain
into chilled cordial glass.*

SEX ON THE BEACH

¼ oz. black raspberry liqueur
¼ oz. melon liqueur
¼ oz. vodka
¼ oz. pineapple juice
¼ oz. cranberry juice

*Shake first four ingredients
with ice and strain into
chilled cordial or shot
glass. Top with cranberry
juice.*

SHAVETAIL

½ oz. peppermint
   schnapps
½ oz. pineapple juice
½ oz. half-and-half

*Shake with ice and strain
into chilled cordial glass.*

SILVER SPIDER

½ oz. vodka
½ oz. light rum
½ oz. triple sec
½ oz. white crème
   de menthe

*Stir with ice and strain into
chilled shot glass.*

SOUR APPLE

¼ oz. vodka
¼ oz. apple liqueur
½ oz. melon liqueur
½ oz. lemon-lime soda

*Shake first three ingredients
with ice. Add lemon-lime
soda and strain into cordial
glass.*

STALACTITE

1¼ oz. sambuca
¼ oz. Irish cream liqueur
¼ oz. black raspberry
   liqueur

*Pour sambuca into cor-
dial glass. Using back of
barspoon, float Irish cream
(see page 18) on top.
Carefully pour raspberry
liqueur, drop by drop, as top
layer. The raspberry liqueur
will pull the Irish cream
through the sambuca and
settle on the bottom.*

STARS AND STRIPES

½ oz. grenadine
½ oz. heavy cream
½ oz. blue curaçao

*Float carefully (see page
18), in order given, over
back of barspoon into chilled
cordial or shot glass, so that
each ingredient layers on
preceding one.*

TERMINATOR

½ oz. coffee liqueur
½ oz. Irish cream liqueur
½ oz. sambuca
½ oz. Mandarine Napoléon
½ oz. vodka

*Float carefully (see page 18),
in order given, over back of
barspoon into chilled cordial
glass, so that each ingredient
layers on preceding one.*

DEVILS TAIL

FROZEN MATADOR

EL TIBIO

PEANUT BUTTER HOT CHOCOLATE

GOLDEN EGGNOG

CLARET CUP

WHITE SANGRIA

INGRID BERGMAN

TO THE MOON

½ oz. coffee liqueur
½ oz. amaretto
½ oz. Irish cream liqueur
½ oz. 151-proof rum

Stir with ice and strain into chilled shot glass.

TRAFFIC LIGHT

½ oz. crème de noyaux
½ oz. Galliano
½ oz. melon liqueur

Float carefully (see page 18), in order given, over back of barspoon into chilled cordial or shot glass, so that each ingredient layers on preceding one.

WOO WOO

½ oz. peach schnapps
½ oz. vodka
1 oz. cranberry juice

Shake with ice and strain into chilled shot glass.

SHOOTERS

FROZEN DRINKS

FROZEN DRINKS ARE certainly perfect for summertime sipping, but they're also enjoyed year-round—much like ice cream. In fact, some are creamy concoctions made with ice cream. Others are tropical in nature, combining spirits or liqueurs with fruit juices, blended with ice. Served in tall, generous glasses and garnished with an assortment of seasonal fruits, they're best sipped slowly—to prevent brain-freeze—through a straw.

Ice cream–based frozen drinks, often mixed with liqueurs such as crème de cacao, amaretto, or Irish cream and topped with whipped cream, also make delicious dessert substitutes. Just imagine sipping a strawberry shortcake or a raspberry cheesecake after a meal, and you sort of get the picture.

The most important ingredient to consider when planning to mix up frozen drinks is ice—and more than you think you could possibly need. Depending on the size and shape of the ice you use, it will melt differently when mixed with warm mixers and alcohol, and it will blend differently, too. And speaking of blending, having an electric blender to pulverize the ice will allow you to make professional-style smoothies at home. Otherwise, you'll need a hand-cranked crusher—or a Lewis bag and a mallet.

You'll find plenty of delicious recipes for every season in this section. Next time it's 90 degrees in the shade, you and your blender can quickly dispatch a Tidal Wave or a Maui Breeze to cool down. And when you have a hankering for a creamy treat any time of year, you'll find a recipe that will put you on cloud nine.

APPLE COLADA

2 oz. apple schnapps
1 oz. cream of coconut
1 oz. half-and-half
Garnish: Apple slice, maraschino cherry

Process ingredients with 1 cup crushed ice in blender until smooth. Pour into highball glass and serve with straw. Garnish with apple and cherry.

APPLE GRANNY CRISP

1 oz. apple schnapps
½ oz. brandy
½ oz. Irish cream liqueur
2 scoops vanilla ice cream
Garnish: Graham cracker crumbs, whipped cream, ground cinnamon

Process ingredients in blender until smooth. Pour into hurricane glass. Top with crumbs, whipped cream, and cinnamon.

APPLE RIVER INNER TUBER

1 oz. brandy
1 oz. dark crème de cacao
1½ scoops vanilla ice cream
Garnish: Half-ring spiced apple

Process ingredients with 1 cup crushed ice in blender until smooth. Pour into hurricane glass. Garnish with spiced apple.

APRICOT CREAM SPRITZ

2 oz. milk
2 oz. apricot nectar
1 oz. apricot-flavored brandy
2 oz. sparkling wine

Process first three ingredients in blender with ¼ cup crushed ice until smooth. Pour into red-wine glass. Top with sparkling wine. Stir gently.

BANANA DI AMORE

1 oz. amaretto
1 oz. crème de banana
2 oz. fresh orange juice
½ oz. simple syrup
½ oz. fresh lemon juice
Garnish: Orange half-wheel,
   banana slice

*Process ingredients with
1 cup crushed ice in blender
until smooth. Pour into red-
wine glass. Garnish with
orange and banana.*

BANANA FOSTER

1½ oz. spiced rum
½ oz. banana liqueur
2 scoops vanilla ice cream
1 medium banana, sliced
Garnish: Ground cinnamon

*Process ingredients in
blender until smooth. Pour
into large snifter. Top with
cinnamon.*

BAY CITY BOMBER

½ oz. vodka
½ oz. light rum
½ oz. blanco tequila
½ oz. gin
½ oz. triple sec
1 oz. fresh orange juice
1 oz. pineapple juice
1 oz. cranberry juice
½ oz. simple syrup
½ oz. fresh lemon juice
¼ oz. 151-proof rum
Garnish: Orange half-wheel,
   maraschino cherry

*Process all ingredients except
rum with 1 cup crushed ice
in blender until smooth.
Pour into hurricane glass.
Slowly pour rum on top.
Garnish with orange and
cherry.*

BEACH BUM'S
COOLER

1¼ oz. Irish cream
   liqueur
¾ oz. light rum
¼ oz. banana liqueur
2 oz. pinapple juice
1 tsp. cream of coconut
¼ ripe banana, sliced
2 scoops vanilla ice cream
1 splash half-and-half
Garnish: Pineapple wedges,
   paper umbrella

*Process ingredients in
blender until smooth.
Pour into hurricane glass.
Garnish with pineapple and
umbrella.*

THE BIG CHILL

1½ oz. dark rum
1 oz. pineapple juice
1 oz. fresh orange juice
1 oz. cranberry juice
2 tsp. cream of coconut
Garnish: Pineapple wedge,
  maraschino cherry

Process ingredients in blender with 1 cup crushed ice until smooth. Pour into hurricane or pilsner glass. Garnish with pineapple and cherry.

THE BLIZZARD

1 oz. brandy
1 oz. Irish cream liqueur
1 oz. coffee liqueur
1 oz. light rum
2 scoops vanilla ice cream
1 splash half-and-half
Garnish: Freshly ground
  nutmeg

Process ingredients in blender until smooth. Pour into large snifter. Top with nutmeg.

BLUE CLOUD COCKTAIL

1 oz. amaretto
½ oz. blue curaçao
2 scoops vanilla ice cream
Garnish: Whipped cream,
  maraschino cherry

Process ingredients in blender until smooth. Pour into snifter. Top with whipped cream and cherry.

BLUE VELVET

1 oz. black raspberry liqueur
1 oz. melon liqueur
2 scoops vanilla ice cream
Garnish: Whipped cream, blue
  curaçao, maraschino cherry

Process liqueurs and ice cream in blender until smooth. Pour into hurricane glass. Top with whipped cream and drizzle with blue curaçao. Garnish with cherry.

BLUSHIN' RUSSIAN

1 oz. coffee liqueur
¾ oz. vodka
1 scoop vanilla ice cream
4 fresh or frozen strawberries
Garnish: Chocolate-covered
  strawberry

Process ingredients in blender until smooth. Pour into hurricane glass. Garnish with strawberry.

THE BRASS FIDDLE

1 oz. grenadine
2 oz. peach schnapps
¾ oz. Tennessee whiskey
2 oz. pineapple juice
1 oz. fresh orange juice
Garnish: Pineapple wedge,
  maraschino cherry

Swirl grenadine inside hurricane glass to coat inside. Do not discard excess. Process remaining ingredients in blender with 1 cup ice until smooth. Pour into glass. Garnish with pineapple and cherry.

BUNKY PUNCH

1½ oz. vodka
1 oz. melon liqueur
1 oz. peach schnapps
2 oz. fresh orange juice
1½ oz. cranberry juice
½ oz. Concord grape juice
Garnish: Lime wheel

Process ingredients with 1 cup crushed ice in blender until smooth. Pour into hurricane glass. Garnish with lime.

CANYON QUAKE

¾ oz. Irish cream liqueur
¾ oz. brandy
1 oz. amaretto
2 oz. half-and-half

Process all ingredients with 1 cup crushed ice in blender until smooth. Pour into large snifter.

CAVANAUGH'S SPECIAL

1 oz. coffee liqueur
1 oz. white crème de cacao
1 oz. amaretto
2 scoops vanilla ice cream
Garnish: Whipped cream, chocolate sprinkles

Pour coffee liqueur into snifter. Process next three ingredients with 1 cup crushed ice in blender until smooth. Pour over coffee liqueur. Top with whipped cream and chocolate sprinkles.

CHAMPAGNE CORNUCOPIA

1 oz. cranberry juice
2 scoops rainbow sherbet
1 oz. vodka
¾ oz. peach schnapps
1 oz. chilled Champagne or sparkling wine
Garnish: Orange half-wheel

Pour cranberry juice into oversized red-wine glass. Process sherbet, vodka, and schnapps in blender until smooth. Pour over cranberry juice to produce a swirl effect and pour Champagne on top. Garnish with orange.

FROZEN DRINKS

CHERRY REPAIR KIT

Use imported cherries for the best flavor.

6 Italian preserved cherries or domestic maraschino cherries
½ oz. half-and-half
½ oz. white crème de cacao
½ oz. amaretto
½ oz. maraschino liqueur
Garnish: Italian preserved cherry in syrup or domestic maraschino cherry

Process 6 cherries with the remaining ingredients with 1 cup crushed ice in blender until smooth. Pour into hurricane glass. Garnish with remaining cherry and serve with straw.

CHI-CHI

1½ oz. vodka
1 oz. cream of coconut
4 oz. pineapple juice
Garnish: Pineapple slice,
    maraschino cherry

*Process ingredients with
1 cup crushed ice in blender
until smooth. Pour into red-
wine glass. Garnish with
pineapple and cherry.*

CHILLY IRISHMAN

3 oz. cold brewed espresso
1 oz. Irish whiskey
½ oz. coffee liqueur
½ oz. Irish cream liqueur
1 scoop vanilla ice cream
1 dash simple syrup

*Process all ingredients in
blender with 1 cup crushed
ice until smooth. Pour into
hurricane glass.*

CHOCO-BANANA SMASH

1¼ oz. Irish cream liqueur
½ oz. half-and-half
½ scoop vanilla ice cream
½ ripe banana, sliced
½ tsp. vanilla extract
Garnish: Maraschino cherry
    and banana chunk on
    cocktail pick, whipped
    cream, chocolate sprinkles

*Process ingredients with
1 cup crushed ice in blender
until smooth. Pour into hurricane glass. Garnish with
skewered cherry and banana,
and top with whipped cream
and chocolate sprinkles.*

CHOCOLATE ALMOND CREAM

1 oz. amaretto
1 oz. white crème de cacao
2 scoops vanilla ice cream
Garnish: Chocolate shavings

*Process ingredients in
blender until smooth. Pour
into hurricane glass. Garnish
with shaved chocolate.*

CITRUS BANANA FRAPPÉ

2 oz. dark rum
1 oz. soda water
1 oz. fresh orange juice
1 oz. milk
½ oz. fresh lime juice
½ ripe banana, sliced
1 tsp. light brown sugar

*Process all ingredients with
1 cup crushed ice in blender
until smooth. Pour into
Collins glass.*

CLOUD 9

1 oz. Irish cream liqueur
1 oz. amaretto
½ oz. black raspberry
    liqueur
2 scoops vanilla ice cream
Garnish: Whipped cream,
    chocolate–peanut butter
    cup, notched

*Process ingredients in
blender until smooth. Pour
into hurricane glass. Top
with whipped cream, and
perch a chocolate–peanut
butter cup on the rim.*

COOL OPERATOR

1 oz. melon liqueur
½ oz. vodka
½ oz. light rum
4 oz. fresh grapefruit juice
2 oz. fresh orange juice
½ oz. fresh lime juice
Garnish: Melon wedge,
    maraschino cherry

*Process ingredients
with 1 cup crushed ice
in blender until smooth.
Pour into hurricane glass.
Garnish with melon and
cherry.*

CRANBERRY COOLER

1½ oz. bourbon whiskey
1½ oz. cranberry juice
½ oz. fresh lime juice
½ oz. simple syrup

*Process all ingredients with
1 cup crushed ice in blender
until smooth. Pour into hurricane glass.*

CREAMY GIN SOUR

2 oz. gin
1 oz. triple sec
½ oz. fresh lime juice
½ oz. fresh lemon juice
1 oz. heavy cream
1 oz. simple syrup

*Process all ingredients
with 1 cup crushed ice in
blender until smooth.
Pour into large red-wine
glass.*

DEATH BY CHOCOLATE

1 oz. Irish cream liqueur
½ oz. vodka
½ oz. dark crème de cacao
1 scoop chocolate ice cream
Garnish: Whipped cream,
    chocolate curls

*Process ingredients in
blender with 1 cup crushed
ice until smooth. Pour into
hurricane glass. Garnish
with whipped cream and
chocolate curls. Serve
with straw.*

FROZEN DRINKS

DEVIL'S TAIL

1½ oz. light rum
1 oz. vodka
1½ tsp. apricot-flavored
    brandy
1 tbsp. fresh lime juice
1½ tsp. grenadine
Garnish: Lime twist

*Process ingredients in
blender with 1 cup crushed
ice until smooth. Pour into
champagne flute. Add lime
twist.*

DI AMORE DREAM

1½ oz. amaretto
¾ oz. white crème de cacao
2 oz. fresh orange juice
2 scoops vanilla ice cream
Garnish: Orange wheel

*Process ingredients in
blender until smooth. Pour
into hurricane glass. Garnish
with orange.*

DREAMY MONKEY

1 oz. vodka
½ oz. crème de banana
½ oz. dark crème de cacao
½ ripe banana, sliced
2 scoops vanilla ice cream
1 oz. half-and-half
Garnish: Whipped cream,
    banana half

Process ingredients in blender until smooth. Pour into hurricane glass. Top with whipped cream and insert banana half as garnish.

FROSTY NOGGIN

1½ oz. light rum
¾ oz. white crème de menthe,
    plus more for garnish
3 oz. prepared nonalcoholic
    eggnog
2 scoops vanilla ice cream
Garnish: Whipped cream,
    green crème de menthe,
    chocolate-mint cookie

Process ingredients in blender until smooth. Pour into hurricane glass. Top with whipped cream, drizzle with green crème de menthe, and garnish with cookie.

FROZEN BERKELEY

1½ oz. light rum
½ oz. brandy
½ oz. passion fruit syrup
½ oz. fresh lemon juice

Process ingredients in blender with 1 cup crushed ice until smooth. Pour into champagne flute.

FROZEN CAPPUCCINO

For glass: Orange wedge,
    superfine sugar, ground
    cinnamon
½ oz. Irish cream liqueur
½ oz. coffee liqueur
½ oz. hazelnut liqueur
1 scoop vanilla ice cream
1 dash half-and-half
Garnish: Cinnamon stick

Rim hurricane glass with orange and blend of sugar and cinnamon. Process remaining ingredients in blender with 1 cup crushed ice until smooth. Pour into glass. Sprinkle with cinnamon and serve with a straw.

FROZEN CITRON NEON

1½ oz. citrus-flavored vodka
1 oz. melon liqueur
½ oz. blue curaçao
½ oz. fresh lime juice
½ oz. simple syrup
½ oz. fresh lemon juice
Garnish: Lemon wheel,
    maraschino cherry

Process ingredients in blender with 1 cup crushed ice until smooth. Pour into hurricane glass. Garnish with lemon and cherry.

FROZEN DAIQUIRIS

CLASSIC FROZEN DAIQUIRI

1½ oz. light rum
1½ oz. fresh lime juice
½ oz. simple syrup
Garnish: Maraschino cherry

Process ingredients in blender with 1 cup crushed ice until smooth. Pour into champagne flute. Garnish with cherry.

FROZEN BLUEBERRY DACQUIRI

⅓ cup fresh or frozen blueberries
1½ oz. light rum
1½ oz. fresh lemon juice
¾ oz. blueberry syrup
Garnish: 1 mint sprig

Process ingredients in blender with 1 cup crushed ice until smooth. Pour into white wine glass. Garnish with mint sprig.

FROZEN STRAWBERRY DACQUIRI

4 large strawberries, hulled and sliced
1½ oz. light rum
1½ oz. fresh lime juice
¾ oz. strawberry syrup
Garnish: 1 whole strawberry

Process ingredients in blender with 1 cup crushed ice until smooth. Pour into white wine glass. Garnish with whole strawberry perched on rim of glass.

BANANA FROZEN DAIQUIRI

1½ oz. light rum
½ oz. triple sec
1½ oz. fresh lime juice
½ oz simple syrup
1 medium banana, sliced
Garnish: Maraschino cherry

Process ingredients in blender with 1 cup crushed ice until smooth. Pour into champagne flute. Garnish with cherry.

MINT FROZEN DAIQUIRI

2 oz. light rum
¾ oz. fresh lime juice
6 fresh mint leaves
¾ oz. simple syrup

Process all ingredients in blender with 1 cup crushed ice until smooth. Pour into old-fashioned glass.

PINEAPPLE FROZEN DAIQUIRI

2 oz. light rum
4 (2-inch) pineapple chunks
¾ oz. fresh lime juice
¾ oz. simple syrup

Process all ingredients in blender with 1 cup crushed ice until smooth. Pour into champagne flute.

FROZEN DRINKS

FROZEN FUZZY

1 oz. peach schnapps
½ oz. triple sec
½ oz. fresh lime juice
½ oz. grenadine
1 splash lemon-lime soda
Garnish: Lime wedge

Process ingredients in blender with 1 cup crushed ice until smooth. Pour into champagne flute. Garnish with lime.

FROZEN MARGARITA

Vary the flavor of your Frozen Margarita by substituting fruit schnapps for the triple sec and adding ½ cup of the desired fruit. Depending on the fruit's sweetness, you may need to add simple syrup. Try berries in season, mango, or melon.

1½ oz. tequila
¾ oz. triple sec
1 oz. fresh lime juice
Garnish: Lemon or lime wheel

Process ingredients in blender with 1 cup crushed ice until smooth. Pour into cocktail glass. Garnish with lemon or lime.

FROZEN MATADOR

1½ oz. blanco tequila
2 oz. pineapple juice
½ oz. fresh lime juice
Garnish: Pineapple wedge

Process ingredients in blender with 1 cup crushed ice until smooth. Pour into old-fashioned glass. Garnish with pineapple.

FRUITY SMASH

1 oz. cherry-flavored brandy
1 oz. crème de banana
1 scoop vanilla ice cream
Garnish: Maraschino cherry

Process ingredients in blender with 1 cup crushed ice until smooth. Pour into cocktail glass. Garnish with cherry.

GAELIC COFFEE

1½ oz. dark crème de cacao
¾ oz. Irish whiskey
¾ oz. Irish cream liqueur
2 oz. milk
1 tsp. instant coffee or 1 oz. cold brewed espresso
Garnish: Whipped cream, green crème de menthe

Process ingredients in blender with 1 cup crushed ice until smooth. Pour into Irish coffee glass. Top with whipped cream and drizzle with crème de menthe.

GEORGIO

1 oz. coffee liqueur
1 oz. Irish cream liqueur
½ ripe banana, sliced
2 oz. half-and-half
Garnish: Whipped cream, unsweetened cocoa powder, fresh mint sprig

Process ingredients in blender with 1 cup crushed ice until smooth. Pour into hurricane glass. Top with whipped cream, sprinkle with a dusting of cocoa, and garnish with mint.

GOLDEN CADILLAC

2 oz. white crème de cacao
1 oz. Galliano
1 oz. half-and-half

Combine with ½ cup crushed ice in blender on low speed for 10 seconds. Pour into chilled champagne flute.

GULF STREAM

For glass: Lime wedge, superfine sugar
1 oz. blue curaçao
1 oz. Champagne or sparkling wine
½ oz. light rum
½ oz. brandy
4 oz. lemonade
1 oz. fresh lime juice
Garnish: Whole strawberry

Rim hurricane glass with lime and sugar. Process remaining ingredients in blender with 1 cup crushed ice until mooth. Pour into glass. Garnish with strawberry.

HUMMER

1 oz. coffee liqueur
1 oz. light rum
2 large scoops vanilla ice cream

Process all ingredients in blender until smooth. Serve in highball glass.

ICED COFFEE À L'ORANGE

2 oz. cold or tepid espresso
1½ oz. triple sec
2 scoops vanilla ice cream
Garnish: Orange wheel

Process ingredients in blender until smooth. Pour into hurricane glass. Garnish with orange wheel.

ICY RUMMED CACAO

1 oz. dark rum
1 oz. dark crème de cacao
2 scoops vanilla ice cream
Garnish: Chocolate shavings

Process ingredients in blender until smooth. Pour into highball glass. Top with chocolate shavings.

IRISH DREAM

¾ oz. dark crème de cacao
½ oz. hazelnut liqueur
½ oz. Irish cream liqueur
2 scoops vanilla ice cream
Garnish: Whipped cream, chocolate sprinkles

Process ingredients in blender with 1 cup crushed ice until smooth. Pour into pilsner glass. Top with whipped cream and chocolate sprinkles.

ITALIAN DREAM

1½ oz. Irish cream liqueur
½ oz. amaretto
2 oz. half-and-half

Process all ingredients in blender with 1 cup crushed ice until smooth. Pour into hurricane glass.

FROZEN DRINKS

JACK'S JAM

½ oz. peach schnapps
½ oz. apple schnapps
½ oz. strawberry liqueur
¼ oz. banana liqueur
2 oz. fresh lemon juice
1 oz. fresh orange juice
1 tsp. superfine sugar
Garnish: Fresh mint sprig, maraschino cherry

Process ingredients in blender with 1 cup crushed ice until smooth. Pour into hurricane glass. Garnish with mint and cherry.

JAMAICAN BANANA

½ oz. light rum
½ oz. white crème de cacao
½ oz. crème de banana
2 scoops vanilla ice cream
1 oz. half-and-half
1 ripe banana, sliced
Garnish: Freshly grated nutmeg, banana slices, whole strawberry

Process ingredients in blender until smooth. Pour into large snifter. Top with nutmeg and garnish with banana and strawberry.

KOKOMO JOE

1 oz. light rum
1 oz. banana liqueur
5 oz. fresh orange juice
2 oz. pineapple juice
1 oz. cream of coconut
½ ripe banana, sliced
Garnish: Orange wheel

Process ingredients in blender with 1 cup crushed ice until smooth. Pour into hurricane glass. Garnish with orange.

LICORICE MIST

1¼ oz. sambuca
½ oz. coconut liqueur
2 oz. half-and-half
Garnish: Licorice stick (cut off both ends to use as a straw)

Process ingredients in blender with 1 cup crushed ice until smooth. Pour into hurricane glass. Add licorice stick "straw."

MOVE IT

Be a roving bartender and keep a wary eye. Avoid long involved conversations with guests. Everyone likes a friendly bartender, but everyone loves a bartender who makes his rounds, increasing the customers' rounds.

—DALE DeGROFF (aka King Cocktail), author of *The Craft of the Cocktail*

LONELY NIGHT

1¼ oz. Irish cream liqueur
1¼ oz. hazelnut liqueur
¾ oz. coffee liqueur
1 scoop vanilla ice cream
Garnish: Whipped cream,
    chocolate shavings

*Process ingredients in
blender with 1 cup crushed
ice until smooth. Pour
into hurricane glass. Top
with whipped cream and
chocolate.*

MAUI BREEZE

½ oz. amaretto
½ oz. triple sec
½ oz. brandy
½ oz. simple syrup
½ oz. fresh lemon juice
2 oz. fresh orange juice
2 oz. guava juice
Garnish: Pineapple spear,
    maraschino cherry

*Process ingredients in
blender with 1 cup crushed
ice until smooth. Pour into
hurricane glass. Garnish
with pineapple and cherry.*

MISSISSIPPI MUD

1½ oz. Tennessee sour mash
    whiskey
1½ oz. coffee liqueur
2 scoops chocolate ice cream
Garnish: Chocolate shavings

*Process ingredients in
blender until smooth. Pour
into cocktail glass. Top with
chocolate.*

MONT BLANC

1 oz. black raspberry liqueur
1 oz. vodka
1 oz. half-and-half
1 scoop vanilla ice cream

*Process all ingredients in
blender until smooth. Pour
into oversized red-wine glass.*

FROZEN
DRINKS

NUTTY COLADA

3 oz. amaretto
1½ oz. canned coconut milk
3 Tbs. canned crushed
    pineapple with juices

*Process all ingredients in
blender with 1 cup crushed
ice until smooth. Pour into
Collins glass and serve with
a straw.*

ORANGE BLOSSOM
SPECIAL

1 oz. peach schnapps
2½ oz. lemon-lime soda
1 scoop orange sherbet
1 scoop vanilla ice cream
2½ oz. half-and-half
Garnish: Orange half-wheel,
    maraschino cherry

*Process ingredients in
blender with 1 cup crushed
ice until smooth. Pour into
hurricane glass. Garnish
with orange and cherry.*

ORANGE TREE

1½ oz. amaretto
¾ oz. crème de noyaux
1½ oz. fresh orange juice
1 scoop vanilla ice cream
Garnish: Whipped cream,
   orange half-wheel

*Process ingredients in
blender until smooth. Pour
into hurricane glass. Top
with whipped cream and
garnish with orange.*

OVER THE RAINBOW

2 oz. spiced rum
1 oz. orange curaçao
2 scoops rainbow sherbet
4 peeled fresh peach slices
2 whole strawberries
Garnish: Fresh peach slice,
   whole strawberry

*Process ingredients in
blender with 1 cup ice until
smooth. Pour into hurricane
glass. Garnish with peach
and strawberry.*

PEACH MELBA
FREEZE

¾ oz. peach schnapps
¾ oz. black raspberry liqueur
¾ oz. hazelnut liqueur
2 scoops vanilla ice cream
¾ oz. half-and-half
1 oz. melba sauce or
   raspberry jam
Garnish: Fresh peach slice

*Process ingredients in
blender until smooth. Pour
into hurricane glass. Garnish
with peach.*

PEACHY AMARETTO

2 oz. amaretto
4 canned peach slices
   with juice or fresh peach
   slices
2 scoops vanilla ice cream

*Process all ingredients in
blender until smooth. Pour
into hurricane glass.*

RASPBERRY
CHEESECAKE

1 tbsp. cream cheese,
   softened
1 oz. white crème de cacao
1 oz. black raspberry
   liqueur
2 scoops vanilla ice cream

*Process all ingredients in
blender with 1 cup crushed
ice until smooth. Pour into
hurricane glass.*

ROAD RUNNER

For the glass: Orange wedge,
   superfine sugar, freshly
   grated nutmeg
1 oz. vodka
½ oz. amaretto
2 tsp. cream of coconut
Garnish: Freshly grated
   nutmeg

*Rim edge of chilled cham-
pagne flute with orange
and a mixture of sugar and
nutmeg. Combine remaining
ingredients in blender with
½ cup crushed ice for 15
seconds. Pour into glass. Top
with nutmeg.*

STRAWBERRIES AND CREAM

1 oz. strawberry schnapps
1½ oz. simple syrup
2 oz. half-and-half
2 strawberries, sliced
Garnish: Whole strawberry

Process first three ingredients in blender with 1 cup crushed ice until smooth. Add sliced strawberries and blend for 10 seconds. Pour into hurricane glass. Garnish with whole strawberry and serve with straw.

STRAWBERRY ALEXANDRA

1 oz. white crème de cacao
1 oz. brandy
½ c. partially thawed frozen sliced strawberries in syrup
1 scoop vanilla ice cream
Garnish: Whipped cream, chocolate curls

Process ingredients in blender until smooth. Pour into white-wine glass. Top with whipped cream and chocolate curls. Serve with a straw and a spoon.

STRAWBERRY BANANA SPRITZ

1½ oz. crème de banana
1 c. frozen strawberries
1 scoop vanilla ice cream
¼ c. soda water
Garnish: 1 whole strawberry

Process ingredients in blender until smooth. Pour into hurricane glass. Garnish with whole strawberry.

STRAWBERRY DAWN

1 oz. gin
2 tsp. cream of coconut
½ c, sliced fresh or frozen strawberries
Garnish: Fresh strawberry slice, fresh mint sprig

Process ingredients in blender with 1 cup crushed ice until smooth. Pour into cocktail glass. Garnish with strawberry slice and mint.

STRAWBERRY SHORTCAKE

1 oz. amaretto
¾ oz. white crème de cacao
½ c. thawed frozen strawberries in syrup
2 scoops vanilla ice cream
Garnish: Whipped cream, whole strawberry

Process ingredients in blender until smooth. Pour into oversized red-wine glass. Top with whipped cream and garnish with strawberry.

SURF'S UP

½ oz. crème de banana
½ oz. white crème de cacao
5 oz. pineapple juice
1 oz. half-and-half
Garnish: Orange wheel, maraschino cherry

Process ingredients with 1 cup crushed ice until smooth. Pour into hurricane glass. Garnish with orange and cherry.

FROZEN DRINKS

SWEET-TART

2 oz. vodka
3 oz. cranberry juice
3 oz. pineapple juice
½ oz. fresh lime juice
Garnish: Lime wheel

Process ingredients in blender with 1 cup crushed ice until smooth. Pour into hurricane glass. Garnish with lime.

TENNESSEE WALTZ

1¼ oz. peach schnapps
2 oz. pineapple juice
1 oz. passion fruit juice
2 scoops vanilla ice cream
Garnish: Whipped cream, peach slice

Process ingredients in blender until smooth. Pour into hurricane glass. Garnish with whipped cream and peach.

TEQUILA FROST

1¼ oz. tequila
1¼ oz. pineapple juice
1¼ oz. fresh grapefruit juice
½ oz. honey
½ oz. grenadine
1 scoop vanilla ice cream
Garnish: Orange wheel, maraschino cherry

Process ingredients in blender until smooth. Pour into hurricane glass. Garnish with orange and cherry.

TIDAL WAVE

1¾ oz. melon liqueur
½ oz. light rum
1 oz. pineapple juice
1 oz. fresh orange juice
½ oz. coconut syrup
¾ oz. simple syrup
¾ oz. fresh lemon juice
Garnish: Lime wheel, maraschino cherry

Process ingredients in blender with 1 cup crushed ice until smooth. Pour into hurricane glass. Garnish with lime and cherry.

TIDBIT

1 oz. gin
1 oz. dry sherry
1 scoop vanilla ice cream

Blend ingredients in blender at low speed and pour into old-fashioned glass.

TROLLEY CAR

1¾ oz. amaretto
4 fresh or frozen strawberries
2 scoops vanilla ice cream
Garnish: 1 whole strawberry

Process ingredients in blender until smooth. Pour into hurricane glass. Garnish with whole strawberry.

HOT DRINKS

HOT TODDIES, simple mixtures of hot water, sugar or honey, and a single spirit—usually bourbon, but any whiskey, rum, brandy, or even gin could be used—are remembered by many as old-fashioned cold remedies, especially by people who remember the first edition of this book. While it was thought that the spirit made you feel better, it was really the heat combined with the spirit that did the trick. Indeed, toddies are one of those classic comforts that we are loath to abandon even today. That's probably because hot drinks are both comforting and stimulating. Sipping in front of a fireplace is recommended but optional.

Remember that the best hot drinks are made with high-quality ingredients: piping hot, freshly brewed coffee or tea; old-fashioned hot chocolate made with real cocoa and milk instead of a mix; cream you've whipped yourself (really, it only takes a couple of minutes); and freshly ground spices.

At home, it's no challenge to heat the ingredients for these drinks on the stove. At a bar, use a hot plate, a microwave oven, or even the steamer of an espresso machine to do the job. Be sure that your serving utensil is heatproof. As an extra precaution against hot beverages cracking cups, you may want to place a spoon in the cup before adding hot liquids. Stemmed Irish coffee glasses are usually tempered and crack-proof. Irish coffee glasses are nice, but large coffee mugs work, too.

Perhaps the most important tip is to serve the drinks in preheated glasses. Pour very hot water into the serving cup, let it stand for a minute or two to warm the cup, and toss out the water.

ALMOND TEA TODDY

Created by JONATHAN POGASH, New York, NY

1 oz. Plymouth gin
½ oz. orange liqueur
½ oz. orgeat or almond syrup
4 oz. hot brewed chai or orange-spiced tea
Garnish: Orange half-wheel

Stir in preheated Irish coffee glass or mug. Garnish with orange.

AMARETTO TEA

6 oz. hot brewed black tea
2 oz. amaretto
Garnish: Whipped cream

Pour hot tea into preheated Irish coffee glass. Add amaretto, but do not stir. Top with whipped cream.

AMERICAN GROG

1½ oz. light rum
¾ oz. fresh lemon juice
1 sugar cube
4 oz. boiling water

Put rum, lemon juice, and sugar cube in preheated Irish coffee glass. Fill with hot water. Stir to dissolve sugar.

APRIHOT

2 oz. apricot-flavored brandy
4 oz. boiling water
Garnish: 1 dash ground cinnamon, orange or lemon wheel

Pour ingredients into preheated Irish coffee glass. Top with ground cinnamon and garnish with citrus wheel.

BLACK GOLD

¼ oz. triple sec
¼ oz. amaretto
¼ oz. Irish cream liqueur
¼ oz. hazelnut liqueur
4 oz. hot brewed coffee
1 dash cinnamon schnapps
Garnish: Whipped cream, chocolate shavings, cinnamon stick

Pour first four ingredients into preheated Irish coffee glass. Add coffee and schnapps and stir. Top with whipped cream and chocolate and add cinnamon stick.

BLUE BLAZER

Dim the lights and bring out your inner performer with this pyrotechnic specialty of "Professor" Jerry Thomas. Try this only when you have your wits about you.

2½ oz. rye whiskey
2½ oz. boiling water
½ oz. simple syrup
Garnish: Lemon twist

Warm two large, silver-plated mugs with handles with boiling water; pour out water. Put whiskey into one mug and fresh boiling water into other mug. Ignite whiskey. While whiskey flames, pour into mug with boiling water. Repeat pouring from one mug into the other, extending stream to a foot or so. If done well, this will have the appearance of a continuous stream of liquid fire. Sweeten with syrup. Pour into preheated Irish coffee glass and add lemon twist.

BOSTON CARIBBEAN COFFEE

For glass: Orange wheel, superfine sugar
1 oz. dark crème de cacao
1 oz. dark rum
4 oz. hot brewed coffee
Garnish: Whipped cream, ground cinnamon, cinnamon stick

Rim preheated Irish coffee glass with orange and sugar. Pour first two ingredients into glass. Fill with coffee. Top with whipped cream and sprinkle with ground cinnamon. Add cinnamon stick.

BOURBON SPICE LATTE

Created by JONATHAN POGASH, New York, NY

1 oz. bourbon
½ oz. coffee-flavored liqueur
¼ oz. allspice liqueur (pimento dram)
1 tsp. agave nectar
1 pinch pumpkin pie spice
4 oz. hot milk
Garnish: Star anise pod

Stir in preheated Irish coffee glass. Float star anise on top.

HOT DRINKS

BRANDY BLAZER

2 oz. brandy, warmed
1 sugar sugar
1 orange twist

Combine first two ingredients in preheated old-fashioned glass. Light with a match and stir with barspoon for a few seconds. Pour into preheated Irish coffee glass. Add orange twist.

BRANDY TODDY (HOT)

½ oz. simple syrup
4 oz. boiling water
2 oz. brandy
Garnish: Lemon wheel, freshly grated nutmeg

Pour syrup into preheated Irish coffee glass or mug. Fill with boiling water. Add brandy and stir. Add lemon and sprinkle with nutmeg.

CAFÉ & CACHAÇA

Created by JONATHAN POGASH, New York, NY

¾ oz. Coffee-Infused Cachaça (recipe follows)
½ oz. cream liqueur, such as Coole Swan
¼ oz. triple sec
4 oz. hot brewed coffee
Garnish: Freshly grated nutmeg

Stir in preheated Irish coffee glass. Top with nutmeg.

COFFEE-INFUSED CACHAÇA

Combine ⅓ cup dark roast (Italian or French) coffee beans with 1 cup cachaça in a jar. Cover tightly and let stand at room temperature for 5–7 days. Strain into bottle and store, refrigerated, for up to 1 month.

CAFÉ L'ORANGE

½ oz. cognac
1 oz. Mandarine Napoléon
½ oz. triple sec
4 oz. hot brewed coffee
Garnish: Whipped cream, finely chopped orange zest

Pour first three ingredients into preheated Irish coffee glass. Fill with coffee. Top with whipped cream and sprinkle with orange zest.

CAFFÈ DI AMARETTO

2 oz. amaretto
4 oz. hot brewed coffee
Garnish: Whipped cream

Pour amaretto into preheated Irish coffee glass. Fill with coffee. Top with whipped cream.

CAPRICCIO

For glass: Orange wheel, superfine sugar, ground cinnamon
1 oz. amaretto
1 oz. simple syrup
½ oz. brandy
½ oz. crème de café or coffee liqueur
4 oz. hot brewed coffee
Garnish: Whipped cream, toasted sliced almonds, maraschino cherry

Rim preheated Irish coffee glass with orange and blend of sugar and cinnamon. Pour next four ingredients into glass. Fill with coffee and stir. Top with whipped cream, sliced almonds, and cherry.

CHOCOLATE-BERRY MOCHA

Created by JONATHAN POGASH, New York, NY

½ oz. black raspberry liqueur
¾ oz. dark crème de cacao
1 tsp. chocolate syrup
½ oz hot milk
4 oz. brewed hot coffee
Garnish: Mini marshmallows, pinch of cocoa powder

Stir in preheated Irish coffee glass. Top with marshmallows and cocoa.

CHOCOLATE COFFEE KISS

¾ oz. coffee liqueur
¾ oz. Irish cream liqueur
1¼ oz. dark crème de cacao
1¼ oz. Mandarine Napoléon
1½ oz. chocolate syrup
4 oz. hot brewed coffee
Garnish: Whipped cream, chocolate shavings, maraschino cherry

Pour first five ingredients into preheated Irish coffee glass. Fill with coffee and stir. Top with whipped cream, chocolate, and cherry.

DOUBLEMINT

1 oz. spearmint schnapps
4 oz. hot brewed coffee
Garnish: Whipped cream, green crème de menthe

Pour schnapps into preheated Irish coffee glass. Fill with coffee and stir. Top with whipped cream and drizzle with crème de menthe.

EL TIBIO

Created by CHRIS CARLSSON, Rochester, NY

½ oz. dark rum
¼ oz. ginger liqueur
1 tsp. honey
5 oz. hot brewed Earl Grey tea
Garnish: 1 dash Creole bitters, cinnamon stick wrapped in long lemon zest

Combine rum, liqueur, and honey in preheated Irish coffee glass or mug. Add tea and stir. Add bitters and cinnamon stick.

HOT DRINKS

GIN TODDY (HOT)

4 oz. boiling water
1 sugar cube
2 oz. gin
Garnish: Lemon half-wheel,
    freshly grated nutmeg

*Pour boiling water and sugar
into preheated Irish coffee
glass or mug and stir to dissolve sugar. Add gin and
stir again. Add lemon and
sprinkle with nutmeg.*

HANDICAPPER'S CHOICE

1 oz. Irish whiskey
1 oz. amaretto
4 oz. hot brewed coffee
Garnish: Whipped cream

*Pour whiskey and amaretto
into preheated Irish coffee
glass. Fill with hot coffee and
stir. Top with whipped cream.*

HOT APPLE TODDY

Created by JONATHAN POGASH,
New York, NY

4 oz. apple cider
1 tsp. mulling spices
1 oz. Calvados
½ oz. vanilla liqueur
Garnish: Orange half-wheel
    studded with 3 whole cloves

*Heat cider and spices
together over low heat for
10 minutes. (Mixture does
not need to boil.) Strain into
preheated Irish coffee glass
or mug. Add Calvados and
liqueur and stir. Garnish
with clove-studded orange.*

HOT BRANDY ALEXANDER

¾ oz. brandy
¾ oz. dark crème de cacao
4 oz. steamed milk
Garnish: Whipped cream,
    chocolate shavings

*Pour ingredients into pre-
heated Irish coffee glass.
Top with cream and
chocolate.*

HOT BRICK TODDY

½ oz. simple syrup
1 tsp. unsalted butter
1 pinch ground cinnamon
2 oz. rye or bourbon whiskey
4 oz. boiling water

*Put first three ingredients into
preheated Irish coffee glass.
Add whiskey, fill with boiling
water, and stir.*

HOT BUTTERED RUM

Hot buttered rum is perhaps
the ultimate chill-chaser. If you
don't have Demerara syrup,
dissolve 1 tsp. Demerara sugar
(or light or dark brown sugar) in
the boiling water.

½ oz. simple syrup or
    Demerara Syrup (page 25)
4 oz. boiling water
2 oz. dark rum
1 tsp. unsalted butter
Garnish: Freshly grated nutmeg

*Put syrup into preheated
Irish coffee glass or mug. Fill
with boiling water. Add rum
and butter and stir. Top with
nutmeg.*

HOT BUTTERED WINE

6 oz. muscatel or other sweet wine
¼ cup very hot water (not boiling)
2 tsp. maple syrup
1 tsp. unsalted butter
Garnish: Freshly grated nutmeg

Pour wine and water into preheated Irish coffee glass. Add maple syrup and butter and stir. Top with nutmeg.

HOT CINNAMON ROLL

1½ oz. cinnamon schnapps
4½ oz. apple cider, heated
Garnish: Whipped cream, cinnamon stick

Pour schnapps into pre-heated Irish coffee glass. Add cider and stir. Top with whipped cream and add cinnamon stick.

HOT GOLD

2 oz. amaretto
6 oz. fresh orange juice, heated until very warm
Garnish: Cinnamon stick

Pour amaretto into pre-heated red-wine glass or Irish coffee glass. Add orange juice and stir. Add cinnamon stick as stirrer.

HOT KISS

1 oz. Irish whiskey
½ oz. white crème de menthe
½ oz. white crème de cacao
6 oz. hot brewed coffee
Garnish: Whipped cream, chocolate-covered mint

Pour whiskey and liqueurs into preheated Irish coffee glass. Add coffee and stir. Top with whipped cream and garnish with a chocolate-covered mint.

INDIAN SUMMER

For glass: Lemon wedge, superfine sugar
2 oz. apple schnapps
4 oz. apple cider, heated
Garnish: Cinnamon stick

Rim preheated Irish coffee mug or glass with lemon and sugar. Add schnapps and cider and stir. Add cinnamon stick, if using.

IRISH COFFEE

2 sugar cubes
4 oz. hot brewed coffee
1½ oz. Irish whiskey
Garnish: Lightly whipped cream

Stir sugar cubes and coffee in preheated Irish coffee glass to dissolve sugar. Add whiskey. Float cream over back of barspoon to fill glass.

HOT DRINKS

ITALIAN COFFEE

½ oz. amaretto
4 oz. hot brewed coffee
1 small scoop coffee ice
    cream
Garnish: Ground coriander

Pour amaretto into pre-heated Irish coffee glass. Fill with coffee and stir. Top with ice cream and sprinkle with coriander.

JAMAICA COFFEE

1 oz. coffee-flavored brandy
¾ oz. light rum
½ oz. simple syrup
4 oz. hot brewed coffee
Garnish: Whipped cream,
    freshly grated nutmeg

Pour brandy, rum, and syrup into preheated Irish coffee glass. Fill with coffee and stir. Top with whipped cream and nutmeg.

KEOKE COFFEE

See Coffee Nudge, page 234.

LUMBERJACK

Created by CHARLES MYERS,
O'Fallen, MO

2 oz. bourbon
1 tsp. light brown sugar
½ tsp. unsalted butter
8 oz. apple juice, heated
Garnish: Ground cinnamon

Stir in preheated Irish coffee glass. Top with cinnamon.

MEXICAN COFFEE

1 oz. coffee liqueur
1 oz. blanco tequila
4 oz. hot brewed coffee
Garnish: Whipped cream

Pour coffee liqueur and tequila into preheated Irish coffee glass. Fill with coffee and stir. Top with whipped cream.

MEXITALY COFFEE

For glass: Maraschino cherry
    juice, superfine sugar,
    ground cinnamon
¾ oz. coffee liqueur
¾ oz. amaretto
4½ oz. hot brewed coffee
Garnish: Whipped cream,
    chocolate shavings

Rim preheated Irish coffee glass with cherry juice and blend of sugar and cinnamon. Pour liqueurs into glass. Fill with coffee and stir. Top with whipped cream and chocolate.

MULLED CABERNET

5 oz. cabernet sauvignon
1½ oz. fresh orange juice
½ oz. simple syrup
1 pinch ground cinnamon
1 pinch freshly ground nutmeg
1 dash Angostura bitters
Garnish: Cinnamon stick

Heat ingredients together until hot but not boiling. Serve in preheated Irish coffee glass or mug. Add cinnamon stick.

MULLED WINE

Created by JONATHAN POGASH,
New York, NY

The steamer spout of an
espresso machine does a great
job of heating the wine with the
spices. If you don't have one,
be careful not to let the rum
and spice come to a boil. Make
it in quantity for a large group.

1½ oz. malbec, zinfandel, or
    other red wine with spicy
    notes
1 tsp. mulling spices
1½ oz. dark rum
1 tsp. honey
Garnish: Lemon wheel

*Heat wine and spices in
metal latte jug with steamer
spout of espresso machine.
(Or heat in a small saucepan over very low heat
just until steaming.) Pour
into preheated Irish coffee
glass or mug. Add rum and
honey and stir. Garnish with
lemon.*

PEANUT BUTTER HOT
CHOCOLATE

Created by JONATHAN POGASH,
New York, NY

1 oz. Castries Peanut Rum
    Crème Liqueur
¾ oz. light rum
4 oz. hot chocolate
Garnish: Mini marshmallows,
    pinch of cocoa

*Stir in preheated Irish cof-
fee glass or mug. Top with
marshmallows and cocoa.*

PEANUT COFFEE

Created by JONATHAN POGASH,
New York, NY

1 oz. Castries Peanut Rum
    Crème Liqueur
¾ oz. dark rum
4 oz. hot brewed coffee

*Stir in preheated Irish coffee
glass.*

RAZZMATAZZ

1 oz. black raspberry liqueur
½ oz. crème de cassis
½ oz. coffee liqueur
4 oz. hot brewed coffee
Garnish: Whipped cream,
    fresh seasonal berries

*Pour liqueurs into preheated
Irish coffee glass. Fill with
coffee and stir. Top with
whipped cream and berries.*

HOT DRINKS

RUEDESHEIM KAFFE

3 sugar cubes
1½ oz. brandy, warmed
4½ oz. hot brewed coffee
Garnish: Whipped cream,
    chocolate shavings

Place sugar cubes in preheated Irish coffee glass. Add brandy and ignite. Let burn until it extinguishes itself (or cover tightly after 1 minute to extinguish). Fill with coffee and stir. Top with whipped cream and chocolate.

RUM TODDY (HOT)

1 sugar cube
4 oz. boiling water
2 oz. light or dark rum
Garnish: Lemon wheel,
    freshly grated nutmeg

Stir sugar and water in preheated Irish coffee glass or mug to dissolve sugar. Add rum and stir. Add lemon and sprinkle with nutmeg.

RUSSIAN COFFEE

½ oz. coffee liqueur
½ oz. hazelnut liqueur
1 oz. vodka
4 oz. hot brewed coffee
Garnish: Whipped cream

Pour liqueurs and vodka into preheated Irish coffee glass. Fill with coffee and stir. Top with whipped cream.

SNOW BUNNY

1½ oz. Grand Marnier
5 oz. hot chocolate
Garnish: Cinnamon stick

Pour liqueur into preheated Irish coffee glass. Fill with hot chocolate and stir. Add cinnamon stick.

SPANISH COFFEE

1½ oz. Spanish brandy
4½ oz. hot brewed coffee
Garnish: Whipped cream

Pour brandy into preheated Irish coffee glass. Fill with coffee and stir. Top with whipped cream.

SPICED APPLE CIDER

Created by JONATHAN POGASH,
New York, NY

1 oz. rye whiskey
¾ oz. allspice liqueur
½ oz. Honey Syrup (page 25)
4 oz. hot cider
Garnish: Orange half-wheel
    studded with 3 whole
    cloves

Stir in preheated Irish coffee glass or mug. Garnish with clove-studded orange.

STEAMING PEACH

2 oz. peach schnapps
4 oz. boiling water
Garnish: Orange wheel

Pour schnapps into preheated snifter. Add boiling water and stir. Float orange on top.

TOM AND JERRY

"Professor" Jerry Thomas popularized this warming drink, and it is still served as a Christmastime beverage. Here is his original recipe. It makes enough for many servings, so it would be best in a professional bar setting.

Makes about 28 servings
ORIGINAL TOM AND JERRY BATTER
3 eggs, separated
¼ tsp. cream of tartar
2¼ c. superfine sugar
2 oz. light rum
1 tsp. ground cinnamon
½ tsp. ground cloves
½ tsp. ground allspice
For 1 serving
2 oz. brandy
1 oz. Original Tom and Jerry Batter
4 oz. boiling water
Garnish: Freshly grated nutmeg

To make batter, beat egg whites and cream of tartar in medium bowl to stiff peaks. Beat yolks in another medium bowl until slightly thickened. Gradually beat in 1 cup of the sugar. Mix in rum, cinnamon, cloves, and allspice. Mix in remaining 1 cup sugar. Fold in whites. Cover and refrigerate until ready to serve, up to 2 days. Makes 3½ c. batter, enough for about 28 drinks.

For 1 serving, combine brandy and batter in preheated punch cup or coffee mug. Fill with boiling water and stir well. Top with nutmeg.

TOM AND JERRY (CREAMY)

Richer and headier than the original, this Tom and Jerry is made with hot milk. This is the perfect hot punch to serve at your holiday parties.

Makes 10 servings
TOM AND JERRY BATTER
6 eggs, separated
2 c. superfine sugar
⅓ c. brandy
⅓ c. light rum
¼ c. bourbon
For 1 serving
1 oz. Tom and Jerry Batter
5 oz. hot milk, as needed
Garnish: Freshly grated nutmeg

To make batter, beat egg whites in large bowl to stiff peaks. Beat yolks in medium bowl until thickened. Gradually beat in sugar until very thick and pale yellow. Mix in brandy and rum. Fold in whites. (If you have a Tom and Jerry serving bowl, transfer batter to bowl.) Cover and refrigerate until ready to serve, up to 1 day.

For each serving, spoon batter into preheated punch cup or coffee mug. Add milk to fill and stir. Top with nutmeg.

TOM AND JERRY FOR TWO

Makes 2 servings
Instead of the brandy, substitute light rum, or use a combination of brandy and rum.

1 egg, separated
3 tbsp. superfine sugar
1 oz. brandy
12 oz. hot milk
Garnish: Freshly grated nutmeg

Beat egg white until soft peaks form. Beat egg yolk with sugar until thick and pale yellow. Fold in white. Divide batter, brandy, and milk between two preheated punch cups or coffee mugs and stir well. Top with nutmeg.

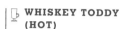

WHISKEY TODDY (HOT)

1 sugar cube
4 oz. boiling water
2 oz. rye, bourbon, or blended whiskey
Garnish: Lemon wheel, freshly grated nutmeg

Stir sugar and water in pre-heated Irish coffee glass or mug to dissolve sugar. Add whiskey and stir. Add lemon and sprinkle with nutmeg.

EGGNOGS AND PUNCHES

E GGNOG FIRST BECAME popular during colonial times. Rum was the favorite spirit of the early Americans; they mixed it with milk, eggs, and sugar. Over the years, whiskey and brandy have been used as substitutes for rum. Today, eggnog is enjoyed mostly as a holiday drink, which is a shame.

Raw eggs can carry a bacterium that causes salmonella poisoning, but fortunately, there are solutions to the problem. One, use a prepared mix such as Mr. Boston Egg Nog. Two, use large prepasteurized eggs, available at many supermarkets. Three, if using unpasteurized eggs, make cooked eggnog on page 283. Float a block of vanilla ice cream (removed in one piece from its packaging) in the eggnog's punch bowl—the ice cream will chill and flavor the nog as it melts.

Punches are ideal for serving a large number of guests. Recipes for both cold and hot punches can be found in this section, as well as for several nonalcoholic punches. While cold punches in smaller quantities can be mixed in and served from a pitcher, larger recipes are usually served in a punch bowl from which guests help themselves. Use a block of ice, not ice cubes, to keep punch chilled.

Hot punch should be served at the proper steaming temperature. For an informal party, ladle up the drink right from the pot on the stove, or put the pot in the party area on a hot plate, keeping in mind that you might need an electric source. At a bar, the latte steamer of an espresso machine renders drinks mixed from cold ingredients hot in a few seconds.

EGGNOGS

AMBASSADOR'S MORNING LIFT

Makes 10 to 12 servings
1 qt. eggnog, chilled
¾ c. cognac
3 oz. Jamaican rum, brandy, or bourbon
3 oz. dark crème de cacao
Garnish: Freshly grated nutmeg

Combine ingredients in large punch bowl. Serve in punch cups and top each serving with nutmeg.

APRICOT BRANDY EGGNOG

Makes 10 to 12 servings
1 qt. eggnog, chilled
1¼ c. apricot-flavored brandy
2½ oz. triple sec
Garnish: Freshly grated nutmeg

Combine ingredients in large punch bowl. Serve in punch cups and top each serving with nutmeg.

BALTIMORE EGGNOG

Makes 10 to 12 servings
1 qt. eggnog, chilled
⅔ c. brandy
⅔ c. Jamaican rum
⅔ c. madeira
Garnish: Freshly grated nutmeg

Combine ingredients in large punch bowl. Serve in punch cups and top each serving with nutmeg.

BRANDY EGGNOG

Makes 10 to 12 servings
1 qt. eggnog, chilled
1½ c. brandy
Garnish: Freshly grated nutmeg

Combine ingredients in large punch bowl. Serve in punch cups and top each serving with nutmeg.

🍵 EGGNOG (COOKED)

Makes 8 to 10 servings
3 c. half-and-half
¾ c. sugar
9 large egg yolks
¾ c. golden rum
1 c. heavy cream
Garnish: Freshly grated
    nutmeg

Heat half-and-half and sugar in medium saucepan over medium heat, stirring to dissolve sugar. Whisk egg yolks in large heatproof bowl until thickened; gradually whisk in hot mixture. Return to saucepan and stir with wooden spoon over medium-low heat until custard coats spoon and reads 185°F on instant-read thermometer. Strain through wire sieve into preheated large punch bowl; let cool. Stir in rum. Cover and refrigerate until chilled, at least 4 hours. Whip cream to soft peaks and fold into custard. Serve in punch cups and top each serving with nutmeg.

🍵 CHRISTMAS YULE EGGNOG

Makes 10 to 12 servings
1 qt. eggnog, chilled
1 cup bourbon whiskey
½ cup light rum
Garnish: Freshly grated
    nutmeg

Combine ingredients in large punch bowl. Serve in punch cups and top each serving with nutmeg.

EGGNOGS AND PUNCHES

🍸 EGG CRUSHER

1 c. eggnog
1 oz. light rum
1 oz. coffee liqueur
Garnish: Freshly grated
    nutmeg

Shake with ice and strain into oversized snifter. Top with nutmeg.

🍸 FROSTY NOG

½ c. eggnog
1 oz. amaretto
Garnish: Toasted sliced
    almonds, freshly grated
    nutmeg

Process eggnog, amaretto, and 1 cup crushed ice in blender on medium speed until smooth. Pour into hurricane glass. Top with almonds and nutmeg.

GOLDEN EGGNOG

Created by JONATHAN POGASH,
New York, NY

Your guests will feel very
special when presented with
gold-topped cups of nog. To
transfer the edible gold (or
silver) leaf to the drink, use the
tip of a fine-tipped artist's brush
to lift a large flake of the gold
from its tissue. Touch the edge
of the flake onto the surface
of the eggnog and remove the
paintbrush without getting the
bristles wet.

1 large egg, separated
1 tsp. superfine sugar
1½ oz. vanilla liqueur
1½ oz. whole milk
Garnish: Freshly grated
    nutmeg, edible gold leaf

*Beat egg white with ½ tsp.
sugar until soft peaks form.
Beat yolk well with remaining ½ tsp. sugar until pale
and thickened. Add white
and gently fold together. Add
liqueur and milk and mix
gently. Pour into ice-filled
cocktail glass. Top with nutmeg and gold leaf.*

GOLDEN EGGNOG
(LARGE BATCH)

Created by JONATHAN POGASH,
New York, NY

Makes 6 servings
6 large eggs, separated
2 Tbs. superfine sugar
9 oz. vanilla liqueur
9 oz. whole milk
Garnish: Freshly grated
    nutmeg, edible gold
    leaf

*Beat egg whites with
1 Tbs. sugar until soft
peaks form. Beat yolks
well with remaining 1 Tbs.
sugar until pale and
thickened. Add whites
and gently fold together.
Add liqueur and milk and
mix gently. Pour into ice-
filled cocktail glasses. Top
each with nutmeg and
gold leaf.*

IMPERIAL EGGNOG

Makes 10 to 12 servings
1 qt. eggnog, chilled
1¼ cups brandy
2 oz. apricot-flavored
    brandy
Garnish: Freshly grated
    nutmeg

*Combine ingredients
in large punch bowl. Serve
in punch cups and top
each serving with
nutmeg.*

MAPLE EGGNOG

Makes 8 servings
1 qt. eggnog
½ c. pure maple syrup, preferably grade B
½ c. bourbon whiskey
Garnish: Freshly grated nutmeg

Combine ingredients in large pitcher and chill. Stir before serving. Serve in punch cups and top each serving with nutmeg.

NASHVILLE EGGNOG

Makes 10 to 12 servings
1 qt. eggnog, chilled
¾ cup bourbon whiskey
3 oz. brandy
3 oz. Jamaican rum
Garnish: Freshly grated nutmeg

Combine ingredients in large punch bowl. Serve in punch cups and top each serving with nutmeg.

NOG DE CACAO

1½ oz. white crème de cacao
1½ oz. eggnog, chilled

Pour over ice in old-fashioned glass and stir.

OLD-FASHIONED EGGNOG

Makes 8 to 10 servings
6 large eggs
1 c. sugar
½ tsp. salt
1 c. golden rum
1 pt. half-and-half
1 pt. milk
Garnish: Freshly grated nutmeg

In a large bowl, beat eggs until pale and foamy. Add sugar and salt, beating until thickened. Stir in rum, half-and-half, and milk. Chill at least 3 hours. Serve in punch cups and top each serving with nutmeg.

PORT EGGNOG

Makes 10 to 12 servings
1 qt. eggnog, chilled
2¼ c. tawny or ruby port
Garnish: Freshly grated nutmeg

Combine ingredients in large punch bowl. Serve in punch cups and top each serving with nutmeg.

RUM EGGNOG

Makes 10 to 12 servings
1 qt. eggnog, chilled
1½ c. light rum
Garnish: Freshly grated nutmeg

Combine ingredients in large punch bowl. Serve in punch cups and top each serving with nutmeg.

EGGNOGS AND PUNCHES

RUSSIAN NOG

1 oz. vodka
1 oz. coffee liqueur
1 oz. eggnog

Pour into ice-filled old-fashioned glass and stir.

SHERRY EGGNOG

Makes 10 to 12 servings
1 qt. eggnog, chilled
2¼ c. cream sherry
Garnish: Freshly grated
    nutmeg

Combine in large punch bowl. Serve in punch cups and top each serving with nutmeg.

WHISKEY EGGNOG

Makes 10 to 12 servings
1 qt. eggnog, chilled
1½ c. blended or bourbon
    whiskey
Garnish: Freshly grated
    nutmeg

Combine in large punch bowl. Serve in punch cups and top each serving with nutmeg.

THE WORLD BAR EGGNOG

Created by JONATHAN POGASH,
New York, NY

1 large egg, separated
2 tsp. superfine sugar
1 oz. heavy cream
⅛ tsp. pure almond extract
⅛ tsp. pure vanilla extract
1½ oz. dark rum
Garnish: Ground cinnamon,
    freshly ground nutmeg

Beat egg white with 1 tsp. sugar until soft peaks form. Beat egg yolk well until pale and thick. Add white and gently fold together. Beat cream, almond, and vanilla extracts with remaining 1 tsp. sugar until stiff. Add to egg mixture and gently fold together. Fold in rum. Pour into ice-filled punch cup or cocktail glass. Top with cinnamon and nutmeg.

◯ THE WORLD BAR EGGNOG (LARGE BATCH)

Makes 18 to 20 servings
10 eggs, separated
1 c. superfine sugar
3 c. heavy cream
2 Tbs. almond extract
2 Tbs. vanilla extract
2 c. dark rum
Garnish: 1 tsp. freshly grated nutmeg, 1 tsp. ground cinnamon

Beat egg whites with ½ cup sugar until soft peaks form. Beat egg yolks well until pale and thickened. Add whites and gently fold together. Beat cream, almond and vanilla extracts, and remaining ½ cup sugar until soft peaks form. Add to egg mixture and gradually fold together. Fold in rum. Cover and refrigerate until chilled, at least 4 hours or overnight. Pour into punch bowl and top with nutmeg and cinnamon. Serve, without ice, in punch cups or cocktail glasses.

COLD PUNCHES

☐ APRICOT ORANGE FIZZ

Makes 6 servings
1½ c. fresh orange juice
½ c. light rum
¼ c. apricot-flavored brandy
1 oz. fresh lime juice
Soda water
Garnish: Lime wheels

Combine first four ingredients in pitcher and stir. Pour into ice-filled Collins glasses, about ⅔ full. Top each with soda water and stir. Garnish with limes. Serve in punch cups.

◯ BOMBAY PUNCH

Makes 60 servings
1 (1-liter) bottle brandy
1 (1-liter) bottle dry (fino) sherry
3 c. fresh lemon juice
1½ c. simple syrup
½ c. maraschino liqueur
½ c. triple sec
4 (750-ml) bottles Champagne, chilled
2 qt. soda water, chilled
Garnish: Fresh seasonal fruit

Stir first six ingredients into large punch bowl. Add Champagne and soda water and stir. Add large block of ice. Garnish with fruit. Serve in punch cups.

EGGNOGS AND PUNCHES

☕ BOOM BOOM PUNCH

Makes 36 servings
2 (1-liter) bottles light rum
1 qt. fresh orange juice
1 (750-ml) bottle sweet
   vermouth
1 (750-ml) Champagne,
   chilled
Garnish: Sliced bananas

*Stir first three ingredients
in large punch bowl. Add
Champagne and stir again.
Add large block of ice.
Garnish with bananas.
Serve in punch cups.*

☕ BRANDY PUNCH

Makes 36 servings
1.75 liters brandy
1 qt. soda water
3 c. fresh lemon juice
2 c. fresh orange juice
2 c. simple syrup
1 c. grenadine
1 c. triple sec
2 c. cold strong brewed
   black tea
Garnish: Fresh seasonal fruit

*Stir in large punch bowl.
Add large block of ice.
Garnish with fruit. Serve
in punch cups.*

PUNCH BOWL ICE BLOCKS

In addition to the punch itself, a punch bowl should always hold a block of ice to keep the drinks properly chilled. Simply pour cold water into a flexible plastic container, and freeze until the ice is solid, being sure to allow plenty of time (at least overnight). Just pop the ice out of the container and transfer it into the bowl. If your sense of aesthetics requires a crystal-clear ice block, it is easily done. Dissolved air is the cause of cloudy ice, but it is removed by boiling. Boil the water in a saucepan, let it cool, then boil it again. Use the cooled, double-boiled water for your ice block, which will be impressively transparent.

JONATHAN POGASH,
The Cocktail Guru

☕ BRUNCH PUNCH

Makes 40 servings

3 qt. tomato juice, chilled
1 (1-liter) bottle light or dark rum
2½ tsp. Worcestershire sauce
⅔ c. fresh lemon or lime juice
Salt and freshly ground black pepper to taste
Garnish: Lemon or lime wheels

Combine in large punch bowl and stir well. Add large block of ice. Garnish with citrus. Serve in punch cups.

☕ CAPE CODDER PUNCH

Makes 40 servings

3 (32-oz.) bottles cranberry-apple drink
3 c. vodka
2 c. fresh orange juice
1 c. simple syrup
⅔ c. fresh lemon juice
1 (28-oz.) bottle mineral water, chilled

Stir in large punch bowl. Add large block of ice. Serve in punch cups.

SQUEEZE FRUIT WARM

Never store lemons, limes, or oranges that are meant for juicing in the refrigerator because cold fruit is stingy with juice. If the fruit is cold, soak it in warm water for 15 or 20 minutes, then roll it under the palm of your hand to break the cells and release the juice. Follow these simple steps and you'll almost double the amount of juice from the same fruit.

—DALE DeGROFF (aka King Cocktail),
author of *The Craft of the Cocktail*

☕ CARDINAL PUNCH

Makes 42 servings
2 qt. red wine, such as merlot
1 qt. soda water
3 c. fresh lemon juice
2 c. fresh simple syrup
2 c. brandy
2 c. light rum
2 c. cold strong brewed
    black tea
1 split Champagne
1 c. sweet vermouth

*Stir in punch bowl. Add
large block of ice. Serve in
punch cups.*

🍸 CHAMPAGNE CUP

Makes 6 servings
¾ c. soda water
2 oz. brandy
1 oz. triple sec
1 oz. simple syrup
1 pt. Champagne, chilled
Garnish: Fresh seasonal fruit,
    3 long strips of cucumber
    peel, bunch of fresh mint

*Pour first four ingredients
into pitcher and stir. Half-
fill with ice and top with
Champagne. Garnish with
fruit. Insert cucumber peels
inside pitcher and top with
mint. Serve in red-wine
glasses.*

☕ CHAMPAGNE PUNCH

Makes 32 servings
3 c. fresh lemon juice
2 c. simple syrup
2 c. brandy
1 c. maraschino liqueur
1 c. triple sec
2 (750-ml) bottles
    Champagne, chilled
2 c. cold soda water
2 c. cold strong brewed
    black tea
Garnish: Fresh seasonal fruit

*Stir in large punch bowl.
Add large block of ice.
Garnish with fruit. Serve
in punch cups.*

☕ CHAMPAGNE
SHERBET PUNCH

Makes 20 servings
3 c. pineapple juice, chilled
¼ c. fresh lemon juice,
    chilled
1 bottle (750-ml)
    Champagne, chilled
1 qt. pineapple sherbet

*Stir pineapple and lemon
juices and Champagne in
punch bowl. Add sherbet.
Serve in punch cups, adding
a portion of sherbet to each
glass.*

CITRUS-BEER PUNCH

Makes 8 servings

8 lemons
2 c. sugar
1 c. fresh grapefruit juice
2 (12-oz.) cans chilled lager beer
Garnish: Lemon wheels

Remove zest from 6 lemons with vegetable peeler and reserve. Juice lemons; you should have 2 cups Bring 2 cups water and sugar to a boil in large nonreactive saucepan. Add lemon zest and remove from heat. Cover and let stand 5 minutes. Add lemon juice and grapefruit juice. Strain into large pitcher, cover, and refrigerate until chilled. Just before serving, add beer. Serve in punch cups, garnished with lemon wheels.

CLARET CUP

Also known as a Loving Cup, make this with a full-bodied, fruity red wine.

Makes 6 servings

1 pt. red wine, such as cabernet-merlot blend or claret
¾ c. soda water
2 oz. brandy
2 oz. simple syrup
1 oz. triple sec
Garnish: Fresh seasonal fruit, 2 long strips of cucumber peel, bunch of fresh mint

Pour ingredients into large pitcher. Stir. Fill with ice. Garnish with fruit. Insert cucumber peels inside pitcher and top with mint. Serve in red-wine glasses.

CIDER PUNCH:
Substitute apple cider for the red wine.

EGGNOGS AND PUNCHES

CLARET PUNCH

Makes 40 servings

3 (750-ml) bottles red wine, such as cabernet-merlot blend
1 qt. soda water
1 qt. cold strong brewed black tea
3 c. fresh lemon juice
2 c. brandy
1 c. simple syrup
1 c. triple sec

Pour over large block of ice in punch bowl. Stir well. Serve in punch cups.

EXTRA-KICK PUNCH

Makes 24 servings

2 qt. hot water
1 c. packed light or dark brown sugar
2 c. dark rum
1 c. brandy
1 c. fresh lemon juice
1 c. pineapple juice
¼ c. peach brandy

Stir hot water and brown sugar in large heatproof bowl to dissolve sugar; let cool. Stir in remaining ingredients. Cover and chill. Pour over block of ice in punch bowl. Serve in punch cups.

FISH HOUSE PUNCH

The Schuylkill Fishing Company, a gentleman's club in Philadelphia, is also known as the "Fish House," and it is the place of origin for this heady punch.

Makes 40 servings

3 c. fresh lemon juice
2 c. simple syrup
2 (750-ml) bottles brandy
1 (1-liter) bottle peach-flavored brandy
2 c. light rum
1 qt. soda water
1 pt. cold strong brewed black tea (optional)
Garnish: Fresh seasonal fruit

Stir in punch bowl. Add large block of ice. Garnish with fruit. Serve in punch cups.

KENTUCKY PUNCH

Makes 32 servings

2 (6-oz.) cans frozen orange juice concentrate, thawed
2 (6-oz.) cans frozen lemonade concentrate, thawed
1 c. fresh lemon juice
1 (1-liter) bottle bourbon whiskey
2 (2-liter) bottles lemon-lime soda

Stir all ingredients except soda in large container and chill. Pour into punch bowl over large block of ice and stir in soda. Serve in punch cups.

MINT JULEP PUNCH

Makes 44 servings

1 c. mint jelly
6 c. pineapple juice
1 (750-ml) bottle bourbon
  whiskey
½ c. fresh lime juice
7 c. lemon-lime soda
Garnish: Lime wheels, fresh
  mint leaves

Cook mint jelly and 2 cups water in large nonreactive saucepan over low heat, stirring until jelly melts. Let cool. Stir in pineapple juice, bourbon, 2 cups cold water, and lime juice. Cover and chill. Pour over block of ice in punch bowl. Slowly pour in soda, stirring gently. Garnish with lime and mint. Serve in punch cups.

RHINE WINE CUP

Makes 6 servings

1 pt. semidry white wine,
  preferably Rhine wine
2 oz. simple syrup
2 oz. brandy
1 oz. triple sec
Garnish: Fresh seasonal fruit,
  3 long strips of cucumber
  peel, bunch of fresh mint

Pour ingredients into large pitcher. Stir. Fill with ice. Garnish with fruit. Insert cucumber peels inside pitcher and top with mint. Serve in white-wine glasses.

SANGRIA PUNCH

Makes 10 servings

1 (750-ml) bottle red or
  rosé wine, preferably
  Spanish
½ c. simple syrup
1 orange, thinly sliced
1 lime, thinly sliced
¾ c. soda water
Garnish: Fresh seasonal
  fruit

Pour wine, syrup, and ½ cup water into pitcher and stir. Add orange and lime. Half-fill pitcher with ice. Add soda water and stir gently. Add fruit. Serve in red-wine glasses, adding fruit to each glass.

TEQUILA PUNCH

Makes 40 servings

4 (750-ml) bottles dry white
  wine, such as pinot grigio,
  chilled
1 (1-liter) bottle tequila,
  chilled
1 (750-ml) bottle
  Champagne, chilled
2 c. simple syrup
1 c. fresh lime juice
2 quarts assorted fresh fruits,
  such as berries and melon
  balls

Pour first five ingredients into large punch bowl and stir. Add large ice block and fruit. Serve in punch cups.

EGGNOGS AND
PUNCHES

WEST INDIAN PUNCH

Makes 48 servings
2 (1-liter) bottles light rum
1 (750-ml) bottle crème de banana
1 qt. pineapple juice
1 qt. fresh orange juice
1 qt. lemon juice
1½ cups simple syrup
1 tsp. freshly grated nutmeg
1 tsp. ground cinnamon
½ tsp. ground cloves
¾ cup soda water
Garnish: Sliced bananas

Pour ingredients into large punch bowl. Stir. Add large ice block. Garnish with bananas. Serve in punch cups.

WHISKEY SOUR PUNCH

Makes 32 servings
3 (6-oz.) frozen lemonade concentrate, thawed
1 (1-liter) bottle bourbon whiskey
3 c. fresh orange juice
1 (2-liter) bottle soda water, chilled
Garnish: Orange wheels

Combine ingredients over block of ice in punch bowl. Stir gently. Garnish with oranges. Serve in punch cups.

WHITE WINE CUP

Makes 6 servings
1 pt. dry white wine, such as pinot grigio or sauvignon blanc
2 oz. simple syrup
2 oz. brandy
1 oz. triple sec
Garnish: Fresh seasonal fruit, 3 long strips of cucumber peel, bunch of fresh mint

Pour ingredients into large pitcher. Stir. Fill with ice. Garnish with fruit. Insert cucumber peels inside pitcher and top with mint. Serve in white-wine glasses.

HOT PUNCHES

HOT APPLE BRANDY

Makes 8 servings
6 c. apple juice
1½ c. apricot-flavored brandy
3 cinnamon sticks
½ tsp. ground cloves

Simmer all ingredients over low heat for 30 minutes. Serve warm in snifters.

HOT BURGUNDY PUNCH

Makes 8 to 10 servings
¼ c. Demerara or packed light brown sugar
1 c. apple juice
Zest of of ½ lemon, removed with vegetable peeler
1 cinnamon stick
6 whole allspice berries
5 whole cloves
1 (750-ml) bottle domestic pinot noir or burgundy
Garnish: Freshly grated nutmeg

Bring sugar and 1½ cups water to a boil in large nonreactive saucepan over medium heat, stirring to dissolve sugar. Add apple juice, lemon zest, cinnamon, allspice, and cloves, and bring to simmer. Cook over medium heat for 15 minutes. Strain into another saucepan and add wine. Simmer over low heat but do not boil. Serve in punch cups and top each serving with nutmeg.

HOT RUMMED CIDER

Makes 8 servings
1½ qt. apple cider
⅓ cup Demerara or packed light brown sugar
3 tbsp. unsalted butter
1½ c. light rum
Garnish: Cinnamon sticks

Bring cider and sugar to a boil in large saucepan. Reduce heat and add butter. When butter is melted, add rum. Serve in punch cups, with cinnamon sticks.

SMUGGLER'S BREW

Makes 8 servings
1½ c. dark rum
1 qt. cold strong brewed black tea
3 tbsp. unsalted butter
½ c. sugar
½ tsp. freshly grated nutmeg
½ c. brandy

Heat first five ingredients in large saucepan until boiling. Heat brandy in small saucepan until barely warm and add to rum mixture. Serve in punch cups.

WARM WINTER CIDER

Makes 18 to 20 servings
1 gal. apple cider
6 cinnamon sticks
1½ c. spiced rum
1 c. peach-flavored brandy
¾ c. peach schnapps
Garnish: Cinnamon sticks, apple slices

In large saucepan, bring cider and cinnamon to a full boil over medium heat. Reduce heat and add rum, brandy, and schnapps, stirring until heated through. Serve in punch cups garnished with cinnamon sticks and apples.

EGGNOGS AND PUNCHES

NON-ALCOHOLIC PUNCHES

BANANA PUNCH

Makes 40 servings

3 c. superfine sugar
2 (6-oz.) cans frozen orange juice concentrate, thawed
1 (46-oz.) can pineapple-grapefruit juice
4 ripe bananas, mashed
4 qt. soda water

Mix 1½ quarts water and sugar in large bowl to dissolve. Add juices and bananas. Pour into 4 (1-quart) freezer containers and freeze overnight. About 1 hour before serving, unmold and transfer to large punch bowl to melt slightly. Stir in club soda. Serve in punch cups.

DOUBLE BERRY PUNCH

Makes 25 to 30 servings

2 qt. cranberry juice
3 c. raspberry-flavored soda, chilled
1 qt. raspberry sherbet
Garnish: Fresh raspberries

Chill cranberry juice with ice block in punch bowl. Just before serving, slowly pour in soda and stir gently. Add sherbet. Serve in punch cups, adding sherbet and raspberries to each serving.

FUNSHINE FIZZ

Makes 6 to 8 servings

2 c. fresh orange juice, chilled
2 c. pineapple juice, chilled
1 pint orange sherbet
1 c. soda water, chilled

Combine first three ingredients in blender in batches, blending until smooth. Pour into pitcher and stir in soda water. Serve in Collins glasses.

TROPICAL CREAM PUNCH

Makes 22 servings

1 (14-oz.) can sweetened condensed milk
1 (6-oz.) can frozen orange juice concentrate, thawed
1 (6-oz.) can frozen pineapple juice concentrate, thawed
1 bottle (2-qt) soda water, chilled
Garnish: Orange wheels

Whisk condensed milk and juice concentrates in punch bowl. Add club soda and stir gently. Add block of ice and garnish with orange. Serve in punch cups.

WINE AND BEER IN MIXED DRINKS

OME COCKTAILS EMPLOY classic varietal wines like chardonnay, claret (another name for Bordeaux or cabernet), or merlot. But wine is a broad term for several subcategories less familiar to classic wine drinkers until you say their names—many of which are proprietary. Do Fernet-Branca, Dubonnet, and Lillet sound familiar? How about vermouth? All of these are examples of wines that are aromatized—the basic grape flavor is augmented with the addition of flavorings such as spices, herbs, flowers, nuts, honey, quinine, or even pine resin.

Proprietary aromatics are often sipped solo in Europe either before or after a meal, whereas in the United States they more often show up in cocktails. Anyone who drinks Martinis or Manhattans is familiar with vermouth, a wine infused with herbs, alcohol, sugar, caramel, and water. There are three types of vermouth: dry, sweet, and half-sweet (sometimes called bianco).

Sparkling wine or Champagne is used in many cocktails, often splashed on top to add a touch of fizz. In the classic Champagne Cocktail, the bubbly is the main ingredient; unless specified, use a dry (brut) style of Champagne or an American wine, Spanish cava, or Italian prosecco. When chilling sparkling wine cocktails with ice, fold the ingredients together very carefully to avoid bursting the bubbles.

And don't forget beer as a mixer for cocktails. Its effervescence and slight bitterness make it the ultimate thirst quencher. Try a Shandy, where beer meets lemonade in a very happy marriage, and you'll find yourself craving another.

1815

2 oz. Ramazzotti Amaro
½ oz. fresh lemon juice
½ oz. fresh lime juice
Ginger ale
Garnish: Lemon and lime
    wedges

Shake first three ingredients with ice and strain into ice-filled Collins glass. Top with ginger ale. Garnish with lemon and lime.

THE ALLSPICE FLIP

Created by NATASHA DAVID,
New York, NY

1½ oz. ruby port
½ oz. Demerara Syrup
    (page 25)
½ oz. heavy cream
¼ oz. allspice liqueur
    (pimento dram)
1 egg
1 oz. German white wheat
    beer, such as Erdinger
Garnish: Freshly grated nutmeg

Shake first five ingredients without ice. Add ice and shake again. Strain through wire sieve into chilled Collins glass. Top off with beer. Sprinkle with nutmeg.

AMERICANO

2 oz. sweet vermouth
2 oz. Campari
Soda water
Garnish: Lemon twist

Pour vermouth and Campari into ice-filled highball glass. Fill with soda water and stir. Add lemon twist.

ANDALUSIA

1½ oz. dry sherry
½ oz. Spanish brandy
½ oz. light rum

Stir well with ice and strain into chilled cocktail glass.

APPLE-CINNAMON SPARKLER

Created by JONATHAN POGASH, New York, NY

1 oz. apple cider
½ oz. Cinnamon Syrup (page 25), or use store-bought
¼ oz. fresh lemon juice
4 oz. sparkling wine or Champagne, plus 1 splash to finish
Garnish: Red apple slice

Gently fold ingredients with ice in mixing glass. Strain into chilled champagne flute. Top with extra splash of sparkling wine or Champagne. Add apple.

BELGIAN ORANGE

Created by VAN SCOTT JONES, Hollywood, CA

14 oz. white Belgian ale, such as Blue Moon
1½ oz. orange-flavored vodka
Garnish: Orange half-wheel

Fill 1-pt. beer mug or pilsner glass with ale, leaving room at the top for the vodka. Pour in vodka. Garnish with orange.

BELLA ROSSA

Created by ROBERT KRUEGER, New York, NY

1¼ oz. bianco vermouth
1 oz. Campari
½ oz. fresh lemon juice
½ oz. simple syrup
½ large strawberry, sliced
2 oz. ginger beer

Shake first five ingredients with ice, shaking hard to break up strawberry. Strain into ice-filled old-fashioned glass. Top with ginger beer.

BELLINI

Make your own puree from peeled and pitted fresh peaches, or buy online.

1 ounce peach puree, preferably white peach
5 ounces chilled prosecco

Pour puree into chilled Champagne flute. Carefully fill glass with prosecco (watch out for foaming).

BISHOP

1 oz. fresh orange juice
¾ oz. fresh lemon juice
½ oz. simple syrup
Red wine
Garnish: Fresh seasonal fruit

Shake first three ingredients with ice and strain into ice-filled highball glass. Fill with wine, and stir well. Garnish with fruit.

▽ BLACKBERRY FIZZ

Created by JONATHAN POGASH,
New York, NY

2 large fresh blackberries
¾ oz. fresh lemon juice
¾ oz. simple syrup
1 oz. Lillet Blanc
1 oz. gin
2 oz. chilled sparkling wine
Garnish: Fresh blackberry

*Muddle blackberries, lemon
juice, and syrup in mixing
glass. Add Lillet, gin, and
ice and shake. Strain into
chilled champagne flute.
Top with sparkling wine.
Garnish with blackberry.*

▽ BRAZIL COCKTAIL

1½ oz. dry vermouth
1½ oz. dry sherry
1 dash Angostura bitters
1 dash anisette

*Stir with ice and strain into
chilled cocktail glass.*

▽ BROOKLYN TAI

Created by JONATHAN POGASH,
New York, NY

1 oz. dark rum
½ oz. orgeat syrup
½ oz. fresh lime juice
12 oz. lager beer, preferably
    Brooklyn Lager
Garnish: Fresh mint sprig,
    lime wheel

*Shake first three ingredients
with ice and strain into 1-pt.
beer mug. Gently pour in
beer. Garnish with mint and
lime wheel.*

▽ BROKEN SPUR COCKTAIL

¾ oz. sweet vermouth
1½ oz. tawny port
¼ oz. triple sec

*Stir with ice and strain into
chilled cocktail glass.*

▽ CHAMPAGNE COCKTAIL

1 sugar cube
2 dashes Angostura bitters
Chilled Champagne
Garnish: Lemon twist

*Place sugar and bitters in
champagne flute and fill with
Champagne. Add lemon
twist.*

▽ CHERRY-VANILLA SPARKLER

Created by JONATHAN POGASH,
New York, NY

1 oz. cherry puree
½ oz. maraschino liqueur
½ oz. vanilla liqueur
¼ oz. vanilla syrup
3 oz. sparkling wine or
    Champagne, plus 1 splash
    to finish

*Gently fold ingredients
with ice in mixing glass.
Strain into chilled cham-
pagne flute. Top with extra
splash of sparkling wine or
Champagne.*

CHRYSANTHEMUM COCKTAIL

1½ oz. dry vermouth
¾ oz. Bénédictine
3 dashes absinthe or pastis
Garnish: Orange twist

Stir with ice and strain into chilled cocktail glass. Add orange twist.

CLARET COBBLER

2 oz. soda water
½ oz. simple syrup
3 oz. red wine, such as claret or cabernet sauvignon
Garnish: Fresh seasonal fruit

Pour soda water and syrup into ice-filled red-wine glass. Add wine and stir. Garnish with fruit. Serve with straws.

CRANBERRY SPICED CHAMPAGNE

Created by JONATHAN POGASH, New York, NY

6 fresh cranberries
¼ oz. fresh lemon juice
1 tsp. agave nectar
1 pinch pumpkin pie spice
4 oz. sparkling wine or Champagne, plus 1 splash to finish
Garnish: 3 fresh cranberries

Muddle 6 cranberries with lemon juice, agave nectar, and pumpkin pie spice in mixing glass. Add sparkling wine or Champagne and ice and gently fold. Strain into chilled champagne flute. Top with extra splash of sparkling wine or Champagne. Float 3 cranberries on top.

DEATH IN THE AFTERNOON

1 oz. absinthe or pastis
5 oz. chilled Champagne

Pour absinthe into chilled flute glass. Top with Champagne.

DIPLOMAT

1½ oz. dry vermouth
½ oz. sweet vermouth
2 dashes Angostura bitters
½ tsp. maraschino liqueur
Garnish: Lemon half-wheel, maraschino cherry

Stir with ice and strain into chilled cocktail glass. Garnish with lemon and cherry.

WINE AND BEER

EL MAESTRO

Created by TED KILGORE,
St. Louis, MO

1 cucumber slice
1½ oz. oloroso sherry
½ oz. gin
½ oz. elderflower liqueur
½ oz. Cynar
2 dashes celery bitters
Garnish: Cucumber slice

*Muddle 1 cucumber slice in
mixing glass. Add remaining
ingredients and stir with
ice. Strain into ice-filled
highball glass. Garnish with
cucumber slice.*

FALLING LEAVES

2 oz. Alsatian riesling or
   semidry white wine
1 oz. pear eau-de-vie
½ oz. Honey Syrup
   (page 25)
½ oz. orange curaçao
1 dash Peychaud's bitters
Garnish: Star anise pod

*Shake ingredients with ice
and strain into chilled cocktail glass. Garnish with star
anise pod.*

KIR ROYALE

Félix Kir, mayor of the French
city of Dijon, popularized this
drink in the years after World
War II.

5½ oz. chilled Champagne
½ oz. crème de cassis

*Pour into large champagne
flute or white-wine glass.*

FAR EAST SIDE

Created by KENTA GOTA,
New York, NY

2 fresh shiso leaves
2 oz. sake
¾ oz. elderflower liqueur
½ oz. blanco tequila
¼ oz. fresh lemon juice
1 pinch yuzu pepper
Garnish: Fresh shiso leaf

*Muddle 2 shiso leaves in
mixing glass. Add remain-
ing ingredients and stir with
ice. Strain through wire
sieve into chilled cocktail
glass. Garnish with shiso
leaf.*

FIELD BLEND

Created by NATASHA DAVID,
New York, NY

3 cucumber slices
3 oz. dry riesling
¾ oz. Cocchi Americano
¼ oz. pear brandy
1 oz. soda water
1 oz. sparkling wine

*Put cucumber slices in red-
wine glass and add ice. Pour
in remaining ingredients,
and stir gently.*

FROSTED APRICOT

Created by MARK A. WEDDLE, Greensboro, NC

2 oz. late-harvest riesling or ice wine
¾ oz. apricot-flavored brandy
¾ oz. elderflower liqueur
1 oz. white cranberry juice
½ oz. fresh lemon juice
Garnish: Orange twist

Shake with ice and strain into chilled cocktail glass. Add orange twist.

THE GATHERING

Created by MARK A. WEDDLE, Greensboro, NC

2 oz. Belgian white ale
2 oz. sauvignon blanc
1 oz. elderflower liqueur
½ oz. fresh lemon juice
Garnish: Lemon twist

Pour into ice-filled white-wine glass. Add lemon twist.

GINGER-PASSION SPARKLER

Created by JONATHAN POGASH, New York, NY

½ oz. ginger liqueur
1 oz. passion fruit puree
4 oz. sparkling wine or Champagne
Garnish: Candied ginger slice

Gently fold ingredients with ice in mixing glass. Strain into chilled champagne flute. Top with extra sparkling wine or Champagne. Garnish with ginger.

THE GRAPEVINE

Created by JONATHAN POGASH, New York, NY

3 lime wedges
8 fresh mint leaves
½ oz. simple syrup
1½ oz. cabernet sauvignon
½ oz. Grand Marnier
½ oz. light rum
Soda water

Muddle limes, mint, and syrup in mixing glass. Add next three ingredients and ice and shake. Strain into ice-filled Collins glass. Top with soda water.

INGRID BERGMAN

Created by MIKE SAMMONS, Houston, TX

For an Ingmar Bergman, substitute dry vermouth for the sweet.

11 oz. cold lager beer
1 oz. sweet vermouth
3 dashes Angostura bitters
Garnish: Orange twist

Pour ingredients, in order given, into pilsner glass. Add orange twist.

LONDON SPECIAL

Large orange twist
1 sugar cube
2 dashes Angostura bitters
Chilled Champagne

Put a orange twist into champagne flute. Add sugar and bitters. Fill with Champagne and stir.

WINE AND BEER

MIMOSA

1 oz. fresh orange juice
5 oz. chilled Champagne
Garnish: Orange half-wheel

Pour orange juice into chilled champagne flute. Gradually add Champagne (watch out for foaming). Garnish with orange.

MODERN LEMONADE

1 lemon, cut into quarters
1 oz. simple syrup
1½ oz. dry sherry
1 oz. sloe gin
Soda water

Muddle lemon quarters and syrup in mixing glass. Add sherry and sloe gin. Shake with ice and strain into chilled Collins glass. Fill glass with soda water.

PEAR FIZZ

Created by Brendan Kirby, St. Louis, MO

1 dash lemon bitters
1 oz. pear brandy
3 oz. cold sparkling wine
2 drops orange blossom water
Garnish: Pear slices

Add lemon bitters to ice-filled old-fashioned glass. Pour in brandy and then slowly top with sparkling wine. Add orange blossom water. Garnish with pear slices.

PEAR-VANILLA SPARKLER

Created by JONATHAN POGASH, New York, NY

¾ oz. pear puree
½ oz. vanilla liqueur
½ oz. pear liqueur
3½ oz. sparkling wine or Champagne, plus 1 splash to finish
Garnish: Freshly grated nutmeg

Gently fold ingredients with ice in mixing glass. Strain into chilled champagne flute. Top with extra splash of sparkling wine or Champagne. Sprinkle with nutmeg.

RED DIESEL

A relative of the Shandy, with beer, cider, and a shot of currant liqueur to give the color that gives the drink its name.

8 oz. cold apple cider
8 oz. cold beer
1 oz. crème de cassis

Pour cider and beer together into chilled beer mug and stir briefly. Add crème de cassis.

SANGRIA

SANGRIA (WINTER)

3 oz. fruity red wine, such as merlot
¾ oz. dark rum
½ oz. allspice liqueur (pimento dram)
½ oz. orange liqueur
½ oz. Honey Syrup (page 25)
½ oz. fresh lemon juice
Garnish: Cinnamon stick, orange twist studded with 3 whole cloves

Shake with ice and strain into ice-filled red-wine glass. Garnish with cinnamon and orange twist.

SANGRIA (RED)

Created by Jonathan Pogash, New York, NY

1 oz. brandy
¾ oz. black raspberry-flavored liqueur
½ oz. fresh lemon juice
½ oz. fresh orange juice
½ oz. simple syrup
2 oz. red wine, such as merlot
Garnish: Orange half-wheel

Shake with ice and strain into ice-filled red-wine glass. Garnish with orange.

SANGRIA (WHITE)

1 oz. brandy
¾ oz. passion fruit puree
½ oz. orange liqueur
½ oz. fresh lemon juice
½ oz. simple syrup
3 oz. dry white wine, such as sauvignon blanc
Garnish: Lime half-wheel

Shake with ice and strain into ice-filled white-wine glass. Garnish with lime.

SANGRIA (ROSÉ)

3 (1-inch) watermelon chunks
1 oz. brandy
½ oz. orange liqueur
½ oz. fresh lemon juice
½ oz. simple syrup
2 oz. rosé wine
Garnish: Fresh berries

Muddle watermelon in mixing glass. Add remaining ingredients with ice and shake. Strain into ice-filled white-wine glass. Add berries.

WINE AND BEER

SHANDY

This mix of beer and lemonade is one of the most refreshing drinks ever invented.

8 oz. cold lemonade
8 oz. cold ale or lager beer

Pour into chilled beer mug and stir briefly.

▽ SHISO NO NATSU

4 fresh shiso leaves
1½ oz. sake
1 oz. gin
½ oz. dry vermouth
Garnish: 1 shiso leaf

Muddle 4 shiso leaves in mixing glass. Add remaining ingredients. Stir with ice and double-strain into chilled cocktail glass. Garnish with shiso leaf.

▽ STRAWBERRY MIMOSA

½ cup partially thawed frozen sliced strawberries in syrup
2 oz. fresh orange juice
4 oz. chilled Champagne or sparkling wine
Garnish: Orange half-wheel, whole strawberry

Process strawberries and orange juice in blender until smooth. Pour into ice-filled hurricane glass. Fill with Champagne. Garnish with orange and strawberry.

▽ STRAWBERRY-VANILLA SPARKLER

Created by JONATHAN POGASH, New York, NY

1 strawberry, sliced
¼ oz. simple syrup
¼ oz. fresh lemon juice
½ oz. vanilla liqueur
4 oz. sparkling wine or Champagne, plus 1 splash to finish
Garnish: Strawberry slice

Muddle sliced strawberry, syrup, and lemon juice in mixing glass. Add remaining ingredients with ice and gently fold. Strain into chilled champagne flute. Top with extra splash of sparkling wine or Champagne. Garnish with strawberry.

▽ TRIDENT

1 oz. dry sherry
1 oz. Cynar
1 oz. aquavit
2 dashes peach bitters
Garnish: Lemon twist

Stir with ice and strain into chilled cocktail glass. Add lemon twist.

NONALCOHOLIC DRINKS

THERE'S A VERY GOOD chance that, among your circle of friends and acquaintances, there are those who do not consume alcohol at all. While it's certainly important that you respect their personal choice not to drink, there's no reason why nondrinkers cannot raise their glasses in a toast with a libation that's prepared with the care and creativity with which all mixed drinks and cocktails are made.

Most everyone has heard of a Virgin Mary and Shirley Temple, and recipes for these old standards are included here. But there are also nonalcoholic versions of other popular cocktails, such as the Unfuzzy Navel and Punchless Piña Colada. From the frosty Summertime Breeze to the refreshingly tangy Yellowjacket, you'll find quaffs to offer nondrinkers that are a giant step above plain old soft drinks.

You may want to make one for yourself when you're the designated driver, or order one when you're at a business meal or important meeting. Feel free to be creative and experiment with omitting the alcohol in some of the standard cocktail recipes throughout this book, especially those made with a variety of fresh fruit juices. (After all, without the alcohol, a Lime Rickey is Limeade.) And, of course, don't forget that presentation is just as important with these drinks as with any other.

APPLE-CINNAMON SODA

Created by JONATHAN POGASH, New York, NY

¾ oz. Cinnamon Syrup (page 25), or use store-bought syrup
3 oz. apple cider
3 oz. ginger beer
Garnish: Red apple slice

Pour into ice-filled pilsner glass and stir briefly. Garnish with apple.

BEACH BLANKET BINGO

3 oz. cranberry juice
3 oz. varietal white grape juice, such as chenin blanc
Soda water
Garnish: Lime wedge

Pour juices into ice-filled highball glass. Top with soda water and stir. Add lime.

BLACKBERRY SODA

Created by JONATHAN POGASH, New York, NY

4 blackberries
1 oz. Honey Syrup (page 18)
½ oz. fresh lemon juice
5 oz. ginger ale
Garnish: Blackberry and lemon wheel, skewered together

Muddle blackberries with honey syrup and lemon juice in mixing glass. Add ice and shake. Strain into ice-filled pilsner glass. Top with ginger ale and stir briefly. Garnish with skewered blackberry and lemon.

BUBBLETART

3 oz. cranberry juice
1 oz. fresh lime juice
3 oz. soda water
Garnish: Lime wheel

Shake juices with ice and pour with ice into chilled highball glass. Fill with soda water. Garnish with lime.

BUBBLY ORANGEADE

¾ oz. frozen orange juice concentrate, thawed
6 oz. soda water
Garnish: Orange half-wheel

Stir together in Collins glass and add ice. Garnish with orange.

COFFEE ALMOND FLOAT

Makes 4 to 6 servings
1 qt. milk
⅓ c. cold brewed espresso or French roast coffee
2 tbsp. brown sugar
¼ tsp. almond extract
Chocolate ice cream

Combine milk, coffee, brown sugar, and almond extract in pitcher. Stir well. Pour into ice-filled hurricane glasses. Top each with a scoop of ice cream.

COFFEE-COLA COOLER

Makes 3 or 4 servings
2 c. cold brewed coffee
1 tbsp. maple syrup
1½ c. cola, chilled
Garnish: Lemon wheels

Combine coffee and maple syrup in pitcher. Slowly stir in cola. Pour into ice-filled Collins glasses. Garnish with lemon.

CREAMY CREAMSICLE

1 c. fresh orange juice
2 scoops vanilla ice cream
Garnish: Orange wheel

Combine orange juice and ice cream in blender on low speed until smooth. Pour into highball glass. Garnish with orange.

CROW'S NEST

4 oz. fresh orange juice
1 oz. cranberry juice
1 tsp. grenadine
Garnish: Lime wheel

Shake with ice and strain into ice-filled old-fashioned glass. Garnish with lime.

CUCUMBER PEACH SODA

Created by JONATHAN POGASH, New York, NY

2 (1-inch-thick) cucumber slices, chopped
1 oz. peach puree
½ oz. fresh lemon juice
1 tsp. agave nectar
3 oz. soda water
Garnish: Cucumber slice

Muddle chopped cucumber, peach puree, lemon, and agave nectar in mixing glass. Add ice and shake. Strain into ice-filled highball glass. Top with soda water and stir briefly. Garnish with cucumber slice.

FLAMINGO

3 oz. cranberry juice
1½ oz. pineapple juice
1½ oz. fresh lemon juice
3 oz. soda water
Garnish: Lime wedge

Shake juices with ice and strain into ice-filled highball glass. Top with soda water and stir. Garnish with lime.

NONALCOHOLIC DRINKS

FRUIT SMOOTHIE

1 c. fresh orange juice
1 ripe banana, sliced
½ c. berries, such as
   blueberries, raspberries, or
   sliced strawberries
Garnish: Banana slice, fresh
   berries, orange wheel

*Process ingredients in
blender on low speed until
smooth. Pour into highball
glass. Garnish with fruits.*

FUZZY LEMON FIZZ

4 oz. peach nectar
2 oz. lemon-lime soda
Garnish: Lemon twist

*Pour ingredients into ice-
filled highball glass. Garnish
with lemon twist.*

GINGER-POMEGRANATE SODA

Created by JONATHAN POGASH,
New York, NY

1½ oz. Grenadine (page 26),
   or use store-bought
6 oz. ginger beer
Garnish: Candied ginger, lime
   wedge

*Pour into ice-filled pilsner
glass and stir briefly. Add
ginger and lime.*

GRAPEBERRY

3 oz. cranberry juice
3 oz. fresh grapefruit juice
Garnish: Lime wedge

*Combine juices in large ice-
filled red-wine glass. Garnish
with lime and serve with a
short straw.*

ICED MOCHA

Makes 3 to 4 servings
2 c. milk
⅓ c. chocolate syrup
2 oz. cold brewed
   espresso or Italian
   roast coffee
Garnish: Whipped cream,
   chocolate shavings

*Combine ingredients in
pitcher and stir well. Pour
into ice-filled Collins glasses.
Top with whipped cream and
chocolate.*

INNOCENT PASSION

4 oz. passion fruit juice
1 oz. cranberry juice
½ oz. fresh lemon juice
2 oz. soda water
Garnish: Maraschino
   cherry

*Combine juices in ice-filled
highball glass. Top with soda
water and stir. Garnish with
cherry.*

LAVA FLOW

½ c. light cream
½ oz. cream of coconut
⅓ c. pineapple juice
½ ripe banana
½ c. sliced strawberries

*Process first four ingredi-
ents in blender with 1 cup
crushed ice until smooth. Put
strawberries at the bottom
of a parfait glass. Quickly
pour in blended mixture for
a starburst effect.*

LEMONADE

1 oz. fresh lemon juice
1 oz. simple syrup, or more
 to taste
Soda water or plain
 water
Garnish: Lemon slice,
 maraschino cherry
 (optional)

*Stir lemon juice and syrup
in Collins glass. Add ice,
fill with water, and stir
again. Garnish with lemon
and cherry, if using.*

LEMONADE
(RASPBERRY)

1 oz. fresh lemon juice
1 oz. raspberry syrup
½ oz. simple syrup
Soda water or plain water

*Stir first three ingredients
in Collins glass. Add ice,
fill with water, and stir
again.*

LIMEADE

3 oz. fresh lime juice
1 oz. simple syrup
Soda water or plain
 water
Garnish: Lime wedge,
 maraschino cherry
 (optional)

*Stir juice and syrup in
Collins glass. Add ice,
fill with water, and stir
again. Add lime and
cherry, if using.*

LIME COLA

½ oz. fresh lime juice
Cola
Garnish: Long lime twist

*Add juice to ice-filled Collins
glass. Fill with cola and stir.
Add lime.*

LIME COOLER

½ oz. fresh lime juice
Tonic water
Garnish: Lime wedge

*Add juice to ice-filled Collins
glass. Fill with tonic water
and stir. Garnish with lime.*

LITTLE ENGINEER

3 oz. pineapple juice
3 oz. fresh orange juice
1 oz. grenadine
Garnish: Paper flag

*Pour over ice in hurricane
glass. Garnish with paper
flag.*

ORANGE AND TONIC

3 oz. fresh orange juice
4 oz. tonic water
Garnish: Lime wedge

*Pour juice into ice-filled
highball glass. Fill with tonic
water and stir. Garnish with
lime.*

NONALCOHOLIC
DRINKS

ORANGEADE

3 oz. fresh orange juice
½ oz. simple syrup
4 oz. soda water or plain
    water
Garnish: Orange wheel,
    maraschino cherry
    (optional)

*Stir juice and syrup in
Collins glass. Add ice, fill
with water, and stir again.
Garnish with orange and
cherry, if using.*

PASSION FRUIT
SPRITZER

½ c. passion fruit juice, chilled
3 oz. soda water
Garnish: Lime wedge

*Pour juice into champagne
flute and fill with soda water.
Garnish with lime.*

PEACH MELBA

1 c. peach nectar, chilled
2 scoops vanilla ice cream
½ ripe peach, pitted and
    sliced
⅓ c. fresh raspberries
Garnish: Fresh raspberries

*Process ingredients in
blender on low speed until
smooth. Pour into highball
glass and garnish with
raspberries.*

PINEAPPLE-MINT
SODA

Created by JONATHAN POGASH,
New York, NY

2 oz. pineapple juice
¾ oz. fresh lime juice
1 oz. Demerara Syrup
    (page 25)
4 oz. soda water
Garnish: Fresh mint sprigs

*Shake first three ingredients
with ice and strain into ice-
filled pilsner glass. Top with
soda water and stir briefly.
Garnish with mint.*

POMEGRANATE-
ALMOND SODA

Created by JONATHAN POGASH,
New York, NY

1 oz. pomegranate juice
1 oz. almond or orgeat syrup
5 oz. soda water
Garnish: Lime wedge

*Pour into ice-filled pilsner
glass and stir briefly. Add
lime.*

PUNCHLESS PIÑA
COLADA

1 oz. cream of coconut
1 oz. pineapple juice
¼ oz. fresh lime juice
Garnish: Pineapple slice,
    maraschino cherry

*Process ingredients in
blender with 1 cup crushed
ice until smooth. Pour into
Collins glass. Garnish with
pineapple and cherry.*

RUMLESS RICKEY

1 oz. fresh lime juice
1 tsp. grenadine
1 dash Angostura bitters
4 oz. soda water
Garnish: Long lime twist

Add juice, grenadine, and bitters to ice-filled old-fashioned glass. Fill with soda water and stir. Garnish with lime.

RUNNER'S MARK

4 oz. vegetable-tomato juice, such as V8
2 drops hot red pepper sauce
2 drops fresh lemon juice
1 dash Worcestershire sauce
Garnish: Celery stalk or scallion

Combine all ingredients in ice-filled old-fashioned glass. Stir. Garnish with celery or scallion.

SHIRLEY TEMPLE

½ oz. grenadine
Ginger ale
Garnish: Orange slice, maraschino cherry

Add grenadine to ice-filled Collins glass; top with ginger ale. Garnish with orange and cherry.

STRAWBERRY WONDERLAND

½ c. frozen strawberries
⅓ c. pineapple juice
1 oz. cream of coconut
½ oz. simple syrup
½ oz. fresh lemon juice
Garnish: Whipped cream, fresh strawberry

Process ingredients in blender with 1 cup crushed ice until smooth. Pour into snifter. Top with whipped cream and garnish with strawberry.

SUMMERTIME BREEZE

Makes 2 servings
½ c. sliced fresh strawberries
½ c. chopped fresh pineapple
½ c. fresh grapefruit juice
Garnish: Pineapple wedges, whole strawberries

Process ingredients in blender with 1 cup crushed ice until smooth. Pour into Collins glasses. Garnish with pineapple and strawberries.

SUNSHINE SPLASH

2 oz. pineapple juice
2 oz. fresh orange juice
½ oz. simple syrup
½ oz. fresh lemon juice
½ oz. grenadine
Lemon-lime soda
Garnish: Pineapple wedge

Stir first five ingredients in hurricane glass. Add ice, fill with lemon-lime soda, and stir. Garnish with pineapple.

NONALCOHOLIC DRINKS

TOMATO COOLER

4 oz. tomato juice
1 oz. fresh lemon or lime juice
2 oz. tonic water
Garnish: Lime wedge, dill sprig, cucumber stick

Combine juices in ice-filled highball glass. Fill with tonic water. Garnish with lime, dill, and cucumber.

UNFUZZY NAVEL

2 oz. peach nectar
2 oz. fresh orange juice
½ oz. fresh lemon juice
¼ oz. grenadine
Garnish: Orange wheel

Shake with ice. Strain into chilled red-wine glass. Garnish with orange.

VIRGIN MARY

½ c. tomato juice
½ tsp. Worcestershire sauce
1 dash fresh lemon juice
2 drops hot red pepper sauce
1 pinch salt
1 grind freshly ground black pepper
Garnish: Lime wedge

Add ingredients to ice-filled large red-wine glass and stir. Garnish with lime.

WAVEBENDER

1 oz. fresh orange juice
½ oz. fresh lemon juice
1 tsp. grenadine
Ginger ale

Shake juices and grenadine with ice and strain into ice-filled highball glass. Fill with ginger ale and stir.

YELLOWJACKET

3 oz. pineapple juice
3 oz. fresh orange juice
½ oz. fresh lemon juice
Garnish: Lemon wheel

Shake with ice and strain into ice-filled old-fashioned glass. Garnish with lemon.

RESOURCES

GENERAL BAR SUPPLIES

Bar Equipment World
www.barequipmentworld.com
  The name says it all.

A Best Kitchen
www.akitchen.com
  Great prices on all sorts of barware.

Barproducts.com
www.barproducts.com
  Mainly for the trade but open to consumers, it is a great resource for all kinds of bar supplies, from equipment to accessories.

Co-Rect Products
www.co-rectproducts.com
  Bar and restaurant supplies specifically for the trade.

The Boston Shaker
www.thebostonshaker.com
  This site, with a retail shop in Somerville, MA, sells only the very best cocktail equipment for the home mixologist.

BAR EQUIPMENT

PUG! Muddler

www.wnjones.com/pug

The makers of PUG! Muddlers—sturdy wood muddlers with a simple, beautiful design.

Riedel Vinum Martini Glasses

www.williams-sonoma.com

Among their many top-of-the-line barware products, Williams-Sonoma carries the beautiful, classic-sized Riedel Vinum Martini Glasses.

Schott Zwiesel Cocktail Glasses

www.surlatable.com

Sur La Table's Schott Zwiesel Cocktail Glasses have a retro look and are reasonably sized.

Tovolo Perfect Cube Silicone Ice Cube Trays

www.amazon.com

A substantial square of ice won't melt as quickly as the standard cube from your freezer's ice dispenser. Use distilled water or double-boiled and cooled water for sparkling clear cubes.

DRINKS DATABASES

Ardent Spirits

www.ardentspirits.com

A website by Gary and Mardee Regan, perhaps the most prolific authors on the subject of cocktails and spirits today; they've written several must-have books, including *New Classic Cocktails*, *The Martini Companion*, and *The Joy of Mixology*.

B.A.R.

www.beveragealcoholresource.com

Comprehensive spirits and mixology training programs designed to provide a well-rounded education in mixology and spirits can be found here.

Cocktail.com
www.cocktail.com

Paul Harrington's site's mission is simple: to bring the drink aficionados and bartenders of the world the best cocktail recipes and advice.

CocktailDB
www.cocktaildb.com

CocktailDB is the brainchild of Martin Doudoroff and Ted Haigh (aka Dr. Cocktail), offering an extensive anthology of cocktails authenticated in print, coupled with a massive ingredients database.

Cocktail Guru
www.thecocktailguru.com

The site of this book's master mixologist, Jonathan Pogash, with terrific recipes, information about his cocktail classes, and other services.

Cocktail Spirit
www.smallscreennetwork.com

Home of the wildly popular educational podcast "The Cocktail Spirit with Robert Hess."

DrinkBoy
www.drinkboy.com

Robert Hess's scholarly database incorporates history, tips, advice, and recipes—just like a proper barman.

Esquire Drinking Database
www.esquire.com/drinks

A great collection of cocktail recipes and wisdom, including much imparted by resident spirits expert David Wondrich. Every week it showcases a new recipe worth checking out.

Imbibe Magazine
www.imbibemagazine.com

Get the latest information on all beverages, from cocktails to coffee, from this lively and colorfully produced magazine.

Inside Food and Beverage

www.insidefandb.com

Insider news on the restaurant and hotel industry, with special attention paid to the importance of the spirits to the bottom line.

King Cocktail

www.kingcocktail.com

One of the most recognized bartenders in America and author of *The Craft of the Cocktail*, Dale DeGroff shares insights and recipes, plus great tips and advice.

Liquor.Com

www.liquor.com

Their motto is "An expert guide to cocktails and spirits," and they are right.

Miss Charming

www.miss-charming.com

Cheryl Charming, author of *Miss Charming's Book of Bar Amusements*, provides useful information and resources to both budding and experienced bartenders.

The Modern Mixologist

www.themodernmixologist.com

The cyberhome of one of the smoothest mixmasters on the planet, Tony Abou-Ganim, where you'll find tips and tricks of the trade. His video *Modern Mixology: Making Great Cocktails at Home* is worth seeking out.

Spirit Journal

www.spiritjournal.com

Writer Paul Pacult's newsletter rating spirits, wine, and beer.

BITTERS

Adam Elmegirab Bitters

www.atthemeadow.com

This online store, with brick-and mortar locations in New York City and Portland, OR, offers an amazing selection of bitters.

Bittermen's Bitters

www.bittermens.com

With flavors like Xocotl Mole and 'Elemakule Tiki, this firm is dedicated to expanding the possibilities for making cocktails. They also have an outlet, Bittermen's General Store, in New York City's East Village.

Fee Brothers Bitters

www.kalustyans.com

The Fee Brothers of Rochester, NY, have been making bitters and cocktail flavorings for decades, and their experience shows in their six different bitters flavors.

Peychaud's Bitters/Regan's Orange Bitters

www.buffalotrace.com

A great source for these bar essentials.

Scrappy's Bitters

www.scrappysbitters.com

High quality, small-batch bitters that are worth searching out.

FLAVORINGS AND SWEETENERS

B. A. Reynold's Syrups

www.okolemaluna.com

Handmade exotic syrups, with an emphasis on ingredients for Polynesian-style drinks.

Depaz Cane Syrup

www.igourmet.com

An excellent substitute for simple syrup, try it in Mojitos and other tropical drinks.

Elderflower Cordial and Wild Hibiscus Flowers in Syrup

www.chefswarehouse.com

It's fun to browse at this well-stocked site.

Kalustyan's

www.kalustyans.com

If you've never heard of it, they have it. A good place to get such exotics as orange blossom and rose water, orgeat, and rose syrup (mymoune).

Pink Sanding Sugar

www.amazon.com

You will find many other food products for your bar at amazon.com, too.

Sonoma Syrup

www.sonomasyrup.com

Great fruit and spice syrups for every cocktail.

FRUIT JUICES AND PUREES

Boiron

www.emarkys.com

French fruit purees prepared without sugar and bursting with natural flavor, the only drawback is that they come in 1kg (2.2-pound) containers, so make plans for using your entire purchase.

Ceres Juices

www.ceresjuices.com

You might find these excellent juices with minimum sweeteners at your local specialty grocer. They specialize in tropical flavors, such as passion fruit, and their pineapple is superior to the supermarket variety.

Perfect Purée of Napa Valley
www.perfectpuree.com

The Perfect Purée Company of Napa Valley produces a wonderful selection of fruit and vegetable purees, including a fabulous White Peach elixir that's perfect for Bellinis.

GARNISHES

Luxardo Cherries
www.amazon.com and www.kegworks.com

Two recommended places to buy Italian marasca cherries in syrup.

Les Parisiennes Cherries in Brandy
www.emarkys.com

Second only to real marasca cherries, these are perfect for Manhattans.

Cocktail Onions
www.sableandrosenfeld.com

A Gibson isn't a Gibson without proper onions. Sable and Rosenfeld sells other top-notch cocktail garnishes, such as a full line of flavored green olives, too.

GLOSSARY

The following list is meant to serve as a brief explanation for the ingredients and terminology used in this book.

Absinthe Banned for many years because of its supposed (and disproven) hallucinogenic qualities, absinthe is back on the market. It is a green not-too-sweet liqueur with a high alcohol content that turns cloudy when mixed with water.

Absinthe Substitutes When absinthe was illegal, licorice-flavored substitutes made without the wormwood were produced. Still sold, examples include Pernod (French) and Herbsaint (American). (See Pastis.)

Ale A type of beer, top-fermented with malt and hops (meaning that the mashed grains float on top of the liquid during fermentation) at warm temperatures.

Allspice Liqueur Also called pimento dram (pimento is another name for allspice), this Jamaican rum-based product is used in some Caribbean-style drinks.

Amaretto Italian almond-flavored liqueur distilled from bitter and/or sweet almonds.

Amaro "Bitter" in Italian, a variety of digestif liqueur with bitter herbal flavors. Some have specific proprietary names (such as Campari, Cynar, and Fernet-Branca) and others are branded by their producer (Amaro Ramazzotti and Amaro Averna).

Amer Picon A French apéritif wine with bitter orange flavor, it is currently not distributed in the United States. Torani Amer, a domestic product made in California, is an excellent substitute.

Anisette A very sweet anise-flavored liqueur.

Apéritif A liquor, often made from fortified and flavored wine, served before a meal as an appetite stimulant. (*Apéritif* comes from the Latin *aperire*, which means "to open.") Like digestifs, which are their opposite because they are served after a meal, they can also be ingredients in mixed drinks. Examples are Dubonnet, Lillet, and vermouth.

Aperol An Italian apéritif, with a discernable bitter orange flavor.

Apple Brandy A liquor distilled from fermented apples and barrel aged.

Applejack American apple brandy, originally distilled from frozen apple juice, a process called jacking. Laird's Applejack from New Jersey is the most common brand, and it is excellent.

Apricot Brandy A naturally or artificially apricot-flavored liqueur that must contain brandy.

Apricot Liqueur An apricot-flavored liqueur that does not contain brandy and is not as sweet as apricot brandy.

Aquavit A clear to light yellow distilled Scandinavian spirit flavored with herbs and caraway and other spices.

Armagnac Gascony, a region in southwest France, is the home of this brandy made from white grapes and aged in oak.

Batavia Arrack Similar to rum, a liquor distilled from sugar cane and rice, native to Indonesia. Other Asian countries make arrack from palm sugar and coconut flowers. **Arak** is an anise-flavored liquor drunk in eastern Mediterranean countries.

Beer Brewed from grain (often malted—sprouted and dried—but not always) and flavored by hops, this beverage is often drunk by itself, but makes a good mixer in the right cocktail. **White beer** is brewed from wheat.

Bénédictine Legend says that the original recipe for this sweet French liqueur with strong herbal flavors comes from a Benedictine monastery. The DOM on the label stands for *Deo Optimo Maximo*, which in Latin means "To God, most good, most great."

Black Raspberry Liqueur Chambord is a common and richly flavored brand of this sweet berry liqueur.

Bourbon Whiskey A uniquely American spirit is distilled from a mash of grains that must contain at least 51 percent corn (and can also include malted barley, rye, or corn). Bourbon is aged in new, charred barrels for at least two years before bottling. The name refers to Bourbon County, Kentucky, from which the whiskey was originally distributed.

Brandy Many countries, including France, Spain, and America, make this alcoholic liquor distilled from fermented grapes (although there are brandies made from other fruits, such as apples and apricots).

Cachaça Brazilian liquor made from sugar cane and similar to rum, it is the base liquor of a Caipirinha.

Calvados Apple brandy specifically from a region in Normandy, France.

Campari A high-alcohol Italian apéritif with bitter and herbal flavors.

Canadian Whisky Whisky produced in Canada is usually light-bodied, with a smooth taste, and made from a blend of whiskies distilled from multiple grains.

Cava A Spanish sparkling wine.

Chartreuse Richly flavored with herbs, this French liqueur is made by Carthusian monks from over 130 herbs. There are two colors, green (which gets its natural hue from chlorophyll) and yellow (which is lower proof, milder, and less sweet).

Cherry Brandy Red, cherry-flavored brandy, such as Cherry Heering, made from black cherries.

Cider Filtered apple juice. If allowed to ferment and develop alcohol content, it is called hard cider.

Claret A term for Bordeaux-style red wine.

Cocchi Americano An aromatized white wine from Asti, Italy, that often serves as a substitute for Kina Lillet (which has been discontinued) and can be enjoyed like dry vermouth.

Coffee Liqueur Kahlúa and Tia Maria are examples of this kind of liqueur.

Cognac Brandy made in Cognac, France, from white grapes that are good for distilling into spirits but not for fermenting into wine.

Cointreau An orange liqueur in the clear-colored, triple sec–style.

Cream of Coconut A thick, sweetened coconut puree used to make Piña Coladas and other tropical drinks.

Crème de Cacao Chocolate liqueur available dark (brown-colored) and white (clear).

Crème de Cassis Black currant liqueur.

Crème de Menthe Mint-flavored liqueur, sold in two colors: green and white (clear).

Crème de Mure Blackberry liqueur.

Crème de Noyaux Brandy-based almond liqueur.

Crème de Violette A pale purple liqueur with a floral violet flavor and aroma.

Crème Yvette An American version of crème de violette with a more pronounced vanilla flavor.

Curaçao A citrus-flavored liqueur made with the peel of the orange-like laraha fruit, a product of the island of Curaçao. It is sold in three colors: blue, white (clear), and orange.

Cynar Italian digestif made from artichokes and herbs.

Digestif A liquor containing herbs and other ingredients with traditional medicinal properties, drunk after dinner to aid digestion, but increasingly used as a cocktail ingredient. (See Amaro).

Drambuie A Scotch whisky liqueur.

Dubonnet An example of a *quinquina* (quinine-flavored) apéritif, originally developed to fight malaria. Sold in Rouge (red) and Blanc (clear pale yellow) varieties.

Falernum A spicy Caribbean syrup, it is sold in a nonalcoholic version, but many bartenders prefer John D. Taylor's Velvet Falernum liqueur.

Fernet A kind of amaro, Fernet-Branca and Luxardo Fernet are just two brands of many.

Fortified Wine Spirits (usually brandy) were added to wine to help preserve it on long ship voyages. Examples include madeira, marsala, port, sherry, and vermouth.

Galliano A very sweet bright yellow Italian liqueur made from over 30 herbs and spices, but with a distinct vanilla flavor. Named for a hero of the First Italo-Ethiopian War of the late nineteenth century.

Genever Also called *genièvre*, is a type of gin made in Holland that is the origin of today's liquor. There are two styles, young and old, which have nothing to do with age, but rather with how they are made. *Jonge* (young) is clear and almost neutral in flavor, like vodka. *Oude* (old) is made from malted grains and aged in barrels, like whiskey. In this book, genever refers to the oude style.

Gin A clear spirit made from a mash of cereal grain and flavored with botanicals (mainly juniper). London dry gin in made in a style traditionally popular in that city; Plymouth gin is similar, but must be made in Plymouth, England.

Grand Marnier Cognac-based French liqueur flavored with bitter Seville oranges.

Grappa An Italian brandy distilled from grape pomace (the remains from pressing grapes), and not from grape juice.

Hazelnut Liqueur Frangelico is a popular brand.

Irish Cream Thick-bodied cream-based liqueur flavored with Irish whiskey. Store in the refrigerator after opening.

Irish Whiskey Made in a manner similar to Scotch whisky, but distilled three times. Barley, either malted or not, is the main grain used for the mash.

Licor 43 Also known as Cuarenta y Tres, this bright yellow Spanish liqueur has citrus and vanilla flavors derived from its forty-three ingredients.

Lillet A French apéritif based on Bordeaux wine and citrus liqueur, sold in both Rouge (red) and Blanc (white) versions. Kina Lillet, a third version, was discontinued in 1986. (See Cocchi Americano.)

Limoncello An Italian lemon liqueur, traditionally made in Southern Italy from lemons.

Madeira A Portuguese fortified wine from the island of Madeira.

Mandarine Napoléon A tangerine-flavored liqueur.

Maraschino A clear Italian liqueur made from marasca cherries, bearing no resemblance to American maraschino flavoring or cherries.

Mezcal A relative of tequila, made from maguey plants, primarily near Oaxaca, Mexico.

Pastis A French licorice-flavored absinthe substitute, it turns cloudy when mixed with water. Pernod is a notable brand.

Pimm's No. 1 There were originally six different kinds of this liqueur, but the gin-based No. 1 is the only one still sold in the United States.

Pisco A colorless brandy made in Chile and Peru, with some argument as to which country can claim it as its own.

Port Originally a fortified wine from Portugal, but now made in other wine-producing countries. It is available in the following styles: white (made from white grapes), ruby (aged under four years in casks), tawny (a blend of white and ruby), late-bottle vintage (aged four to six years, then bottled, which stops the aging), and vintage (highest quality port aged for two years in the cask, then bottled, where it continues to age). For cocktails, ruby or tawny port are good choices.

Punt e Mes An Italian apéritif similar to sweet vermouth, but more bitter.

Rum Distilled from sugar products (either molasses, sugarcane juice, or a syrup made from reduced sugarcane juice), the three main styles are light, medium, and dark. Also sold are spiced or flavored rum, aged rum, and high-proof rum.

Rye A whiskey that must include at least 51 percent rye in its mash.

Sake A brew (not quite a wine and not quite a beer) made from fermented rice. Traditionally made in Japan, there are also domestic sakes.

Sambuca Made from elderberries and anise, an Italian liqueur usually served as an after-dinner drink with three espresso beans added to the glass.

Schnapps A light-bodied, very sweet liqueur that comes in a wide variety of flavors.

Scotch The common name for Scottish whisky (spelled without an "e") from malted barley that has been dried over smoldering peat. Blended whisky is created from a combination of whiskies from different barrels. Single malt whisky is the product of a single distillery and aged for at least three years in charred oak barrels (many of which are imported from America after being used to age bourbon). The flavor of the Scotch is often dictated by the distiller's location—Islay and Skye produce the smoky whiskies called for in some cocktails.

Sherry Spanish fortified wine made in Andalucía. Varieties encompass fino (the driest flavor), manzanilla (richer than fino, but still dry), amontillado (half-dry, with nutty flavor notes), oloroso (sweet and full-bodied), cream (also sweet and heavy-bodied), and Pedro Ximénez (very sweet and rich). Use the sherry indicated in the recipe, because, as you can see, the flavors range enormously.

Sloe Gin A red liqueur made from sloe plums, but only the best versions have a gin base.

Tequila Mexican liquor distilled in the Jalisco region from blue agave, sold in four distinct styles: *blanco* (also called clear or silver), *oro* (gold, artificially colored to give the appearance of aging and generally disdained by the best bartenders), *reposado* (blanco aged in oak barrels for up to one year), and *añejo* (aged in oak for over one year).

Triple Sec A colorless orange liqueur made in the curaçao style.

Tuaca Originally Italian, and now produced in Kentucky, a liqueur with predominant citrus and vanilla notes.

Vanilla Liqueur A liqueur where the vanilla flavor is dominant without citrus or spice notes.

Vermouth A fortified wine-based apéritif aromatized with over fifty herbs and spices, in red (sweet) and white (dry) styles.

Vodka A colorless, virtually flavorless spirit distilled from grain, potatoes, or buffalo grass. Flavored vodkas, with flavors ranging from lemon to chile pepper, are also available.

Whisk(e)y A spirit distilled from cereal grains (mainly barley, corn, or rye, alone or in combination with oats and wheat), and often aged in oak barrels. (See Bourbon, Irish Whiskey, Rye, Scotch, and White Whiskey.)

White Whiskey Also called white lightning, a colorless unaged whiskey distilled from corn that was the traditional homemade liquor of the South.

Wine The fermented juice of grapes or other fruits.

INDEX

A

Abbey Cocktail, 72
Absinthe Special Cocktail, 232
Academic Review, 194
Accoutrement, 50
Adderly Cocktail, 194
Admiral Perry, 170
Affinity Cocktail, 195
Air Mail, 122
Akogare, 195
Alabazam, 50
Alamo Splash, 152
Alaska Cocktail, 72
Alexander cocktail(s), 53, 72, 274
Alfie Cocktail, 170
Algonquin, 195
Allegheny, 195
Allen Cocktail, 73
Amante Picante, 152
Amaretto and Cream, 232
Amaretto Rose, 232
Amber Amour, 233
American Beauty Cocktail, 50
American Trilogy, 195
Americana, 195
Ancient Mariner, 122
Angel's Share, 195
Angler's Cocktail, 73
Apollo, 73
Apple Brandy Cocktail, 51
Apple Pie, 233
Aquarius, 195
Aqueduct, 170
Archangel, 73
Arise My Love, 233
Artillery, 73
Astoria Bianco, 73
Audrey Fanning, 73
Autumn Leaves, 196
Aviation, 46, 74
Aztec's Mark, 196

B

Babbie's Special Cocktail, 52
Bahama Mama, 122
Bajito, 123
Banana Cow, 123
B&B, 52
Banshee, 233
Bar, basics of, 1–26
Barbary Coast, 74
Baron Cocktail, 74
Basil 8, 170
Basil's Bite, 74
Basin Street, 196
Beachbum, 123
Beachcomber, 123
Beautiful Day, 196
Beauty Beneath, 122
Beauty-Spot Cocktail, 74
Bee's Kiss, 122
Bee's Knees, 75
Bee Sting, 75
Beer Buster, 170. See also Wine(s)
    and beer(s)
Belgian Orange, 199
Bella Fragolia, 171
Bella Rossa, 199
Bellini, 299
Belmont Cocktail, 75
Bennett Cocktail, 75
Bensonhurst, 197
Berliner, 75
Bermuda Bouquet, 75
Bermuda Triangle, 124
Betsy Ross, 52
Bianca, 171
Big Crush, 171
Big Red Hooter, 152
Bikini, 171
Bishop(s), 45, 126, 220, 299
Bitches' Brew, 124
Bitter, Dark & Stormy, 124

Black Cat, 76
Black Cherry Chocolate, 171
Black Devil, 124
Black Feather, 53
Black Hawk, 197
Blackjack, 233
Black Magic, 171
Black Maria, 124
Black Russian, 172
Blackthorn, 233
Black Widow, 125
Blanche, 233
Blarney Stone Cocktail, 197
Blinker, 197
Blood and Samba, 125
Blood and Sand, 197
Blood Orange(s), 76, 172
Bloody Bull, 172
Bloody Maria, 152
Bloody Mary(s), 43–45, 172
Bloody Scotsman, 198
Bloomsbury, 76
Blue Hawaiian, 125
Blue Lagoon, 172
Blue Moon Cocktail, 76
Bobbo's Bride, 76
Bobby Burns Cocktail, 198
Bocce Ball, 233
Bolero, 125
Bombay Cocktail, 53
Bone, 198
Boomerang, 76
Bordeaux Cocktail, 173
Borinquen, 125
Bosom Caresser, 53
Bossa Nova Special Cocktail, 125
Boston Cocktail, 76
Boston Gold, 173
Bourbon à la Crème, 198
Bourbon and Elder, 199
Bourbon Renewal, 199
Brandied Madeira, 53
Brandied Port, 53
Brandy Alexander. See Alexander
    cocktail(s)
Brandy Cassis, 53
Brandy Cocktail, 54
Brandy Gump Cocktail, 55
Brandy Vermouth Cocktail, 56
Brave Bull, 153
Bravo, 152
Bridal, 77
Bronx Cocktail, 77
Brooklyn, 196
Brooklyn Wanderer, 77
Brothers Perryman, 77
Brunswick Street Cocktail, 56

Buccaneer, 126
Buck(s), 45, 102, 140
Buck Jones, 126
Bull and Bear, 199
Bull Shot, 173
Bull's Blood, 126
Bull's Eye, 57
Bull's Milk, 57
Bulldog Cocktail, 56
Bullfrog, 173
Bum's Rush, 153
Burning Sun, 234
Bushwhacker, 234

C

Cabaret, 77
Cable Car, 126
Cablegram, 200
Cactus Berry, 153
Cadiz, 57
Caesar, 173
Café Cabana, 224
Calvados Cocktail, 57
Cameron's Kick Cocktail, 200
Camino Del Ray, 153
Canadian Breeze, 200
Canadian Cherry, 201
Canadian Cocktail, 201
Canado Saludo, 127
Cantaloupe Juice, 81
Cape Codder, 173
Cappuccino Cocktail, 173
Capriccio, 273
Capricious, 78
Captain's Blood, 127
Cara Sposa, 57
Caribbean Cruise, 174
Caribbean Ginger, 127
Caribbean Romance, 127
Caricature Cocktail, 78
Carré Reprise, 201
Carroll Cocktail, 57
Casino Cocktail, 78
Castaway, 128
Champagne Flamingo, 174
Champs Élysées Cocktail, 57
Chancellor Cocktail, 201
Chantilly Cocktail, 128
Chapala, 154
Chapel Hill, 201
Chaplin, 201
Character Development, 201
Charles Cocktail, 57
Chas, 202
Chef's Pain, 202
Cherie, 128

Chef's Pain, 202
Cherie, 128
Cherry Blossom, 58
Chet Baker, 128
Chicago Cocktail, 58
Chinchona, 154
Chinese Cocktail, 128
Chin Up, 78
Chocolate-Covered Strawberry, 234
Chocolate Italian, 78
Chocolate Rum, 128
Chupa Cabra, 154
Ciders, 254, 274, 275, 278, 291, 295
Cinnamon Sugar, 126
Cinquecento, 174
Claridge Cocktail, 79
Classic Cocktail, 58
Cloister, 79
Clover Club, 79
Club Cocktail, 79
Cobbler(s), 45, 54, 87, 144, 227, 301
Cocktail classics, 31–53
Cocomacoque, 128
Coffee drinks, 58, 202, 234, 262, 270, 271, 272, 273, 275, 276, 277, 278, 309. See also Iced coffee(s)
Coffee Nudge, 224
Colada(s), 9, 129, 147, 254, 312
Cold Deck Cocktail, 58
Collins, 45, 54, 114, 144, 163, 176, 189, 190, 211, 227, 240
Colonial Cocktail, 79
Commodore Cocktail, 202
Company B, 154
Concrete Jungle, 129
Confidential Cocktail, 79
Continental, 129
Cooler(s), 52, 63, 79, 86, 87, 97, 107, 113, 125, 145, 174, 175, 178, 191, 198, 208, 212, 213, 224, 237, 239, 255, 259, 309, 311, 314
Cooperstown Cocktail, 80
Cordials and liqueurs, 231–242
Corkscrew, 130
Cornwall Negroni, 80
Corpse Reviver(s), 42, 58, 80
Correct Cocktail, 80
Cosmopolitan, 46, 174
Count Camillo's Paloma, 154
Count Currey, 80
Cream Puff, 130
Crème de Café, 59
Crème de Menthe Frappé, 234
Creole, 130
Creole Club Cocktail, 130
Creole Lady, 203
Crimson Cocktail, 80

Crusta(s), 45, 54, 199
Crux, 59
Crystal Slipper Cocktail, 81
Cuba Libre, 130
Cuban Cocktail No. 2, 59
Cuban Special, 130
Cubeltini, 175
Cure and the Cause, 131
Currant Affair, A, 72

D

Daiquiri(s), 38–40, 45, 123, 131, 132, 148, 261
Daisy(s), 45, 54, 87, 110, 112, 143, 145, 155, 191, 201, 227
Daisy de Santiago, 132
Daisy Dueller, 203
Daisy Mae, 81
Damn-the-Weather Cocktail, 81
Darb Cocktail, 82
Dark 'n Stormy, 132
D'Artagnan, 59
Day at the Beach, A, 122
Deauville Cocktail, 59
Debonair, 203
Deep Blue Sea, 82
Deep Sea Cocktail, 82
De La Louisiane, 203
Delmarva Cocktail, 204
Demonico No. 1, 82
Dempsey Cocktail, 82
Depth Bomb, 59
Depth Charge, 234
Derby, 204
Deshler, 204
Devil's Soul, 204
Diablo, 154
Diabolo, 132
Diana Cocktail, 235
Dinah Cocktail, 204
Dingo, 132
Dirty Daisy, 155
Dirty Harry, 204
Diva Quaranta, 82
Dixie Whiskey Cocktail, 204
Doc Daneeka Royale, 82
Doctor Funk No. 2, 132
Doff Your Hat, 83
Dolores, 59
Dream Cocktail, 59
Dubliner, 205
Duboudreau Cocktail, 205
Dutch and Butterscotch, 83

Easterner, 206
East India Cocktail No. 1, 60
Easy Like Sunday Morning Eastside, 83
Eden, 84
Eggnogs, 281–287
1815, 198
Elder Statesman, 84
Electric Jam, 175
El Molino, 155
El Niño, 155
El Oso (The Bear), 155
El Presidente Cocktail(s), 133
El Profesor, 60
Emerson, 84
Emperor Norton's Mistress, 206
English Channel, 84
English Rose Cocktail, 85
Ethel Duffy Cocktail, 60
Everybody's Irish Cocktail, 206

F

Fair-and-Warmer Cocktail, 133
Falernum, 7
Fallen Angel, 85
Fallen Leaves, 60
Fancy Brandy, 60
Fancy-Free Cocktail, 206
Fancy Gin, 85
Fancy Whiskey, 206
Fantasio Cocktail, 60
Fare Thee Well, 85
Fat Like Buddha, 134
Ferrari, 235
Final Ward, 206
Fine-and-Dandy Cocktail, 85
Fitzgerald, 86
Fix(es), 45, 55, 88, 144, 145, 227
Fizz, 46, 52, 55, 72, 80, 81, 82, 88,
    90, 91, 93, 103, 106, 110, 111,
    142, 210, 239, 241, 287, 296,
    299, 304, 310
Flamingo Cocktail, 86
Flip(s), 46, 137, 202, 203, 205,
    216, 242, 298
Florida, 86
Floridita(s), 124
Flower Power, 156
Flying Scotchman, 206
Fog Cutter, 134
Fontainebleau Special, 60
Fox River Cocktail, 206
Francis the Mule, 207
Fratelli Cocktail, 207
French Connection, 235
French Fantasy, 235

French Quarter, 61
French "75", 86
Frisky Witch, 176
Frostbite, 156
Froupe Cocktail, 61
Frozen drinks, 253–268
Fuzzy Navel, 235

G

Garnet, 86
Garnishes, 9–12
Gaugin, 134
Gentle Ben, 176
Georgia Mule, 176
Georgia Peach, 176
Gershwin, 86
Gibson (Gin), 87
Gilchrist, 207
Gilroy Cocktail, 61
Gimlet, 6, 87, 177, 191
Gin Aloha, 87
Gin and Bitters, 87
Gin and Sin, 88
Gin and Sip, 89
Gin and Tonic, 90
Gin Gin Mule, 89
Gin Squirt, 89
Gin Suck, 87
Gin Thing, 89
Girl from Cadiz, 90
Glass Tower, 176
Goat's Delight, 61
Godchild, 177
Godfather, 207
Godmother, 177
Golden Dawn, 61
Golden Daze, 90
Golden Dream, 235
Golden Eclipse, 135
Golden Friendship, 135
Goldrush, 207
Golf Cocktail, 90
Goober, 235
Gotham, 61
Grande Guignol, 135
Grandfather, 207
Grape Nehi, 177
Grasshopper, 191, 236, 246
Green Dragon, 90
Greenpoint, 207
Grenadine, 7
Greyhound (Gin), 90
Grounds for Divorce, 208
Groupie, 178
Guadalajara, 156
Gypsy Cocktail, 91

H

Hai Karate, 135
Harlem Cocktail, 91
Harrington, 178
Harvard Cocktail, 62
Harvest Moon, 208
Harvest Nectar, 135
Harvey Wallbanger, 178
Hasty Cocktail, 91
Havana Cocktail, 135
Hawaiian Cocktail, 91
Headless Horseman, 178
Heather Blush, 208
Heather's Kiss, 208
Heat Wave, 236
Heavenly Dram, 208
Hebrides, 208
Hemingway's Nog, 136
Highball, 46, 51, 55, 58, 75, 85,
    88, 96, 145, 199, 210, 219, 221,
    227, 237
High Cotton, 208
High Plains Drifter No. 1, 156
Hill Dog, 208
Hokkaido Cocktail, 91
Hole-in-One, 208
Holy Roller, 136
Homemade Grenadine, 26
Homestead Cocktail, 91
Honeymoon Cocktail, 62
Honolulu Cocktail(s), 92
Hoot Mon Cocktail, 208
Hop Toad, 136
Horse's Neck (with a Kick), 208
Hoskins, 92
Hospitality Holdings, 143
Hot drinks, 269–280, 294–295
Hotel d'Alsace, 208
Hot Pants, 156
Hudson Bay, 92
Hula-Hula Cocktail, 92
Hummingbird Down, 92
Humpty Dumpty, 178
Huntsman Cocktail, 179
Hurricane, 136
Hurricane Leah, 136
Hush and Wonder, 137

I

I.A.P, 210
Ibiza, 179
Ideal Cocktail, 92
Iced coffee(s), 234, 263
Iced tea(s), 182, 184, 185
Imperial Cocktail, 92

Incider Cocktail, 210
Income Tax Cocktail, 93
Indian Summer, 275
Inscription, 93
Interesting Cocktail, 156
Irish Coffee, 275
Irish Shillelagh, 210
Irish Whiskey Cocktail, 210
Irresistible, 137
Italian Sombrero, 236
Italian Surfer, 236

J

Jackie-O, 179
Jack-in-the-Box, 62
Jack Maples, 62
Jack Rose Cocktail, 62
Jacqueline, 137
Jade, 137
Jamaica Glow, 93
Jamaica Granito, 62
Jamaican Crawler, 137
Jamaican Ginger, 137
Jamaican Ten Speed, 179
Japanese, 62
Jasmine, 93
Jersey Lightning, 62
Jewel Cocktail, 93
Jinx Cocktail, 157
Jockey Club Cocktail, 36, 93
Joe Lewis, 211
Johnnie Cocktail, 236
Johnny Appleseed, 63
Jollity Building, 94
Joulouville, 94
Journalist Cocktail, 94
Judge Jr. Cocktail, 94
Judgette Cocktail, 94
Julep(s), 46, 55, 61, 211, 215, 293
Jungle Juice, 180
Juniper Breeze No. 1, 94
Jupiter, 94

K

Kara Sutra, 237
Katana, 180
Keegan, 211
Kentucky Blizzard, 211
Kentucky Cocktail, 211
Kentucky Colonel Cocktail, 212
Kentucky Longshot, 212
King Cole Cocktail, 212
Kiss in the Dark, 94
Kiss on the Lips, 212
Knickerbocker Cocktail(s), 95, 138

Knockout Cocktail, 95
Ko Adang, 138
Kretchma Cocktail, 180

L

La Bicyclette, 95
La Bomba, 157
La Campanile Cocktail, 95
Ladies' Cocktail, 212
Lady Be Good, 63
Lady Finger, 95
La Jolla, 63
La Louche, 95
La Perla, 157
Last Word, 95
La Tavola Rotonda, 212
La Tazza D'eva, 95
La Ultima Palabra, 157
La Vita Dulce, 138
Lawhill Cocktail, 212
Leapyear, 96
Leave-It-to-Me Cocktail(s), 96
Leaves of Grass, 180
Lemonade(s), 174, 184, 200, 304,
    305, 311
Lemon Crush, 180
Lemon Drop, 46, 181
Lemony Snicket Cocktail, 96
Leo de Janeiro, 96
Le Paradini, 181
Levelheaded Cocktail, 138
Liberal, 213
Liberty Cocktail, 63
Light and Day, 96
Lights on the Plaza, 181
Lillypad, 157
Limestone Cocktail, 213
Linstead Cocktail, 213
Liqueurs and cordials, 231–242
L'Italienne, 181
Little Devil Cocktail, 138
Little Princess Cocktail, 138
Loch Lomond, 213
London Cocktail, 97
Londoner, 97
Long Island Iced Tea, 182. See also
    Iced tea(s)
Look Out Below, 138
Loop, 182
Louisville Lady, 213
Lounge Lizard, 138
Lover's Kiss, 237
Lumination, 139
Luxury Cocktail, 64
Lychee Lucy, 182

M

Madras, 182
Magnolia Maiden, 213
Maiden's Blush Cocktail, 97
Maiden's Plea, 97
Mai-Tai(s), 41–43, 139, 233
Major Bailey, 97
Malmaison, 139
Mamie Gilroy, 213
Mandeville, 139
Manhasset, 214
Manhattan(s), 32–33, 99, 163,
    214, 331
Manuscript, 214
Maracuya Mosquito, 182
Margarita(s), 38–40, 153, 157, 162,
    163, 262
Mariposa, 139
Marlowe, 97
Marmalade, 237
Martinez Cocktail, 34, 97
Martini(s), 33–38, 78, 85, 86, 91,
    98, 103, 113, 145, 175, 176,
    183, 184, 185
Martinique Rose, 139
Mary Pickford Cocktail, 139
Maurice Cocktail, 98
Maxim, 98
Maxwell's Return, 98
McCelland Cocktail, 237
McCoy, 214
Melon Stand, 99
Mercy, Mercy, 99
Merry Widow Cocktail, 99
Metropole, 214
Metropolitan Cocktail, 64
Mexican Firing Squad, 158
Mexican Madras, 158
Mexican Monk, 158
Mexicana, 158
Mexicola, 158
Miami Beach Cocktail, 215
Midnight Cocktail, 64
Midnight Express, 140
Mikado Cocktail, 64
Mimosa(s), 304, 306
Mint Julep. See Julep(s)
Miss Jones, 183
Mocha Express, 183
Modern Cocktail, 215
Mojito, 140
Mon Sherry, 64
Monarch, 99
Moneypenny, 100
Monkey Gland, 100
Monkey Wrench, 140

Miss Jones, 183
Mocha Express, 183
Modern Cocktail, 215
Mojito, 140
Mon Sherry, 64
Monarch, 99
Moneypenny, 100
Monkey Gland, 100
Monkey Wrench, 140
Montana, 64
Monte Carlo, 215
Monte Carlo Imperial Cocktail, 100
Montmartre Cocktail, 100
Moondream, 100
Moonlight, 64
Moonquake Shake, 140
Morning Cocktail, 65
Morro, 100
Moscow Mule, 183
Moto Guzzi, 215
Moulin Rouge, 237
Mr. 404, 183

N

Narragansett, 215
Negroni, 101
Netherland, 65
Nevada Cocktail, 140
Nevins, 215
New Amsterdam, 101
New York Cocktail, 216
Nicky Finn, 65
Night & Day, 65
Night Cap, 140
Nightmare, 101
Nijinsky Blini, 183
19th Century, 194
No. 8, 158
Nomad South, 158
Non Ci Credo, 101
Nonalcoholic drinks, 296, 308–314
Nonotchka Cocktail, 183
Normandy, 65
Novara, 101
Nutcracker, 216

O

Obituary Cocktail, 101
Oh, Gosh!, 140
Old Bay Ridge, 216
Old Cuban, 141
Oldest Temptation, 159

Old-Fashioned Whiskey
    Cocktail(s), 28–31, 74, 145, 159,
    164, 202, 216, 221
Old Goat, 101
Old Pal Cocktail, 217
Olympic Cocktail, 65
Opal Cocktail, 102
Opera, 102
Orange Blossom, 102
Orange Oasis, 102
Orgeat, 7
Oriental Cocktail, 217
Orient Express, 103
Oscar Wilde, 238
Outsider, 103

P

Pacific Sunshine, 159
Paddington, 141
Paddy Cocktail, 217
Pall Mall, 103
Palm Beach Cocktail, 103
Palmetto Cocktail, 141
Paloma(s), 159
Pancho Villa, 159
Paradise Cocktail, 65
Paris When It Sizzles, 141
Parisian, 104
Park Avenue, 104
Peach Melba(s), 238, 266, 312
Pearl Button, 141
Pearl White, 104
Penicillin, 217
Peppermint Iceberg, 238
Peppermint Stick, 238
Peppermint Twist, 238
Perfect 10, 104
Perfect Cocktail, 104
Peter Pan Cocktail, 104
Petit Zinc, 184
Piccadilly Cocktail, 104
Pickleback, 249
Pickled Pink, 184
Pimm's Cup, 238
Piña Agave, 160
Piña Colada, 9, 129
Pineapple Cocktail, 141
Pink Creole, 142
Pink Gin, 104
Pink Lady, 105
Pink Paradise, 142
Pink Pussycat, 184
Pink Squirrel, 238
Pisco Punch, 66
Pitbull, 217
Planter's Cocktail, 142

Presto Cocktail, 66
Pretty in Pink, 184
Prince of Wales, 67
Prince's Smile, 105
Princeton Cocktail, 105
Priority Cocktail, 185
Prizefighter, 239
Prohibition Cocktail, 105
Pulitzer, 106
Punches, 63, 66, 67, 122, 143, 172, 199, 279, 281–282, 287–196
Purple Mask, 185
Purple Pancho, 160
Purple Passion, 185
Purple Ruby, 185

Q

Quaalude, 239
Quaker's Cocktail, 143
Quarter Deck Cocktail, 144
Quebec, 218
Queen Elizabeth, 106
Quetzalcoatl, 160

R

Raspberry Romance, 239
Reconciliation, 218
Red Apple, 185
Red Baron, 106
Red Cloud, 107
Red Hook, 218
Red-Hot Passion, 218
Red Raider, 218
Refuge, 160
Remember the Maine, 218
Renaissance, 67
Renaissance Cocktail, 107
Restless Native, 144
Revolver, 219
Rickey(s), 46, 51, 52, 88, 135, 145, 210, 221, 227, 241, 313
Ringo Starr, 144
Robert Burns, 219
Robin's Nest, 185
Rob Roy, 219
Robson Cocktail, 144
Rolls-Royce, 107
Rory O'More, 219
Rose Cocktail(s), 108
Rosemary Clementine Sparkle, 186
Rosita, 160
Rouxby Red, 186
Royal Smile Cocktail, 67
Ruby Red, 186

Rum Relaxer, 145
Russian Bear Cocktail, 186
Rusty Monk, 108
Rusty Nail, 219
Rye Cocktail, 219

S

Saint Lucy Bracer, 146
Salty Dog(s), 6, 108, 187
Sambuca Con Mosca, 239
Sampan Shipwreck A, 186
S&V, 146
San Francisco Cocktail, 240
Sangaree(s), 46, 55, 66, 88, 228
Sangria(s), 293, 305
San Martin Cocktail, 108
San Sebastian, 108
Santiago Cocktail, 146
Santiago Scotch Plaid, 219
Saratoga Cocktail(s), 67, 68
Sargasso, 147
Satan's Whiskers, 109
Satin Sheets, 161
Saucy Sue Cocktail, 68
Sazerac (Rye), 220
Scofflaw, 220
Scotch Bonnet, 220
Scotch Bounty, 220
Scotch Royale, 221
Scottish Bandit, 222
Scottish Guard, 221
Screwdriver(s), 146, 179, 187, 248
Seaboard, 222
Sea Breeze, 187
Seals Cocktail, 196
Sea of Cortez, 161
Seelbach Cocktail, 222
Sensation Cocktail, 109
Seventh Heaven Cocktail, 109
Sevilla 75, 68
Sfozando, 161
Shady Grove, 109
Shady Lady, 161
Shalom, 187
Shamrock, 222
Shangri-Lita, 240
Sheer Elegance, 240
Shirley Temple, 313
Shiprock 109
Shoot, 222
Shooters, 243–251
Shriner Cocktail, 68
Shruff's End, 222
Siberian Sleighride, 187

Sidecar(s), 38–40, 52, 68, 69, 78, 126
Sidewinder, 161
Silent Third, 222
Silk Stockings, 161
Silver Bullet, 109
Silver Cocktail, 109
Silver Lining, 223
Silver Streak, 110
Simple Syrup, 7, 25
Sir Walter Cocktail, 147
1626, 194
Sleeping Monk, 223
Sling(s), 46, 55, 103, 112, 160,
    191, 228
Sloeberry Cocktail, 240
Sloe Driver, 240
Sloe Gin Cocktail, 240
Sloe Starter, 241
Sloe Vermouth, 241
Slope, 223
Sloppy Joe's Cocktail(s), 68, 147
Smart Alec, 68
Smash(es), 46, 56, 89, 165, 228,
    258, 262
Smokey Hollander, 110
Snowball, 110
So Cue, 110
Solomon, 111
Sombrero, 68
Something Different, 241
Sonic Blaster, 187
Soother Cocktail, 69
Sorriso, 111
Sour(s), 46, 51, 56, 81, 89, 134,
    148, 165, 181, 191, 205, 207,
    211 216, 221, 228, 232, 236,
    259, 294
Southern Belle, 223
Southern Bride, 111
Southern Lady, 223
Southern Peach, 224
South of the Border, 162
South-Side Cocktail, 111
Soviet, 187
Spanish Town Cocktail, 157
Spencer Cocktail, 111
Spice of Life, 162
Sputnik, 187
Standard, 112
Stanley Cocktail, 112
Star Cocktail, 69
Stiletto, 224
Stinger(s), 52, 69, 191, 221, 232
Stirrup Cup, 69
Stockholm 70, 188
Stone Cocktail, 147

Stone Fence, 224
Stone Wall, 147
St. Patrick's Day, 239
Straight Law Cocktail, 112
Straight Rye Witch, 224
Strawberry Fields Forever, 241
Strawberry Shortcake, 267
Stupid Cupid, 188
Summer Cabinet, 112
Summer of Love, 188
Sun Also Rise, 113
Sun Kiss, 242
Sunday Confession, 163
Sunset at Gowanus, 148
Sunrise(s), 156, 165, 175, 180,
    236, 241
Surf Rider, 188
Susie Taylor, 148
Sweet Maria, 188
Swiss Family Cocktail, 224
Swizzle(s), 47, 56, 89, 124, 129,
    146, 196, 228, 234
Syrups, 6–7, 25–26, 203

T

Tabby Cat, 188
Tahiti Club, 148
Tailspin, 113
T&T, 113
Tango Cocktail, 113
T-Bird, 224
Temper Cocktail, 69
Tequila(s), 151–167, 268, 293
Thanksgiving Special, 69
Third-Degree Cocktail, 114
Third-Rail Cocktail, 148
Three Card Monty, 114
Three Miller Cocktail, 148
Thunderclap, 114
Tía Juanathan, 166
Tiger Tanaka, 189
Tijuana Taxi, 168
Tillicum, 114
Tipperary Cocktail, 224
Titian, 189
Toasted Almond, 242
Toasted Drop, 189
Toddy, 47, 56, 90, 146, 217, 270,
    272, 274, 278, 280
Tom and Jerry(s), 279, 280
Tombstone, 225
Top Banana, 189
Toreador, 166
Torridora Cocktail, 149
Trident(s), 189, 306

Trilby Cocktail, 225
Tropica Cocktail, 149
Tropical Cocktail, 242
Tropical Special, 114
Tulip Cocktail, 70
Turf Cocktail, 115
Tuxedo Cocktail, 115
21st Century, 167
Twentieth-Century Cocktail, 115
"23", 50
Twin Hills, 225
Twin Peach, 242
Twister, 189
Typhoon, 115

U

Underneath the Mango Tree, 190
Union Cocktail, 115
Union Jack, 115
Urban Anxiety, 149

V

Vacation Cocktail, 149
Vagabond, 225
Vagabundo, 167
Valencia Cocktail, 70
Valentino, 115
Vanderbilt Cocktail, 70
Van Vleet, 149
Velvet Peach Hammer, 190
Venial Sin, 167
Verrazano, 225
Vesper, 43, 116
Victor, 116
Vieux Carré, 225
Vieux Mot, 116
Virgin Mary, 314
Virginia Dare, 149
Viva Villa, 167
Vodka and Apple Juice, 190
Vodka and Tonic, 190
Vow of Silence, 116

W

Waikiki Beachcomber, 116
Waiting on Summer, 167
Wallick Cocktail, 116
Wallis Blue Cocktail, 116

Walters, 226
Ward Eight, 226
Warsaw Cocktail, 191
Washington Apple, 226
Water Lily, 117
Watermelon, 242
Weeski, 226
Welshman, 226
Wembly Cocktail, 117
Western Rose, 117
West Side, 192
Whimsy, 226
Whip Cocktail, 70
Whiskey Orange, 227
Whiskey Squirt, 228
Whispers-of-the-Frost Cocktail, 228
White Lady, 117
White Lily Cocktail, 150
White Lion Cocktail, 150
White Russian, 192
White Spider, 117
White Way Cocktail, 117
Whoa, Nellie!, 228
Widow's Kiss, 70
Wiki Waki Woo, 150
Will Rogers, 117
Windy Corner Cocktail, 70
Wine(s) and beer(s), 170, 275, 277, 297–306
Wink, 117
Winkle, 118
Wolf's Bite, 118
Woodstock, 118
Woodward Cocktail, 228
Woolworth, 228

X

Xanthia Cocktail, 116
X.Y.Z. Cocktail, 150

Y

Yale Cocktail, 119
Yellow Parrot Cocktail, 242
Yellow Rose of Texas, 167
Yokahama Romance, 119

Z

Zombie, 150